Gerigt Van Een balcon of bedeckte Stoep.
De bloemparken te

RUSSIAN PARKS

PETER HAYDEN

AND GARDENS

FRANCES LINCOLN

Frances Lincoln Ltd
4 Torriano Mews
Torriano Avenue
London NW5 2RZ
www.franceslincoln.com

ISBN 0 7112 2430 7

Designed by John Morgan studio
Printed and bound in China

9 8 7 6 5 4 3 2 1

Previous pages: One of Nicolaas Bidloo's drawings
(*c*.1730) of his garden in Moscow.

CONTENTS

Introduction 6

1 The Earliest Russian Gardens 8

2 The Formal Parks and Gardens of St Petersburg 16

3 The Formal Parks and Gardens of Moscow and the Provinces 52

4 Catherine the Great and the English Style of Landscaping 76

5 The Landscape Parks of Paul I and Maria Fyodorovna 108

6 Landscape Parks in and around St Petersburg 144

7 Landscape Parks in and around Moscow 164

8 Some Landscape Parks in the Provinces 186

9 From the Emancipation of the Serfs to the Revolution 214

10 The Soviet Period 226

Plans 239
Notes 242
Bibliography 246
Index 250
Acknowledgments 255

INTRODUCTION

In spite of a climate which makes gardening difficult, some of the world's greatest parks were created in Russia. They owed much to the enthusiasm and genius of Tsar Peter the Great and two German empresses, Catherine the Great and Maria Fyodorovna. Peter was inspired by the parks and gardens he had seen in western Europe and spared no expense in enlisting leading architects and gardeners from Germany, France, Italy and Holland to work for him in Russia. Virtually unlimited resources were available for materials; statues and plants were imported from abroad regardless of cost; and an enormous workforce was available, composed of soldiers, serfs and Swedish prisoners of war. The great park at Peterhof was the exceptional result. Catherine was largely responsible for the introduction of the English landscape style to Russia with outstanding success at Tsarskoe Selo; while Maria Fyodorovna's great park at Pavlovsk was influenced by those she had known in Germany and France. The parks created for all three of them outshone the parks which had inspired them, with styles which had evolved in western Europe attaining their highest expression in Russia.

Other notable parks in Russia were created by the few families which had amassed the immense resources needed to make them. Some of the founders of these dynasties had been richly rewarded by tsar or empress for exceptional service on the battlefield, Peter's Field Marshal Boris Sheremetev among them, or in the bedchamber, as was the case with the Empress Elizabeth's favourite Alexis Razumovsky. One or two, notably Count Grigory Orlov and Prince Grigory Potemkin, served with distinction in both arenas. They were all rewarded with considerable sums of money, vast tracts of land and thousands of serfs. The Golitsyns, the Strogonovs and the Demidovs owed their fortunes to ironworks in the Urals.

When, following legislation in 1762 and 1785, the nobility were no longer required to spend most of their lives in state service and were able to devote their time instead to developing their country estates, it was the landscape style, adapted to Russian conditions, which they favoured, and those who could afford to sought to employ British gardeners.

Major problems began in the nineteenth century with Napoleon's 1812 invasion; this brought catastrophe to the properties his forces overran. Declining fortunes were another factor, since the adoption of extravagant western lifestyles, with new palaces, parks and everything which went with them, cost even some of the very rich more than they could afford and led to massive debts. The abolition of serfdom in 1861 deprived those who had owned serfs of their free labour without ending the unrest and class hatred that led to the 1905 revolution. The revolution of 1917 brought the overthrow of the nobility and put an end to private ownership. While a few of the outstanding parks were given state protection as the creation of the peasants who had worked on them, the rest were put to other uses or left to pillage and to nature. The Second World War brought horrendous damage to all the great parks, but most of them were admirably restored in the decades which followed.

With the end of communism and the restoration of private ownership it will be interesting to see what today's *nouveaux riches* make of the properties they acquire.

Parks and gardens in countries now independent, Ukraine and the Baltic states, have been included, since they were once part of the Russian empire.

Some passages in the book have already appeared in *A Sense of Place* and in articles in *Garden History, The Garden, Country Life, Landscape Design* and *Historic Gardens Review*.

My photographs were all taken with Rolleiflex cameras using Professional Ektachrome and Fujichrome film.

In transliterating from Russian, the letters я, ё and ю are represented by ya, yo and yu. In words with endings which would transliterate as -ii or -yi, the ending has been changed to -y. The soft sign (') has been omitted except in the bibliography and the endnotes. Where another form of transliteration has been generally used for a name, such as Potemkin, that form has been retained.

A lion sculpture in the park at Arkhangelskoe, decorated by a visitor.

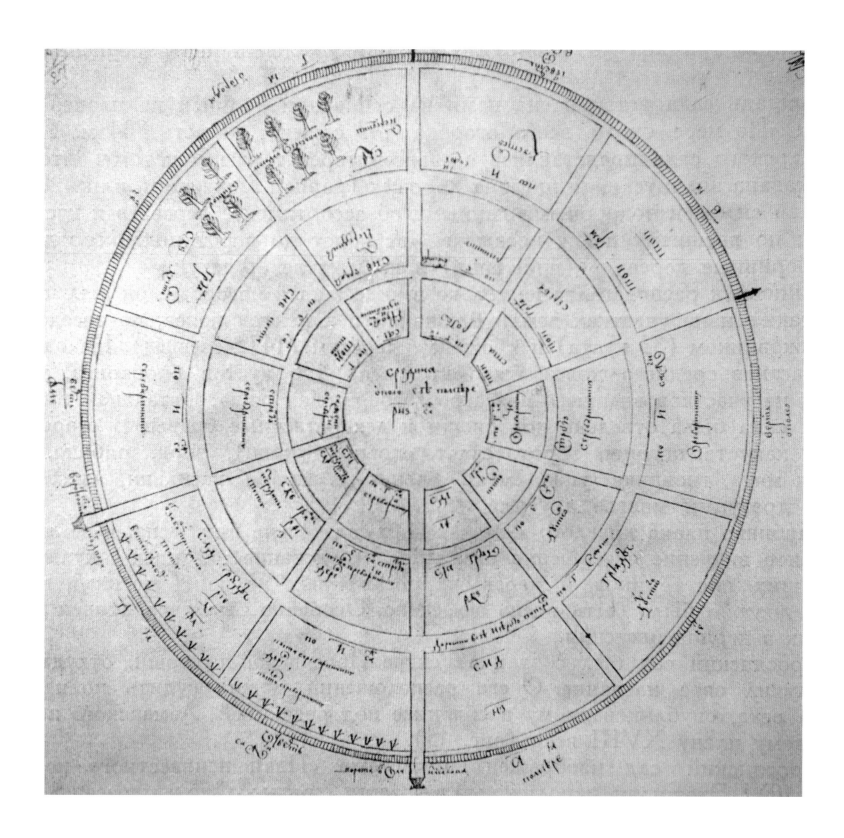

1

THE EARLIEST RUSSIAN GARDENS

Some of the earliest Russian gardens were in Kiev, for it was around Kiev in the tenth century that the Russian state first developed, when Kievan princes asserted their authority over East Slavic tribes and established Kievan Rus. The conversion to Christianity, in the late tenth century, of Prince – later Saint – Vladimir was of exceptional significance through the cultural contacts which it brought with Byzantium. There were great benefits to architecture, and the first cathedral of the 990s was followed by S. Sophia half a century later, inspired by the great sixth-century S. Sophia in Constantinople. Gardens, too, were probably influenced by Byzantium, where there were many hanging gardens – gardens at upper floor levels – with flowers, pavilions and water features. Prince Yuri Dolgoruky had an estate called a *rai* (paradise) outside the city by the River Dnieper, which may well have had a hanging garden, since there was one at his other estate in Suzdal, which Greek gardener-monks had helped to create. There is also evidence of other gardens in Kiev, belonging to nobles and monasteries, and of Greek gardeners working in them, cultivating apples, pears, cherries, plums, currants, raspberries and gooseberries.[1] In commercial vegetable gardens around Kiev and other cities, cabbages, peas, turnips, onions, garlic and pumpkins were grown.[2]

In the eleventh century the territory of Kievan Rus embraced Suzdal and Novgorod and extended to the Baltic coast, where the city of St Petersburg would later be established, but it comprised numerous princedoms, which led to civil conflicts, and there were frequent rebellions. In 1169 Prince Andrei Bogolyubsky of Suzdal, the son of Yuri Dolgoruky, attacked and overwhelmed Kiev, won for himself the title of Grand Prince and transferred the capital to Vladimir. In 1240 Kiev was overrun by the Mongols and suffered immense damage.[3]

Under Andrei Bogolyubsky and, after his death in 1174, his brother Vsevolod, Suzdal and Vladimir were for a time the main centre of power in Russia. Prince Andrei had a hanging garden on his estate in Vladimir, the work of Greek gardener-monks, as his father's had been in Suzdal. It seems that the nobility and monasteries enjoyed similar gardens.

Novgorod, far to the north of Kiev, with a population of thirty thousand, was another important early Russian city and centre of power. While Kiev was being sacked by the Mongols, Alexander Nevsky was leading an army from Novgorod to victory against the Swedes on the banks of the Neva and then rescued Pskov, Novgorod's 'little brother', from the Teutonic Knights. As a result he became Prince of Novgorod and then Grand Prince of Russia. Novgorod was the most democratic of Russian cities and was governed by a town council, who could appoint and dismiss its prince. It was also the most important Russian trading centre with a strong and affluent middle class, many of whom had contacts abroad. There were 'gardens with fruit trees and bushes – apple, cherry, plum, currant, raspberry, gooseberry' in Novgorod at that time,[4] and it has been established that there were public gardens.[5]

A contemporary plan of the seventeenth-century Apothecary's Garden at Izmailovo.

But it was in Moscow that the first major Russian gardens were established. According to a chronicle the Grand Prince Yuri Dolgoruky 'laid the foundations of the town of Moscow',[6] implying that he built the city wall, in 1156. Its eventual emergence at the head of a centralized Russian state owed much to its geographical location. It was on the route between Kiev and the increasingly important north-east, and its proximity to four major rivers – the Oka, the Volga, the Don and the Dnieper – made it an ideal centre from which to expand.

Moscow established its pre-eminence over the other Russian cities in the fourteenth century. Ivan I (1325–40) made an important contribution by persuading the Metropolitan of the Russian Church to settle there, making Moscow the spiritual centre of Russia. Between the first half of the fourteenth century and 1462 the territory controlled by Moscow increased from 600 square miles to 15,000 square miles.[7] By the year 1500 the Mongols, who had been exacting tribute from the Russians for a century and a half, ceased to be a threat, and the borders were pushed further back under Ivan III (1462–1505). Ivan IV (1533–84), the Terrible, was the first Russian head of state to be crowned tsar, in a Byzantine-inspired ceremony, and during his troubled reign Russia advanced into Siberia.

In the fifteenth century there were already some quite extensive gardens in parts of Moscow. The Pokrovsky Monastery is known to have had gardens, and most monasteries would have grown their own fruit and herbs. Producing food was the main concern of most gardeners. A sixteenth-century manuscript gave advice on how to plant and maintain fruit gardens, how to make hot beds for melons, how to prepare seeds, how to protect plants from frost, how to combat pests and how to graft.[8] Large gardens were usually designed to be pleasing to the senses as well as productive, combining groves of cedar (then newly introduced from Siberia) and birch, meadows, fruit trees, cereals, fish ponds, bee hives under the limes, sweet-smelling herbs and flowers.

During the reign of Ivan IV the Apothecary's Garden was laid out for the Tsar between the Borovitsky and Troitsky Gates and planted with fruit trees and bushes and aromatic and medicinal herbs. East of the Kremlin, beyond the walls of Kitaisky Gorod, was the Vasiliev Garden. Opposite the Kremlin on the right bank of the river was Tsaritsyn Meadow with a patterned parterre.[9] At Borisovo, the palace of Tsar Boris Godunov (1598–1605) by the River Protva, six miles south of Moscow, a large artificial lake with an island in the middle was formed by a dam. There were boats on the lake and a pavilion of some sort on the island. There was also a swannery and apple and cherry orchards.

Of particular interest among the seventeenth-century gardens of Moscow are the hanging gardens of the Kremlin Palace, laid out on terraces outside rooms on upper floors. They were very substantially supported and were lined with soldered lead plates to prevent water leaking through. They had paths, flowerbeds and pools. The beds were edged with boards and the plants grown in them included lilies, peonies, carnations, tulips and apple trees.

One of the hanging gardens of the Kremlin, the upper garden, constructed by gardener Nazar Ivanov in 1623 and reconstructed in 1635 by gardeners Tit Andreev and Ivan Telyatevsky, was on a corner of the building. It was surprisingly large – 63 feet wide, 182 feet long on the façade of the building and 280 feet long at the side. The pool measured 35 × 28 feet, was almost 5 feet deep and was probably stocked with fish. There was a pumping machine for raising the water to it. Brightly painted towers stood at the corners of the garden, and there were fine views from the windows in the stone walls. The lower garden, dating from the 1680s, had a pool and a water tower, and the walls were decorated with perspective paintings, apparently by an English artist, named as Peter Englez. There may have been orangeries in both of the gardens in the 1690s.

There were other hanging gardens in the Kremlin. Patriarch Joachim had an upper and a lower garden at his court there, and it is recorded that three hundred tulips were obtained for these gardens in 1680. Kitchen produce was also grown there including melon plants. Boyars and other leading dignitaries of the church also had hanging gardens.[10]

The earlier Patriarch Nikon, who had enjoyed considerable power from 1652 until he was deposed in 1668, had a luxurious palace in the Kremlin, with rooms larger than those in the Tsar's palace, and would almost certainly have had a garden. Nikon founded the famous New Jerusalem Monastery in 1656 at Istra, some 25 miles north-west of Moscow. The Church of the Resurrection there was modelled on the Church of the Holy

Above: This plan of Moscow (c.1600) seems to indicate that there were many gardens there then.

Right: The Church of the Resurrection, modelled on the Church of the Holy Sepulchre in Jerusalem, at the New Jerusalem Monastery at Istra, where the adjacent landscape was made to represent the topography of Jerusalem.

Sepulchre in Jerusalem from plans and drawings made by one of his monks who was sent to Palestine for that purpose.[11] The setting of the monastery was made to represent the topography around Jerusalem. The River Istra became the Jordan, which was joined by the Euphrates, the Garden of Gethsemane and various other landscape features. Chapels and crosses were erected, and signs indicated what features of Jerusalem were represented. A visitor to the New Jerusalem in the early nineteenth century described his guided tour:

> As the convent bears the appellation of New Jerusalem, the villages, hills, and country around, have likewise assumed the names of Palestine. Here I saw the mounts Carmel and Taber, the sea of Galilee, the Jordan, the village of Emaus, &c, &c.
>
> Our pious conductor, who pointed out these scenes with religious awe, was about thirty-two or thirty-three. . . . He led us to a spacious tower that overlooked one of the rivers, the banks of which were richly shaded with trees. 'This', said he, 'is the house of David, whence he beheld Bathsheba bathing: and those are the gardens of Uriah. . . .'
>
> We passed out at a little gothic gate, and shaped our course along the foot of the embattled walls, and through a romantic wood, gradually descending the hill on which the New Jerusalem towered above us. We soon found ourselves on an extended plain beautifully enriched with trees, and watered by the Jordan and Euphrates. To be sure the latter river has made rather a jump from the plains of Babylon to meet the Judean flood under the walls of this monastery. But if the Patriarch could bring the Jordan from its native springs so far, it required very little more stretch of power to transport the Euphrates also; and he was very right to fulfill all his wishes while he was about it. Here then flowed the two famous rivers of Palestine and Assyria; and though in miniature, the effect was fine and solemn. . . .
>
> Our pious abbot conducted us through another avenue in the wood to a little white building embosomed amid drooping arches. In this austere spot did the austere Nichon spend most of the days in twenty years.[12]

It was to the New Jerusalem that Nikon had retired after his deposition.

At the Monastery of the Trinity and St Sergius in Sergiev (now Zagorsk) in the seventeenth century there were extensive orchards outside and within the walls. When the monastery was besieged by Polish troops in 1611 it was recorded that a battle took place there 'on the field of cabbages'. In the late eighteenth century Patriarch Platon followed the New Jerusalem example

and attempted to recreate the landscape of Jerusalem by the monastery in Sergiev.[13]

Estates outside Moscow were mostly situated on the high banks of rivers to take advantage of the views. Gardens were laid out, pools were formed by damming or excavation and stocked with fish, many fruit trees and bushes were planted and bees were kept. Birch groves, already provided by nature or planted, were particularly admired as picturesque features in the landscape.

Among the estates of the Tsar outside Moscow in the seventeenth century were Pokrovskoe-Rubtsovo, Preobrazhenskoe, Kolomenskoe and Izmailovo. Rare plants were grown at Pokrovskoe-Rubtsovo, where the garden was made in 1635. There was a pool with boats at Preobrazhenskoe. At Kolomenskoe, where some of the marvellous buildings may still be seen, there were numerous orchards planted with apples, plums, cherries, currants and raspberries, and there were wonderful views of the water meadows and the high hill with the Church of the Ascension.

The best-recorded seventeenth-century Russian gardens are those at Izmailovo, thanks to the survival of a number of detailed drawings of various gardens, which not only present interesting geometrical layouts but also provide information about the planting. Izmailovo, the estate of Tsar Aleksei Mikhailovich (1645–76), father of Peter the Great, is situated on the River Serebrianka, a tributary of the Yauza. A pool was formed here in

Above: The seventeenth-century Bridge Tower and Pokrovsky Cathedral at Izmailovo survive between later buildings.

Left: The Cathedral of the Assumption at the Monastery of the Trinity and St Sergius at Sergiev (now Zagorsk), where there was also an attempt in the eighteenth century to recreate the landscape of Jerusalem.

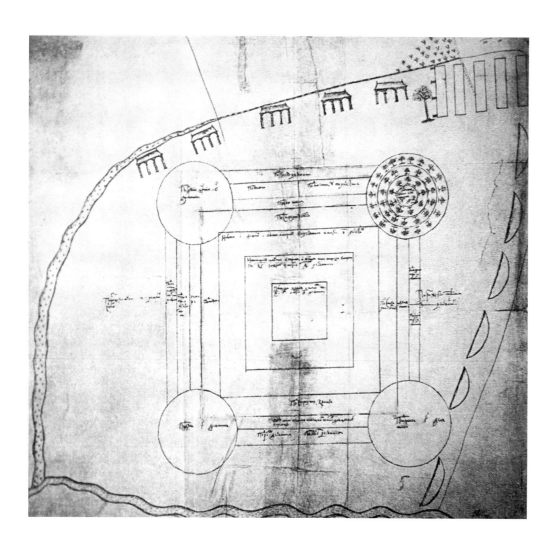

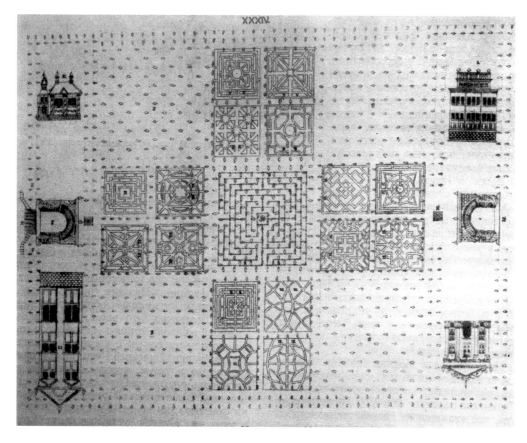

Left, above: A contemporary plan of the seventeenth-century Vineyard Garden at Izmailovo.

Left: A seventeenth-century plan for a 'Pleasure Palace with a Garden' at Izmailovo.

the seventeenth century by damming the river, with an island in the middle where a cathedral, the Tsar's palace and a number of service buildings were built. The gardens were laid out in different parts of the surrounding forest and were not compositionally linked with the palace or with each other.

Aleksei Mikhailovich was a great innovator in agriculture and horticulture, and Izmailovo is notable for the work done there on the acclimatization of plants. Melons were grown, and gardeners were brought to Moscow from Astrakhan with several tons of appropriate soil in which to cultivate the melons. Attempts were also made to grow grapes and to introduce the mulberry to establish a silk industry.

In the Vineyard Garden, which in 1687 covered 40 acres, fruit and agricultural crops were grown in a simple but striking design of a series of diminishing squares, one within another, and with circles at the outside corners of the design. In each of the square strips a different crop was planted – buckwheat, rye, wheat, barley, poppies, white currants, flowers and herbs. In the four circles a different kind of fruit was planted in concentric rings – pears, white and red cherries and plums. At the centre of the design stood two painted garden buildings and sundials. The plan of the garden also shows what appear to be five tables and five sheds which must have been used for sorting and storing the produce. It was in this garden that attempts were made to establish vines with an elderly gardener from Kiev to care for them, protecting them with mats in winter. Some success was initially recorded but it was not maintained, and the experiment was eventually abandoned.

The Apothecary's Garden was circular; it had a diameter of 920 feet and covered 15 acres, and its design was again based on simple geometric forms. Three broad concentric bands were each divided by ten straight paths radiating from the centre (see page 8). Details of the planting were given on the plan and included sweet briars, mulberries, apples, rowan, a birch grove, gooseberries, berberries, cabbage, cucumbers, peas, lettuce, carnations, poppies, mint, dill and various medicinal herbs which gave the garden its name.

The square Prosyansky Garden was surrounded by forest and enclosed by a wooden fence, painted red. Here again there were diminishing squares one inside another. At the centre of the garden a pavilion was surrounded by four fountains in the form of winged animals and then by a square of flowerbeds. Outside these were fruit trees – apples, cherries, plums and pears – which in turn gave way to agricultural crops – flax, millet, rye, barley, buckwheat, hemp and peas.

The plan for a 'Pleasure Palace with a Garden' is a much more complex design and shows the influence of contemporary Western European garden design. Of particular interest is the large central, square maze, possibly the first in a Russian garden. Along its paths blackcurrants and cherries were planted. On each side of the maze a square parterre was laid out, each divided into four further squares, sixteen in all, with very elaborate patterns, no two of which were the same. The key to the plan gives details of how these squares were planted – one with various tulips,

another with tulips and other flowers, another with white and yellow narcissus, another with scented herbs, and so on. The square blocks between the parterres were planted with fruit trees.

Among the other gardens at Izmailovo were a raspberry garden, a strawberry garden and the mulberry garden. The latter seems to have been vast since three hundred soldiers were used to plant it. Gardeners were brought from the Lower Volga and Terek to tend the mulberry trees, which, like the vines, were protected by mats in winter. There were also bird farms, where 484 swans were recorded, and a collection of wild animals which included bears, leopards, lynx and wolves.[14]

Tsar Aleksei died in 1676 and his successor Fyodor III six years later, when Peter Alekseevich was only ten. Peter became joint Tsar with his feeble half-brother Ivan, while his capable half-sister Sophia was appointed regent. In 1689 there was a plot among Sophia's associates to put her on the throne at the expense of Peter and Ivan, and Peter, fearful for his life, hurriedly left Preobrazhenskoe, where he was living, and sought sanctuary at the Monastery of the Trinity and St Sergius in Sergiev, 45 miles north-east of Moscow. In the confrontation which followed Peter won majority support, including, invaluably, that of the Patriarch Joachim, and Sophia was obliged to spend the rest of her life in a nunnery. For five years Peter was content to leave government in the hands of his mother, Natalya Naryshkin, but after her death in 1694, when he was twenty-two, he took charge himself.

By the end of the seventeenth century there had been an immense expansion of Russian territory with settlements as far away as the Chinese border and Kamchatka by the Pacific; but there was only one seaport, Archangel, by the White Sea, which was ice-bound from November to May. Access to the Baltic and the Black Sea was very badly needed, and it would be won by force of arms from Sweden and Turkey in the eighteenth century under two great leaders, Peter and Catherine. They would also direct the creation of two of the world's greatest parks, while numerous other notable parks would further enhance the territories they conquered.

2

THE FORMAL PARKS AND GARDENS OF ST PETERSBURG

An engraving by S. Galktionov from a painting by S.F. Shchedrin of the Hermitage Cascade at Peterhof, which was created by A.N. Voronikhin at the end of the eighteenth century. In the 1850s, A.I. Stakenschneider reconstructed it, adding a three-sided colonnade of fourteen columns. It then became known as the Lion Cascade on account of bronze statues of lions. Destroyed during the German occupation, it was eventually restored in time for the tercentenary of St Petersburg in 2003.

Peter's first military encounter as Tsar was with the Turks, but he soon turned his attention to Sweden in what was to become the Great Northern War. After an initial heavy defeat by the young Charles XII at Narva in 1700, Field Marshal Count Boris Sheremetev led the Russian army to victories in Livonia and Estonia in the two following years, and in 1703 Peter was able to found his great city of St Petersburg on the banks of the Neva. There was a further famous victory over the Swedes at Poltava in Ukraine in 1709, and eventually, in 1721, Sweden ended the war by admitting defeat, ceding Livonia, Estonia, Ingermanland and Karelia to Russia by the Treaty of Nystad.

No country owes more to a leader, in so many spheres, than Russia owes to Peter the Great; and in architecture and in the art of laying out parks great progress was made during his reign. While St Petersburg was being developed, all other major building activity in Russia ceased. All noblemen who owned thirty families of serfs were obliged to build a house in the new city, and many were compelled to settle there. St Petersburg had first call on building materials, and the use of stone was forbidden elsewhere. During Peter's reign and beyond, the making of notable parks and gardens was virtually restricted to the new capital, and the great achievements in this field owed much to the personal involvement of the Tsar.[1]

This commitment would have surprised some of the owners of the gardens he visited during his travels in Western Europe, where his main purpose was to study shipbuilding and navigation. In England he and his followers earned a reputation for riotous behaviour at John Evelyn's Sayes Court, where Admiral John Benbow was Evelyn's tenant: 'There is a house full of people, and right nasty,' wrote Evelyn's servant to his master.[2] According to tradition, the Russian visitors pushed one another, including Peter, in a wheelbarrow into a fine holly hedge, to its considerable detriment, and extensive damage was caused elsewhere in the garden. A claim was made to the king, and substantial compensation was paid.[3] In Berlin the Margravine of Bayreuth declared that Peter and his companions had left Monbijou looking 'like Jerusalem after the sack', although everything fragile had been removed before their arrival.[4]

Nevertheless Peter was very impressed by many of the parks and gardens he visited. In Berlin he admired Charlottenburg and Oranienburg as well as Monbijou. He knew the major Dutch parks, including Het Loo, and was a frequent visitor to a park called Petersburg on the River Vecht, the home of a merchant, Christoffel Brants, who traded with Russia and was an agent of the Tsar. Peter's first visit to Holland was in 1697–8. During his second visit in 1716–17 he visited the gardens of Zorgvliet, Watervliet, Rijksdorp, Ouderhoek and Honselaarsdijk, as well as Het Loo and Petersburg.[5] In 1717, he also went to France, where he saw Versailles, the Trianon, St Cloud and Marly.[6]

He accumulated an exceptional collection of books and manuscripts concerning the making of gardens which is preserved with the rest of his library at the Academy of Sciences in St Petersburg. G.A. Böckler's *Nova architectura curiosa* contains much information about the construction of fountains and water amusements with many illustrations. Another book about fountains by Salomon de Caus, *Les Raisons des forces mouvantes avec diverses machines tant utiles que plaisantes*, which was taken to Russia by Le Blond, also covered water organs. A set of engravings of the outstanding gardens of Europe has Peter's notes in the margins. Two manuscript volumes presented to him in France contain plans drawn by Le Nôtre of Versailles and Marly.[7] In 1705 he ordered the publication in Amsterdam of *Simvoly i emblemy* (Symbols and emblems), since symbols were to play an important role in the educational content of the new gardens.[8] Peter made much use of these and other books when he presided over the creation of new parks and gardens. He instructed agents abroad to buy statues, particularly from Rome and Venice.

Most important of all, he engaged leading architects and gardeners to help create parks and gardens in his new capital. Among the distinguished foreign specialists who were persuaded to work for Peter were the architects Domenico Tressini, Johann Braunstein, Nicolo Michetti, Andreas Schlüter and Jean-Baptiste Alexandre Le Blond,[9] the sculptor Carlo Rastrelli and his son Bartolomeo, and the gardeners Jan Roosen and Leonard Hernichfelt.[10] At the same time, Peter placed great emphasis on the training of Russian specialists. Schools of architecture and gardening were set up, and the contracts of architects and gardeners engaged from abroad usually included a clause requiring them to train Russian pupils. It seems that they did not always take this part of their duties very seriously, and that those they were supposed to teach were sometimes exploited. One unfortunate pupil, Mikhail Petrov, complained in writing to the Chancellery of Building:

> I am humbly enrolled to study architecture with architect Johann Braunstein, with whom I have been for nine years, and up till now he has shown me only how to make copies of drawings, and during this time I have lived in poverty, and his wife makes us do all kinds of household work, and I have carted hay in from the country and looked after the stove and always looked after the birds . . . and put fire in the cooker and boiled water for tea and have done the cooking.

Some very able Russian architects and gardeners were trained, nevertheless, and there was no shortage of opportunities for them in the developing city.[11]

A vast number of trees had to be obtained for all the new parks and gardens. Many came from the villages around Moscow, particularly Kolomenskoe, Alekseevsky and Izmailovo, where there were large quantities of fruit trees and groves of limes and cedars. Flowering plants and bulbs, too, were provided from these villages, among them roses, peonies, tulips, narcissi and sweet-smelling herbs. Large quantities of trained trees and yew and box came from nurseries abroad, but the yew and the box failed to thrive in the Russian climate and were sometimes replaced by juniper (*Juniperus communis*) and red whortleberry (*Vaccinium vitis-idaea*).[12] Apple trees came from Sweden, roses and berberis from Danzig, and limes by the thousand from Holland. In a letter to the Russian ambassador in Holland, Boris Kurakin, in 1712, Peter wrote: 'If in Holland, near Haarlem, there are any lime trees grown from seeds (and not from wild ones) in sandy places. . . . work on this, in order to get some two thousand. . . . And having planted them with roots in sand on board of the ship, which is put as ballast, send them to Petersbourg in the same autumn.'[13]

Other species, such as birch and fir, of which many were planted, could be found in local woods. For Peterhof 40,000 elms and maples were brought from Moscow and 6,000 beeches from Rostov.[14] In 1708 orange and lemon trees were ordered by Peter from Persia and transported through Astrakhan and along the Volga. 'And have heated huts made for them to overwinter so that they don't die from frost.'[15]

It was also necessary to establish nurseries in St Petersburg. The plan of the first, the 'imperial reserve garden', was made and signed by Le Blond and has survived.[16] The site measured 950 × 1375 feet and was divided into several plots, with basins to provide water for the plants. The largest was for trees of various kinds, another was for fruit trees, including peaches and apricots, while a third was for oranges, lemons and southern plants. Although there was covered winter accommodation, it soon became clear that the range was excessively optimistic in this climate, and changes were made.

The Summer Garden

Peter's first garden in St Petersburg was the Summer Garden, begun in 1704. Ivan Matveev was responsible for much of the work until his death in 1707, though Peter himself no doubt took a hand in the planning. From 1711 to 1716 the Dutch gardener Jan Roosen was in charge. During the following three years Le Blond produced plans for the Summer Garden which do not seem to have been realized. Mikhail Zemtsov in the 1720s and, after Peter's death, Bartolomeo Rastrelli in the 1730s and 1740s both made considerable contributions.

Today the Summer Garden covers 27 acres, but in the eighteenth century it was substantially larger, extending over what are now the Field of Mars and the Mikhailovsky Garden.

Right, above: The Summer Garden is still the most popular open space in St Petersburg, but when the ground is soft after the thaw it has to be kept closed to the public.

Right: An early eighteenth-century bust of Flora in the Summer Garden.

Far right: An engraving by A. Zubov of the Summer Garden (1717).

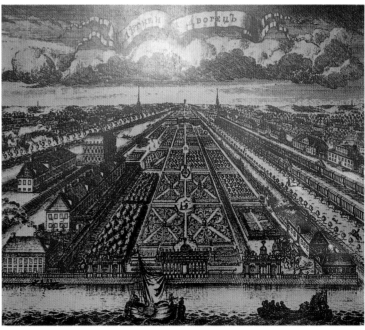

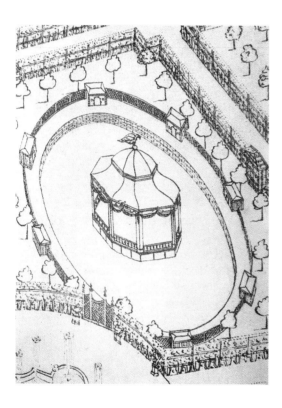

It was intended to be a venue where various ceremonies, festivals and firework displays might be held, and the principal areas were inspired by the gardens Peter had seen in Holland as well as by French gardens, which at that time he knew only from books and engravings. There were walks with statues, clipped green walls, covered ways formed with trained and clipped trees, a grotto and many fountains fed from the river, which thus earned its name Fontanka. The most interesting were those in the labyrinth which incorporated statues and sculptural groups, many of animals, illustrating Aesop's fables. Most of the animals were life-size and gilded. Peter's aim was educational – to introduce Russians to ideas from Western Europe – and a card with an explanatory text was placed by each fountain. Peter also enjoyed explaining the fables personally to visitors. Unfortunately most of the fountains were lost during the great flood of 1777.

The architects Andreas Shlüter, Georg Mattarnovy, Michetti, Le Blond and Zemtsov all took part in building the grotto, which probably stood where the Rossi Pavilion now stands in the Mikhailovsky Garden. It was divided into three halls, the walls of which were decorated with tufa, shells, coloured stones and glass, and it was intended to give the appearance of a cave. In the central hall there was a fountain with a statue of Neptune with seahorses, and there were other fountains. When the fountains played the water flowing through the pipes brought the water organ into play. On the parapet over the grotto stood statues of Flora, Navigation, Architecture, Fortune, Terpsichore and Zephyr. Sadly the grotto was also destroyed during the flood of 1777.[17]

After the death of Le Blond in 1719 Peter himself directed the introduction of an oval pool in a bosket near the main avenue with a summerhouse on a small island. A skiff was tied up by the side of the pool for Peter's use to reach the island when he wanted to be alone – reminiscent of the much more elaborate arrangements for imperial seclusion in the Marine Theatre at Hadrian's Villa.[18]

There is still a notable collection of ninety early eighteenth-century statues and busts in the Summer Garden, including works by Pietro Baratta, Antonio Bonazza and Zorzoni, but in 1736 the collection exceeded two hundred. In Peter's time the most important statue was an antique Venus which is now in the Hermitage. The Pope was reluctant to allow its export, but there were some holy relics among the war booty the Russians had taken from the Swedes. St Peter's successor in Rome could hardly refuse to release a pagan statue when offered a holy relic; while, in St Petersburg, an outstanding masterpiece of ancient art would have seemed well worth the additional cost of a small portion of the mortal remains of the Blessed Bridget.[19]

Peter's small Summer Palace – the work of Domenico Tressini – still survives in the corner of the garden near the river and has been well restored. Another palace was built for his wife, Catherine, at the other end of the garden in the present Mikhailovsky Garden, but it was demolished in the second half of the eighteenth century. Further palaces for the Empresses Anna and Elizabeth, both by Rastrelli, have also gone. According to Hirschfeld, Catherine had a small garden, planted by a Swedish gardener, which was approached by a bridge over the canal. On

Top: *View of the Summer Garden and the grotto from the River Fontanka* (1753), an engraving by G. Kachalov from a drawing by M. Makhaev.

Above: Peter's island retreat in the Summer Garden, from P.A. de Saint Hilaire's perspective plan of St Petersburg (1764–73).

the same site the Empress Elizabeth later had a summer palace with a pretty hanging garden outside her bedroom.[20]

Tressini was one of the ablest, most versatile and most influential of the foreign architects who worked in Russia. Born in Switzerland and trained in Italy, it was after building a palace for Frederick IV of Denmark, Peter's ally and personal friend, that he agreed in 1703 to work in Russia for a year and spent the rest of his life there. In addition to the Summer Garden, he was the architect for the Peter and Paul Fortress and Cathedral, the third Winter Palace, the ground floor of the Twelve Colleges and the fortifications, powder magazines, canals and living quarters on Kronstadt. He also produced a range of model plans for the residences and gardens of estates of all sizes, which the owners generally were obliged to follow.[21]

When the landscape style was introduced to Russia and the great landscape parks were made outside St Petersburg, the Summer Garden became rather neglected, but magnificent wrought-iron railings were added by Yuri Velten between 1770 and 1784. Carlo Rossi's Coffee House was added in 1826, Ludovik Charlemagne's Tea House in 1827 and Pyotr Klodt's monument to the Russian fabulist Krylov, with figures from his fables on the pedestal, in 1855.

The Summer Garden is still the favourite open space in St Petersburg, as it was during the nineteenth century. The trees have long been allowed to grow naturally and the original formal appearance of the garden has changed considerably. The statues no longer benefit from a background of clipped

Above: Peter's small palace in a corner of the garden by the river.
Below left: One of Tressini's model plans for residences and gardens in St Petersburg, to which owners were required to conform (*c.*1720).
Below: A model plan for a garden by Le Blond (*c.*1718).

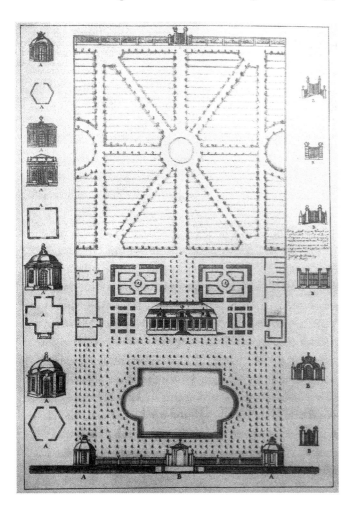

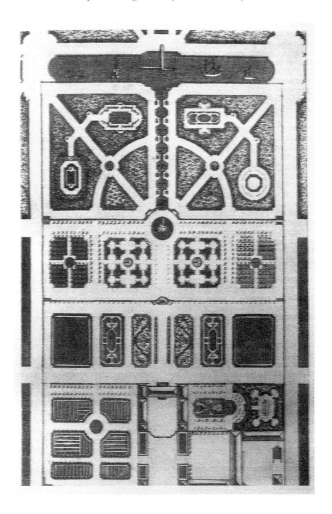

green hedges. Plans to restore some of the lost formality have been drawn up firstly by Tatyana Dubyago and, more recently, by Natalia Tumanova. Some restoration has already been undertaken. Now, in 2004, the Summer Garden is the responsibility of the Russian Museum, and a plan for further impressive restoration has been approved. It is intended to restore the fountains and the formally clipped hedges behind the statues. One hopes that the scheme will gain the support of the Ministry of Culture and that the necessary funds will be made available.

Peterhof

In few cities is one so constantly and so agreeably aware of the presence of water as in St Petersburg, with its many canals, great river and, not far away, the Gulf of Finland, the vital sea link with the West and the reason Peter the Great chose to establish his new capital here in 1703. Water is also an essential element in the gardens and parks created in and near the city by Peter and his successors, though the ways in which it was used varied with the changing fashions in gardening and landscaping. At Peterhof it is the main element in the park, and in no other park in the world has it been used so impressively.

Peter had a wooden palace at Peterhof several years before he began to create his great complex of palaces and gardens. It was a convenient place to stay during his frequent visits to Kronstadt where the fortress and dockyard, so vital to Russia's future, were being developed. It also gave him the opportunity to consider the capabilities of the site he favoured by the Gulf of Finland, which he was to use so effectively.

The massive iron pipes through which the water passes on the last stage of its 15-mile journey to the fountains at Peterhof.

The situation of the palace at Peterhof (also called Petrodvorets in Russia), near the edge of a natural terrace, about 50 feet above and some 2,000 feet away from the sea, lent itself to waterworks, and this is a very great water garden. A number of architects worked in the park, including Le Blond who made a major contribution, although he was there only from 1716 until his death in 1719. However, he was required to consult Peter about everything he proposed, and Peter frequently imposed his own revisions.

He rejected Le Blond's proposal that a sufficient supply of water should be obtained by damming two rivers and then raising it by means of a windmill and a special pumping machine 24 feet high and worked by horses. He had become familiar at Versailles and Marly with the practice of raising water artificially, but he looked for a simpler solution and went in search of other sources of water. He found one in 1720 near Ropsha, some 15 miles away. Hundreds of soldiers were pressed into service when work began shortly afterwards on a system of canals and reservoirs under the direction of hydraulic engineer Vasily Tuvolkov, who had studied in France.[22] On 8 August 1721, Peter went again to Ropsha personally to connect the new water system to the river Kavashi, and the fountains played for the first time the following morning. Additions and improvements continued throughout the eighteenth century and into the nineteenth, and there are now 25 miles of canals and eighteen reservoirs with a total surface area of almost 250 acres and a capacity of 300,000,000 gallons. And so, unlike Versailles, which Peter sought to outshine, Peterhof has an excellent supply of water, and some 660 gallons a second are now used there for ten to twelve hours a day during the summer months.

Mieczyslaw Pilsudski, who was in charge of the work of reconstructing the original fountain system in the 1850s, wrote a detailed account of the course followed by the water from the village of Olkhova near Ropsha, mainly by canal but partly by the channel of a small river. Along the bottom of the final length of canal it reaches the large pipe which later disappears underground and passes under the Upper Garden to the main pipe as well as branching out to all the other fountains. Pilsudski concluded:

> One may boldly say that there is no summer residence in the world like Peterhof. One may meet with more luxury, more wealth, but one cannot find a situation corresponding better to its purpose, more magnificent and beautiful. Having been abroad several times I base this on personal conviction. For twenty years I have shown the sights of Peterhof to foreigners. All without exception gave Peterhof precedence before the other pleasure palaces of Europe. The fountains of Versailles play for several hours a month and then not all at once. Such a spectacle costs about 30,000 francs a time. Here at Peterhof they play every day in summer and all of them without exception.[23]

The Upper Garden, designed as a formal approach to the palace, is rectangular in shape and covers about 37 acres. In Peter's time it was a simple, rather utilitarian area without special ornament. The monumental main gate and railings, replacing a much simpler earlier fence, date from 1754 and were designed by Bartolomeo Rastrelli. A wide central parterre with basins and impressive fountains is flanked by boskets and covered green ways. In 1738 the architects Ivan Blank and Ivan Davydov constructed treillage pergolas with niches in which cages of singing birds were hung.

The first fountains encountered on entering the Upper Garden are the threatening dragon and four leaping dolphins in the circular Mezheumny (Midway) Basin (diameter 100 feet) on the main axis. When these fountains were installed in the late 1730s to Carlo Rastrelli's plans, there was also a fountain-statue group of Perseus on horseback, holding the head of the gorgon Medusa and protecting Andromeda from the dragon, but by 1773 only the dragon and the dolphins survived, and they were rearranged. In 1858 they were replaced by a vase to the design of Andrei Stakenschneider, and it became the Vase Fountain. After total destruction during the German occupation the dragon and the dolphins were recreated from eighteenth-century drawings.[24]

The central Neptune Fountain group in a large rectangular basin (300 × 110 feet) is quite exceptional. The gilded statue of Neptune in his chariot, which had been placed on the Ruin Cascade in the Lower Park in 1723, was moved here on a large limestone base and surrounded by four tritons on horseback,

Below: The Neptune Fountain, decorated with dolphins and tritons.

Bottom: The Dragon and Dolphins Fountain.

tritons blowing into conch shells, and dolphins. By the end of the eighteenth century Neptune and his chariot had become badly misshapen and were replaced in 1799 by the present Neptune fountain group, bought by Paul I in Nuremberg. It was the work of Christoph Ritter in the 1650s and 1660s for the city centre, but the water supply had proved inadequate, and it had been put into storage. Neptune is surrounded by two female figures with oars, representing the Rivers Rednitz and Pegnitz, which flow through Nuremberg, riders on hippocampi, four infant tritons on dolphins, a sea lion and a dragon. During the occupation the Germans dismantled it and took it back to Germany, but it was recovered in 1947 and restored. At one end of the basin a bronze statue of Apollo Belvedere, based on an antique original, stands on a low marble column by a small cascade. It was installed here in 1800, replacing an earlier statue of Winter.[25]

The basin of the Oak Fountain, between the Neptune Fountain and the palace, is circular and similar in size to the Mezheumny Basin. It is called the Oak Fountain because there was originally a cascading gilded oak tree, with a group of dolphins and tritons underneath, by Carlo Rastrelli, no doubt inspired by the Oak Fountain at Versailles. In 1746 they were replaced by a tufa starfish with six dolphins and a horn of plenty. In 1929, during restoration, the horn of plenty was replaced by a gilded marble Cupid putting on a mask.

The two matching rectangular basins in front of the side galleries of the south façade of the palace were proposed by Le Blond to hold water for the Great Cascade. They were constructed in 1719 and 1720. In the west basin a sculptural group of Diana and the Nymphs by Carlo Rastrelli was installed in 1737. In 1770–3 six gilded spouting dolphins were added. At the same time a sculptural group of Arethusa and Alpheus and six similar dolphins were installed in the east basin. During restoration after 1945 the statue in the west pool was replaced by Venus and in the east by the young Apollo. There are also marble statues of Zephyr, Flora, Vertumnus and Pomona near by, all by Antonio Bonazza.[26]

Master gardener Leonard Hernichfelt was in charge of work in the gardens from the beginning until after Peter's death. His chief assistant was Anton Borisov and other gardeners were transferred to Peterhof from Izmailovo and Kolomenskoe, the imperial estates on the outskirts of Moscow. Hernichfelt was also responsible for the school of gardening at Peterhof, where pupils did practical work from April to October and then theory with lessons in natural history, Latin, German, mathematics and drawing plans. There would have been no shortage of trained gardeners, while a great deal of unskilled labour was also available. In 1721 more than two thousand soldiers and peasants were working at Peterhof and this number doubled in the following three years.[27]

In 1714 Johann Braunstein was appointed first architect for the main palace, but his plans were revised by Le Blond when he arrived in Russia two years later. The building which resulted was only the size of a country mansion, reflecting the modest tastes of the patron, who had, of course, closely supervised its development. In the early 1720s Michetti added matching pavilions on each side, linked to the central section by galleries decorated with statues and vases. Every part of the extended palace was covered by a handsome iron roof. Between 1747 and 1755 the palace was considerably enlarged for the Empress Elizabeth by Bartolomeo Rastrelli, who added a storey to the existing two-storey building and extended it further with three-storey wings.

The most important water feature in the park is the Great Cascade, which flows from grottoes below the terrace on the north front of the palace down to the Samson Fountain and Pool and then to the canal which leads to the Gulf of Finland. This is a quite extraordinary combination of architecture, sculpture and fountains, while it seems very much an integral part of the palace itself on the terrace above. The Small Grotto, the gilded Triton Fountain and two large gilded fountain wall-masks of Neptune and Bacchus are on the terrace just below the palace. On each side of this terrace a steeply stepped cascade, flanked by fountains, gilded statues, gilded vases and other ornaments, descends to the level below. Here the massive arched masonry of the Great Grotto, with its statues and shell-encrusted walls, seems to be supporting the palace. In front of the grotto the Basket Fountain makes a spectacular centrepiece. Twenty-eight curving jets weave together to appear to form a flower basket, while an inner ring of jets rises up high inside to suggest flowers.

The water flows on down the three steps of the central cascade to the Samson Pool, with personifications of the Rivers Neva and Volkhov adding to the flow, and Naiad, Siren, Triton and Dolphin Fountains joining in the fun. It all culminates with the figure of Samson forcing apart the jaws of the lion to release a column of water which rises 70 feet into the air, towering far above all the other fountains. A lion figures in the Swedish coat of arms, and this is an allegorical celebration of Russia's defeat of Sweden and the recovery of her access to the sea. While most of the Great Cascade was completed in Peter's lifetime, Carlo Rastrelli's fountain-statue of Samson was installed to mark the twenty-fifth anniversary of the Battle of Poltava where Russia gained a decisive victory on St Samson's Day 1709.[28]

On the Great Cascade there are 37 statues, 29 bas-reliefs, 108 consoles. 2 large and 5 small wall masks, 18 vases and 18 herms – all gilded. Statues of Jupiter, Juno, Aphrodite Callipygus, Neptune, Flora, Perseus, Galatea, Ganymede, Actaeon, a gladiator, a discobolus, an amazon, tritons, sirens, naiads, dolphins and frogs combine to extol the victory and Russian mastery of the sea. Myths from Ovid's *Metamorphoses*, depicted on the bas-reliefs on the steps of the cascade, allegorize the progress of Russia's struggle with Sweden. Pluto's abduction of Proserpina and the centaur Nessus' fatal attempt to ravish Deianeira, the wife of Hercules, reflect Sweden's seizure of

The Great Cascade, with fountains and gilded statues extolling Russian victory over Sweden and mastery of the sea.

Russian territory. Perseus' rescue of Andromeda from the sea monster, his beheading of Medusa, and Apollo's flaying of Marsyas allude to the defeat and humiliation of Sweden. Phaethon, shot down in flames by Jupiter, stands in for the Swedish king, Charles XII. This must be the most impressive victory celebration in garden architecture.

In 1720 British merchants in St Petersburg, Hill Thomas Evans and William Elmsall, contracted to supply some of the lead sculpture for Peterhof from England, including 'recumbent figures from underneath which water flows', 'two frogs which spurt water', six tritons, ten dolphins, lead consoles and lead frames; in the following year eighteen bas-reliefs and six figures of sirens and naiads were ordered for the grotto. Twelve statues, representing the months, and twelve urns were obtained from Holland. Other sculptured figures for the Great Cascade were cast in the St Petersburg workshops of Carlo Rastrelli and François Wassoult, some from moulds of ancient originals, as well as bas-reliefs, large masks and six figures of centaurs.[29]

The original gilded lead statues were showing considerable signs of wear by the end of the century, and in 1799 it was decided that they should be replaced by gilded bronze statues. This work was completed by 1806. While some of the replacements were copies of antique originals in the Academy of Arts, others were original works by the Russian sculptors I.P. Prokofev, Ivan Martos, Feodosy Schedrin and Fedot Shubin, and Jean Dominique Rachette. Mikhail Kozlovsky was responsible for Samson and the Lion.

The two colonnaded pavilions with gilded vase-fountains on the roofs near to the Samson Pool were added in 1803 by Voronikhin. In Peter's time there were wooden colonnades here, and it was intended to embellish them with statues, fountains and musical instruments worked by water, but by 1724 there was only a glockenspiel – a water organ with crystal bells – in the eastern colonnade. In 1745 another water organ was installed in the western colonnade with moving figures, accompanied by sound effects, of dogs, deer, a huntsman with a horn, birds and two satyrs playing flutes.[30]

Voronikhin's pavilions are on either side of the Sea Canal, which bisects the Lower Park and is flanked by twenty-two fountains. They were placed further away from the canal when they were first installed. At that time the canal was enclosed in trellis screens with twenty-two niches for fountains. Fountain-statues representing fables from Aesop – *Two Serpents, A Dragon Gnawing at an Anvil, A Mountain gives Birth to a Mouse* and *The Hen and the Kite* – were placed in four of the niches, while the other eighteen niches contained multi-jet wooden vase-fountains. In 1735 all the fountains were brought nearer to the banks of the canal in limestone basins, while the water outlets in the walls of the canal were covered with gilded lead masks. By 1860 new marble bowls were made for the fourteen fountains nearest to the palace and all the fountains had 13-foot

The Samson Fountain and the canal leading to
the Gulf of Finland.

single jets. The canal makes an impressive link with the sea, and the presence of the sea, as background, as foreground and symbolically, contributes very significantly to the character and impact of Peterhof. It was always intended that it should be approached by sea, and the best way of visiting the palace today is by hydrofoil. The canal and the small harbour to which it leads were dug out by Swedish prisoners of war living in wretched conditions.[31]

The Great Fountains stand on the extensive parterres below the palace terrace on either side of the Samson Pool: the French Fountain to the east and the Italian to the west. The fountains are identical, 4 feet wide marble bowls on monumental marble pedestals, standing at the centre of pools some 25 feet wide and edged in marble. One was built by the French hydrotechnical expert Sualem, the other by Giovanni and Giuliano Barattini. The original bowls were of oak. The replacements were made in 1854 at the Peterhof Stone Works to Stakenschneider's designs.[32]

Elaborate parterres of embroidery, as they were called, were laid out by Hernichfelt and Borisov to the designs of Le Blond. They are said to have been bordered with closely clipped box, but this seems unlikely. It may have been red whortleberry, *Vaccineum vitis-idaea*, which was sometimes used as substitute for box in Russia and Sweden. When the palace was extended by Rastrelli, he and master gardener Bernhard Fock created new parterres to accord with it. Their intricate patterns of crushed marble, crushed brick and shells against a background of grass were the basis of the present restored parterres.

Like the Great Cascade with its Samson fountain, the Marly and the Ruin Cascades both celebrated the victories on land and at sea which had led to Russia's recovery of her land by the Baltic. Marly was Peter's favourite French garden and he had studied the water system there with great interest. The two principal cascades at Marly, the Water Staircase (*Rivière d'eau*) and the Agrippine Cascade, were illustrated in the Marly album which Peter had been given, and he intended his Marly Cascade to have the look of the Water Staircase and his Ruin Cascade to reflect the Agrippine Cascade, but the situation and conditions were different at Peterhof and there is no close resemblance.

To the east of the canal, the Ruin Cascade, now called the Dragon Cascade or the Chessboard Hill, was built on a steep slope 70 feet high with four terraces cut into the face. In 1721 Michetti designed a small marble cascade with two tower-ruins, and two years later it was decided to place a sculptural group, *Neptune in his Chariot* by Carlo Rastrelli, at the top of the cascade. In the 1730s new plans were made, and the cascade was decorated with tufa, wooden dragons and Italian statues. Later it was painted in black and white squares. In 1874 metal dragons were cast in Germany to replace the wooden ones, but they were destroyed during the 1941–5 war, while the statues, which had been buried, survived. New bronze dragons were made in 1953 based on eighteenth-century drawings.[33]

For his Marly Cascade, west of the canal, Peter instructed Michetti to draw up a plan copying the French model, but the

The view across the Marly Cascade and the
Marly Palace to the Garden of Venus and the
Gulf of Finland.

Top: The Marly Palace.

Above: Statues of Neptune, a triton, a nymph and
gilded masks of Medusa at the head of the Marly
Casacde.

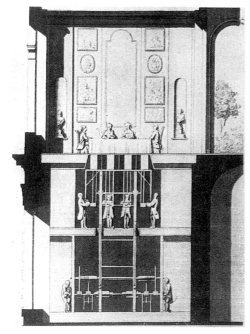

number of steps had to be reduced to suit the incline of the slope. Peter later asked Zemtsov to design a sculptural group of Hercules overcoming the seven-headed Hydra, while Carlo Rastrelli created the three gilded masks of the head of Medusa, from the jaws of which water flowed on to the cascade. After Peter's death there was a break in the work until 1731 when Zemtsov was ordered to complete the cascade, and he added marble statues of Neptune, a triton and a nymph on the wall above the masks and Andromeda and Venus with a cupid by the bottom steps. When the Germans invaded in 1941 the masks and the statues were hidden and survived.

Close by, the Marly Palace was built to the plans of Braunstein on a narrow strip of land surrounded by artificial stretches of water. It is a particularly elegant small country mansion and Peter was very attached to it. It looks out across a very large rectangular pool. The semi-circular pool behind is divided into four equal segments by radial walls supporting paths with a patterned surface and ornamental railings. The pools were a source of fish for the kitchens – carp, tench and other kinds according to an eighteenth-century visitor. It is said that Peter used to sound a bell to summon the fish to be fed.

The large garden of fruit trees between the Marly Palace and the embankment by the sea was given the name Garden of Venus by Peter. The massive embankment, about 13 feet high and 835 feet long, was built to protect the garden from the winds blowing across the Gulf of Finland. The earth extracted when the Marly pools were being excavated – by up to a thousand soldiers and peasants – was used, reinforced by stone, to form a base on which to build the stone and brickwork wall. The wall was then stuccoed, coloured with ochre and surmounted by a balustrade. The many wide niches in the wall were planted with cherry trees, attached to wooden frames, and embellished with marble vases on pedestals. During the early years of the garden there was a pigeon house, designed by Zemtsov, with a high roof crowned with a lantern and a tall spire.[54]

Hermitages – pleasure pavilions where small parties could be entertained in some seclusion – were a fairly common feature in formal gardens in the eighteenth century. The Hermitage at Peterhof, close to the shore between the Marly Palace and the canal, was the first of this kind in Russia. It is surrounded by a moat, intended to be filled with water and originally crossed by a drawbridge. Intimate dinner parties were held on the first floor – the Upper Hall – which was reached by a chair lift, now replaced by a staircase. On the ground floor there was a machine to raise and lower the central section of the dining table with its fourteen walnut place mats. All the service, course by course, was provided on the ground floor, and the meal could be freely enjoyed without the inhibiting presence of servants. Through the windows there were splendid views of the park and the Gulf of Finland, and an outstanding collection of pictures covered the walls.[55]

Peter's first and favourite residence in the park was the Monplaisir Palace on the east side of the canal. He chose the site at the sea's edge so that he might view passing ships and his

fortress island Kronstadt. He contributed towards the planning with the participation of Braunstein, Le Blond and Michetti. It is not very large and was inspired by the pleasingly unpretentious houses which Peter had admired in Holland. The central and original part of the building has a high mansard roof and there is a long gallery, added later, leading to a small pavilion on each side. Although modest in size the construction and the interior decoration were of a very high standard.

The Monplaisir garden lies on the south side of the palace and is enclosed to the east and the west by identical single-storey service buildings. The garden is divided into four square compartments by two intersecting paths. Peter himself, as so often, decided on the outlines of the garden, and his sketch, showing the quartered garden and three paths radiating from it, has survived. Master gardener Leonard Hernichfelt laid out the garden between 1714 and 1716. Fertile soil was spread over the site, paths were made, the four quarters were edged with box (or perhaps a box substitute), flowering plants were introduced and at the sides of the garden young limes, maples and chestnuts were planted. The garden was enclosed by trellis on three sides, and there were covered green allées. Near the entrance to the palace there was a sundial on a marble pedestal.

In the early 1720s a number of gilded lead statues designed by Michetti were installed. There was a gilded cloche fountain surmounted by a gilded statue in each of the four quarters, while the Sheaf Fountain stood in a basin surrounded by tufa at the centre of the garden where the paths crossed. The two trick Bench Fountains at the ends of the side allées have been recreated.[36] The present flower garden does not quite reproduce the garden of the early eighteenth century.

Peterhof has some of the best surviving eighteenth-century trick fountains. The Umbrella Fountain, which is a particular favourite of children visiting the park, surrounds those who walk under it with a wall of water, while the Bench Fountain is liable to soak the unwary who sit on it. When the dilapidated oak tree was removed from its basin in the Upper Garden the surviving pieces were used to make a new one, which was placed with the tulip fountains near the Bench Fountain in the hope that visitors would decide to sit down to admire them. All the trick fountains were destroyed during the war, but restoration began in the late 1940s. Skilled craftsmen recreated the Oak Fountain from a drawing of 1828 and a record left by Pilsudski. The replacement has 500 hollow branches and several thousand leaves, and there are five tulips. The three Fir Tree Fountains, first made in 1784, were recreated from an old drawing in 1958. These surviving water jokes date from the second half of the eighteenth century. There were numerous other earlier trick fountains in the Lower Park, in the Great Grotto, and in front of the Ruin Cascade.

The Sun Fountain, a golden disc from which a circle of jets radiates, revolves above a ring of spouting dolphins in the Menagerie Pool not far from Monplaisir, so called because Peter intended it to be part of a menagerie – in the sense of an enclosure for birds or animals, not a zoo – and swans and other

Top: Enthusiastic visitors under the Umbrella Trick Fountain.

Above left: The Sun Fountain.

Above right: The Aviary.

ornamental birds were kept there. At each side of the pool there was an aviary for singing birds; one of them has survived, but without prisoners. Later in the eighteenth century the Menagerie Pool became a swimming and boating pool for the imperial family and was surrounded by an unfortunate high wall, with painted decoration, which remained until 1926.

The Pyramid Fountain is one of the most elaborate, with 505 jets rising above each other in seven tiers from a four-sided pyramid on a stepped marble base. Michetti had proposed a fountain based on the Obelisk Fountain at Versailles, but Peter decided on a pyramid. It was constructed by Braunstein, Zemstov and Sualem. It stands in a basin on a large square raised platform with balustrades and vases; the water cascades down a short flight of steps on each of the four sides.

Two of the most prominent features in the Lower Park are the Adam and Eve Fountains, standing at key points on the Marly Avenue which runs from the Marly Pool in the west to the boundary of the park 1¼ miles away in the east. Eve is on the west side of the canal, Adam on the east, each of them on pedestals surrounded by sixteen powerful jets at the centre of deep octagonal basins 60 feet across. Paths radiate from the basins, part of the system of paths *en étoiles* – in star formation – introduced by Le Blond, so the statues are seen from various points in the park. They were commissioned in 1718 from the Venetian sculptor Giovanni Bonazza; he was inspired by Antonio Rizzi's statues in the Doges' Palace.[37] Peter must have thought that these former residents of Paradise would feel at home at Peterhof.

The imposing two-tiered Roman Fountains on the extensive grass parterre with flowered borders in front of the Dragon Cascade were constructed in 1738–9 to designs by Blank and Davydov, inspired by the fountains in St Peter's Square, Rome. They were originally made of wood lined with sheet lead, but their replacements at the end of the eighteenth century were of granite faced with marble and ornamented with lead masks, festoons, wreaths, garlands and shells. They were restored in 1954.

The palatial two-storey orangery, completed in 1725 with a sheet-iron roof from the foundries of the Demidovs in the Urals, was probably designed by Michetti. It was intended for the cultivation of exotic flowering plants and for the winter protection of plants in pots and tubs, which were placed outside in milder seasons for the enhancement of the palaces, parterres, fountains, basins and grottoes. There is a notable fountain in the Orangery Garden of a triton struggling with a sea monster on an island of tufa with four spouting turtles in attendance.

One other fountain which must be mentioned is the Favoritka, situated behind Voronikhin's Western Colonnade, which features a pug chasing four ducks round a small basin. It has survived – though with considerable restoration – since 1725 and was based on Aesop's fable of *The Four Ducks and the Poodle*. Originally there was an acoustic device which made the dog bark and the ducks quack.[38]

Above: The Eve Fountain.

Below: One of the two Roman Fountains.

Above left: The Favoritka Fountain, with a pug chasing four ducks.

Above: The Nymph Fountain.

Left: The Triton and Sea Monster Fountain.

Right: A Triton cloche fountain.

When the German army invaded Russia in 1941 and advanced towards Leningrad, urgent attempts were made to move as much of the contents as possible from the great palaces and museums to Sarapul and Novosibirsk, but a good deal was also moved to St Isaac's Cathedral in Leningrad. Marina Tikhomirova, the former chief custodian of Peterhof, lived in Leningrad throughout the blockade, helping to look after the vast quantity of very valuable objects, with many packing cases marked Peterhof, Pushkin (Tsarskoe Selo) and Pavlovsk, along with colleagues from those palaces and from Gatchina. She later wrote an absorbing account of her experiences there and of the enormous task of restoration after the German retreat – *Pamyatniki, Liudi, Sobytiya* (*Monuments, People, Events*).

It was intended to send the bronze statues from the Great Cascade to one of the distant depositories to the east, and some were packed in crates and taken to the goods section of the Oktyabrsky railway station in Leningrad, where they spent the war when the way was closed to them. The one exception was Perseus, who, a sword in one hand and Medusa's head in the other, occupied the porch at St Isaac's, suggesting that the Germans would soon share the fate of the Swedes. There had not been time to move the rest of the bronze statues, and, with the German army approaching and Peterhof under fire from artillery and from the air, a small group of palace-museum workers stayed behind long enough to move most of them to a secret tunnel near the Great Grotto. Samson and some other statues by the Samson Pool were too heavy to move and had to be left where they were.

Life was grim in Leningrad between 1941 and 1944, the winters were dire, there was little food and fuel, there were constant air and artillery attacks, and very many died. Peterhof was finally liberated on 19 January 1944, Pushkin, Pavlovsk and Gatchina a day or two later. On 31 January Marina Tikhomirova and her colleagues from the other palaces set off in a bus, through a landscape badly scarred and littered with the debris of recent battles, to report on the condition of the buildings and the parks they had had to leave. When Tikhomirova reached Peterhof she was appalled by what she saw beyond the ruined gates and railings of the Upper Park:

> Indescribable chaos, ruins half-covered in snow, an enormous anti-tank trench cutting through the whole garden and beyond it the burnt-out ruins of the Great Palace, without its gold cupolas, dark-red against the dazzlingly white snow. But that was only the start of the tragic discoveries on a day that sticks in the memory.[39]

During the siege of Leningrad much of the treasure from the great palaces was stored under the dome of St Isaac's Cathedral.

Narrow paths led past snow drifts, broken branches of trees and notices warning of mines – 'Achtung! Minen'. She found the Marly Cascade half-destroyed and the Marly Palace another burnt-out ruin. The Hermitage had lost its elevating table, and there was a gun on the upper floor with its barrel jutting out of a gap in the wall and directed towards Kronstadt. Many thousands of trees had been destroyed. Not only was the Great Palace burnt out, but the central section had been blown up along with the terrace outside. She was soon to learn of similar situations in all the great palaces and parks.

There were mines and booby-traps everywhere, and it was dangerous to attempt anything until the sappers had done their work. In Peterhof and the surrounding area 35,000 mines and booby-traps and 15,000 shells were dealt with, and some fifteen sappers were killed and twenty seriously injured. Those who died share a common grave and memorial by the road leading to Old Peterhof. There were booby-traps even in the underground passages leading to the fountains, where, among the iron pipes, mine-detectors were ineffective. Their place was very successfully taken by Jim, a collie-sapper, with several thousand sniffed-out mines to his credit already.[40]

Once the ground was cleared the task of restoring statues and fountains could get under way. Finding the marble statues which had been buried in the garden was more difficult than had been anticipated. When they were buried their location was recorded in relation to some object near by, but too often the object they had been related to had disappeared in the general destruction. Some of the statues survived their interment fairly well, others less so. While Adam needed very little repair, Eve was exhumed in several pieces and required a great deal of expert attention.

A major problem was the loss not only of Samson but of the Tritons, the Neva and the Volkhov, which had all been carried off by the Germans and not recovered, and new statues had to be made. Replacements were also needed for the bas-reliefs, consoles, masks and herms. The bas-reliefs with scenes from Ovid were a particular problem, since there was no satisfactory pictorial record of the scenes sculpted on them.[41] Aids to their recreation were found in the illustrations to early French, German and Dutch editions of the *Metamorphoses*. A collection of scenes from a Nuremburg edition of Ovid of 1699 was published in Russia in 1721, and there were scenes from Ovid on some Russian medals. Similar scenes on bas-reliefs on Peter's Summer Palace were also of considerable assistance. The work on the statues and all the sculptured ornament was carried out by a group of Leningrad sculptors under the direction of Innokenty Suvorov.

When the former imperial parks were restored after the war the most symbolic and the most important event was the restoration of the statue of Samson and the Lion at Peterhof, and in 1946 the task was entrusted to the Soviet sculptor Vasily Simonov.[42] Again there was no satisfactory pictorial record and no measurements apart from the height – 10 feet – and the weight. What was needed was a range of photographs from different angles and that was not available. An appeal was made in the press for snapshots, and hundreds were sent in. Almost all of them were taken from the same limited range of viewpoints, but eighteen which were more useful were selected. Drawings were made from them with the image on each adjusted to a height of 12 inches (a tenth of the height of Kozlovsky's Samson) and eighteen silhouettes were made. These were then transferred on to tracing paper and set into a screen, and Simonov viewed them there with the 12-inch sketches he had made for the sculpture, seeking a complete correspondence between the two in every detail. Subsequently he compared from different angles the first small model he made with the images on the screen. Then, with valuable assistance from fellow sculptor Nikolai Mikhailov, he spent many days recreating Samson and the Lion, which was cast with great pride in fourteen parts by the workforce at the Monumentsculptura foundry.

On 31 August 1947, a clear and sunny day, the bronze sculpture, 10 feet tall and weighing 5 tons, was mounted on the back of a lorry with its makers and set off through the streets of Leningrad to the surprise and delight of the passers-by. It was a Sunday, so many were out on Nevsky Prospect to applaud and cheer the hero's return. Groups of military personnel stood to attention and saluted as they would a general, traffic police held up the city transport at all crossroads to ensure a clear passage, and a stream of small vehicles formed a procession to escort Samson far out of the city on his way home. On arriving at Peterhof sleeves were rolled up for the far from easy task of hoisting him back into place, and then everything was ready for the further celebration when the fountains were turned on again.

While work had been continuing on the fountains, it was also in progress on the water system which fed them. New sluices and new dams had to be constructed as well as brick tunnels and hundreds of yards of iron pipe. It was vitally important to find someone who really understood how fountains work and how to control them to produce every shade of variation for the range of effects that were required. They were very lucky to get P.P. Lavrentyev, who turned out to be a complete master of the art.

On 14 September many thousands flocked to Peterhof for the great occasion. As midday approached, in front of the still-ruined palace, a naval guard stood in attendance, an orchestra played, choristers sang and poets declaimed the verses they had written, anticipating this event, during the blockade. Two miles away a rocket was fired to signal that the sluice had been opened in the restored water system, and shortly afterwards a column of water shot triumphantly into the air from the mouth of the lion to the immense satisfaction of all present. And on the terrace above, the musicians played Glinka's *Slava*, the Russian Hymn of Victory, to accompany this celebration in water of Russia's latest triumph, for now the lion represented not Sweden but the defeated armies of the Third Reich.

Left: A photograph of the ruined palace after the German occupation, *c*.1945.

Right: Great symbolic importance was attached to the restoration of the Samson Fountain after the end of the war. The palace was restored later.

Strelna

Peter's other great park at Strelna began at much the same time as Peterhof. They are only 3 miles apart and are both picturesquely situated on the same high terrace overlooking the Gulf of Finland. At first a small wooden palace was built for Peter with a church not far away and two cottages for visitors. There was a small flower garden, in which tulips and daffodils were grown, and fir trees were planted round it clipped as pyramids. Near by stood an old lime tree with a treehouse approached by a spiral staircase round the trunk. Glasshouses, fruit gardens, vegetable gardens and a carp pool followed.[45]

In 1710 Peter decided on the site for the intended great stone palace and its grounds. In 1715 Carlo Rastrelli and his son, Bartolomeo, were contracted to work on the planning of the building, gardens and fountains, but in the following year Peter turned to Le Blond for an alternative scheme. Le Blond's very impressive plan survives in the State Hermitage Museum, showing the palace on the edge of the terrace, looking across the lower garden, which was divided by three canals, flanked by lime avenues and linked with the gulf. The spaces between them were divided by a transverse canal. A great variety of detail included many boskets, fountains and a central cascade. The water for the cascade and the fountains was to be brought by pipes from a source a few miles away. Le Blond also proposed that the level of the avenues should be raised by 3 feet to protect them from flooding from the sea. He estimated that four thousand workmen would be required. In the spring of 1717 fifty

thousand trees were planted on the upper terrace, a great deal of work was done in the lower park, and pipes for the fountains were ordered.

But, for some reason, Peter was not satisfied with Le Blond's efforts and ordered a new scheme from the Italian architect Sebastiano Cipriani, who had trained Russian students in Italy. His plan, sent from Italy, seems to have been altogether inferior to Le Blond's and it, too, failed to satisfy Peter who turned next to Nicolo Michetti in 1718. Where the transverse canal crossed the central canal on Le Blond's plan there was an island with an artificial hill surmounted by a pavilion, the Water Castle. This was also shown on Cipriani's plan. Peter rejected this feature because it would have shut out the view of the sea and passing ships. Instead he is said personally to have sown seeds of pines on the small flat island, which had been gathered in the Harz mountains of Germany, and to have ordered that there should be a clearing across the island to keep open the view to the sea. Michetti's plan reflects Peter's wishes on this point.

Dubyago was not able to study Michetti's plan and did not know whether it still existed when she wrote about Strelna in 1963: 'Michetti's general scheme for the park is not known. Archival documents, contemporary plans of the ensemble and study of the park as it is now suggest that Michetti added another transverse canal to the system of canals, dividing off that part of the park at the foot of the palace where flowerbeds were laid out. It is very probable that at the same time the system of diagonal avenues in the park was devised, traces of

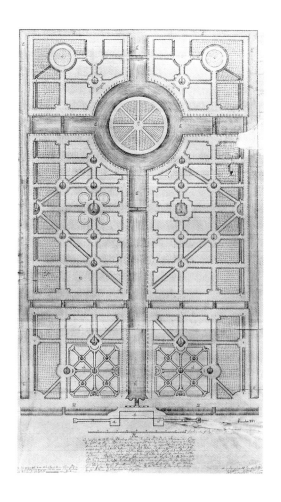

Above: The remains of the great park at Strelna. The palace became a naval college during the Soviet period.

Far left: Le Blond's plan for Strelna (1717).

Left: Michetti's plan for Strelna (c.1719).

Right: An overgrown canal in the park.

Far right: The remains of the grotto under the palace.

which still survive.'[44] Michetti's plan, which is in the Nationalmuseum in Stockholm, is reproduced here and confirms the details anticipated by Dubyago. In 1746 Friedrich von Bergholz, who had spent much of his life in Russia, was dismissed as tutor to the future Peter III. When he left Russia for Sweden he took with him a large collection of Russian architectural drawings, all of which, including Michetti's plan, are now in the Nationalmuseum.[45]

After the death of Le Blond in 1719 the foundations of the palace were laid in 1720 and work continued on Michetti's scheme until 1722. The French gardener Denis Brocket was in charge in the gardens, and many alders, limes and maples were planted, but a considerable proportion of them died because of the marshiness of the land. Covered ways were to play a considerable part and a thousand arches were made for them.

After he had visited the site in the early 1720s Bergholz wrote:

> Three terraces of unusual length, descending by slopes from the hill to the garden, are already finished and provided with pipes for the fountains, which will play on all sides, and which, I have heard, have already cost the Tsar a significant sum. In the middle of the upper terrace the foundations have already been laid of an extensive palace which will be almost more magnificent than Versailles in France. From the main body of the palace across all the terraces a large, wide cascade descends into the garden with a vault inside from which emerges something like a grotto. . . . It is incomprehensible how the Tsar, in spite of the hard and lengthy war, could in such a short time build St Petersburg, the harbours in Reval and Kronstadt, a considerable navy and so many pleasure castles and palaces.[46]

Strelna and Peterhof were being developed at the same time, and during the early years Peter seemed to give Strelna precedence as his principal residence and for expenditure on fountains. However, the supply of water was better at Peterhof, and the terrace from which it would flow was rather higher, and it was probably these factors, together with the loss of so many trees, which led to a decline in Peter's enthusiasm. Attention was now concentrated on Peterhof and turned towards another park at Dubki.

The Strelna Palace, which was largely rebuilt by Andrei Voronikhin and Luigi Rusca after a major fire in 1803, was still well preserved until the Second World War, and the outlines of the park remained impressive, although the early plans were never fully realized; however, both palace and park suffered immense damage during the German occupation.

Dubki

In addition to Peterhof, Strelna and the Summer Palace, Peter also had three residences on the north coast of the Gulf of Finland between St Petersburg and Sestroretsk, namely Dubki (The Oaks), which was also called Far Dubki, New Dubki and Old Dubki. Peter needed a residence near Sestroretsk when visiting the armaments factory there. Virtually nothing remains of them now, but there are references to them in the archives including Peter's field journal. On 16 September 1720 he was 'in Far Dubki measuring the site for the garden'.[47] Old Dubki was the first to be built, but little is known about it and virtually nothing remains.

At Dubki there is still a large grove of old oaks where it was built, and it is possible that they were already there and attracted Peter to the site, and that he added to them. That some of the oaks along this stretch of coast have been there for about four hundred years has been shown by counting the annual growth rings on an old stump. Like Monplaisir the palace was built at the sea's edge on an artificial embankment jutting out into the sea at the southern end of the Dubkovsky Promontory, and there was a viewing terrace protected by a sea wall. A large harbour had been made near by. Both the house and the garden were designed by the Dutch architect Steven van Swieten, whose plan, dated 1722, is in the State Hermitage Museum. The garden was behind the palace and was surrounded by canals faced with stone. As was then typical of Dutch gardens, it was divided by two avenues of trees forming a cross into four rectangles with parterres and fountains. Two hundred and seventy five chestnuts and other trees were planted in 1723, and the main road was also planted with chestnuts. In the boskets both chestnuts and limes were planted. Peter insisted on chestnuts, which he particularly liked – 'the place is very warm, the soil is good'. He was well informed, since it seems that this is the only place in the vicinity of St Petersburg where young chestnuts are not killed by frost. Among the oaks beyond the garden a system of paths was formed *en étoiles*, and there were pavilions and summerhouses. Peter ordered the transfer of a large part of the Strelna workforce to Dubki, where he intended to install fountains which would rival Peterhof, using water pumped up from the overflow resulting from the construction of a dam. Floods, however, proved to be a considerable problem, and Old Dubki did not survive long. A plan of 1740 shows only the remains of the palace and the completely neglected garden, and nothing can be seen there now apart from traces of the canals.

A surviving plan of New Dubki, also called Near Dubki, between Lakhta and Sestroretsk, indicates that the site was almost square, bounded by canals and divided into four parts by a transverse canal crossing the main avenue, with a round island at the intersection, reminiscent of the island at Strelna. There were glasshouses in one of the divisions including a vine house. By combining archival research with fieldwork Dubyago succeeded in finding the outlines of the New Dubki estate among the undergrowth in the forest park.[48]

Ekaterinhof

Ekaterinhof, the small palace of Peter's wife Catherine by the River Ekaterinhofka, dates from 1714 or a little earlier. As Zubov's engraving shows, it was quite a modest residence, approached by a short length of canal which divided the garden into two parts, each with a flower garden enclosed by a covered way and a treillage summerhouse by the river. It soon suffered considerable damage from flooding, and new plans were sought from Le Blond. To reduce the risk of repeated flooding he suggested raising the site by 3 feet and surrounding the garden by canals terminating in octagonal basins. He also proposed the installation of a water-raising machine for fountains and suggested that his fellow-countryman Denis Brocket should undertake the work. No action seems to have been taken. Even smaller palaces, Annenhof and Elizavethof, were built near by for Peter's daughters, but they never reached the stage of having gardens.

Above: An engraving by A. Zubov of Ekaterinhof (*c*.1717).

Top: The canal that ran through the garden to the palace is all that remains of Ekaterinhof.

In the late 1730s work began at Ekaterinhof on a vast new hunting park for the Empress Anna Ivanovna. Much of it was intended for deer, and there was to be an impressive radial system of avenues, as was usual in hunting parks. There were also to be boskets for hares, an aviary and pools for waterfowl. A Temple of Diana was to be built at the centre of the deer park and there would be other temples and pavilions. The death of the Empress brought an end to this development.

In the nineteenth century a landscape park was added at Ekaterinhof and it became a popular resort for celebrations and fêtes. While the small palace finally burned down in the 1920s, the canal that led to it can still be seen.[49]

Kamenny Island

Count Gabriel Golovkin's estate on Kamenny Island was one of the most important in St Petersburg. At first there was a wooden house and a large formal garden divided into a series of rectangular areas; these were surrounded by clipped green walls with openings giving access to the fruit and vegetable gardens enclosed in them. It was described as 'a fine garden embellished

Below: Engraving (1753) from a drawing by M. Makhaev showing the Hermitage in the garden of the Bestuzhev-Ryumins on Kamenny Island.

Bottom: Engraving (1753) from a drawing by M. Makhaev showing the Gallery on Kamenny Island.

with various avenues', but after it had been acquired by the Bestuzhev-Ryumins it became even finer, as the engravings seen here testify. Members of the public were admitted and another engraving shows a notice by the entrance reading in three languages 'for all honest people'. The Hermitage and the Gallery were fine park buildings, while the presence of the river further enhanced their settings.[50]

The best of the small estates in St Petersburg in Peter's time were by the Rivers Moika and Fontanka. While some of the early buildings survive, little or nothing remains of the gardens, but the graphic evidence of plans of the city made in 1753 and 1764–73 indicates that the standard of garden design was uniformly quite impressive. This was because the owners were obliged to follow the model designs of Domenico Tressini. There was a whole range of these from which a choice could be made according to the size of the site and the financial circumstances of the owner.[51] The Peterhof Road, leading along the coast from the city to Peterhof, was already the most favoured residential area outside the city, and Tressini's plans must have been used by those lucky enough to secure plots.

Vasilevsky Island

The estate of Prince Alexander Menshikov on Vasilevsky Island was laid out at about the same time as the Summer Garden. Menshikov was Peter's close and trusted associate, who lost no opportunity of putting his privileged position to considerable personal advantage. His was the first residence in St Petersburg to be approached by its own canal. The estate covered some 30 acres and was maintained by a large team of gardeners, said to number sixty-seven in 1728. There were flowerbeds, basins, labyrinths, *cabinets de verdure* and covered allées. Bergholz considered it to be the most remarkable garden in St Petersburg after the imperial gardens.

When Peter died in 1725 he was succeeded by his wife Catherine I, who had been Menshikov's mistress before transferring her affections to Peter. Menshikov was now the most powerful figure in the land, and, when Catherine died only two years later, he was able to ensure that her successor would be the eleven-year-old Peter II, Peter I's grandson, and to arrange the engagement of the new Tsar to his daughter Maria. His luck ran out when Peter turned against him, and he died in exile in Siberia in 1729. Sadly Peter died of smallpox in 1730, and this brought to the throne Anna Ivanovna (1730–40), the daughter of Ivan, Peter I's inadequate half-brother and co-Tsar. By this time Menshikov's estate on Vasilevsky Island was declining rapidly and Anna authorized its transfer to the cadet corps. In 1745 the Empress Elizabeth (1741–61), Peter I's daughter, decreed that 25,000 mature trees 'and if possible more' should be transplanted from the garden to the new area which had been added to the Summer Garden. Now no trace of Menshikov's garden remains.[52]

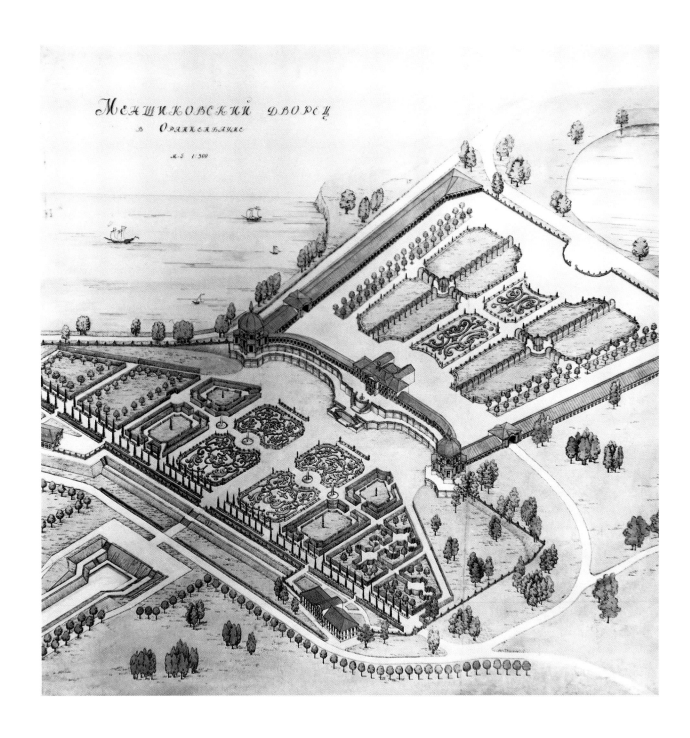

Oranienbaum

Oranienbaum, or Lomonosov as it became known during the Soviet period, was another residence of Menshikov's. Like Peterhof and Strelna it was situated on the terrace by the Gulf of Finland with a view across to, and easy access to, the island of Kronstadt, where Menshikov was responsible for the development of the fortress and dockyard. The architects of the palace, which was grander than Peter's at Peterhof, were Giovanni Fontana and Gottfried Schädel. The central block was probably built between 1710 and 1716 and then a curvilinear gallery and a pavilion were added to each side.

There was a steep slope down from the terrace on which the palace stood to a large formal central parterre with fountains and carved wooden statues painted to imitate marble (three fountains and forty-six statues according to a 1720 report). The parterre was flanked by boskets of clipped plants and beyond it

there was a small harbour to which a canal led from the sea. A Swedish master gardener worked here from 1709 to 1728.[53]

After Menshikov's exile in 1727 Oranienbaum was confiscated and became dilapidated, but in 1743 it became the property of Peter Fyodorovich, later Peter III. The further development of Oranienbaum will be described in Chapter Four.

The palace, the upper garden and the lower garden at Oranienbaum, with part of the canal and the basin bottom left. From P.A. de Saint Hilaire's axonometric plan of 1775.

Tsarskoe Selo

The first imperial building at Tsarskoe Selo was a small wooden house for Peter's wife Catherine with two smaller buildings for servants. The garden, 100 × 100 sazhens (700 × 700 feet) was divided by two avenues of clipped trees in the form of a cross into four squares. Niches with treillage and summerhouses were formed in the avenues. By damming the river a basin was created and two canals to provide an outflow from it.

In 1718 the wooden house was replaced by a stone palace to the plans of Johann Braunstein, and the garden was refashioned by the gardener Jan Roosen to harmonize with it. He submitted a report in which he referred to projected terraces and gave calculations for the earthworks necessary for their construction and for reinforcing the beds of two basins.

The garden was laid out on a series of terraces, parallel with the façade of the palace, with slight differences of level and with gently descending flights of steps. There were flowerbeds on the first terrace enclosed by espaliers of maple and trellis. On the second terrace there were covered allées, probably with treillage summerhouses as was usually the case then. On the third terrace there were two identical rectangular basins.

Beyond, in the lower area, there was a radial system of allées, and in this part of the garden the parterres were surrounded by walls of clipped trees, with fruit trees planted inside. In 1718 there were 1,590 apple trees, 800 cherries, 280 gooseberry bushes, 160 redcurrants, 360 blackcurrants, and 22 beds of strawberries. Beyond the large canal a 'wild grove' was planted using 738 birch trees.[54]

In 1718 a hunting park was developed on land to the north-west of the palace, where a large square area was surrounded by a fence, and eight rides were cut through dense woodland leading to a hunting pavilion on an artificial hill. Deer, elk and wild boar were kept there and were hunted by Catherine and later, with great enthusiasm, by the Empress Elizabeth.

In the 1740s and 1750s, during the reign of the Empress Elizabeth (1741–61), major changes were made to the palace, first by Andrei Krasov, then by Savva Chevakinsky and finally by Bartolomeo Rastrelli. As a result the length of the façade was extended to 1,000 feet. The palace was now a ceremonial imperial residence and further changes to the gardens were necessary.

Work began in 1745 on the New Garden on the other side of the palace, between the palace square and the hunting park.[55] Chevakinsky may well have been involved, along with master gardener Conrad Schröder. The New Garden comprised a system of square boskets, each measuring 660 × 660 feet. In the centre of each square was a pavilion or some other ornamental feature. In the first bosket a raised platform in the centre was surmounted by a curious structure of thirty-seven hexagonal wooden pavilions, joined together like a honeycomb, and each with a cupola which was to be gilded. It had not been completed in 1762, when Catherine II ordered its demolition. In the second bosket there was an amphitheatre with a 'green' theatre, where the stage, on a raised earth platform, would have been enclosed on three sides by clipped hedges. There was an artificial hill, Mount Parnassus, in the third, while the fourth seems to have been intended for festivities and entertainments.[56]

The main vista of the New Garden terminated in the open space of the hunting park from where the eight rides radiated. A surprising amount of birch was used in the New Garden, including the main avenues. In 1718 935 birch trees were planted. In later years many of them were replaced by oaks and limes.

The first wooden-framed glasshouse had been built in 1710, followed by a stone orangery in 1722, which was 140 feet long. A further large stone orangery was built in 1747.

In the middle of the eighteenth century three outstanding pavilions, richly ornamented with sculpture and gilding, were built in the park. The Hermitage, then in the centre of the Wild Grove, seems to have involved Krasov, Chevakinsky and Bartolomeo Rastrelli. It has survived but is no longer so richly decorated and is without its original very striking formal setting and the accompanying sculpture. It was then surrounded by a moat with footbridges.

Like the Hermitage at Peterhof it was a two-storey building without a staircase, and guests were conveyed in elevating armchairs to the upper floor, where there was a table which could be lowered to the ground floor for each course to be laid during an intimate meal without the presence of servants.

The equally exceptional Mon Bijou, by Chevakinsky and Rastrelli, was built in the centre of the hunting park. Again it

Left: Statues protected against the winter on the palace terrace at Tsarskoe Selo.

Right: The Hermitage at Tsarskoe Selo, where there was an elevating table, elevating armchairs and no staircase.

was richly decorated and embellished by sculpture in a remarkable formal setting. Very sadly it was later demolished.

The Grotto by the side of the lake, then a large basin, was the work of Rastrelli, who intended it to be surrounded by water on three sides. The interior was finished with tufa and shells, while the exterior was decorated appropriately with masks of Neptune, sculpted shells, entwined dolphins and other sea images. It still plays an important role in the landscape.[57]

Statues were important ornaments in the park although they were used less meaningfully than they had been by Peter. Elizabeth ordered the transfer to Tsarskoe Selo of statues in the Summer Garden – 'twelve white marble statues of human size with white marble pedestals' – which had been moved there from Menshikov's estate after the disgrace and exile of its owner. Twenty busts, four marble figures and six gilded lead figures were transferred from the confiscated garden by the River Moika which had belonged to the Empress Anna Ivanovna's courtier and close confidant Count Reinhold Löwenwolde, now also disgraced. The Steward at Tsarskoe Selo, Udalov, reported that in 1743 he had received forty-seven statues and busts 'from the properties of state criminals'. In 1744 he received 'from Menshikov's house' seventeen marble statues with pedestals and six busts with pedestals.[58]

Another major pavilion by Rastrelli was erected in the 1750s in conjunction with the Coasting Hill (*Katal'naia gora*) designed by the inventor A. K. Nartov, a member of the Academy of Sciences. It stood on what is now the Granite Terrace and was decorated with columns, gilded vases and statues.[59] Coasting hills (*montagnes russes*) are a traditional Russian amusement and the forerunner of the modern roller-coaster. There were ice hills during carnivals on the Neva, each of them

composed of a scaffold of timbers about six fathoms high, having steps on one side for ascending it, and on the opposite side a steep inclined plane covered with large blocks of ice, consolidated together by pouring water repeatedly from the top to the bottom. Men as well as women (the latter however only of the lower orders) in little low sledges descend with amazing velocity this steep hill; and by the momentum acquired by this descent are impelled to a great distance along a large field of ice carefully swept clear of snow for that purpose, which brings them to a second hill: by the side of which they alight, take their sledges on their back and mount it by the steps behind, as they had done the former.[60]

Left: The Grotto, ornamented with masks of Neptune, sculpted shells, dolphins and other images of the sea. It stood by a large formal basin which was transformed by John Busch.

Above: An engraving (1761) by E.G. Vinogradov from a drawing by M. Makhaev of Mon Bijou, another exceptional eighteenth-century pavilion which was sadly demolished to make way for a new development in the park.

A simple coasting or sliding hill was made at the Winter Palace, and everyone was expected to take a turn. No doubt the Empress Anna herself was an enthusiastic spectator, always hoping that the often reluctant performer would end up in a heap and that the ultimate in disarray might be observable. The wife of the British Minister was appalled at the prospect of a fate worse than a broken neck. She wrote:

> Sometimes if these sledges meet with any resistance, the person in them tumbles head over heels; that, I suppose, is the joke. Every mortal that goes to court has been down this slide, as it is called, and no neck has been broken. I was terrified out of my wits, for I had not only the dread of breaking my neck, but of being exposed to indecency too frightful to think on without horror.[61]

At first there seem to have been two rather gentle tracks, winter and summer, at Tsarskoe Selo, one towards the palace and the other away from it. Catherine II must have found them too tame, since in 1763 she commanded that a third track be made, down to the lake, and not long afterwards it was extended over the water to the island. The many other changes Catherine made at Tsarskoe Selo will be discussed in Chapter Four.

Ropsha
It was the water which first attracted Peter the Great to Ropsha, high in the hills some 12 miles south of Peterhof. Valuable medicinal properties were claimed for it — particularly for the stream called the Jordan — and it also became an important source for the fountains at Peterhof.

Peter built a small wooden palace on an artificial terrace near the church, looking out over a formal parterre with pavilions at the corners and with splendid distant views of St Petersburg. There was also an orchard, a vegetable garden and a fish pool, where trout and carp were bred. It seems to have resembled the standard designs for country seats by Domenico Tressini, which those building outside the city were expected to follow. Peter stayed here from time to time for the water cure, but later gave it to Prince Romodanovsky.

Near by there was a country seat belonging to State Chancellor G.I. Golovkin, who was given the land in 1710. After Golovkin's son Michael married Catherine, the daughter of Romodanovsky, he inherited both properties, and a substantial stone palace was built with a park embracing both the earlier sites. However he had crossed Elizabeth Petrovna, and when she became Empress in 1741 he was sent to Siberia; the Ropsha estate was confiscated and given to her favourite Alexis Razumovsky. Razumovsky was from a simple Cossack background in Ukraine, but he had a very fine voice and had come to court as a singer. He was also handsome, and Elizabeth had found him irresistible. Ropsha was one of several important gardens he and his relatives were to own. Alexis' younger brother Kirill enjoyed the benefit of a good education abroad and became President of the Academy of Sciences, a field-marshal and Hetman of Ukraine. Elizabeth was

a frequent visitor to Ropsha and it was developed to cater for her enthusiasm for hunting and fishing. New pools were made and stocked with carp and trout, fishing pavilions were erected by the water and deer were brought in from the imperial parks.

The palace was not large enough for Elizabeth and her entourage, and in 1748 Rastrelli was directed to remodel both it and the park. The extension to the palace was to include a church and a hermitage with a table which could be lowered to the cellar and the kitchen for clearing and replenishing, but the Seven Years War interrupted the building and the hermitage was never realized.

The terrace in front of the palace was edged with a balustrade, and three flights of steps led down to the Lower Garden, which is now meadow. It measured 590 × 700 feet and was divided *en étoiles* by a pattern of crossing paths, a typical Rastrelli plan. It was planted with limes and embellished with statues which were later taken to Gatchina.

The private garden in the courtyard of the palace was divided into squares with flowerbeds and basins. There was a covered walk at each end. A canal ran to the west of the palace, and beyond it a network of straight avenues divided the Upper Garden into sixteen squares, each measuring 300 × 300 feet. Canals and basins virtually surrounded the palace and there were four cascades in the Lower Garden.

Fruit had been cultivated in the garden at Ropsha from the earliest days. During Elizabeth's reign her favourite varieties of apples were grown near the palace — the most outstanding was said to be *bely naliv* (white juice) — and there were three orangeries at one side of the Lower Garden. The latter were moved to a less conspicuous position when it was decided to add further hothouses and other more utilitarian garden buildings.[62] An English gardener, Thomas Grey, worked at Ropsha for many years and is buried in a local churchyard.

Elizabeth died in 1761. Six months later her inadequate successor, Peter III, was forced to submit to a coup and to abdicate in favour of his wife, Catherine, and was sent to stay at Ropsha under guard on 28 June 1762. A week later he was assassinated there by those who were guarding him. Exactly what happened will never be known, but Catherine was disturbed when she was told of the outcome, fearing adverse public reaction, and hastened to express her sorrow in a manifesto:

> On the seventh day of our accession to the throne of Russia, we have been advised that the ex-Tsar Peter III suffered another of his habitual haemorrhoidal attacks, together with a violent colic. Aware of our duty as a Christian, we immediately gave the order to supply him with all necessary care. But to our great sadness we received, last night, the news that God's will had put an end to his life. We have ordered that his mortal remains should be taken to the Nevsky Cathedral and be buried there.[63]

There was no adverse public reaction, and she was now free to apply herself to ruling Russia, and to making gardens, without fear of a counter-coup.

Above: The palace of Ropsha, which was remodelled by Rastrelli, who also laid out the garden.

Right: The paper factory by the Factory Lake, built in 1788–94, is a not unpleasing feature in the park. The architect was Yuri Velten.

Voluptatum genitrix operumque creatrix

DIVÆ FLORÆ

Schetz tot een Tytul voor mijn Huijns Tekeningen

3

THE FORMAL PARKS AND GARDENS OF MOSCOW AND THE PROVINCES

The German Suburb (Nemetskaya Sloboda) covered an extensive area of Moscow by the River Yauza set aside for the residences of foreign diplomats and merchants. It would have been familiar to Peter from an early age, since it was not far from Izmailovo, the Sokolniki wildlife reserve and the Preobrazhensky hunting palace where he had spent much of his boyhood. It was probably in the German Suburb that he acquired an interest in and a taste for western architecture and other aspects of life in western Europe.

Architecturally it stood out from the rest of the city, with the influence of Holland and Germany particularly apparent. Many of the gardens must have reflected the national backgrounds of the foreign residents who owned them. According to Cornelius de Bruyn, a Dutch visitor to Moscow in 1701–2, the gardens of the German residents were neatly laid out with fruit trees and flowers; but the most impressive and influential garden was to be made by Nicolaas Bidloo, Peter's Dutch physician. Bidloo's father, Lambert Bidloo, was an apothecary and botanist. His uncle, Govert Bidloo, held a senior medical post at Leiden University and, from 1701, was physician to William III. He also wrote plays and designed triumphal arches for William's Royal Entry into the Hague in 1691. After studying medicine in Amsterdam Nicolaas matriculated in Leiden in 1696 and successfully defended his thesis there in the following year.[1]

Bidloo made for his children nineteen drawings of his house and garden, which are now in the library of Leiden University. In an accompanying account he expressed his enthusiasm for husbandry and country life, provided for Man by God, and outlined the background to his presence in Moscow:

Left: One of Nicolaas Bidloo's drawings (*c.*1730), showing the entrance from his garden to the hospital garden, which he laid out, and hospital, which he built. The figure sitting by gardening tools and architects' instruments is presumbaly Bidloo himself.

Right: A mid-eighteenth-century engraving of an unidentified Moscow garden.

I sought my livelihood and honour by the practice of medicine; I had as well various other crafts and sciences for my diversion and pleasure, such as painting, drawing, music, mathematics and geometry and some speculative philosophy, but none of these since my youth has given me so much pleasure, nor had so profound or joyous an influence on me, as country life.

After coming to Russia in 1702, as Court-physician to his Imperial Majesty of Most Laudable Memory, and after I had for several years accompanied him everywhere, until prevented from doing so by frailty and ill health, I requested him to allow me to return to my native land. His Majesty then saw fit to order me to build a Hospital next to the German Sloboda or Suburb, to attend to patients there and to teach 50 students there anatomy and surgery. His Majesty granted me a small piece of land next to the garden of the Hospital, where I created for myself a garden and modest country life, so as to indulge my inclinations as much as possible. And because this garden, though small, was orderly planted in harmony with its surroundings, and so well grown, it pleased his Imperial Majesty to honour me with frequent visits, both in my presence and absence. . . .

If it should chance that I end my days here . . . then my children, preserve at least my handwork, and you will always be able to see what simple pleasures refreshed your father. And should you not have the opportunity of owning this garden, then wander through these drawings of your father, and if you feel so inclined, follow his footsteps in seeking such a useful, honest and pleasing diversion.[2]

In building the hospital Bidloo was influenced by Christopher Wren's Greenwich Hospital (which Peter had visited in 1698). He also laid out the large garden, with fine avenues, and the botanic garden; and he established a theatre at the hospital.

Invoking the scriptures and Virgil in his account, Bidloo extolled the virtues of country life. Of all the arts and sciences none could compare with the art of husbandry. God had planted the Garden of Eden to provide Adam and Eve with their needs and delights. After their banishment their descendants 'had spread themselves over the face of the earth, each one in search of a pleasure garden, such as can be found anywhere, for indeed the whole world is but a bower of delight, when perceived with understanding.' Effort was required but good husbandry could lead not just to supplying everyday needs but to a foretaste of Paradise. The prospects were instinctively attractive to all men from sovereign to farmer. Many kings, counsellors and generals had wisely withdrawn from their stations of power to retire to the alternative benefits of a country seat.[3]

Bidloo's small estate by the River Yauza was flanked by meadows, his own cornfield and the hospital garden. A wide allée ran through the centre of the garden to the forecourt, 'upon which carriages can be driven, and from which one can go on foot through the garden', and then the coach yard, with stables, hayloft and granaries. From there a drive continued the line of the allée, past 'land on which all kinds of vegetables can be grown', to the road.[4]

To the left of the allée near the river, Bidloo's modest wooden house looked on to a flower parterre with an urn, a statue of Flora and other statues. A peacock and a hart appear in this scene and on another drawing. One can only speculate whether the hart was a tame animal, a statue or artist's licence. (Diana, who also appeared in the garden, was often represented accompanied by a stag.) On the other side the house was screened from the river by a 'thicket of all kinds of trees, planted in a wild manner'. A transverse allée led from the house across the central allée to a triumphal arch, through which Bidloo entered the grounds of the hospital. On each side of the central allée there were two large compartments formed by tall clipped hedges. One was the site of the flower parterre, while on the other side there was a maze with a statue of Diana and an ornamental basin at the centre 'with very nice waterspouts. . . . This spot is surrounded, in accordance with the shape of the basin, by tall clipped trees, and very pleasant.' The water from this basin apparently flowed under the transverse allée and cascaded into a larger basin at a lower level and was then discharged into the river and supplied a fountain. In the two other compartments fruit and other kitchen produce were probably grown. Beyond them the round courtyard was 'surrounded by a beautiful paling and by very tall firs and lime trees. A dense wood around which one can walk . . .' There was also a landing stage and a steam bath house by the river and a bleaching green surrounded by trees.

Bidloo probably began to plant the garden towards 1710 and, in view of the considerable height of the hedges in the drawings, the latter were probably made in the early 1730s, although some slight inconsistencies between some of them suggest that they were made at different dates.[5]

On the frontispiece to Bidloo's text, the triumphal arch frames a view of the hospital and the major part of its garden, with a figure, no doubt Bidloo, sitting with gardening tools and architects' instruments at his side. There are two large basins in the garden with fountains and extensive flowerbeds with a statue of Flora.

Right: Two of Bidloo's drawings of his garden.

Above, an impressive basin with perhaps exaggeratedly tall hedges; *below*, a view of the garden from the house.

Gezigt vande Grootste Nijver vande Rievier kant naar d'Ereepoort te zien.

Gezigt van Een balcon of bedeckte stoep. Van uijt het huijs naar De bloemparken te zien.

The Lefort and Golovinsky Gardens

Two important gardens on adjacent estates were laid out by the River Yauza towards the end of the seventeenth century: the Lefort Garden and the Golovinsky Garden. François Lefort, a native of Switzerland, had sought a career in the Russian army, attained the rank of general-admiral and became the Governor-General of Novgorod. He was a close associate and favourite drinking companion of the Tsar. His palace seems to have been provided by Peter as a place where they could meet, drink together and enjoy the fellowship of others of the inner circle. Information about the garden is limited, but a stairway led down from a terrace to the lower garden where there was a large pool in the centre with rectangular outline and semi-circular form on one side. There was another artificial pool on the other side of the river.

Fyodor Golovin, who succeeded François Lefort as General-Admiral following the death of the latter in 1699 and subsequently enjoyed a virtually prime-ministerial role in the government of the country until his death in 1706, commissioned Bidloo to design his garden and a garden house for him in 1704. In 1721 Peter purchased the estate from Golovin's heirs and instructed Bidloo to recreate the garden. Bidloo drew up a plan, which seems not to have survived,

although it was recorded in the catalogue of manuscripts and rare books in the library of the Academy of Sciences. In a list of books intended for publication during Peter's reign there is an entry for a manuscript with the title 'The Proposal of Nikolai Bidloo to Peter the Great about the construction of a garden and a dam for fountains'. This appears to refer to the Golovinsky Garden. However, Peter evidently countermanded its publication. Dubyago suggested that this was probably because a clerk had written it for Bidloo in archaic Russian, which displeased Peter.[6]

In the garden it was proposed that two dams should be constructed to provide the required water pressure for the fountains. The breast walls supporting the upper terrace were to become the base for sculptural ornaments linked to cascades and fountains. There were to be two pools, each by a dam and backed by a grotto. Inside the first grotto there was to be a statue of Hercules, representing Peter, with the many-headed dog Cerberus lying fettered at his feet, accompanied by two gilded sphinxes. The exploits of Hercules were also to be featured, presumably in bas-reliefs, on both sides of the dam. Bidloo had written a congratulatory address to Peter after the Battle of Poltava, comparing him to that other slayer of lions, Hercules, and he had designed a triumphal arch embellished with sculpture and bas-reliefs based on the Greek myths of Hercules.

Pools on the site of the Lefort Garden by the River Yauza.

In the second grotto there was to be a statue of Venus surrounded by gilded figures of dolphins. There was also a place for gilded cupids sitting on swans. Both these groups were to be surrounded by lively fountains and cascades.

When the site was acquired there were already a number of buildings, a large fish pond and birch groves. Large-scale work began in 1722–3 to realize Bidloo's plans, with a thousand soldiers from the Moscow garrison involved. In 1724 work on the dams was completed and five pools had been made. A system of canals was added which Peter intended to be used for excursions round the garden by boat.

The palace was a modest wooden building. There were two parterres, skirted by fir trees, and a maple avenue. By the river an area of land which had earlier been part of the estate of François Lefort was added to the Golovinsky Garden, and the Krestovsky and Bolshoi pools were formed.[7]

After Peter II's coronation in Moscow, in January 1728, he refused to return to St Petersburg, which he disliked, and the court stayed in Moscow with him. He died, however, only two years later, and Peter I's niece Anna Ivanovna came to the throne, bringing with her to power her German lover Ernst-Johann Biron (Bühren), who had the rapacity of Alexander Menshikov without the latter's ability. Anna had been living very modestly as the widowed Duchess of Courland (a coastal district of Latvia), but the change in her circumstances aroused extravagant ambitions, one of which was to eclipse in size and splendour the palaces and parks of St Petersburg with a new one in Moscow. This was to be achieved with the help of Bartolomeo Rastrelli on a very extensive site which included the Golovinsky Garden and was now to become Annenhof. Ten thousand limes were ordered, 5,000 maples and 5,000 elms, along with 50,000 trees with which to form covered ways. The two-storey wooden palace, with a façade of 700 feet, was built on the upper terrace, not on the edge, like those by the Gulf of Finland, but in a central position, from where there was a magnificent panorama of Moscow. A new formal garden, with grand parterres, fountains, ornamental basins, intricate flower beds and boskets, was laid out in front of the palace looking towards the old Golovinsky Garden. It was surrounded on three sides by a canal. At the end of the garden a cascade tumbled down the impressive breast wall with twenty fountain-masks to the level below. On one side of the palace there was a maze, on the other an orangery. Rastrelli followed Bidloo's choice of sculpture for the cascade with Hercules and 'a seven-headed snake' (the Lerna Hydra), along with twenty small statues of tritons.

Good progress was made at first, but Anna was used to western style and western ways and she had soon had enough of Moscow and headed for St Petersburg. Rastrelli was there too, rarely visiting Annenhof and merely sending instructions to his assistant architects Evlashev and Shanin and master gardener Brandhof. Even if interest and effort had not waned Annenhof could never have equalled the best of St Petersburg, since the topography was no match for the sites by the Gulf of Finland. At the same time this was a palace and park on a scale which Moscow had not known before and has not seen since. The intended plan was not fully realized, and, although some work continued until 1740, the year of Anna's death, what had been completed was not properly maintained.

When Peter's daughter Elizabeth then became empress (1741–61), a church, a theatre, an opera house and triumphal gates were erected on the site of the Golovinsky Garden in honour of her coronation. She decreed that 'Annenhof henceforth will not be known by that name but will be called the Golovinsky Garden as it used to be'. In 1771 a fire caused irreparable damage to the palace and a new stone palace was built for Catherine II to the plan of Antonio Rinaldi. When William Coxe visited the gardens in 1772 much of Bidloo's contribution was still there, but was due shortly to disappear. Garden fashions had moved on and Coxe was not impressed by it:

> We crossed the Yausa over a raft bridge to a palace, which was constructed for the accommodation of the present empress [Catherine] whenever she may choose to visit Moscow. . . . The gardens, which belonged to the old palace, built by Elizabeth, near the spot where the present structure was erected, are still retained: they are of considerable extent, and contained some of the best gravel-walks I have seen since my departure from England. In some parts the grounds were laid out in a pleasing and natural manner; but in general the old style of gardening prevailed, and continually presented us with rows of clipped yew trees, long straight canals, and a profusion of preposterous statues. Hercules was presiding at a fountain, with a retinue of gilded Cupids, dolphins and lamias; every little structure was a pantheon; and every grove was haunted by its Apollos and Dianas; but the principal deity in the place seemed to be a female figure holding a cornucopia reversed, which, instead of distributing as usual, all kinds of fruit, grain and flowers, poured out crowns, coronets and mitres. But the reign of all these deities was doomed to be very short: under the auspices of her present majesty all these instances of grotesque taste were to be removed, and give place to more natural ornaments.[8]

After Catherine's death in 1796 her palace was used as a barracks, no doubt at the instigation of her son Paul. Paul was an enthusiast for formality in gardens and gave orders 'to clip the trees in the form of cockerels and peacocks and in various geometric figures without the slightest omission.'[9] In 1824 the palace was allocated to the Cadet Corps, and the area of the Annenhof Grove became a field for military training. Worse was to follow. In the early 1930s it became a Park of Culture and Rest. Not much now remains of the Lefort and Golovinsky Gardens and Annenhof, but there are still a few picturesque pools, traces of canals and a little masonry including something of the fine breast wall built by Rastrelli.[10]

Kuskovo

The Sheremetevs, one of the richest and most powerful families in Russia, had owned the estate at Kuskovo, 7 versts (about 5 miles) south-east of Moscow, since the sixteenth century. In 1715 it was bought from his younger brother by Field Marshal Count Boris Sheremetev, a hero of the Battle of Poltava and other battles against the Swedes and Commander-in-Chief of Peter the Great's army. In 1719 it was inherited by his son Peter Borisovich, who enhanced the family's wealth by marrying Princess Cherkasskaya in 1743, adding the adjacent Veshnyakovo estate to Kuskovo. Both the Sheremetevs and the Cherkasskys had impressive gardens to their credit. The Sheremetevs had a notable estate by the Fontanka in St Petersburg, while Cornelius de Bruyn had singled out the large Dutch garden, the work of Jan Roosen, on one of the Cherkassky estates as the best laid-out garden in the country. By the middle of the eighteenth century,

another great garden was being made at Kuskovo.[11]

The French architect Charles de Wailly is thought to have contributed to the pleasingly simple classical design of the palace, which was built between 1769 and 1775 under the direction of Karl Blank. The lower floor is brick and the upper floors wood stuccoed to imitate stone. It is situated on the shore of a large artificial stretch of water created in the 1750s and near to an asymmetrically placed church and service buildings. Opposite the palace a stone-faced canal, 325 yards long and aligned with the central axis of the garden, was dug, leading from the large pool, and a vista was cleared opening up the view of the church in Veshnyakovo, linked with which and closing the perspective is the bell tower (1734), its vertical form strengthened by the addition of a spire in 1755. A basin was formed in the canal with a small circular stone-faced island surrounded by a balustrade with vases, on which an ornate

The Sheremetevs' palace at Kuskovo. The upper
floors are of wood stuccoed to imitate stone.

circular pavilion was built, approached by a bridge. The canal was terminated by an ornamented stone wall with cascading fountains. Another canal encircled the formal garden, and there were small pools in the landscape.

On the garden side the palace looks out to the north across an extensive parterre to the equally wide orangery. An eighteenth-century engraving shows an intricate 'embroidered' parterre surrounded by many tubs containing evergreen shrubs clipped to a great variety of whimsical shapes. Perhaps the artist recording the scene added to the embroidery, but it is not surprising that there has been no attempt at full restoration. An army of dedicated serfs would be required to restore it and then maintain it afterwards, but it is a disappointingly dull area now with rather basic grass masquerading as *boulingrin* (sunken lawn) and only statues and seasonal bedding plants in the borders to help. An appropriate design in coloured gravel could

Top: Part of the parterre in front of the palace, from a 1782 engraving.

Above: A view across the parterre to the orangery. The replica of the Kagul Obelisk at Tsarskoe Selo commemorated Catherine's visit to Kuskovo.

Top: An engraving (1770s) of the Dutch House at Kuskovo, from a drawing by M. Makhaev. Makhaev led a group of Russian artists who sketched views with the aid of a camera obscura.

Above: The Dutch House today.

Opposite
Above: An engraving (1770s) of the Hermitage, from a drawing by M. Makhaev.

Below: The Hermitage today.

go some way towards restoring the intricacies of the past without adding to the burden of maintenance.

The numerous statues are good and make a considerable contribution to the parterre, but they are generally not quite of the same quality as those in the imperial parks of St Petersburg. Among them the River Scamander particularly stands out, a personification of the river on which, according to Homer, Troy stood. A statue of Minerva on a column (1779) and a marble copy of the Kagul Obelisk (1786) at Tsarskoe Selo commemorated the visit to Kuskovo of Catherine the Great.

The large open central area was closed on both sides by tall green walls of meticulously clipped boskets. These were a very important element in the garden, enclosing a succession of spaces which invited the visitor to explore. They still retained their clipped solid forms at the beginning of the twentieth century. Mostly limes were used and now there are groves of trees where once there were boskets.

Fyodor Argunov, one of Sheremetev's serf architects who had trained at the Chancellery of Building in St Petersburg, was responsible for much of the development of Kuskovo, where he was assisted by another serf architect, A.F. Mironov. Argunov's brick-built Dutch House on the western side of the park recreates a corner of Holland. It was built in 1749, the first building in the park, as a memorial to Peter the Great, a copy of whose portrait by Godfrey Kneller hangs inside. The building faces a rectangular pool, and there is a vegetable garden on one side and a flower garden on the other with tulips, narcissi and other appropriate flowering plants. The house was furnished in the Dutch style and aimed at giving the visitor an impression of what it was like to live in Holland. The walls of all the small rooms were covered in ceramic tiles, and there are scenes of Dutch life on the white and blue tiles in the kitchen. There were many marine scenes by Dutch and English artists.[12] The Dutch House stood by a pool and on its bank there were two other substantial buildings, the Chinoiserie Pagodenburg and the Column Pavilion, which have not survived. Near by in summer there was a Persian Tent and a Chinese Tent.

The Hermitage is one of the most impressive buildings at Kuskovo. The architect is not known, but Karl Blank and Fyodor Argunov supervised its construction. It is similar in style to the hermitages in the gardens of St Petersburg and like them it was intended for entertaining small groups of special guests. Here too there was an elevating table, which could be laid downstairs and raised to the upper floor with the guests freed from the constraints of the presence of servants. A new statue of Flora, based on an engraving, has been put back on the dome, which is again surrounded by a balustrade embellished with vases.

Standing by the Italian Pool on the east side of the parterre are the Grotto, the Italian House and the Menagerie (in the sense of an enclosure usually for birds). The Grotto, on the same transverse avenue as the Dutch House, was built between 1755 and 1771 and is reminiscent of Rastrelli's grotto at Tsarskoe Selo. The interior was intended to represent an underwater cave, 'Neptune's Kingdom', offering an escape from the heat of the

Above: The Grotto.

Right: The interior of the Grotto.

Below: The Mengerie under restoration.

Below: The Mengerie under restoration.

Bottom: An engraving (1770s) of the Menagerie, from a drawing by M. Makhaev.

summer sun outside. It is decorated with river- and sea-shells, tufa, pieces of glass and coloured plaster of Paris, modelled to imitate seaweed hanging on the walls. The wrought-iron grilles on the windows and doors are also in the form of seaweed. Everything combines to create a feeling of damp cool shade. Statues of Jupiter, Juno, Venus, Ceres and Flora stand in the niches in the façades, but the statues which once adorned the balustrade on the roof are no longer there.

The Italian House (1754–5), built under the direction of Yuri Kologrivov, is like a miniature palace, with a façade decorated with sculptural elements in the form of wreaths and garlands. On the slightly stepped terraces of a small Italian garden there were fountains and marble statues. The Italian House served as a private museum for the Sheremetevs, with paintings, sculpture and other works of art.

The Menagerie comprised five small pavilions, which are reminiscent of the eight small buildings for ducks by the pool in the Summer Garden, but here there were cranes, American geese, pheasants and pelicans. There was also a large aviary for singing birds in the garden. In this part of the park there was a wide avenue leading to a small artificial hill on which stood the Belvedere, a summerhouse with an observation platform from which to enjoy the surrounding countryside.

The outstanding Orangery, built in 1763 to the design of Argunov, facilitated the raising of large quantities of the wide range of trees, shrubs and flowering plants required for the garden. It was also a winter garden, and there were rooms for games, while concerts and balls were held in the Cupola Hall, a large octagonal central space with a wooden gallery for an orchestra. Two long glazed galleries led to side pavilions, one of which served as the house chapel. Kuskovo had a reputation for horticultural excellence. The gardeners produced oranges and lemons, while coffee and tea plants are said to have grown as well as in their native territory. Among the serf gardeners there were masters of the art of topiary who produced green sculpture of birds, animals and people. The Orangery now houses an impressive museum of ceramics.

A landscape park was laid out in the 1770s on the land north of the Orangery. Although not a large area it had several pavilions and summerhouses bearing such names as 'May You Rest Here', 'Refuge for Good People', as well as a House of Solitude, a Temple of Diana with a statue of the goddess and a Temple of Silence in a labyrinth with a statue of Venus. By the labyrinth there was a Lion's Cave with the figure of a lion. Nothing of this now survives.

Kuskovo is also notable for its green theatre, which was constructed between 1751 and 1763, a garden feature which originated in Italy where the climate was more considerate to outdoor performances than that of Moscow. It stood at the centre of a large bosket. The stage, on a raised earth platform, was enclosed on three sides by clipped hedges, and there were stalls for an audience of about a hundred and a pit for the orchestra. At the sides of the stage there were rooms clipped from the greenery for the actors. The repertoire consisted mainly of ballet and one-act plays performed by serf artists. In the evenings the theatre was illuminated by garlands of coloured lights and lanterns, and performances often ended with a firework display. The green theatre was finally removed in 1894, but it is still possible to trace its contours on the site, and there is a model at Kuskovo showing how it was constructed.

A wooden indoor theatre was built on the estate in the 1760s and was replaced in 1787 by the fine New Theatre built in the landscape park beyond the Orangery, but that too has gone. It was one of more than 170 serf theatres on Russian estates – the Sheremetevs had eight of them. In its heyday the Kuskovo theatre was the best in Russia. Among the 210,000 serfs that they owned there were many talented people, including actors, actresses, ballerinas and singers, as well as architects, artists and craftsmen of all kinds. Those showing particular promise were selected at an early age and given an excellent education and intensive professional training. The French ambassador, the Comte de Ségur, wrote of a performance he attended:

> Notwithstanding my little taste for fêtes, I shall not pass over in silence that which was given by the Count Sheremetoff, at one of his estates situated a league from Moscow.

We found the road brilliantly illuminated. The Count's immense park was decorated with transparencies composed of all colours and exquisitely designed. A grand Russian opera was performed in a very noble theatre; and all who understood the story pronounced it very interesting and well written. . . .

But what appeared to me almost inconceivable was that the poet, and the musical authors of the opera, those who had built the house, the painter who had decorated it, the actors and actresses of the piece and the male and female dancers in the ballets, as well as the musicians in the orchestra, were all slaves of Count Sheremetoff.[15]

The outstanding singer was Praskovya Kovalyova, the daughter of a blacksmith on the Berezino estates of the Sheremetevs in Yaroslavl Province. Her portrait is still in the palace, painted by another serf, Nikolai Argunov, who later received his letter of enfranchisement. After a long liaison Praskovya eventually married Count Nikolai Petrovich, who had inherited the estate on the death of his father.

Below: A wing of the Conservatory.

Bottom: A model of the Green Theatre.

Kuskovo had great popular appeal. On Sundays and festival days, which were widely publicized with invitations to visit posted up by the roadside from Moscow, many thousands flocked there. There was a great deal to entertain them. Beyond the Dutch House, near the canal which surrounds the garden, there was the Avenue of Games with bowling greens, swings and a merry-go-round. Further amusement was provided by life-size cut-out figures of elegantly dressed beaux and belles, some placed singly among the trees, others in groups. 'On the benches situated along the paths leading to the Conservatory there sat comely maidens in bridal veils and further on men in colourful caftans with Persian sashes. They seemed to talk contentedly among themselves.'[114] Near the exit visitors were confronted by a fire-breathing dragon in a cave, and, not far from the cave, very realistic waxworks in two huts, one of a girl with a dish of mushrooms.

Music was provided by a traditional band of hornplayers (each horn could produce only a single note!) and by brass bands, and there was ballet and drama in the green theatre. In the evening, when the park was illuminated by coloured lanterns, and the blaze of bonfires lit up the canal, cannon were fired, oxen were roasted and there were firework displays. On the large pool there was a fleet of colourful pleasure boats – a gilded sailing ship with six cannon, longboats, skiffs, wherries, gondolas and a Chinese junk. An island lent itself to picnicking and to the fireworks, reflected in the mirror surface of the pool, while along its banks there were picturesque artificial ruins, fishermen's huts and summerhouses.

On the far side of the pool there was ancient forest through which avenues were cut, and a large area was enclosed by a stone wall 6 miles long as a wildlife reserve with some six hundred animals, perhaps deer, wild boar and elk, as at Tsarskoe Selo, and, according to Loudon, wolves. At the centre there was a simple circular open pavilion, its roof supported by columns. To one side of the reserve, stables, kennels and a cattle yard were enclosed within a castle-like structure.

Kuskovo declined in the 1790s when Count Nikolai began to lose interest in the estate to which his father had contributed so much. He wanted to achieve something on his own account, reflecting his own talents and enthusiasms, and turned his attention instead to recreating his other Moscow estate, Ostankino. In the nineteenth century much was lost at Kuskovo. The avenues became overgrown, some buildings became ruinous; others, including the theatre, burned down; the

landscape park was replaced by a development of dachas. The disastrous effects of abandonment and neglect were compounded by damage done by Napoleon's soldiers during their temporary occupation of the area in 1812.

On the other hand, the early solidly built structures – the Dutch and Italian Houses, the Grotto, the Hermitage and the Orangery – have mostly survived, and some of the later, ephemeral additions which disappeared were no great loss. By then there were surely too many buildings, in too many styles, too close together. Some restoration was undertaken in the 1850s and 1870s (when N.L. Benois added a Swiss Chalet to the international collection of buildings), but it was in the second half of the twentieth century that comprehensive restoration of a very high standard resulted in the exceptionally fine palace and park which exist today.

Arkhangelskoe

The palace at Arkhangelskoe, some 11 miles from Moscow, is exceedingly well situated at the top of a slope leading gently down to what in the eighteenth century was still the River Moskva, now the former bed of the river. On the other side are meadows, groves and stretches of forest – a quite idyllic scene.

At the end of the seventeenth century it belonged to M. Y. Cherkassky, but it was only a source of food for the Moscow estate, not a residence for the owner. There was a two-storey house there and, unusually at that time, two orangeries producing peaches and tender plants.

In 1703 it was bought by Prince D.M. Golitsyn, a close associate of Peter I, but it was only after he had fallen out of favour with the Empress Anna that he decided to settle at Arkhangelskoe and began to build a palace and to lay out a formal park with maple and lime avenues. A large wooden palace was built in the early 1730s, but further development was discontinued in 1736 following Golitsyn's arrest. Nevertheless, the estate continued to be productive. In 1738 there were bays, figs, lemons, oleanders, geraniums and other exotics in the orangeries, which were heated by tiled stoves. Chestnuts, walnuts, apples, pears, currants, tulips and irises grew in the garden, which was looked after by Fyodor Tyazhelov with the assistance of four apprentices.

When Golitsyn's grandson, Prince Nikolai, visited Arkhangelskoe for the first time in 1773 he was impressed by what he saw and decided that this would be the ideal place to put into practice the ideas he had gathered during extended visits to

Left: An eighteenth-century engraving of a pavilion which stood in the wildlife reserve.

Right: The sculpture of Hercules wrestling with the giant Antaeus on the Upper Terrace.

France, Germany and Italy. His grandfather's palace was demolished, and a new palace was built in the 1780s to a plan of the French architect Charles de Guerne. Its early classical exterior has survived almost as it was then, and subsequent alterations were mainly to the interiors. By the south façade a remarkable system of balustraded terraces and breast walls was designed by Giacomo Trombara at the end of the eighteenth century. They support many of the busts and statues, which are still such a feature of the garden, some two hundred in all.

The Upper Terrace (230 × 230 feet) has the sculptural group of Hercules and Antaeus at the centre of its parterre and statues of female figures, dogs and vases along the balustrades. Menelaus with the body of Patroclus, which was originally here, is now in the main courtyard of the palace. The central feature of the larger Lower Terrace (500 × 80 feet) is a fountain-statue of a group of cupids with dolphins, and there are statues on the parterres of Diana with a stag, Apollo Belvedere and Cupid bending the club of Hercules. On the balustrades on either side of the central staircase are forty-four marble busts of famous Romans, as well as female figures and lions. The breast wall of the Lower Terrace originally had niches containing busts, but these were removed later.

Between the terraces and the river bed, where at this date one might have expected informal landscaping, there is a vast (260 × 75 yards) rectangular *tapis vert* (green carpet) with ten statues and, until recently, a line of tall limes along each side. The *tapis vert* is seen as a formal representation of the Russian meadow and, because of its size, it blends very well with the open landscape beyond. Between the limes and the river stood the two original orangeries surrounded by flower gardens and statues until 1937, when they were replaced by two four-storey sanatoria. While the limes were still there not much could be

Above: Fountain-statue of cupids with dolphins.

Opposite left: The sculpture of Cupid bending the club of Hercules on the Lower Terrace.

Left: A lion decorated by a visitor to the park.

seen of them, but then someone thought it would be a good idea to fell the trees and replace them with covered ways – wooden carcasses with trees trained over them to form green tunnels. The result, needless to say, was starkly disastrous. The sanatoria, though perfectly good buildings, are totally out of place in this setting.

After the death of Golitsyn in 1809 Arkhangelskoe was bought by Prince Nikolai Yusupov (1751–1831), one of the richest men in Russia. He continued to make improvements to the estate and brought to it his exceptional collections of pictures, antique sculpture, porcelain and rare books. There were twenty-four thousand volumes in his library in the palace.

When Napoleon invaded Russia and estates were threatened by French occupation, owners had to resort to the same tactics to protect valuable possessions as those which were to be employed here and elsewhere in 1941 in the face of the approaching German army. Many of the valuable items from Arkhangelskoe were transported to Astrakhan and others were buried in the grounds of the estate, but much of what was left was plundered by the French and a great deal of damage was done. In 1941 the collections were sent to the Urals and the statues buried in the park, but air raids destroyed some of what remained.

There is a further display of sculpture along Pushkin Avenue, including a bust of the poet, who visited Arkhangelskoe

Left: The view across the garden with the statues protected against the winter. The limes were still standing when this photograph was taken and almost completely screened the sanatoria.

Above: The framework of a covered way in the park.

Right: After the limes were felled and replaced with covered ways the sanatoria were starkly exposed on both sides of the *tapis vert*.

Above: The Church of the Archangel Michael.

Far left: Fountain-statue of Cupid with a swan.

Left: The Yusupov Mausoleum, designed by Roman Klein.

in 1827 and 1830. Another avenue leads to a small memorial temple by Evgraf Tyurin with a statue of Catherine II, presented as Themis, the Goddess of Justice. There is also a library pavilion and a small tea house, but none of these buildings contribute much to the park. Much more impressive is the Church of the Archangel Michael (1660s), which still adorns the estate.

A theatre was added to the estate in 1817–18, built to the design of Pietro Gonzaga. Stage sets and a curtain designed by Gonzaga and some of his sketches, together with nine watercolours by serf artists of his backdrops, may still be seen in the museum. Although he was primarily a theatre and stage designer, Gonzaga had also achieved exceptional success as a landscape designer at Pavlovsk, as we shall see in Chapter Five.

After the death in a duel of Nikolai F. Yusupov (1883–1908), a commanding colonnaded mausoleum to the design of Roman Klein was built on the estate. It was completed in 1916, too late to be of much continuing use to the family. After the Revolution Arkangelskoe became a museum. It has one of the latest eighteenth-century formal parks in Russia and one of the best. Both the palace and the park have, with the exception of the felling of the limes, been very well restored and maintained.[15]

Riga

Parks were also made in the former Russian province of Livonia (now partly in Latvia and partly in Estonia) which Russia had won from the Swedes. In July 1710 Riga had capitulated to Field Marshal Boris Sheremetev, and Reval (Tallinn) to Lieutenant-General Bauer two months later. Both were officially conceded to Russia by the Treaty of Nystad in 1721.[16]

A bust of Pushkin (1903), a late commemoration of his visits to Arkhangelskoe in 1827 and 1830.

Peter the Great was a frequent visitor to Riga and before long had three residences there, one in the city and two on the outskirts. Peter's palace in the city was formed from a number of existing buildings. He wanted a garden and, since there was no space for one on the ground, a hanging garden was made at first-floor level on a massively supported terrace overlooking the River Daugave. A late-eighteenth-century plan records that four chestnuts, which had been obtained from Danzig, still survived in the garden. Apart from the trees there were also peonies, white and yellow narcissi, Dutch carnations and many aromatic and medicinal plants.

Alexandershantz, named after Alexander Menshikov, was a fortress built by the river in 1710 during the siege of Riga, and it was here that Peter chose to build a palace and park. He was there on 24 April 1721 measuring the site of the garden, and in 1722 thirty thousand trees of various kinds were planted. The palace was built on a hill at the edge of a steep slope, which was reinforced by a breast wall with deep niches. There was a good supply of water and a basin on the upper terrace to supply the fountains below. In the lower garden there were wide lime and chestnut avenues and boskets, two rectangular basins, summerhouses, figuratively clipped trees and a rose parterre. Some of the boskets were embellished with covered green ways and there were many enclosed sections with lawns and a variety of trees. The plan of the garden was apparently based on a design by Le Blond in A.-J. Dézallier d'Argenville's *La Théorie et la pratique du jardinage*, but with adjustments necessitated by the terrain in this very picturesque setting. After the death of Peter, Alexandershantz was neglected, and by the end of the century the palace had gone and the garden was completely overgrown. In the 1960s part of the site was occupied by a psychiatric hospital.

Peter's third residence, Peterholm, was built at about the same time as Alexandershantz, and the plan of the garden drew inspiration from the same source. Peter is said to have made the plan for the large wooden palace, which was placed on a terrace jutting out into the river. As with Dubki and Monplaisir it looked out across the water and turned its back on the garden, which was divided into two parts: one ceremonial, the other domestic with a kitchen garden. There was the usual combination of parterre, rectangular basin, boskets and avenues. Many Dutch limes were planted, and there were fruit trees in the boskets. The whole of the territory was surrounded by a fosse. A nursery was established near by to help supply the many trees and shrubs which were required. The citizens of Riga were allowed access to the gardens of both Peterholm and Alexandershantz when Peter was not in residence. Peterholm was also allowed to decline after Peter's death, but some of the avenues still survive in what is now a public park, Viestura.[17]

Kadriorg

In 1714 Peter bought a modest house in Tallinn, said to resemble a Dutch burgher's house. When Alexander I visited Tallinn in 1804 the house was in a semi-ruinous condition and he ordered its repair. Unfortunately it was modernized rather than properly restored, but some parts of the original and its contents remain including seven busts intended for the garden of Kadriorg, the palace Peter was building near by for his Estonian wife Catherine. Nicolo Michetti was the architect for the palace and the park and he accompanied Peter to the site in 1718. He was assisted by Mikhail Zemtsov. The very fine baroque palace was built on the levelled slope of a terrace with the Lower Garden in front and the Upper Garden behind. The latter was divided into two parts: the Flower Garden and the so-called 'Mirage', on different levels. The gardener was Ilya Surmin, whose annual salary of 400 roubles, decreed by the Tsar, indicates that he was highly regarded.[18]

In the Lower Garden there were three wide avenues running the length of the garden and crossed by three wide transverse avenues. Between the avenues there were narrower crossing paths. At the crossing points of the avenues and the paths there were circular spaces for arbours, fountains, seats, sculpture and urns. A large circular open space with a basin is similarly placed to the island at the crossing of the canals at Strelna. At each side of the garden there was a stone-faced canal, crossed by two bridges. Beyond the canals there was a considerable area of natural landscape with trees. At the end of the garden there was a semi-circular colonnaded gallery with trellis, supporting climbing plants, attached to the columns. The avenues were flanked by limes and by boskets.

In front of the palace there was a parterre in ten sections, with roses, tulips, peonies and narcissi planted to form various designs, and in summer sixty stands with flowers in urns were placed in the avenues.

The large Swan Pool near the Lower Garden has a round island at its centre reinforced by a stone-faced retaining wall sloping to the water. This, too, is reminiscent of that island at Strelna. The trees growing on the Kadriorg island are probably as old as the park.

The Flower Garden in the Upper Garden comprised two flower parterres with fountains and a similar range of flowering plants to those in the Lower Garden. Six fountains were planned but only two were constructed. Here, too, there were covered galleries, which were open on the side towards the garden. By the Flower Garden was the Mirage Wall, with staircases and panels, each of the latter ornamented by a fountain with a gilded lead mask. There was also a cascade. It was intended to display fifty-four statues and twenty mask fountains, but the plan was only partly realized by fountain master Giuliano Barattini.

On the higher terrace the baroque basin with a stone-lined island was called the Mirage Pool because of the intended waterworks. There was to have been an obelisk 'with four figures of Neptune' on the island, but that also failed to materialize. Unfortunately nothing now remains of the Upper Garden.

Next to Peter's cottage is the site of the orchard, where there used to be many apple, pear, cherry and plum trees, blackcurrant and gooseberry bushes and forty pots with orange trees in summer. There was also a chestnut garden where young chestnut plants from Holland were acclimatized before being sent on to St Petersburg. The remains of the ice house may still be seen.

After the death of Peter, Catherine was no longer interested in Kadriorg and the garden was never completed. In the 1930s there was drastic reconstruction. At the end of the Upper Garden the large ornamental basin was filled in, and a new government building was erected. It is quite a good building but not at all appropriate here. It later became the Praesidium of the Supreme Soviet of the Estonian Socialist Soviet Republic. The palace is now a museum, and what is left of the park is well maintained.[19]

Kadriorg Palace.

Above: An avenue of chestnuts in the park at Kadriorg.

Right: The island in the Swan Pool.

4
CATHERINE THE GREAT AND THE ENGLISH STYLE OF LANDSCAPING

When Catherine II first met Peter III she was Sophia of Anhalt Zerbst and he was Charles Peter of Holstein. They had both been brought up in Germany and they were about ten years old. Charles Peter was the son of Peter the Great's daughter Anna and in 1743, then fifteen, he was taken to St Petersburg to be proclaimed Grand Duke Peter Fyodorovich, heir to the throne. In the following year Sophia was invited to St Petersburg to be considered as a prospective bride, was approved by the Empress Elizabeth and, after the marriage, became the Grand Duchess Catherine Alekseevna. It was not a happy marriage, remaining long unconsummated, and Catherine found consolation elsewhere.[1]

One of her first lovers was Stanislaus Augustus Poniatowski, who arrived in St Petersburg in 1755 with the English envoy, Sir Charles Hanbury-Williams, and fathered the Princess Anna Petrovna who died in infancy. During the many hours he spent with Catherine at Oranienbaum, the Grand Duke's summer residence, often in a secluded garden pavilion which she visited '*sous prétexte de bains*', they may sometimes have found time to discuss gardening, in which she was interested, and it was probably from him that she learned about the new ideas from England, particularly from Stowe, which he had visited in 1754, when he was conducted round the gardens by Earl Temple. He wrote in his memoirs:

> The house and gardens at Stowe, the most extensive then owned by any private individual in England, engaged my attention all the more because this place is the first where the Chinese taste was displayed. When I was there this taste had already been refined and perfected on other estates. Stowe, however, was still regarded with veneration, because it was the cradle of this new taste, which decried symmetrical gardens, the sad family of clipped yews and all the Dutch gew-gaws which William III had introduced to England.[2]

While he had reservations at first about abandoning all the features of formal gardens, this visit must have made a lasting impression, and he would have acquired copies of Benton Seeley's guidebook, *A Description of the Gardens of Lord Viscount Cobham at Stowe in Buckinghamshire*, first published in 1744 and frequently revised and reissued, and of Seeley's companion volume, *Views of the Temples and other Ornamental Buildings in the Gardens at Stowe*, which appeared in 1750. After he became King of Poland, thanks largely to Catherine, Poniatowski personally supervised the development of his summer residence at Łazienki – with an English park and buildings inspired by Greece, Rome and China – which was later to be the home of Catherine's grandson the Grand Duke Constantine Pavlovich.

An engraving by N.I. Utkin, after a painting by V.L. Borovikovsky (1794), showing Catherine with an Italian greyhound in front of the Kagul Obelisk at Tsarskoe Selo.

Oranienbaum

Catherine recorded in her memoirs that it was in 1755 that she 'first took a fancy to form a garden at Oranienbaum. . . . I began then to plan and plant, and as this was my first whim in the construction line, my plans assumed very grand proportions.'[5] What she achieved seems not to have been recorded. The Grand Duke Peter, who venerated Frederick II and his military system, was more interested in playing at soldiers than in making gardens and commissioned Antonio Rinaldi to build a small fortress town in the park for his Holstein troop. It had five bastions, with twelve cannon, and was surrounded by a moat with a drawbridge and an earth embankment. There were barracks, a commandant's house, a guardhouse, officers' quarters, a Lutheran church, an arsenal and a small two-storey palace for Peter. Only the restored palace, the stone gateway and some traces of the earthworks remain. Near by, along the bank of the winding River Karost,

Above: Axonometric plan by P.A. de Saint Hilaire of the small fortress town of Grand Duke Peter, later Peter III at Oranienbaum (1775). Rinaldi's park by the river may also be seen.

Below: The Stone Hall, also known as the Concert Hall, may have been designed by Rastrelli.

Right: A view of the Chinese Palace, so called because of the Chinese rococo style in some of the rooms.

Rinaldi laid out a park with terraces, cascades, arched stone bridges, fountains and other interesting features, including a circular menagerie with twelve pavilions for birds and animals, an octagonal pavilion called the Pavilion of Nightingales and a hermitage with a Chinese-inspired roof.[4]

When Catherine became empress in 1762, Rinaldi built the outstanding Chinese Palace for her, so called not for its architecture but because of the Chinese rococo style of some of the rooms. Rinaldi also built the Coasting Hill Pavilion, which is the most striking of all the buildings at Oranienbaum. It was once a viewing stand and a place of rest and refreshment, and it gave access to the starting platform of the remarkable Coasting Hill, which was built between 1762 and 1769. This was 582 yards long with a series of descents and ascents, switchback fashion. Riders sat in gilded carriages in the form of triumphal chariots, gondolas and saddled animals. There were three tracks, each 20 feet wide, the centre track for coasting and the two outer tracks for winding back the vehicles by cable.[5]

One contemporary writer observed:

> The coach-hill is probably the largest scale of any in the country. It consists of steep declivities built of timber, the highest end being ten fathoms above the ground, and borne upon an arch. The impetus acquired by rapidly descending the first forces the carriage up the second, which having turned it is carried up a third, and so proceeds in diminishing altitudes with amazing velocity. The carriages are made to contain one person, or two seated facing each other, the wheels running in grooves to which they are fitted by the length of the axeltree, and thus the company proceed, not without great alarm to novices of the sport, topping one hill after the other till the carriages naturally stop in an elegant alcove on the horizontal plane. Along this course, on either side, is a covered colonnade of a hundred pillars, which, taken all together, produce an effect wonderfully magnificent.[6]

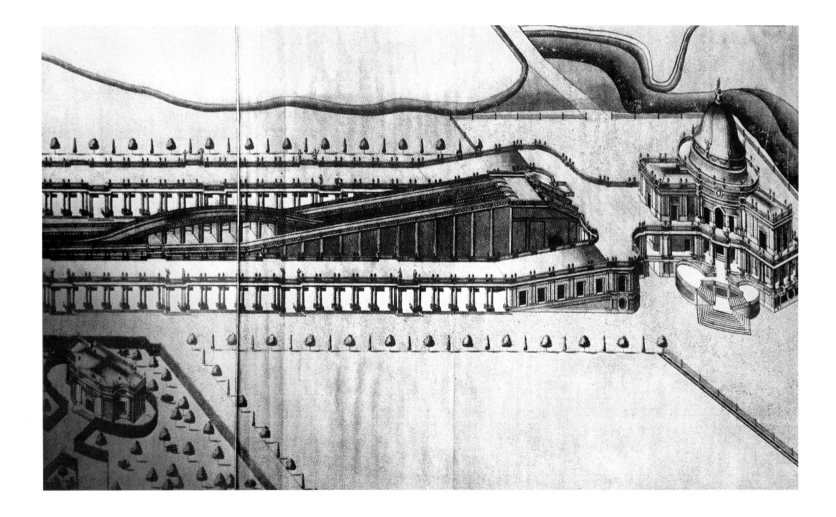

Left: The Coasting Hill Pavilion, which gave access to the starting platform of the Coasting Hill.

Above: Part of the Coasting Hill and the Coasting Hill Pavilion, from P.A. de Saint Hilaire's axonometric plan of 1779.

The upper level of the colonnade was for promenading. Today a flowery meadow marks the site of the track, but the pavilion has been very well restored.

Rinaldi also attempted to introduce an element of landscaping at Oranienbaum. His plan for the gardens on both sides of the track of the Coasting Hill – regular on one side, irregular on the other – is reminiscent of, and may well have been inspired by, Batty Langley's early attempts to introduce irregularity in his plans in *New Principles of Gardening* (1728), with paths not so much winding as writhing and twisting. Rinaldi's landscaping may well not have impressed Catherine, but, in any case, she was turning away from Oranienbaum, because of its associations with Peter III, and devoting all her attention to Tsarskoe Selo, where she spent most of her time. Oranienbaum was made available to naval cadets, but in 1796 it passed to the Grand Duke Alexander and in 1831 it became the summer residence of the Grand Duke Michael Pavlovich.[7]

Tsarskoe Selo

Orders were given in 1762 to stop the formal clipping of most of the trees at Tsarskoe Selo and some attempts at the English style were made. Catherine 'told her architect and gardener, that in future, when making gardens, they should endeavour to follow nature; but this they could neither feel nor comprehend. They made various attempts to please the Empress, but always without success.'[8] In 1769 Charles Sparrow from Scotland may have been the first British gardener engaged by Catherine, and he went to work at Gatchina. Shortly afterwards Thomas Cloase at Hampton Court considered a similar move, and 'Capability' Brown wrote to the Russian ambassador in his support that 'he thought him a Person very fit for the Place he wishes to undertake, being a perfect Master of the Kitchen Garden, Hotwalls, Stoves and Greenhouses. If he should meet with his Excellency's approbation, Mr Brown will be happy to give him any assistance in Plans, or other things, that may be of use to her Imperial Majesty or him.' However, Cloase was not appointed or decided not to go.[9]

When, in 1771, John Busch[10] arrived in St Petersburg to work for Catherine – probably recruited by the Russian ambassador in London, Count Aleksei Musin-Pushkin, as James Meader was to be later – she acquired one of the most significant gardeners the eighteenth century produced, as well as one with whom she could converse in German. Born in Hanover (and christened Johann), he moved to London towards 1750 and established a nursery in 1756 in Hackney, which, under his successor, Conrad Loddiges,[11] also a native of Hanover, was to become for a time the best in the world. From this nursery Busch became a driving force in the development of Germany's earliest landscape parks. As well as supplying appropriate plants for them, he also provided engravings of English parks and instruction on how to create them. It is not clear what training he had, but he may have served an apprenticeship at George II's garden in Hanover (as Conrad

Above: Rinaldi's 1760s plan for a formal garden on one side of the track of the Coasting Hill and for an irregular garden on the other side.

Opposite: The Catherine Palace at Tsarskoe Selo. Catherine ordered that the trees in front of the palace, which had been clipped to form green walls, should be allowed to grow naturally.

III.^{cme} VUE DE TSARSKO-CELO, PROMENADE DE CATHERINE II.

Loddiges did).[12] At the nursery he specialized in American trees and other plants obtained from John Bartram and Peter Collinson.[13] These were ideal for planting in landscape parks. Many of the German owners who were trying to landscape their parks visited the nursery and bought plants, and when some of them sent their gardeners to tour English parks, they also arranged for them to receive instruction from Busch. When the son of the Princess of Hessen-Darmstadt's head gardener was to visit Hackney, Busch, in a letter dated 4 July 1766 to Friedrich August, Baron de Veltheim, the owner of the Harbke estate near Helmstdt, promised to do all he could for him; he also mentioned that the previous September he had escorted the Duke of Zweibrücken's gardener on a 300-mile tour of English parks 'to show him the best places'.[14] Another German gardener, Johann Andreas Graefer, spent a year at the nursery and then secured a post at Lord Coventry's Croome Court, which had been laid out by 'Capability' Brown. This was followed by a spell at James Vere's Kensington Gore, and he was later appointed head gardener to the King of Naples and laid out a landscape garden at Caserta.[15] Busch was on friendly terms with the Prince of Anhalt-Bernburg-Zerbst, who was

related to Catherine, and this friendship may have led to his call to Russia. In December 1770 Catherine sent the architect Vasily Neyelov and his son Pyotr to England to 'visit all the notable gardens and, having seen them, to lay out similar ones here'.[16] It may well be that Busch had been invited to work for Catherine before the visit of the Neyelovs and that he arranged their tour of English parks and accompanied them.

After arriving in St Petersburg in 1771 John Busch wrote to Lord Coventry from Oranienbaum on 20 September:

> May it please Your Lordship
> I have the Honer to acquaint you that I and family are safe arrived at Petersburg after 9 days passage from England, her Imperial Majesty recd me very graiciously & placed me in one of her palaces called oranienbaum, I have sent your Lordship a Box of plants[17] mark'd C No 3

Catherine with her family and Italian greyhounds walking in the park at Tsarskoe Selo. An engraving based on a painting by M. Domam-Memortre (c.1790).

Consign'd to Dr Fothergill,[18] pr Ship General Conway Captn Robert Lumley, which I hope will come safe, next spring when the plants are in bloom I hope we shall find more sorts, it is dangerous in these woods to collect plants there being large bears and wolves,

    I am Your Lordships Most Humble & obiedt servt, John Bush

The plants he sent were vaccinium,[19] creeping vaccinium, a 'black stalk fern', another fern, birch, pyrola, water aloe, geranium, dwarf bramble, ten plants of rhododendron, 'Lilly de valle miner', 'Lilly de valle major', six plants of orach and three unidentified plants, one of which had sweet-scented flowers. He requested payment of £5.5.0. 'please to pay the money to Mr Mello No 36 Fenchurch Street please To direct for me to the Care of Messrs Weltden Baxter & Freederick at St Petersburg'.[20] How long Busch stayed at Oranienbaum and what he achieved there has not been established, but it was at Tsarskoe Selo that he was to make his major contribution.

In 1772 Catherine wrote to Voltaire: 'I now love to distraction gardens in the English style, the curving lines, the gentle slopes, the pools in the form of lakes, and I scorn straight lines and twin allées. I hate fountains which torture water in order to make it follow a course contrary to its nature; statues are relegated to galleries, halls, etc; in a word, anglomania rules my plantomania.'[21] A year later she placed an order through the Russian Consul in London for the famous Green Frog dinner service, with 1,244 different British views on 952 pieces of Queen's ware, which Wedgwood and Bentley delivered in 1774. Many of the views were of parks and gardens, at her request, and it seems that she also asked that all the buildings represented should be in the Gothic style, since Wedgwood wrote to Bentley on 29 March 1773: 'As to our being confin'd to Gothique buildings only, why there are not enough I am perswaded in Great Britain to furnish objects for this service.'[22] That the service should have a Gothic character is also indicated in Wedgwood's letter dated 3 April 1773: 'What do you think of the Etruscan, long pointed border, the same as Ld. Stormonts Desert, I think it is nearly as much Gothick as Etruscan.'[23] This is the figured band which frames the views on the dessert pieces in the service.

Catherine intended to keep the service at the Kekerekeksinensky Palace, designed by Yuri Velten, a small staging palace on the Moscow road between St Petersburg and Tsarskoe Selo. The palace and the church, which was built in association with it, were among the earliest examples of Gothic Revival architecture in Russia. They were to commemorate the brilliant Russian victory over the Turkish fleet at the Battle of Chesme in 1770, and the choice of the Gothic style seems to indicate that this had been a triumph for ancient Northern virtues in the spirit of the crusades. The plan of the palace was based on the late-sixteenth-century Longford Castle in Wiltshire. The plan and two elevations of Longford Castle had been published in 1771 in the fifth volume of

Vitruvius Britannicus, and this, one assumes, was the source used by Velten at Catherine's direction. Longford Castle, which was the original of the castle of Amphialus in Sir Philip Sidney's *Arcadia*, appeared on the cover of a dish in the dinner service. Velten also designed the pink and white Gothic church,[24] which was built between 1777 and 1780 and which, unlike the palace, has been restored. The lanterns on the roof are reminiscent of those on the Gothic Temple at Stowe.

The green frog device, which, as Catherine wished, accompanies every view on the service, derives from the original Finnish name for the location of Chesme, Kekerekeksinen, simulating the sound of croaking (compare the 'brekeke-kex' chorus of *The Frogs* of Aristophanes) and signifying 'place of frogs'. The first Russian name for the palace was Kekerekeksinensky Dvorets, which Catherine translated as La Grenouillère. In 1780 Chesme became the

A glacier from the Wedgwood Green Frog dinner service with a view of Beaudesert in Staffordshire. The figures on the lid – Ice, Cold and Winter – are thought to have been modelled by Josiah Wedgwood.

name of both place and palace. The latter was also known as *Chesmensky dvorets*.

Considering the extent of the undertaking, the service was designed and manufactured with remarkable speed, and it is not surprising to find the selection of parks and the relative prominence given to them a little arbitrary and parochial. Merit sometimes gave way to availability, as well as to Wedgwood's desire to flatter certain rich proprietors.

Stowe, pre-eminent among English parks and the most likely to have been singled out for inclusion by Catherine, was the most comprehensively illustrated, with forty-eight views, and was followed by Kew, the second most widely known abroad, with twenty-five, and then Enville with twenty-one, Windsor with nineteen, Shugborough and West Wycombe with fourteen each, and Mount Edgcumbe and Studley Royal with thirteen each. Booth's Hall in Cheshire, Bradgate in Leicestershire, Chiswick, Esher, Foot's Cray, Gatton, Hall Barn, Castle Howard, Ingestre, Oatlands, Painshill, Shobdon Court, Stourhead, Tabley, Trentham, Whitton, Wilton, Wimpole, Woburn Farm and Wrest Park were each represented by four or more views. Some of these seats are now almost forgotten, and it is a little surprising to find them with more views than Blenheim, Hagley, Claremont, Wentworth or Chatsworth, though this comparison does not take into account the size and importance of the pieces carrying the views. One looks in vain for The Leasowes, Rousham, Bowood, Badminton, Piercefield, Petworth, Caversham, Whiteknights, Kedleston, Woburn Abbey, The Vyne and Longleat, all of them more celebrated than, say, Booth's Hall, Butterton, Barlaston, Whitmore, Keele and Swynnerton – but they were also much further from Etruria. It must be added, however, that posterity has gained from the choice of minor parks, since the views of some of them would not otherwise have been recorded.

The use of the Green Frog service is referred to in court records of occasions when Catherine visited the palace with important guests. On 6 June 1777, she went there with her cousin, Gustav III of Sweden, to lay the foundation stone of the church, and lunch was served off the service to a company of thirty-six. It was also used for the fifty-six guests on 24 June 1780, when Catherine entertained Joseph II of Austria.[25] This was the tenth anniversary of the Battle of Chesme, and it was on this day that the name of the palace was officially changed.[26] A more intimate occasion was the visit of the British envoy, Sir James Harris, later Lord Malmesbury, on 3 June 1779. He had

> the good fortune to have made myself not disagreeable to the Empress. . . . She admits me to all her parties of cards, and a few days ago carried me with only two of her courtiers, to a country place. . . She calls this place *la Grenouillère*; and it was for it that Wedgwood made,

some years ago, a very remarkable service of his ware, on which a green frog was painted. It represented the different country houses and their gardens in England. This, also, we were shown, and this led to a conversation on English gardening, in which the Empress is a great adept.[27]

An early assignment given to John Busch was on a hill at Pulkovo, a few miles from St Petersburg. 'In 1774 the Empress paid her first visit to this place. On entering the garden, and seeing a winding shady gravel walk planted on both sides, she appeared struck with surprise, and exclaimed, "This is what I wanted!" This walk led to a fine lawn, with gravel walks round it, which seemed to strike her still more forcibly, and she again said, "This is what I have long wished to have!" The following year the Tsarskoe Selo gardens were given to John Busch',[28] where he distinguished himself both as a cultivator and as a landscape designer.

Elizabeth Dimsdale, the wife of Catherine's English physician, Thomas Dimsdale, was impressed by the main greenhouse under his care, 'the largest I ever saw' with several hundred orange, lemon and citron trees, and by 'a great number of Hot Houses for all kinds of fruits, and I think the best Melons I ever eat of Mr Bush's raising, and plenty of Water Melons, Peaches and Nectarines very good: and what surprised me most a very great plenty of China Oranges . . . Mr Bush shewed me the foundation of a hot house which was building, of eight hundred Feet in Length.'[29] James Meader, an English gardener who went to St Petersburg in 1779 to landscape the grounds of the English Palace at Peterhof for Catherine, was also impressed. 'The gardens at Tsarskoe Selo are very extensive and beautiful, ornamented with a greater variety of plants than you can possibly conceive in this climate.' He was also impressed by the size and quantity of the carp.[30]

Working with Vasily Neyelov, Busch landscaped a large part of the park, reshaping the surface of the ground to resemble nature, planting many trees, transforming the formal basin into an irregular lake with bays and promontories and additional islands, and creating new pools and water courses, fed by a new water system linked to sources at Taitsy some 10 miles away.[31] Together, under the Empress's critical eye, they laid the foundations for the first great Russian 'English garden', as the Russians called their landscape parks. At the same time an area of the earlier formal garden was retained.

Numerous architectural features were to be added to the setting they had created, and the inspiration for most of them came from plans in English publications. As one result of the Neyelovs' tour, Catherine would almost certainly have been in possession of the 1769 edition of Benton Seeley's *Stowe: A Description of the Magnificent House and Gardens of the Right Honourable Richard Grenville Temple, Earl Temple, Viscount and Baron Cobham*, which combined Seeley's two earlier publications. Other British sources included books of Chinese

Trees in the landscape park at Tsarskoe Selo.

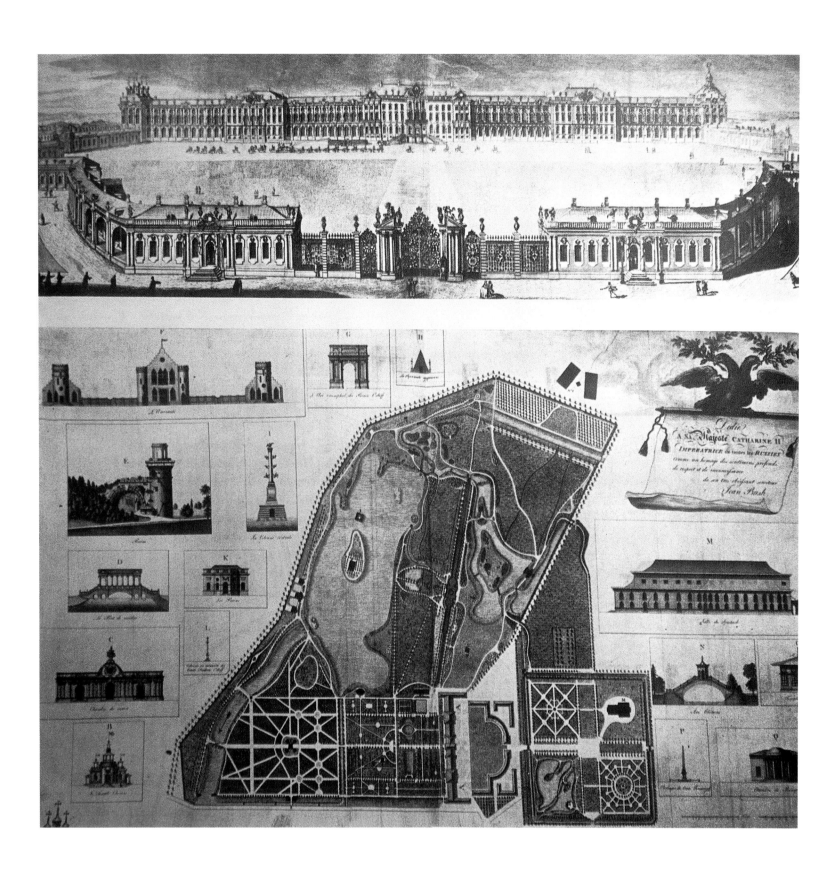

Above: Joseph Busch's plan of the park at Tsarskoe Selo (1789), engraved by Tobias Müller.

Right, top: Yuri Velten's Chinese or Creaking Pavilion.

Right, middle: Part of the Chinese Village, where the houses were let to courtiers and other privileged people.

Right, bottom: One of Cameron's Chinese bridges over the canal which frames the New Garden.

designs by William Chambers, J. & W. Halfpenny, Charles Over and P. Decker.[32] Catherine was very impressed by François-de-Paule Latapie's French translation (1771) – a German translation appeared in the same year – of Thomas Whately's *Observations on Modern Gardening* (1770), and she began to prepare a version of it aimed particularly at the owners of estates along the Peterhof Road, but it never reached publication.[33]

It has often been assumed that the Palladian Bridge at Tsarskoe Selo, which Vasily Neyelov added soon after his return from England, was inspired by the similar bridge at Wilton, but, in view of Catherine's enthusiasm for Stowe, it seems more probable that the view, plan and elevation in Seeley's guide were Neyelov's source. James Gibbs's Gothic Temple at Stowe may have awakened Catherine's interest in the neo-gothic, and among the first Russian neo-gothic buildings were Vasily Neyelov's Hermitage Kitchen and his Admiralty by the lake, which provided accommodation for boats and for water birds. A number of engravings of garden scenes which Neyelov had brought back from England – perhaps obtained by Busch – used to hang on the walls of the Admiralty. They are said to have included a view of the Moon Pools at Studley Royal in Yorkshire, which Neyelov later reproduced on one of the terraces of the Old Garden at Tsarskoe Selo.[34]

The English landscape park was perceived to have links with Chinese parks, which were also inspired by nature, and Chinese buildings were widely introduced into parks in western Europe. The most complex of the Chinese buildings at Tsarskoe Selo is Yuri Velten's Creaking Pavilion. It stands by an intricate water landscape of tightly twisting banks and islands, which enhances the Chinese effect and prepares the visitor for the Chinese village. The village was reached by way of Neyelov's Bolshoi Kapriz, inspired by an illustration of an archway in China.[35] Neyelov's archway with its crowning pavilion was placed over what was then the main approach road to the palace from St Petersburg. On both sides of the road the ground was raised by means of artificial hills to give height to the archway.

The village, the largest group of Chinese buildings in Europe, was begun by Vasily Neyelov, perhaps with some contribution from Rinaldi, but the Scottish architect Charles Cameron later took charge of the project. Considerable alterations were made by Stasov in 1817. The houses used to be let to courtiers and other privileged people. Nikolai Karamzin, the distinguished writer and historian, lived here for a time.[36]

Near to the Chinese village Cameron designed Chinese bridges over the canal framing the New Garden, while the Chinese Theatre in one of the quarters of the New Garden was designed by Rinaldi with modifications by Ivan Neyelov, who supervised its construction. It replaced the earlier open-air theatre. Badly damaged during the last war, it has not yet been restored.

Charles Cameron, though he represented himself to Catherine as a Jacobite aristocrat, was born in London of Scottish descent, the son of a carpenter. He studied in Rome and produced a book on the ancient baths there, which was much admired. He came to St Petersburg in 1779 and delighted Catherine with his work as decorator and as architect. Catherine was anxious to recreate classical antiquity at Tsarskoe Selo, and this Cameron succeeded in doing with his Baths, a magnificent series of rooms, lined with marble, agate and jasper, situated on two floors.

In association with these rooms Cameron built a two-storey gallery, projecting into the park, which became known as the Cameron Gallery. Here Catherine could take gentle exercise among statues of ancient gods, heroes and philosophers, while admiring on one side the formal garden and on the other her landscaped park. Through the centre of the gallery there was a long glass-enclosed space where she could walk in bad weather.

Cameron also created the massively rusticated pandus (*pente douce* or gentle slope), leading down to the park from the hanging garden, which was laid out by the gallery and in front of the Agate Pavilion, the upper floor of the Baths. The

Top: The pandus leading down to the park from the hanging garden in front of the Agate Pavilion.

Above: The Agate Pavilion, where Catherine received her conquering Russian heroes.

Above, right: The cathedral of St Sophia in the town Sofia, representing Constantinople, which Catherine dreamed of capturing. The cathedral has now been fully restored.

Right: Statues of ancient gods, heroes and philosophers in the Cameron Gallery, where Catherine liked to take gentle exercise.

Above left: Captain Grenville's Monument at Stowe, a rostral column celebrating naval victories. From Benton Seeley's *Stowe* (1769).

Above right: The rostral column in the lake at Tsarskoe Selo, commemorating the great naval victory over the Turkish fleet at the Battle of Chesme in 1770. To the left, the later Turkish Bath Pavilion.

hanging garden was no doubt intended to recall the hanging gardens of antiquity. The pandus was originally embellished with the statues of the nine muses, Mercury, Venus and Flora, which, after Catherine's death, Paul transferred to Pavlovsk for the Old Sylvia.

The model town of Sofia outside the park, with its Cathedral of St Sophia, designed by Cameron, was an important feature of the view from the gallery. Catherine had decreed that the architect should 'lay out the streets in relation to the roads of the neighbouring garden in such a way that they make one view with it.' In fact all the roads in the town appeared to radiate from the Cameron Gallery; and when Catherine was in residence the streets were lit at night. This town represented Constantinople, which Catherine dreamed of capturing and re-establishing as the centre of Christendom. With this in mind she 'had her second grandson named Constantine, entrusted him to a Greek nurse, and ordered medals struck with a reproduction of S. Sophia!'[37] These features in the landscape formed part of an allegory of victories achieved and political dreams, which Cameron helped to create for her. The Black Sea, leading to the Turkish capital, was represented by the lake, where Rinaldi's rostral column commemorated the great naval victory at Chesme won by Russian sailors under the command of Aleksei Orlov and the Scot, Captain Greig, subsequently promoted to Admiral. Other monuments celebrated victories at Morea and at Kagul, where, the inscription records, a force of 150,000 Turks was routed by 17,000 Russians under General Count Rumiantsev.[38]

When Prince Potemkin, who had done so much to extend Russia's territory by the Black Sea, or some other conquering hero came to visit Catherine, it was intended that he should enter the park through the triumphal Orlov Gate, decorated in his honour. He would then pass first Velten's Tower-Ruin, erected to celebrate the victory at Ochakov. This was in the form of a Doric column under a Turkish pavilion, symbolizing, argues Shvidkovsky, the ancient might of Greece under the Turkish yoke. This was followed by a Turkish pavilion, destroyed in the last war and not rebuilt, and the Turkish Cascade with its two small gothic towers. He then reached the second gallery designed by Cameron for Catherine – the Temple of Memory, a long, raised colonnade, embellished with many sculptures and bas-reliefs, and linked with a triumphal arch.[39] A drawing by Cameron shows such an arch with medallions depicting battle scenes, and this, it seems, is what was built here. The visiting warrior could pause on the colonnade to look across the Black Sea to Constantinople and St Sophia, which had become a mosque under the Turks, before proceeding on the final stage of his journey and climbing the great ramp, with its enhancing muses, deities and huge antique vases, to the hanging garden, with its beds of scented flowers, and the Agate Pavilion, to be received by Catherine amid the aura of classical ideals and antique harmony which Cameron had created for her. Entry to this world and the promise of immortal fame were the rewards for victory and martial valour.

Stowe, too, was a great victory park with an obelisk to General Wolfe and a rostral column to Captain Grenville, both features which appeared at Tsarskoe Selo, while the triumphal Corinthian Arch at Stowe seems to have been the inspiration for Rinaldi's very similar Orlov Gate. Cameron's Temple of

Above: The two small Gothic towers by the Turkish, or Red, Cascade.

Below: The Temple of Concord and Victory at Stowe, here illustrated in Benton Seeley's *Stowe* (1769), was the inspiration for Cameron's Temple of Memory at Tsarskoe Selo, which was demolished on the orders of Paul I even before it was quite completed.

The Temple of Concord and Victory.

Top: The Egyptian Pyramid at Stowe commemorating Vanbrugh. From Benton Seeley's *Stowe* (1769).

Above: The pyramid at Tsarskoe Selo, a mausoleum for Catherine's greyhounds.

Memory[40] echoed Stowe's Grecian Temple, which was rededicated as the Temple of Concord and Victory after the successful conclusion of the Seven Years War under the national leadership of Earl Temple's brother-in-law, William Pitt. It was described by Seeley as 'one of the principal ornaments of the garden – It has six Statues on the Top as big as Life . . .'.[41] Inside the temple the walls were decorated with fourteen medallions representing the taking of Quebec, Montreal, Louisberg and Pondicherry, and other victories on land and sea.

Unfortunately the life of the Temple of Memory was short, for Paul I ordered its demolition in 1797. Among monuments in the park which have served longer to keep memories alive is the pyramid by Cameron, which honours the last resting place of three of Catherine's Italian greyhounds, Sir Tom Anderson, Duchess and Zemire, brought to Catherine from England by Dr Thomas Dimsdale. The epitaph to Zemire came from the pen of the French ambassador in verse; that to Sir Tom Anderson seems not to have been recorded before it became illegible; while of Duchess we read:

Ci-gît
Duchesse
la fidèle compagne
de
Sir Tom Anderson
Elle le suivit en Russe l'an 1770
Aimée et respectée
par sa nombreuse postérité
Elle décéda en 1782, âgée de 15 ans
laissant 115 descendans
tant lévriers que levrettes.[42]

The pyramid at Stowe served not as a mausoleum but as a memorial to Vanbrugh. Elsewhere in the garden, however – at first behind the Temple of British Worthies, later near St Augustine's Cave – a tablet was erected

To the Memory
of
SIGNOR FIDO
an *Italian* of good Extraction;
who came into *England*
not to bite us, like most of his Countrymen,
but to gain an honest livelihood . . .
a faithful Friend,
an agreeable Companion,
a loving Husband,
distinguish'd by a numerous Offspring,
all which he lived to see take good courses.
In his old Age he retir'd
to the house of a Clergyman in the Country
where he finished his earthly Race,
And died an Honour and an Example to the whole Species.

Reader,
this Stone is guiltless of Flattery,
for he to whom it is inscrib'd
was not a Man
but
a Grey-hound.[45]

There are similarities, too, in the choice of statues and the way they were used at Tsarskoe Selo and Stowe. Statues of Hercules were prominently placed in both gardens. The statues of the nine muses flanked the pandus at Tsarskoe Selo; and there were statues of the nine muses (and Apollo) at Stowe, at first

Right: The Palladian Bridge at Stowe. From Benton Seeley's *Stowe* (1769).

Below: The Palladian Bridge at Tsarskoe Selo.

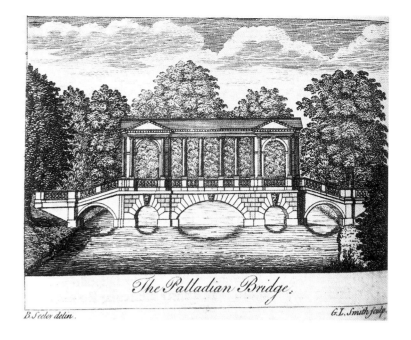

The Palladian Bridge.

B. Seeley delin.

G.L. Smith sculp.

near the house, later by the Doric Arch near the Elysian Fields. The placing of busts of ancient worthies in the Cameron Gallery may have been suggested by the statues of Lycurgus, Socrates, Homer and Epaminondas in the Temple of Ancient Virtue, by the 'Collection of antique Bustoes of Marble' which once stood on the Palladian Bridge, and by the busts in the Temple of British Worthies.

Visitors to Tsarskoe Selo and Stowe today may not be struck by the similarities, but a comparison of the garden Neyelov would have seen at Stowe in 1771 with Catherine's park at the end of her reign reveals the debt of the latter to Stowe and leads to the conclusion that Catherine had Seeley's book at hand as she directed its development.

The Coasting Hill was a favourite entertainment of Catherine's until the carriage in which she was riding came out of its groove and a nasty accident was avoided only by the prompt action of Grigory Orlov, who was standing behind. John Busch told Elizabeth Dimsdale that Orlov strained a leg severely and was lame for some time.[44] According to a later version he broke an arm and the bandages used to repair it included the blue riband.[45] The Coasting Hill fell out of favour and was eventually demolished. When Elizabeth Dimsdale was

there in 1781 she recorded that on one of the hills made for the track of the Coasting Hill 'two very high swings are placed, and a small Chaise to hold one person, and two or three wooden horses that are so constructed that any one might ride round the top of the mount which is boarded, and a Communication is made with wheels underneath worked with an Horse with very great Swiftness.'[46]

Thanks to the Reverend John Glen King, the British chaplain in St Petersburg, we know that there was also an early helter skelter near by. In a letter to the Bishop of Durham he wrote: 'At the same place, there is another artificial mount which goes in a spiral line, and in my opinion, for I have tried it also, is very disagreeable . . .'.[47]

When Quarenghi's Alexander Palace was built in 1792–6, the park was divided into two, the Ekaterininsky and the Aleksandrovsky parks. A landscaped setting by Ilya Neyelov was provided for the new palace with pools on three sides. The formal division of the New Garden (page 46) was retained, though the treatment of the four quarters became less formal.

Beyond the New Garden, on the site of the earlier hunting enclosure, a new romantic park was created by another

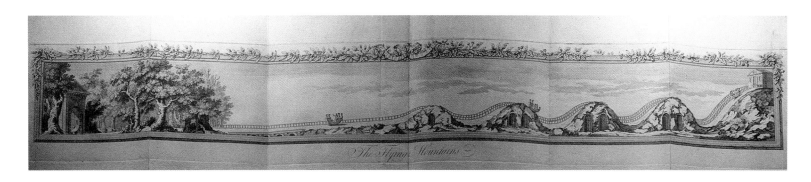

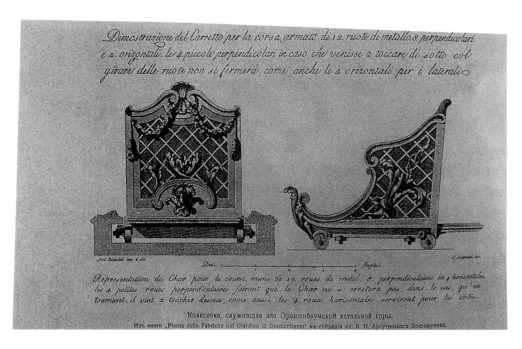

Above: *The Flying Mountain* (Coasting Hill) from Lord Baltimore's *Gaudia Poetica* (1770).

Right: A carriage for the Coasting Hill, from A.N. Benois's book on Tsarksoe Selo (1910).

Opposite: The Alexander Palace, architect Giacomo Quarenghi.

Scottish architect, Adam Menelaws, with winding walks and shady pools and buildings intended to evoke the Middle Ages. Unfortunately this involved the loss of Rastrelli's very fine Mon Bijou pavilion, replaced in 1834 by the neo-gothic Arsenal, which housed the imperial collection of armour.[48] The Chapel was built by Menelaws as a ruin. There were stained-glass windows with biblical scenes and a statue of Christ commissioned by the Dowager Empress Maria Fyodorovna from the sculptor Dannecker in Württemberg.[49] Elsewhere in the park Menelaws designed the retirement stables for horses which had served under the imperial saddle, the farm, the llama house and the elephant house. There was still an elephant in residence in 1911, a good-natured animal which was allowed to wander freely in the summer.[50] Menelaws came to Russia as a master stonemason in 1784 after being recruited, along with many other Scottish craftsmen, by Charles Cameron to work at Tsarskoe Selo. After less than a year with Cameron he left to work on cathedrals for the Russian architect Nikolai Lvov at Mogilev in Belorussia and at Torzhok, some 125 miles north of Moscow; and his association with Lvov led to his advancement from stonemason to successful architect.[51]

The most notable nineteenth-century additions to the Ekaterininsky Park were Rusca's Granite Terrace, the landing stage by the Grotto, the Turkish Bath Pavilion (1852) by Monighetti – a late monument to the 1827–9 war with Turkey – and Sokolov's fountain-statue of the milkmaid with the broken pitcher (1810) based on the fable by La Fontaine. She

The Turkish Bath Pavilion, 1852, a late celebration of victory over the Turks in the war of 1827–9.

had been thinking of the profit she would get from the milk and how she would invest it and get more profit until the milk became a farm in her daydream – and then disaster.

Catherine took an intensely possessive interest in her first grandson, Alexander, the future Emperor, and assumed complete responsibility for his upbringing and education. For his moral guidance she wrote and published fairy tales, which were read to him and his brother Constantine before they went to sleep. As an appropriate moral setting for one of these stories, *A Tale of Tsarevich Khlor*, she ordered an English garden to be made on land which had been given to Alexander. It was called Alexandrova dacha. The designer is not known, but Nikolai Lvov and Charles Cameron have both been suggested.

Catherine's story is set at a time before records began, when a son was born to the Tsar in a town 'on a high mountain in the middle of the forest', and given the name Khlor. 'Behind the palace fruit trees were planted and near them lakes with fish were dug.' Khlor is captured by the Khan of Khirgizia and taken to the steppe, where he is told to go out and find 'the rose without thorns which does not prick'. He is helped by the Khan's daughter, Felitsa, who sends her son, Reason, to accompany him. Nothing remains of Alexandrova dacha and its garden, but it was situated between Tsarskoe Selo and Pavlovsk, and the way to it echoed the route followed by Khlor and Reason, as described in the story. After various encounters they find the rose, which represents virtue, in a temple of seven columns on a hill, and Khlor is praised for being so clever when still so young.[52] Gavrila Derzhavin's *Ode to Felitsa*, with its references to Catherine's tale and its portrayal of her as the Tatar princess Felitsa, a personification of wisdom, delighted the Empress and secured the poet's future prosperity.

Tsarskoe Selo was rightly called *gorod muz*, 'the town of poets', for it must stand out among all the parks of the world for the number of poets associated with it. In the eighteenth century there were Mikhail Lomonosov, the great scientist as well as poet, after whom Oranienbaum was renamed in 1948, and Gavril Derzhavin. In 1811 the lycée, an extended four-storey wing of the palace, was opened, and Alexander Pushkin was among the first to be enrolled. With the inspiration of the beauty of the park and some exceptional teaching, the talents of the pupils were given every encouragement to flourish. During his years there Pushkin became recognized as a poet of great promise, already with more than a hundred poems to his name, many of them published. Two of his fellow pupils, Anton Delvig and Wilhelm Kuchelbecker, would also join the ranks of Russian poets.[53] Living and learning at Tsarskoe Selo was an exceptional formative experience and one to look back on with nostalgia and affection ever afterwards. In Pushkin's view, he and his companions were a race apart and would remain so:

The Milkmaid Fountain. The queue might seem to suggest that the water was considered to have special properties, but when this photograph was taken the local water supply had been cut off.

Wherever fate may choose to toss us,
Wherever destiny would have us go,
We're all as one, the world is foreign to us,
Our fatherland is Tsarskoe Selo.[54]

The poets who followed included Innokenty Annensky, Nikolai Gumilev and, more recently, Anna Akhmatova:

So many lyres are hanging on these boughs,
And yet, it seems, there's still a place for mine.[55]

The town Tsarskoe Selo was renamed Pushkin in 1937.

In 1769 an English poet had arrived at Tsarskoe Selo to lower the tone. Frederick Calvert, the sixth Lord Baltimore, proprietor of Maryland, was described in the *Encyclopedia Americana* as 'selfish, degenerate and mean'. A contemporary publication devoted to his activities suggested that a tour to Constantinople undertaken by him had had the object of obtaining 'intelligence concerning the regulations, laws and customs of the seraglio, with all the ceremonies and methods of treating the sultanas',[56] intelligence which would enable him better to set up a similar establishment in London. It seems that his methods of recruiting were open to misunderstanding, and in 1768, after what had seemed to him a straightforward initiation, he found himself on trial for rape. His acquittal caused a public outcry and, to escape the mob, he embarked on the Northern Tour to the Baltic, describing the highlights in Latin verse, with English and French translations, which he published under the title *Gaudia Poetica*. Though the text is slight, the book was beautifully produced with splendid illustrations.[57]

In Uppsala he won the friendship of Linnaeus with lavish gifts and discovered with pleasure that 'the North abounds in love as well as the East, and the warmest nymphs exist in these cold waves'.[58] In St Petersburg he was presented to Catherine and visited Tsarskoe Selo, to which a section of his poem is devoted. What appealed to him in the park were the mechanical wonders of the Hermitage and the Coasting Hill, and he confines his account of the park to these two features. He provided an illustration of the latter (page 96) as well as describing his sensations as a rider:

Hortus adest magica longe celeberrimus arte;
Ima petit currus, subitoque recurrit in altum
Volvitur in praeceps iterum, iterumque resurgit;
Vis celer exoritar magnis operata ruinis
Proruit et lato sonitu, lapsuque propinquo.
Deficit inde halitus, clauduntur lumina nocte,

Et gelidos motu convulsio corripit artus.
Quinque per excelsos rapide petit aethera montes,
Quinque per infernas decurrit machina valles.
Attoniti, caeci terram superamus, et undam,
Perque nemus, thalamosque volatica membra vehuntur.
Haud procul est lucus magica mirandus ab arte.
Hic dum sublimem stupefactus fertur in arcem
Spectator, solio per sese attollitur imo,
Servus adest nullus, patefactaque gurgite strata
Pandunt, appositam nitido videt ordine mensam.[59]

The adjacent gardens are much admired. A chariot rushes down and soon rises, it rolls headlong and mounts directly, a violent impetus conducts it with a sudden and great noise. Five times it flew rapidly over the lofty hills, and five times it descended into deep valleys. The breath is taken away, the eye sight is obscured, and a cold convulsion seizes all the body. Astonished and blind we passed over land and water, and our flying limbs were carried into woods and rooms. In these enchanting Gardens you are also placed on a Canopy, which carries you of itself aloft into a magnificent apartment, the floor of which opens and a large table rises up, where twenty persons are served without their seeing any body.[60]

The English Park

James Meader arrived in Russia in 1779. In England he had worked for the Earl of Chesterfield and then as head gardener for the Duke of Northumberland at Alnwick Castle and at Syon Park. In 1771 he had had a spot of bother with the law after publishing Thomas Hitt's *The Modern Gardener; or, Universal Kalendar* 'Selected from the diary manuscripts of . . . Mr. Hitt . . . Revised . . . with many new additions, by James Meader'. This was shown to have been largely copied from Thomas Mawe's *Every Man his Own Gardener* – written, in fact, by John Abercrombie, but Mawe had put his name to it. 'The plagiary was so very conspicuous as to cause a lawsuit, in which Meader was convicted; and it was agreed he should never reprint it.'[61] While the text of the plagiarized book is entirely devoted to horticulture, some of the plates, added by Meader with a 'Description and Explanation of the Plans and Designs' instead of an introduction, are concerned purely with landscaping. They illustrate solutions of the sort he was to employ in his work in Russia. 'PLATE VIII is a Design for ornamenting the Back View from the House with Shrubs and Trees. If a River crosses the Ground, the Walks, by Means of Bridges, may be continued through the Plantations beyond. . . . Where a fine Piece of Water presents itself, the View of this should by no means be intercepted from the House by Plantations.'[62] *The Planter's Guide; or Pleasure Gardener's Companion*, published under Meader's own name in 1779, was a very useful guide to trees, shrubs and climbing plants, giving their height, shape, size, a description of their foliage and

advice on cultivation. Both the text and the excellent illustrations suggest how to group them according to their size and shape, and he made out a good case for planting deciduous and evergreen trees separately.

In Russia he had undertaken to work 'wherever Her Imperial Majesty may please to employ me as a Gardener in general and more particularly in those branches of Gardening which consist in planning, designing and laying out of Pleasure Gardens Parks &c. and to take upon me the directive part of planting Trees &c. forming pieces of Water &c. also furnishing Designs for Stoves, forcing Frames, ornamental Buildings or any other Business relative both to the usefull and ornamental part of the hortuary Art.'[63] Count Aleksei Musin-Pushkin, the Russian ambassador in London, had negotiated Meader's contract with him before he left London, and he was to receive an annual salary of 1,000 roubles in silver coin, ninety-six roubles for an interpreter, a hundred and fifty for fuel and thirty-three for candles.

Catherine, who had never liked the main palace at Peterhof and had always chosen to stay at Monplaisir, now engaged Giacomo Quarenghi to build a new palace, which came to be called the English Palace, on adjacent land which had been a hunting park. Meader's task was to lay out an English park to go with it. There were also to be two smaller palaces, one for Paul and Maria Fyodorovna and the other for Alexander and Constantine.

> The spot allotted for me is a park; a great part thereof is full of fine trees. Here are fine pieces of water which want but little help to make them elegant, with a vale where I propose to form a magnificent cascade, the water being above. In these affairs I am under no restraint either to extent of land or water; the bounds are only limited by the gulf of Finland.[64]

At first he was involved in supervising the building of a house for himself, and pine stoves, peach houses and melon frames. There was no lack of money, and a workforce of more than three hundred was available. He was not impressed by the two apprentices allocated to him. 'I have under me two apprentices of the Empress; one of them has been twenty years and the other ten years in the Peterhof gardens. They are both as ignorant of gardening as though they had not been six months.'[65]

The main feature he created in the park was a large pool (circumference 1½ miles) with two islands fed by an artificial river a mile long. A mile and a quarter of paths were laid out, with bridges where there was water to be crossed, hillocks were formed and five thousand deciduous trees of various kinds were planted round the pool. 'I have finished a piece of water

Giacomo Quarenghi's drawing (c.1780) of his English Palace at Peterhof and the park.

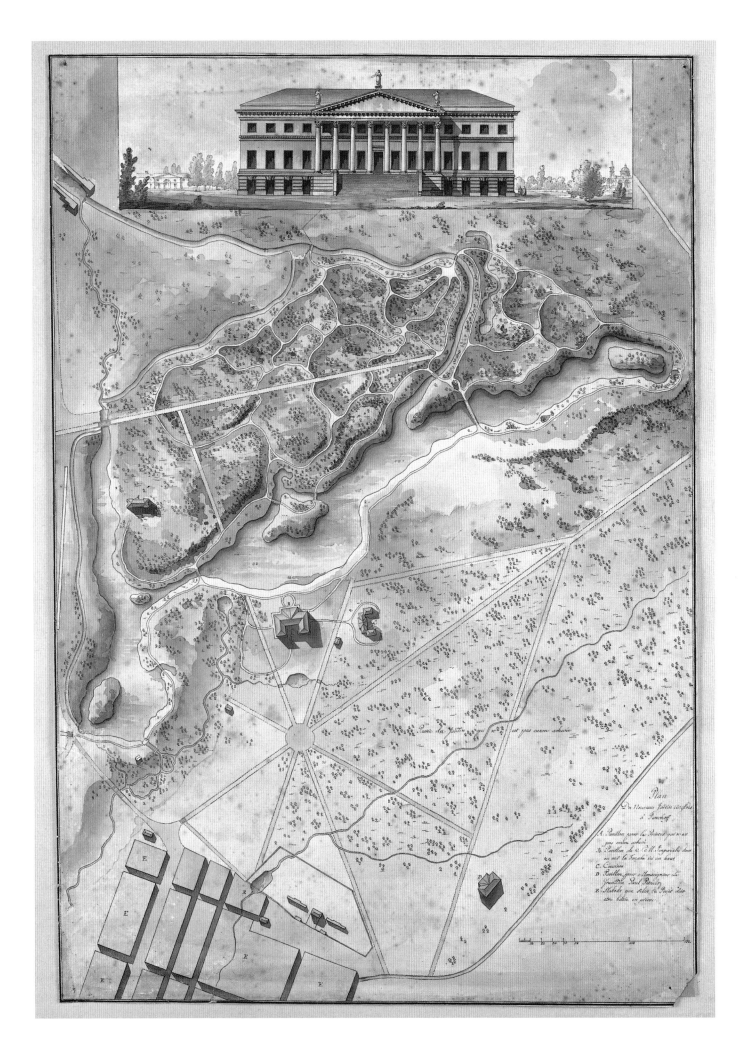

admired by everybody, built a bridge of my own designing which is much noticed, chose a spot for a grand palace in the garden and workmen are employed on the foundation under the direction of a very ingenious Italian architect, the whole to be completed in three years.'[66] He was not exaggerating the enthusiasm of visitors to the park.

Two of the watercolours painted by James Meader of the scenes he created in the English park.

Near Peterhoff, and in the midst of a forest, is a garden executed in the modern English taste – a very delightful spot; and when the natural flatness of the ground is considered, it is amazing what art and taste have been exerted in finishing it. Here are winding rivulets, cascades dashing over moss-clad rocks, antique bridges, temples, ruins, and cottages. In one of the huts I found a collection of prints from the subject of Sterne's *Sentimental Journey*.[67]

Meader was particularly anxious to make a grotto in the park which would surpass the famous grotto at Painshill, created by Joseph Lane, and in the summer of 1782 he complained to his correspondent that he had still not received the Derbyshire spar he had asked for. He received some in 1783 but 'such a bad sample except the few petrefactions that I could not with any propriety show them to the Empress. Those of the sort of Painshill are so short that they were not fit for the purpose of representing icicles, but I have not proceeded in forming the cascade and grotto this year tho' intended owing to a fall.' In 1784 he repeated his request:

> I have shown the Empress a specimen of the spar which she approves of and has ordered me to get a sufficient quantity. Therefore if it is not very inconvenient to you I shall be obliged to you to get me two barrels or hogsheads thereof, but not such short lumps as those you sent me. As I have orders to build a grotto with our petrified stones I want the spar long and thin so as to represent icicles. These stuck to the sides and roof of the grotto will have a most beautiful effect, much superior to Painshill Grott. Therefore let the spar be of the best kind.[68]

There seems to be no reference to a grotto in any description of the English park, so one must conclude that the project was probably never realized.

Meader also frequently asked for vegetable seeds, particularly peas and beans. He was generally able to obtain plants from England and during the years 1785–7 he ordered 200 pineapples, 100 rose bushes, 12 cherry trees, 8 plums and 3 apricots. When he returned to England in 1789 he left in Russia four competent watercolours which he painted in 1782 of scenes in the English park. Further evidence of his versatility comes from J.C. Loudon who says he was a satirical man who wrote verses about his friends and enemies.

The hut with the engravings of Sterne's *Sentimental Journey* was Catherine's little birch house, where she could rest when walking in the park. What appeared to be a simple peasant's hut had a remarkably sophisticated interior and was built at considerable cost by the architect P. Neyelov. There was a dining room, a sitting room, two studies, a divan room and a water closet. They were lined with mirrors – 540 in all – producing an effect of endlessly receding passages. When candles were lit in forty-four French porcelain candlesticks the effect was said to be overwhelming and to have caused some to swoon. Parquet floors, elegant furniture and drapery, eight marble busts and a statue of Cupid all added to the surprise awaiting the visitor to this imperial retreat.[69] Sterne's *Sentimental Journey* was one of Catherine's favourite books – presumably read in translation – which accounts for the engravings.

After the departure of James Meader, William Gould worked here for a time. Paul's hostility towards his mother led him after Catherine's death to attempt to undo whatever she had done. He ordered that the English Palace should become a barracks and that the two small palaces should be demolished, while the park was neglected. Both palace and park were restored under Alexander I, and further improvements were made by Nicholas I, who chose to live at Peterhof. In 1827 the architect I.I. Charlemagne built an enclosure for wild goats and a pheasantry, and the latter was later rebuilt by Stakenschneider. As a result some of the inhabitants of the village of Novaya had to be resettled, since the land on which their homes stood was required for this development.

The English Palace was totally destroyed during the 1941–5 war, and the park was then left to nature.

The Winter Palace

In St Petersburg there were two gardens – summer and winter – on the upper floor and the roof of the Winter Palace. The summer garden was described as having the form of a parallelogram, 'about 392 feet long, divided into numerous parterres, and entirely composed of artificial soil raised forty-two feet above the surrounding ground.' An English visitor was overwhelmed:

> Here, suspended, as it were in the air, the visitor, to his amazement, treads on gravel walks; sees the green turf vivid around him, and finds shrubs, and even trees, growing in luxuriance, under the shelter of which he may take refuge on a couch, and contemplate the execution and fair proportions of some favourite statues, several of which are to be found in the garden. The novelty of the whole scene, and the recollection where it is situated, – not on the ground, but on or near the top of a palace, – added to the overpowering influence of the boundless riches of nature and art which I had just examined, produced an effect which for some time kept me tonguetied, and induced an opinion that the wonders

The site of the English Palace, which was totally destroyed during the 1941–5 war.

of the Hermitage alone are almost worth a journey to Petersburgh.[70]

Another visitor described a visit to the winter garden:

> Here we were joined by another Imperial official who now took the lead, the party following him along the passage before mentioned to an ante-room, gloomy and dark, a preparatory twilight doubtless to the burst of light, and song, and beauty, which broke upon us as we emerged into a gallery, one side of which being composed of glass, presented, beyond, the vision of a miniature Eden – gravel walks, trees, shrubs, fountains, and flowerbeds, suspended as it were in mid-air, and inhabited by numerous feathered choristers of many foreign climes, that filled this Elysée with their songs of gladness. Several superb French lilacs, in full bloom near the entrance of this retreat, appeared to be the favourite resort of numerous canaries, some of which, perched upon the higher branches, were most enthusiastic in their greeting; standing on tip-toe, they sang as if their little throats would burst; while others, more coy, popped out their yellow heads from amidst the profusion of green leaves where they had taken refuge on the entrance of strangers. These birds and flowers are the especial pets of the Empress, some of the former being exceedingly tame.[71]

Tsaritsyno

Catherine, always a reluctant visitor to Moscow, disliked the palaces available to her there. There were several fires at the Golovin Palace, and it was almost completely destroyed by fire in 1771. She liked it no better when it was rebuilt. She commissioned a new palace on the river bank at Kolomenskoe, but that, too, failed to please her.[72] In 1775 she bought Prince Sergei Kantemir's *Chernaya Gryaz* (Black Mud) estate a few miles south-west of Moscow and changed the name to Tsaritsyno.

There were sunny meadows, shady groves, apple and cherry orchards, an orangery, parterres of flowerbeds with peacocks strutting along the paths, birch trees encircling the house, woods and fields stretching into the distance. Catherine was delighted with it and was to describe it as a 'real paradise' in a letter to Baron Grimm. As a temporary measure a small wooden palace was immediately built for her alongside the existing house and she spent the summer of 1775 there.[73]

St Petersburg was a long way from most of Russia, and Catherine must have felt that she needed a more impressive presence in Moscow, particularly in the wake of the revolt of the peasants in 1773–4 led by Emelyan Pugachev, who convinced many that he was Peter III and that he had survived the attempt on his life in 1762. Vasily Bazhenov was the architect chosen to create a vast new palace complex at Tsaritsyno on an elevated plateau between two ravines. It

Above: An engraving, published in 1773 and attributed to N.Ya. Sablin, showing the roof garden at the Winter Palace in St Petersburg.

Opposite: The Grape Gates at Tsaritsyno, designed by Vasily Bazhenov.

was a promising situation, and the resulting picturesque assemblage of buildings included the Great Palace with two identical wings, one for Catherine and one for Paul and his family, the Small Palace for entertaining guests, a pavilion for the ladies-in-waiting, a house for the men-servants, the Bread House, which was the kitchen building, the Opera House, the stable block and two monumental bridges. The combination of red brick and white stone looked back to earlier Russian architecture, but there were also classical and gothic elements.

Bazhenov began to create a landscape park in the surrounding area.

In 1782 two British, probably Scottish, gardeners, Ian Munro and Francis Reid, arrived in St Petersburg to work for Catherine. Munro was to be paid 500 roubles in his first year, 600 in his second year and 700 in his third and subsequent years. Reid was to be paid 100 roubles less per annum than Munro. They were both to receive 900 roubles per annum to cover board, interpreter and all other expenses. There is no

further information concerning Munro's stay in Russia, but in 1784 Francis Reid was sent to Moscow to work at Tsaritsyno.[74] Bazhenov was not pleased and complained that Reid intended to make drastic alterations to the idyllic scenes, such as could hardly be found in England, which he had created.

Worse was to follow for Bazhenov when Catherine visited Tsaritsyno to inspect the new buildings for the first time and was infuriated by what she saw. The likeliest reason for this reaction was Bazhenov's use of masonic symbols in the ornament of the walls of the palace. Bazhenov was a mason, as was his friend Nikolai Novikov, the prominent publisher of progressive books and a source of annoyance to Catherine. She seems to have suspected a masonic plot to promote the Grand Duke Paul as the rightful heir to Peter III. On her orders Bazhenov's palace was demolished, and the architect was at first suspended from service for a year and subsequently discharged permanently. Matvei Kazakov, who was already working on the Petrovsky Palace for Catherine, was commissioned to build a replacement palace at Tsaritsyno.

Meanwhile Reid's plan for the park was soon completed and delivered to the empress, who summoned Karachinsky, the steward, and Reid to St Petersburg to discuss it. On 6 July an order was issued for the repair of the old church at Tsaritsyno; on 7 July an order to clean the pool and to make an island for water fowl; on 9 July Karachinsky received 1,000 and Reid 300 roubles as rewards; and on 13 July it was announced that the plan had been approved and 5,000 roubles made available for its realization. Reid estimated that a workforce of 100 would be needed, and a request to double the amount allotted was agreed. Fifty were working in the park in March 1785, 100 in April, 150 in May, June and for the rest of the summer. Rapid progress was made and the park was practically completed by 1790.[75]

It is not clear how much of Bazhenov's work remained in the park in 1790. Perhaps many of the trees – mainly birch and pine – and he had certainly designed some of the buildings, among them the striking Ceres Pavilion, with a golden sheaf on its sky-blue dome, giving shelter to a statue of the goddess. But in its final form the park was principally Reid's creation with its winding paths, leading the visitor through romantic scenes featuring extensive pools (the length of the largest had been increased by a third), groves, meadows, a variety of pavilions, a tower-ruin, a ruined arch on an island, peacocks and water fowl. There was also an open-air theatre.

After Catherine's death in 1796, work on Kazakov's still unfinished palace was abandoned and Tsaritsyno was never lived in. The park, however, continued to be well maintained during the first half of the nineteenth century and was a favourite resort for the people of Moscow. In 1804 Bazhenov's then dilapidated Milovid Pavilion, overlooking the pool, was replaced by I.V. Egotov's elegant Milovid Pavilion, enclosing a colonnaded gallery with a decorated vaulted roof, which is the most impressive building in the park. It was adorned by three statues and two vases, and there were four busts on pedestals inside the colonnade. A description of the park published in 1815 confirms its excellence:

> The planning of the park is admirable with its variety of views, simple and magnificent, on lofty hills, into impenetrable thickets, on the shore of the lake and on flowery islands, scattered with temples and pavilions, grottoes and statues, the mirror surfaces of clear water, the exuberant animation of the oars of the rowers, the charming groves, the majestic avenues; meadows sown with fragrant flowers and impassable woods – in a word, you will find all the beauty that nature and art have to offer at Tsaritsyno.[76]

The orangeries were also impressive. The very large orangery built by Bazhenov was more than 800 feet long, and by 1825 there were seven other stone-built orangeries producing oranges, peaches, grapes, lemons and pineapples. There were also bays, olive trees and many flowering plants. In Bazhenov's orangery there was a large collection of rare plants, and outside an exhibition of flowers and trees.[77]

During the second half of the nineteenth century Tsaritsyno sadly suffered the same decline as many other Russian estates. In 1860 the government department

Above: The Milovid Pavilion at Tsaritsyno.

Right: The view of the large pool from the Milovid Pavilion.

responsible for the palace advertised buildings for sale subject to removal from the site. The iron roofs were removed from the palace, and the stoves, clad in Dutch tiles, were dismantled. The previous careful maintenance of the park was abandoned and it rapidly became overgrown, with self-sown trees colonizing the open spaces of the meadows. By the end of the century a substantial area became a village of dachas, and the land where the orangeries had stood was built over.

After the Revolution Tsaritsyno was put under state protection, some work was done in the park, and in 1927 a museum was opened. Some of the park buildings and the bridges were restored in the 1950s. In 1984 it was decided that Tsaritsyno should become a museum of applied arts.

After the death of Potemkin, Catherine's former lover and closest associate, in 1791, Catherine bought his Tauride Palace with its park, nursery garden and exceptional winter garden, from his heirs.[78] They will be considered in Chapter Six.

When Catherine died in 1796 she left behind at Tsarskoe Selo one of the world's two greatest landscape parks. The other is at Pavlovsk.

5

THE LANDSCAPE PARKS OF PAUL I AND MARIA FYODOROVNA

When her first grandson, the future Alexander I, was born in 1777, Catherine marked the occasion by a gift to his parents, the Grand Duke Paul Petrovich, later Paul I, and the Grand Duchess Maria Fyodorovna, of an estate two or three miles from her palace and park at Tsarskoe Selo and 20 miles or so from St Petersburg. There were woods, a river valley, two hunting lodges, Krik and Krak, and not much else. They each built a small pleasure house, Paullust and Marienthal, but when these were replaced by the palace designed by Charles Cameron, both it and the park became known as Pavlovsk after the Grand Duke. Paul, however, preferred his palace and park at Gatchina and left Pavlovsk largely to his wife to develop.

The Grand Duchess was born in 1759, the daughter of Duke Friedrich Eugen of Württemberg and his wife Dorothea. She was christened Sophia Dorothea but became Maria Fyodorovna when she was accepted into the Russian Church. Her father served in the Prussian army and earned lasting fame for his valiant defence of Kolberg in the face of superior Russian forces. His favourite occupation was making and improving his parks and gardens, an enthusiasm shared by his wife, who was the daughter of the Margrave of Schwedt and the niece of the owners of the great gardens at Sanssouci, Sanspareil, the Eremitage at Bayreuth and Drottningholm. Maria Fyodorovna's first childhood home was at Treptow on the banks of the Rega, now in Poland, where her mother made a garden about which little is known except that there were covered ways, a conservatory and yew pyramids, but there were probably echoes of the gardens she had been brought up in. The architect Philippe de la Guêpière designed impressive pavilions for Treptow, but there is no evidence that any were built, and nothing now remains of the garden. A chalet was built by a wood, through which vistas were cut radiating from the window of the main room of the chalet, and the princess liked to sit there admiring the view and listening to the nightingales. A small farm was rented near by and a dairy was added which the family frequently visited.[1]

In 1769 the Duke retired from the army and they went to live in Montbéliard, now on the French side of the border with Switzerland, with a summer residence a few miles away at Etupes, where a romantically landscaped garden – a *jardin anglo-chinois* – was soon created. There were bowers of roses, jasmine and honeysuckle, an orangery which could serve as a theatre, a hermit's cell in wild surroundings, and grottoes decorated with sparkling minerals and stalactites, said to be a magical sight when illuminated at night.

> We used to go to the Temple of Flora to admire the statue and took crowns to it and covered it with garlands of daisies. We played bowls and pall-mall on the lawns, to the great despair of the gardeners, and we spent long hours near the aviaries, where all the birds knew us, and we fed them with bread, cake, and fresh herbs. We taught the parrots to speak, and God knows what nonsense the young princes repeated to them.[2]

A watercolour of Pavlovsk in the Devonshire collection at Chatsworth. William Spencer Cavendish, 6th Duke of Devonshire, visited St Petersburg in 1817, when he stayed at Pavlovsk, and again in 1826. He probably brought the painting back with him after one of these visits.

From a high rock a stream cascaded down and flowed under Chinese bridges through flowery meads. A pillar in a quiet grove was dedicated to absent friends, whose initials were carved there, while a weeping willow near by shaded a memorial to a departed friend with an inscription composed by Princess Dorothea. Paths through a wood led to a triumphal arch dedicated to Frederick the Great, constructed from columns and capitals recovered from the remains of the Roman site of Epomandurum. As at Treptow a chalet – 'Rêveries' – was built for the princess near to Etupes, and there was also a dairy and a charcoal-burner's hut, whose simple outward appearance left the visitor unprepared for the elegance within. There were similar buildings in the park at Hohenheim, the home of the Princess Sophia's uncle, the ruling Duke Carl Eugen, and his mistress Franziska von Leutrum.[5] Carl Eugen had lived in splendour at his palace at Ludwigsberg until 1776, but, after being summoned to Vienna and ordered by the Imperial Council to reform the malpractices of his administration, he adopted a much simpler lifestyle with his mistress at Hohenheim, where he created in the park a so-called English village of buildings in Roman, gothic, medieval and Turkish styles. He visited Kew in 1776 before starting this project and was much influenced by the work there of Sir William Chambers, such as the pagoda, mosque, ruined Roman arch and fine orangery.[4] He probably received plants from Kew after this visit, and by 1778 there was an American garden for rare plants in his English village with, according to Hirschfeld, the best collection in Germany.[5] Another uncle, Ludwig Eugen, was a friend and disciple of Rousseau and seems to have been a considerable influence.

Pavlovsk

This then was the gardening pedigree and background of Maria Fyodorovna, strong in the sentimental and the romantic, when she went to Russia to marry Paul. The park at Pavlovsk, which she did so much to create during the following fifty years, had most of its roots not directly in English parks but in the parks on the continent which she had known before her marriage and those which she and Paul visited during a tour of Europe, travelling as the Comte and Comtesse du Nord in 1782. The tour included her family's parks in Württemberg as well as the Petit Trianon, which Maria Fyodorovna greatly admired: 'The gardens are delicious, especially the English part which the queen has just laid out. Nothing is missing; ruins, paths, temples, statues, in short everything which can make it varied and agreeable.'[6] But the park which made the deepest impression on the Grand Duke and Grand Duchess was Chantilly.

Rustic buildings in parks were part of the preoccupation with the simple life made fashionable by Rousseau. Marie Antoinette's *hameau* (a hamlet of simple rustic buildings) had not then been built, but at Chantilly they were entertained in the Prince de Condé's earlier *hameau*, whose simple, thatched exteriors belied the luxury and sophistication within. 'Tout ce gracieux ensemble est préparé pour offrir un asile aux belles dames qui vont en ce lieu jouer à la bergère.'[7] In the dining room

at 'La Grange', the *hameau*'s largest building, skilful painting had created a woodland scene on the walls and ceiling, lit by lanterns which seemed to hang from the boughs of trees. There were other delights at Chantilly. The Duchess of Bourbon, dressed as a naiad, ferried Paul in a gondola to the Temple of Venus on the Island of Love, the inspiration of the Islands of Love at Pavlovsk and Gatchina.

> Chantilly is the most beautiful place in the world. . . .
> The Duke de Bourbon and the Prince de Condé drove the ladies through the grounds, beneath triumphal arches, covered with foliage, and ornamented with bands of ribbon, and the ciphers of their imperial highnesses. . . .
> After the theatricals, we descended to the gardens, which were brilliantly lit up and sparkling with fireworks. The façade of the castle represented the escutcheon of the count and countess du Nord, with their ciphers symbolically entwined *en lac d'amour*.[8]

The Grand Duke told the Prince de Condé that he would give all he had for Chantilly, and he and the Grand Duchess took back to Russia memories of this visit which would be a lasting influence.

Pavlovsk is one of the largest landscape parks (1,500 acres). Charles Cameron, Vincenzo Brenna, Pietro Gonzaga, Andrei Voronikhin and Carlo Rossi all made important contributions, but, for the most part, it was the Grand Duchess who gave the instructions and made the decisions. Cameron was the first architect to work there and his was the major contribution. He was responsible for the outstanding neo-Palladian palace, the Temple of Friendship, the Private Garden, the Aviary, the Lime Avenue and other formal areas near the house, the Apollo Colonnade and other park buildings, and he also landscaped large areas of the park.

Pavlovsk in winter.

The Temple of Friendship in the valley of the
River Slavyanka.

His first building was the Temple of Friendship in the valley of the River Slavyanka, a domed rotunda with Doric columns, which may have been inspired by the Music Pavilion in the park at West Wycombe in Buckinghamshire.[9] Inside there was a statue of Catherine as the goddess Ceres. The form of the temple anticipated the flattened dome and supporting columns of the palace. It is much larger than it appears from a distance and is a key feature in the landscape from many viewpoints in the park. It was the inspiration for numerous garden temples of similar form in Russia.

The palace – later enlarged by Brenna – was modest in size, and its situation at the top of a grassy slope, with its reflection in an expanse of water below, is typical of Russian country estates. The Private Garden by the palace was planned as a formal extension to the interior with the patterned carpeting inside continued by the symmetrically arranged flowerbeds, while the flowers of the garden were echoed by exquisite interior floral decoration. It has much in common with a Dutch flower garden. At the end of the main walk stands the elegant pavilion of sixteen columns designed by Cameron, with Triscorni's sculptural group of the Three Graces. This was based on Canova's original and was carved from a single block of marble.[10]

Cameron's particularly elegant Aviary is a combination of three joined pavilions, a large central pavilion with a smaller one at each side. There were exotic shrubs and trees in tubs,

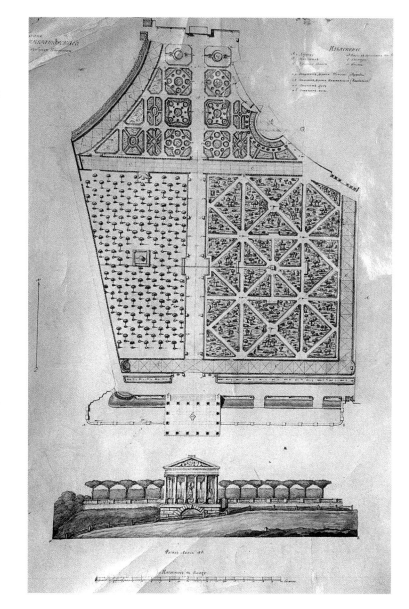

Right: Cameron's plan of the Private Garden by the Palace and the Pavilion of the Three Graces.

Below left: The Private Garden.

Below right: Cameron's Pavilion of the Three Graces.

climbing plants supported by netting and many small birds. A statue of Flora which used to stand in the central pavilion was later moved to the palace, and two small orangeries were replaced by a veranda. Maria Fyodorovna frequently used the Aviary for drawing and for the other crafts she practised. Near to the Aviary a labyrinth was formed to Cameron's intricate design, and many statues were placed there.

The Apollo Colonnade may have been suggested to Maria Fyodorovna by the Apollo Temple at Carlsruhe.[11] With its double ring of columns supporting a circular entablature and enclosing a copy of the Apollo Belvedere, it has stood in its present position on the slope opposite the palace since the year 1800, but it was first placed at the entrance to the park, proclaiming Pavlovsk a sanctuary for the muses and for those who sought beauty and poetry, watched over by Apollo, the protector of valleys and groves, of flocks and herds, and patron of the arts. In 1817 the stream running through the colonnade, no doubt representing the Castalian stream of Mount Parnassus, became a torrent

Left: Triscorni's statue of the Three Graces, carved from a single block of marble. It was buried in the park in 1941 and reinstalled in 1957.

Below: Cameron's Aviary, which contained exotic shrubs and climbing plants as well as many birds.

during a storm and caused part of the structure to collapse. At a time when there was a great interest in ruins, this was seen at once to have enhanced its appearance and it was not restored.

Cameron was commissioned to landscape large areas of the park. The Great Star (320 acres) was a vast tract of mainly coniferous forest, and a pattern of straight paths in star formation radiating from the centre, traditional for a hunting area, was imposed here. A similar system of paths was laid out on the even larger White Birches (620 acres) without any other significant change to its forest character. The valley of the Slavyanka had a great deal more to offer the landscaper with additional features along its banks still to come from Cameron and his successors. Here there was the river itself, now narrow, now spreading out, as it wound its way through the park. The relief of the terrain and the variety of the vegetation, ranging

Left: An eighteenth-century engraving by S. Galaktionov, from S.F. Shedrin's watercolour, of the Apollo Colonnade before part of it collapsed.

Below: The Colonnade was thought to have been improved by the collapse and was not restored.

Top: A natural stretch of the Slavyanka valley.

Above: Cameron's thatched stone dairy, based on the dairy in the park of Maria Fyodorovna's uncle, the Duke of Württemberg, at Hohenheim.

from grassy slopes to dense tree cover, contributed to the changes in the scenery. The palace was dominant from many viewpoints, while Brenna's Great Staircase, the Temple of Friendship, the Iron Bridge, the Great Cascade, the Visconti Bridge, the Amphitheatre, the Peel Tower and the End of the World Column each in turn helped create a new view, until at last the river flowed under two more bridges and out of the park to the fields and meadows beyond. 'Such a distribution of pavilions, bridges and cascades enables each of them to determine the individual character of separate scenes without at the same time destroying the harmonious unity of the general conformation of the landscape.'[12]

Cameron seems to have had no training in or experience of landscaping until his arrival in Russia, but his father-in-law, John Busch, as we have seen, had an impressive record in landscaping and in training others to landscape. Cameron would have followed his work closely in the park at Tsarskoe Selo and would have seen what had been achieved at Gatchina. When he went to Pavlovsk on 25 May 1782, for the ceremony of laying the foundation stone for the palace, he was accompanied by Busch,[13] as he probably was on other occasions. Busch may well deserve a share of the credit for what Shvidkovsky has described as 'one of the greatest achievements of landscape gardening in Russia'.[14]

Cameron was also responsible for a thatched stone dairy, a hermit's cell and a charcoal-burner's hut, of which only the first survives. These were, perhaps, not features he would have wished to introduce into the park, and he seems to have been in no hurry to carry out the Grand Duchess's instructions. 'Has Cameron still not given you anything about the new dairy which I mentioned to you in a letter dated from Rome? Send me his ideas as soon as you can.'[15] Although Cameron's contribution to Pavlovsk was immense, his relations with Maria Fyodorovna seem always to have been difficult and she frequently complained about his delays. Her secretary, Baron von Nicolay (who would also have an exceptional park later, as we shall see in the next chapter, and probably contributed ideas to Pavlovsk), had written to Kuchelbecker, the Director at Pavlovsk, from Rome on 3 March 1782:

> I enclose the plan of the Dairy of his Excellency the Duke of Württemberg in three sheets.[16] Her Imperial Highness wants to have something similar. But you will notice that what is marked on the plan with a + should make a single stable for 5 or at most 6 cows. . . . Her Highness thinks that the best situation for this building would be on the high ground on the edge [of the park] so that the cows can walk straight out of the stalls into the wood. It's also essential that the building should be hidden so that people don't suspect it's there until they draw near to it.

It seems to have been Kuchelbecker's idea to face the external walls with stone, a suggestion which was honoured with the Grand Duchess's approval. The interior, of course, was totally refined, the milk was dispensed from a vessel of Japanese porcelain with a silver tap, and visitors were offered milk, cream and curds. There were not only English, Dutch and Courland cows, but Spanish sheep, peacocks, pheasants, turkeys, ducks and guinea-fowl.[17] 'I want a pretty poultry house near the dairy,' she wrote to Kuchelbecker. Eventually the cows became a nuisance, and a farm was established just beyond the edge of the park.

The interior of the charcoal-burner's hut at Pavlovsk was equally impressive. When a harpsichord was needed for a performance in the theatre Maria Fyodorovna instructed: 'A harpsichord will have to be placed in the orchestra: use the one from the *charbonnier*.'[18] In the case of the Hermitage, with its thatched roof and bark-covered walls, the interior was basic – 'a hearth, in the chimney a kettle on an iron tripod. . . . a table of plain pine, a pine bed with a reed mattress, three simple spoons'.[19]

The Old Chalet at Pavlovsk was closely modelled on the 'Alte Turm' at Hohenheim. It was a single-storey building with a thatched roof, a belfry and an outside staircase leading to a loft. A small kitchen building had been added on one side, and by the veranda there was a hen house that looked like an arbour. Inside the chalet elegance kept company with comfort. Maria Fyodorovna had learned to garden as a child, and it was here that the young Grand Dukes and Grand Duchesses were given lessons in gardening. Their tools – spades, shovels, rakes, etc. – were kept in a small room, with their mother's spinning wheel and a machine for winding thread in another, where she could enjoy the satisfaction accompanying simple, useful activity. In the garden outside, the Grand Dukes prepared the ground, sowed and planted, while the Grand Duchesses weeded and watered. The bell on the roof summoned them to lunch inside the chalet or on the veranda.[20] There are references in the archives to their activities there. When Maria Fyodorovna was abroad in 1782 Kuchelbeker wrote to her: 'They [Alexander and Constantine] spent most of their time near the Chalet where they worked with their spades and rakes. They ordered bigger

tools for themselves – last year's have become too small. Their Highnesses ate cherries and milk and took away with them cream and bunches of flowers.'[21] When a monument was erected at Pavlovsk to the Grand Duchess Alexandra, who died in childbirth at the age of eighteen, the site chosen was the plot where she had gardened as a child.

The Peel Tower in the Slavyanka valley, which was originally a watermill, was another example of a humble exterior concealing unexpected luxury. It has been ascribed to Brenna, but its name seems to suggest that a Scottish building was intended, in which case it may have been by Cameron. Pietro

Above: The 'Alte Turm' in the park at Hohenheim.

Left: The Old Chalet at Pavlovsk in a late-nineteenth-century engraving.

Right, above: A late-eighteenth-century view of the Peel Tower, which was originally a watermill, in the Slavyanka valley.

Right, below: The Peel Tower today.

Top: Apollo Belvedere in the Old Sylvia, where he is surrounded by statues of the nine muses, Mercury, Venus and Flora.

Middle: The Upper Sylvia Pool in the Old Sylvia.

Bottom: Terpsichore, muse of dancing. The exceptionally fine bronze statues of the nine muses were moved to Pavlovsk from Tsarskoe Selo, where they had stood on the pandus (gentle slope) leading up to the palace. They were copied from ancient Roman marble statues (now in the Vatican Museum).

Gonzaga painted it to look like an ancient ruin, roughly repaired and thatched by peasants, but inside, the elegantly furnished sitting room was a favourite retreat of Maria Fyodorovna. It may have been influenced by similar buildings at the Jardin des Mesdames at Bellevue, Châtelet, which Paul and Maria Fyodorovna may have seen during their visit to France.

In choosing to introduce simple country structures at Pavlovsk such as she had known at Etupes, instead of the exotic architecture Catherine had favoured at Tsarksoe Selo, she would have found endorsement in Jacques Delille's advice on garden buildings in his poem *Les Jardins*:[22]

> Their use I grant, but be it not abus'd;
> Far from the garden cast that heap confused
> Of buildings lavished round by fashion's hand,
> A chaos wild, by choice nor reason planned;
> Kiosk, pagoda, obelisk, and dome,
> Drawn from Arabia, China, Greece, and Rome,
> In one small spot, profusely-barren, hurl'd
> Each quarter of the wide extended world.
> There should no idle ornament be seen,
> But each delight should wear an useful mien,
> The farm, the joy and treasure of its lord,
> A constant source of pleasure will afford.[23]

The publication of *Les Jardins* was timed to coincide with the festivities at the Trianon to mark the visit of the Comte and Comtesse du Nord in 1782. It would have been read with delight by the latter and may well have influenced the shaping of Pavlovsk. It was translated into Russian three times in the early nineteenth century, and, in spite of the French literary critic Saint-Beuve's declaration in his *Portraits littéraires* (1862) that Delille was '*mort et bien mort*', a fourth Russian translation by I. Ya. Shafarenko was published in 1987.[24]

Vincenzo Brenna began to play a major role at Pavlovsk from 1786 and, at the wish of his patrons, to give the park a more ceremonial and imposing character in preparation for Paul's accession to the throne which was to follow in 1796. His most important contribution to the park was the Old Sylvia. Here twelve paths radiate from a circular clearing with another statue of the Apollo Belvedere at its centre and the nine muses with Mercury, Venus and Flora in the spaces between the paths on its circumference. There is a further echo here of Chantilly. In the early seventeenth century the poet Théophile de Viau was given sanctuary at Chantilly by the Duchess of Montmorency when under sentence of death, and he referred to her gratefully in his poems as Sylvie. Subsequently there was a Maison de Sylvie, a Jardin de Sylvie and a Parc de Sylvie at Chantilly. There was also a large circular clearing with twelve radiating paths. The New Sylvia, also by Brenna, is a much less formal piece of woodland, a transition between more obviously composed parkland and the natural landscape beyond.

Brenna also laid out the Great Circles, a large formal area on the terrace near the palace. Maria Fyodorovna named it Place

Guillame after Prince Wilhelm, the future German Emperor, had spent several days sitting there recuperating following a bite from Grand Duke Michael's dog. Brenna's impressive Great Staircase with marble lions and vases leads down from the Great Circles to the river bank.

Pietro Gonzaga, distinguished theatre and stage designer and decorator, also made an important contribution to the landscaping at Pavlovsk. After training in Venice he worked at La Scala in Milan before being persuaded to go to Russia, where he worked in the theatres of Moscow and St Petersburg. Examples of his skill as a decorator can be seen in the palace at Pavlovsk, while his work in the park reflects his background of stage design and perspective painting.

The Russians call this '*samoe krasivoe mesto*', the most beautiful place, where visitors are said to have exclaimed 'Ach! Ach!' on seeing this view of Gonzaga's landscaping.

During Paul I's short reign of little more than four years the vast parade ground had been considerably enlarged at the expense of earlier landscaped areas. He spent a great deal of time there reviewing his troops, and it was also the setting of an elaborate, ritualistic ceremony of the Sovereign Order of the Knights of Malta on 23 June 1798. The Order had been virtually destroyed by the French Revolution, when its extensive possessions were confiscated, followed by the French seizure of Malta six years later. An attempt to revive it in Russia with Paul as Grand Master was to prove unsuccessful, but they put on a brave show at Pavlovsk. With Paul at their centre and Guards Officers in attendance, the Knights of the Order went through elaborate rituals and finally marched three times round nine large bonfires, symbolizing purification, observed from a Turkish tent by the Empress and the ladies of the court.[25]

After Paul's death in a scuffle (during a rather heavy-handed attempt to persuade him to abdicate), the parade ground was no longer required. In 1803 Gonzaga was invited to transform it,

and he created a new landscape of meadow, wood and water. His approach to trees is of particular interest. Some trees for him conveyed sadness, others gaiety, gracefulness, pride or majesty, and it was with these characteristics in mind that he selected them and grouped them in his landscape compositions to achieve the effects he wished for. His skill in placing trees singly and in groups enabled him to achieve a great feeling of depth in his landscapes. In the year 1807, 57,000 trees were planted in the former parade ground.

Gonzaga discussed his approach to park design in his fascinating treatise *La Musique des yeux* (1807), in which he compared landscape composition to musical composition. Just as the composer evaluates, selects and arranges sounds, so the landscape designer must distinguish between the different tones emanating from visible objects scattered indiscriminately by Nature and rearrange them into new harmonious compositions. He completed the landscaping of the Slavyanka valley, begun by Cameron, and, over a period of twenty years, refashioned the area called the White Birches. On this extensive flat tract of land (620 acres) he took the northern Russian landscape as his model and created an idealized Russian elysium of meadows and forest, with birch, pine and other native species. It is a landscape of great charm, constantly changing with the weather, the time

Left: The Ring of Birches, planted by Cameron, which seems to echo the Apollo Colonnade, the Temple of Friendship and the columns supporting the dome of the palace at the other end of the park.

Above: The Monument to the Parents, designed by Cameron and funerary sculpture by Ivan Martos.

of the day and the season of the year. There are no buildings in this part of the park, but at the centre stands the ring of white birches which Cameron planted in the 1780s, probably at the request of Maria Fyodorovna, and which Gonzaga retained – a wider echo of the Apollo Colonnade, the Temple of Friendship and the circle of columns supporting the dome of the palace itself at the other end of the park.

Maria Fyodorovna knew much sorrow through the deaths of those dear to her, and monuments were erected in the park to two sisters, a brother, her parents, her husband and to some of her children, five of whom predeceased her. The most notable are the Mausoleum for Paul I and the Monument to the Parents. The placing of funerary monuments in gardens was encouraged by Delille:

> Mid each picture fair,
> Fear not to let an urn or tomb appear,
> Those ever-faithful monuments of woe;
> Who has not wept some sad, some cruel blow;
> Then from the world retir'd unload your heart,
> And to the groves and streams your griefs impart.
> A feeling soul in all will find a friend:
> Already, lo! the yew and fir extend
> Their mournful arms, the quiet grave to shade,
> Where, whom you weep, in lasting night is laid.[26]

Maria Fyodorovna commemorated her parents with a small temple by Cameron and outstanding funerary sculpture by Ivan Martos. On a pedestal of grey marble in the temple's recess, the profiles of the Duke and Duchess of Württemberg are represented on a medallion on a red granite obelisk. Two urns are half-covered with a veil. On the left the figure of Maria Fyodorovna leans on the pedestal with lowered head. On the right the winged Spirit of Death witnesses her grief and draws aside the veil from the urns. There are three bas-reliefs on the lower part of the pedestal. On the left, Mars the god of war calls Frederick into battle, and Saturn shows him the palm of immortality. The centre bas-relief depicts the meeting of the Duke and Duchess beyond the grave. On the right, Hymen joins them in marriage. On the walls of the temple, memorial tablets commemorate her sisters Frederika and Elizaveta and her brother Carl.[27]

The Mausoleum for Paul I, designed by Thomas de Thomon with weeping masks on the frieze, 'stands magnificently and sorrowfully. . . . among long, straight paths, full of mysterious silence and twilight, deep in the heart of the forest'.[28] The sculpture is another exceptional example of the work of Ivan Martos. An obelisk of dark red granite, with a medallion of Paul I, stands in the half-light of the gloomy interior. In front of it a grieving female figure in antique costume and wearing a crown kneels on what appears to be a white marble tombstone and reaches out to an urn.

Brenna's Ruin Cascade was another reminder of life's transience intended to induce melancholy in the visitor to the park. The ground around it was scattered with fragments of ancient statues and broken pieces of marble columns, which may well have been inspired by these lines from *Les Jardins*:

> What awful wonders strike th'astonish'd eye,
> When thrown around the mould'ring ruins lie;
> Where arches, columns, from their bases hurl'd
> Mark time's wide empire o'er the crumbling world . . .
> All human pleasures speedily decay;
> Sports, dances, shepherds soon will fade away.[29]

Happier events were commemorated in the Family Grove. When she already had six children Maria Fyodorovna decided to plant a young tree in memory of the birth of each child so that they and the trees might grow up together. On a headland near the palace six birch trees were planted round an urn which she named the 'Urn of Destiny'. On each tree a small board was attached with the name of the member of the family in whose honour it had been planted. In later years on the occasions of the marriages of their sons and daughters she personally planted trees and affixed small boards with the names of the new members of the family. When she died forty-four trees had been planted.[30]

At Pavlovsk, thanks to a rather milder climate than elsewhere in the region, it was possible to grow a wide range of plants, provided they were given some winter protection. Maria Fyodorovna was a great plantswoman, and it was through her efforts that a very considerable collection of plants reached Pavlovsk from many parts of the world. It was usually she who decided what plants were required and where to obtain them, though some came as unsolicited gifts. Lilies growing by the Black Sea were sent by the officer commanding Russian forces in Georgia, and roses by the Russian ambassador in Constantinople. When a coral tree was expected from Amsterdam in a special container, she left orders that it was to be put in her apartments and not unpacked until she arrived. During a visit to Warsaw in 1818 she sent back seeds of white acacia and chestnut with instructions that they were to be divided equally between three gardeners, who were each to plant half under glass and half in the open ground, so that it could be seen, she wrote, in which conditions they performed better – though, of course, she also wanted to see which gardener was the most successful.

From Vienna she sent Wisler, the gardener, a load of flower seeds, while Baron von Nicolay, her Secretary, wrote to Kuchelbecker to say Wisler must consult the book of Linnaeus about the care of each one. Some of them were marked Jak because Maria Fyodorovna had them from Jacquin in Leiden. Dutch bulbs were sent on numerous occasions. Her devotion to plants and her efforts to add to the collections at Pavlovsk continued throughout her life. In June 1826 she wrote from Moscow to General Frideritsi, the Director and Chief Steward at Pavlovsk from 1820–40: 'The roses are extraordinarily beautiful here and in abundance. I have bought two hundred pots of them, but for no other gardener except Pustinsky, for he will look after them.'[31] A year later she sent 110 rose bushes, 100 lilies and 100 tuberoses.

The Ruin Cascade, where the ground was scattered with fragments of ancient statues and pieces of marble columns to remind visitors of life's transience.

The fruit produced at Pavlovsk included apricots, grapes, peaches and pineapples. The quality of the pineapples was inconsistent: 'Tell Wisler that the pineapples do not have the flavour or the size of last year's, and do not seem to be ripe.'[32] And the quantity produced failed to come up to expectations: 'It is a long time since the gardener gave us any pineapples and of the sixty he promised I have seen only six.'[33]

She had a particular weakness for cherries: 'My dear Kuchelbecker, you promised me a cherry house last year, and I had hoped it had been done, but I have just learned that it hasn't. Be obliging, you know that cherries are my passion.'[34] When cherry trees were ordered, she wrote: 'If they are good, I want them to be planted around the Chalet where the others are; if they are poor by the new dairy.'[35] In March 1782 a convoy of carts brought 200 fruit trees from Count P.A. Rumyantsev, and fruit trees also came from Lübeck. When the Grand Duke and Grand Duchess were in Italy, Kuchelbecker kept her in touch with the progress of the garden. 'The vines and fruit trees are in flower, narcissus, hyacinths have begun to flower and others will soon follow them, the lilies and the bears' ears, from which the gardener is expecting fine flowers, and the roses are in bud. Every time I see them I regret that this spring the greenhouses will not be seen by Your Highness.'[36]

In 1791 Paul's librarian, Franz Lafermière, in a letter to Count Vorontsov, the Russian ambassador in London, asked on Maria Fyodorovna's behalf for seeds for her garden at Pavlovsk: 'I think it's not so much vegetable seeds as flowers and plants to furnish the *clumps* in her English garden.' He suggested that Vorontsov should consult a gardener who would be able to put together an assortment of what she required, 'which would be very much welcomed by the Grand Duchess and would give her great pleasure, the embellishment of her garden being a concern very close to her heart'.[37] Two years later new orangeries and hothouses were being built at Pavlovsk, and she hoped that the Royal Botanic Gardens at Kew might be persuaded to add to her collection of hothouse plants. She was particularly keen to acquire some of the new discoveries from the South Seas. She would probably have known that her uncle, Carl Eugen, had visited Kew in 1776 and 1789. During the second visit he was escorted on a tour of the hothouses by the Superintendent, William Aiton, and his son, William Townsend Aiton. He received plants from Kew after this visit as well as buying plants from the nurseries of James Lee at Hammersmith and Conrad Loddiges at Hackney.[38] Not long afterwards he sent one of his gardeners, George Noe, to train at Kew. A request for plants for Maria Fyodorovna was sent by the British Envoy in St Petersburg to the Foreign Office in 1793. George III, who thought that the Grand Duchess was the Empress Catherine, said he would 'order the seeds wished for the Russian Empress's garden to be collected at Kew and such plants as in the present early state of cultivation can be spared to be sent at the proper season to Petersburgh.'[39] The despatch of the collection was arranged by Sir Joseph Banks. The plants were listed as Stove Plants and Cape House Plants, and, on orders from the King,

plans and elevations of a Stove and a Cape House at Kew were sent with them. They were to be accompanied by one of the King's own gardeners, and the man chosen was George Noe, who had remained at Kew after Carl Eugen's death.

It was regretted that it was not possible to send one of the breadfruit plants Captain Bligh had brought back from Tahiti, since only two remained, one of which was earmarked for Sierra Leone and the other they hoped to propagate from. If their efforts were successful it would be possible to provide the Grand Duchess with a number of plants at a later date. The plant known as New Zealand flax, *Phormium tenax*, was sent, since it was thought that somewhere in 'the extensive dominions of Russia' a suitable climate might be found for its cultivation and that it might be commercially valuable. In a few cases coloured engravings and drawings were sent so that the Grand Duchess would know what to expect when the plants came into flower.

This collection, weighing over three tons with the pots, was sent in the hold of the ship – the *Venus* – on a specially constructed platform. On reaching St Petersburg with very few casualties, the plants were taken first to the Imperial Botanic Garden and then, in fifteen coaches, each with four horses, to Pavlovsk, where they arrived at midnight. When Maria Fyodorovna came to see them at six o'clock the following morning, poor Noe had to beg to be given a few hours to arrange them, and she came back at two in the afternoon with the Grand Duke and seventy attendants. She ordered that the initials G.R. (George Rex) were to be inscribed by Noe on every pot and she spent an hour in the hothouse every day to learn the names of the plants and drew each one as it came into flower. When she and the Grand Duke left Pavlovsk to stay at Gatchina, Noe had to take each plant which flowered there by coach to be inspected. When he left for England, declining the offer of a position, she gave him a gold watch and a sum of money for himself and 300 roubles to buy views of the royal gardens and plants for her.[40]

In 1797 Maria Fyodorovna's brother, Friedrich, who had served in the Russian army and then as Govenor of Viborg, returned to Württemberg as ruling Duke on the death of their father. This was also the year of his marriage to Charlotte, daughter of George III, and of his election as a Fellow of the Royal Society. While in London he asked the King if he could have some plants from Kew, and in April 1798 his Minister of State, Count von Zeppelin, sent to Sir Joseph Banks a list of the plants and seeds which the Prince desired for his gardens from the hothouses of Kew.

John Fraser (1750–1811), who was responsible for the introduction of many new plants from North America to Europe, was another British contributor to Russian gardens. He first visited Russia in 1796 with an impressive collection of plants, which was immediately purchased by Catherine, who is reported to have been 'pleased to command him to put his own price on the collection'.[41] Following Catherine's death soon afterwards, Fraser received an invitation from Count Vorontsov, the Russian ambassador in London, to take a selection of plants for the Empress Maria Fyodorovna at Pavlovsk. He was enthusiastically received, and further orders were placed for Pavlovsk and Gatchina. He was also invited 'to bring from England all such new and approved implements for horticultural and agricultural use as he might consider serviceable in Russia.' In August 1798 he was officially appointed by Paul and Maria Fyodorovna as their 'Botanical Collector, with orders to furnish such other rare and novel plants, as he should recommend for the completion of the Imperial Collections.' As a result of this appointment he and his eldest son, also John, set out to visit unexplored parts of North America and found many new and interesting plants; but when he returned to Russia after the death of Paul and tried to claim reimbursement of the cost of the expedition, his claim was rejected by the Emperor Alexander. 'From the Dowager Empress he received more generous treatment, the gift of a valuable diamond ring being added to the discharge of his account.'[42]

In 1814 Maria Fyodorovna's daughter, the Grand Duchess Catherine Pavlovna, young widow of the Duke of Oldenburg, spent several months in England and on 17 April she visited Kew. This visit was no doubt connected with the second collection of plants her mother received from the Royal Botanic Gardens, for an entry in the Kew Outward Book shows that on 29 June in that year more than 200 plants were sent to the Dowager Empress. Shortly afterwards plants were also sent to Catherine's brother-in-law, the Duke of Saxe-Weimar; and plants and seed were sent to Catherine on a number of occasions after she had become Queen of Württemberg.

When, in 1797, the palace at Pavlovsk was badly damaged by fire, Maria Fyodorovna again looked towards England for plants, writing for help to Count Vorontsov. She told him that her collection of engravings, her library of books and her pictures by Robert and Vernet had suffered grievously, 'but', she continued,

> this kind of trouble is easy to bear when compared with the heart rending suffering I have experienced. . . . Amidst all this misfortune one thing, I must confess, has affected me particularly. The fear that the fire might spread caused them to cut down my magnificent poplars, which I planted and tended. They were taller than the roof. But I console myself with the thought that I shall be compensated for my loss by your efforts, and with this certitude I turn to you, asking you to send me half a dozen or a dozen. Perhaps Lord St Helens [a former British ambassador], who has warm feelings for Pavlovsk, will himself attend to this commission. If the captain is asked to put them on the deck and to roll them along carefully they can be transported without difficulty, and it would be possible to get very big trees. This would lessen my regrets, for I declare that they were one of the finest ornaments of Pavlovsk.[43]

One may be sure that the poplars would have been sent, but perhaps they failed to thrive, since five years or so later Maria

Fyodorovna wrote to Vorontsov for more. He replied in February 1803 that they would be put on the first available vessel in the spring. In July she wrote thanking him for the trees, which were growing 'à merveille', and for seeds which he had sent. In June 1804 Vorontsov wrote to say that he had taken the liberty of sending her a book about English gardens and parks with engravings, which enabled one to see, when a movable slip was lifted, the improvements actually made to the grounds of that park. (In fact, of course, they showed proposed alterations.) 'This is the most highly regarded work on the subject in this country, and since the edition is almost out of print, this book is going to become very rare.'[44] It must have been Humphry Repton's *Observations on the Theory and Practice of Landscape Gardening*, which was published in 1803.

There was a botanical garden at Pavlovsk with a large collection of plants, and when Ivan Weinman, who was later to become well known as a botanist, was brought as head gardener from Gatchina to Pavlovsk in 1815, he suggested to Maria Fyodorovna that a school of botany and horticulture might be established there. She agreed, and in 1816 six boys with a good knowledge of Latin, German and geography were selected from the St Petersburg Foundling Hospital and a similar number from the Moscow Foundling Hospital for a four-year course. This was later reduced to two years. Certificates were awarded to those successfully completing the course, who were then expected to spend six years working in one of the imperial gardens or a similar establishment. A number of financial awards, ranging from 150 to 300 roubles, were made to students who did particularly well. On the Dowager Empress's instructions these sums were not handed over to them but were paid into accounts opened at the savings bank. In 1819 the school was moved to Gatchina, because the facilities for studying fruit production were better, but there continued to be places for four students at Pavlovsk until 1827, when those studying there were moved to the Imperial Botanic Garden in St Petersburg.[45]

Fireworks and illuminations were occasional ornaments in the park, and Maria Fyodorovna took the same personal interest in planning these displays. She gave detailed instructions for a festival at Pavlovsk, on 22 July 1787, celebrating the name-day which she shared with Paul:

> 1. The fireworks will be lit behind the column. There will be two tents for spectators by the column.
> 2. While the Court are watching the fireworks hurry to light the glasses so that, when they return to the palace, the Court will walk along the illuminated avenue.
> 3. The main avenue to the palace will be lit by arches of single-coloured white lights. In each arch will be two garlands, between which will hang coloured lanterns. Many-coloured lights will be suspended from the garlands. Note: For this avenue the supports and arches already used in Pavlovsk may be used, if they are turned as mentioned on the plan. The garlands and lanterns are to be fetched from Gatchina.

4. The courtyard of the palace will be illuminated, as shown on the plan, by six of the pyramids which have been used before, but completely covered with white lights. . . .

5. When they get to the palace, from the balcony of the façade looking out over the garden, the Court will see the lake illuminated in the following manner: On the bank opposite the palace will be placed the temple, which has been used before, on which other devices will be depicted; another transparency on the pediment corresponding to the festival, which in this case will be devoted to His Imperial Highness. . . .

6. On both sides of the temple will be placed pyramids of many-coloured lights. . . .

7. On the lake there will be a pretty boat with sails of laths covered with various coloured illuminations. There will be musicians in it. This boat will sail quietly to and fro in front of the temple in order to provide a beautiful view from the palace. This will undoubtedly produce a splendid effect on account of the reflections of each object in the water, which, doubling the illumination, will bring sparkle and picturesqueness to the scene.

8. All the garden paths will be lined on both sides by earthenware lamps as shown with red dots on the plan.[46]

In the 1790s an amphitheatre had been made by the river to the design of Brenna, and when Maria Fyodorovna arrived in Pavlovsk after a short absence on 25 May 1811, a children's performance was arranged there to welcome her. The *coulisses* (side wings of the stage) were constructed of treillage covered with climbing plants and at the back of the stage stood a pedestal with a bust of the Empress. About thirty courtiers' children took part in the proceedings, which began with a short play in French, written by some of them, and finished with a ballet. The Empress was said to have been delighted and 'touched to tears'. The children were praised for their efforts and entertained to lunch in the Turkish tent.

An aeronautical display was a more unusual event. A French expert attached a cat to a balloon with a cord, to which he fixed a lighted fuse and then allowed the balloon to ascend. After a few minutes the fuse burned down and burned through the cord, releasing the cat, which was equipped with a parachute and descended to the ground in excellent health to be presented to the Empress.

Of all the many events that took place in the park the most important was the celebration at the Rose Pavilion of the return of Alexander following the defeat of Napoleon in 1814. This small pavilion, surrounded by beds of roses, had been completed the previous year with many handcrafted contributions to the furnishings from the Empress and the ladies of the court – chairs and armchairs embroidered with garlands and bouquets of roses, carpets, baskets, footstools, lamps. Originally it was only a small square building, but in 1814, in the space of two weeks, a large hall was added by Voronikhin with more garlands of roses in the decorations by Gonzaga. In the garden a Peace Pavilion was erected, and Gonzaga created the illusion of a Russian village for the staging of plays.

When Alexander and Maria Fyodorovna arrived at the Rose Pavilion on 27 July they were greeted by choirs in Russian costume. Leading opera singers and pupils from the theatre school participated in an interlude of four scenes. Children joined in the first scene, dancing, throwing flowers and rejoicing in the return of their fathers and the Emperor. Young people took part in the second scene; the wives of soldiers, looking forward to their return, in the third; and the parents of soldiers in the fourth. The soldiers whose return was eagerly anticipated

An early twentieth-century photograph of the Rose Pavilion, where Alexander's return following the defeat of Napoleon was celebrated.

were represented by a detachment of the Regiment of Guards, marching and singing through Gonzaga's 'village'.

A French visitor was carried away by the scene at the ball that followed. 'The beauty of the women, their new Parisian dresses, took me back again to Paris as if by magic.' Half way through there was an interval for a spectacular display of fireworks, which ended with the Emperor's monogram burning brightly in a golden tent. After the ball the imperial family and courtiers of the highest rank had supper in the Peace Pavilion, and senior army officers in a marquee in the garden. After the departure of the imperial family to the palace, the crowds of visitors scattered along the illuminated avenues of the park, and some wandered there until morning. 'The Rose Pavilion became a centre of life in Pavlovsk and a symbol of victory and peace.'[47]

Gatchina

The palace and park at Gatchina, 30 miles south of St Petersburg, had had a succession of owners, and in 1765 Catherine II acquired it and gave it to her favourite, Count Grigory Orlov. With its woods and stretches of water it was extremely picturesque and ideal for hunting, which was another pleasure the Count shared with the Empress. Orlov was delighted with it and, with imperial funds amply provided, set about exploiting its natural potential and creating a remarkable residential estate. Antonio Rinaldi was engaged to build a palace, and John Busch provided a plan for the park, where the work was directed by the Scottish gardeners Charles Sparrow

Above: Swan Island on the White Lake at Gatchina.

Right: Gatchina Palace from the White Lake.

Top: Sculpture in the Private Garden.

Above: Gorbaty Bridge spans a water channel which divided Dlinny Island into two parts. There are stone seats on the bridge, from which visitors can enjoy fine views over the White Lake.

and his brother John, with a workforce of five hundred.[48] Before long Orlov wrote to Rousseau, no doubt at Catherine's request, inviting him to stay at Gatchina, where the air was healthy, the water admirable and the walks well suited to contemplation. Comprehensive hospitality was offered. '*Vous auriez la necessaire* [*sic*], *si vous voulez. Si non, vous auriez de la chasse et de la pêche.*' In other words, girls would be available if he wished, if not there was always hunting and fishing. Rousseau declined the offer courteously, saying he would certainly have accepted had he been fitter and younger and had Gatchina been nearer to the sun.[49]

The water is unusually clear at Gatchina, its mirror surfaces reflecting grey willows, dark green conifers and the changing patterns of the sky. Following Busch's plan, the outstanding waterscape of lakes, pools and streams, which we see today, was created during the years of Orlov's ownership. In addition to the English park, an extensive hunting park was developed and many thousands of trees were planted on the estate. After the death of Orlov in 1783, Catherine bought Gatchina from his beneficiaries and gave it to Grand Duke Paul, whose favourite residence it became. Changes to the palace and its setting by Rinaldi after Paul became Emperor gave it a more ceremonial character and reflected Paul's obsession with military matters. The meadow by the palace became a parade ground, flanked by a line of cannon, but a plan to build barracks near by was not realized. Paul engaged an Irish gardener, James Hackett, and new formal gardens appeared at Gatchina, since this was the style Paul preferred. In the *sobstvennyi sad* (private garden) by the palace, overlooked by the rooms usually occupied by Paul, there was a network of straight paths between clipped hedges and treillage, embellished by fourteen marble statues and busts and two marble vases. Two winged sphinxes guarded the terrace. Beyond the private garden were two Dutch gardens, upper and lower, with more statues and formal flower parterres, divided by paths and framed by clipped evergreen shrubs. Paul had intended to install the Neptune fountain he had bought in Nuremberg, but it went to Peterhof instead, and there were no fountains at Gatchina, apparently because of hydrotechnical problems.[50]

Another formal area was the botanical garden, laid out in 1793 by the 'botanical gardener', F. Helmholz, on two terraces covering seven acres. There was a circular basin on the lower terrace and an octagonal basin on the upper, where rare fish were bred and aquatic plants cultivated. The botanical garden was no longer maintained in the nineteenth century, and limes and oaks took over from the less common trees and shrubs that had been planted there earlier.

The principal attraction at Gatchina is the 'English' park with its winding picturesque paths by the side of the White and Silver Lakes and by pools and streams, crossing to and from islands by rather beautiful bridges. At intervals along the route architectural features add to the pleasure. The circular Eagle Pavilion is of unusual design. A semi-circular colonnade of five pairs of columns supports a semi-circular entablature on which a

Right, above: The Eagle Pavilion, claimed to mark the spot where Paul I had shot an eagle.

Right: The Temple of Venus, inspired by the Temple of Venus on the Island of Love at Chantilly.

Above: The Little Birch House, made to look like a
log pile but with an astonishingly refined interior.

Right: A view across the White Lake to the palace.
Engraved from S.F. Shchedrin's watercolour of 1798.

marble eagle once perched, accompanied by a crown and a shield with the coat-of-arms of Paul. The circle is completed by a semi-circular wall supporting a half-cupola. It has been claimed that the pavilion marks the spot where Paul had shot an eagle, which was perching where there is now a marble column surmounted by a bronze eagle. However, an eagle featured on the Orlov coat of arms, and it seems more likely that these sculpted eagles relate to that. Orlov is derived from '*oryol*', Russian for eagle.[51]

The Temple of Venus and the Island of Love on which it stood at Chantilly, which Paul and Maria Fyodorovna had seen in 1782, were the inspiration for similar features at Gatchina some ten years later. The Island of Love is separated from the shore of the White Lake by a narrow channel. On the pediment of the Temple of Venus the attributes of Cupid – a quiver and arrows and a torch – were carved in relief. By the temple there was a miniature formal garden with two statues on pedestals. Inside the temple, above the mirrors on the walls, panels were placed decorated with flowers, flaming hearts, and quivers and arrows. Between the mirrors there were decorative compositions executed in grisaille against a pale gold background. On the ceiling Yakov Mettenleiter painted the Triumph of Venus, which Lansere, writing about Gatchina in *Sredi Kollektsionerov* (*Among Collectors*) considered rather mediocre.[52] Another echo of Chantilly was the area of woodland called Sylvia, which, like the Old Sylvia at Pavlovsk, was formally laid out with a pattern of straight radial avenues. The estate farm was at its northern edge.

The most interesting of all the park buildings is the Little Birch House, which is the ultimate among those rude and simple garden structures with astonishingly refined interiors. First viewed through a grandiose stone portal with sixteen Ionic columns, it appears to be an enormous log pile, but on closer acquaintance the visitor becomes aware of windows and a door. Inside, the walls were covered with looking-glass decorated with

Видъ дворца въ городѣ Гатчинѣ со стороны саду

ЕГО ИМПЕРАТОРСКОМУ ВЕЛИЧЕСТВУ
САМОДЕРЖЦУ ВСЕРОССІЙСКОМУ
ПАВЛУ I.

Vue du Palais de la ville de Gatchine du coté du Jardin.

Dedié a Sa Majesté Imperiale
PAUL I.
EMPEREUR DE TOUTES LE RUSSIES

a pattern of painted treillage, enhanced by a marquetry floor of coloured woods and a beautifully painted ceiling with Zephyr and a garland of flowers. Everything was calculated to create an impression of exquisite luxury. There was also a kitchen with a separate entrance. The architect is not known, but the idea was Maria Fyodorovna's as a surprise for Paul.

By the White Lake a small harbour and a shipyard were constructed, variously known as Holland and the Admiralty. According to one account vessels were built here, but it seems more likely that they were largely built in St Petersburg and that only such finishing touches as the rigging were added at Gatchina. Wherever they were built, the six- or eight-cannon yacht *Mirolyubye* and the sixteen-cannon *Emprenabl* were launched on the White Lake in 1797 and they remained ornaments to the park for many years as they lay at anchor in front of the massively impressive harbour wall with the palace in the background. Skiffs, scouts, gondolas and rafts brought the total of craft in Gatchina's flotilla to twenty-four.

Near the palace kitchen building a remarkable collection of hothouses was erected, with separate houses for grapes, apricots, plums and peaches, and others producing flowers. Some were there during the eighteenth century, more were added in the nineteenth. Palms, almonds and bays were also cultivated under glass. According to one source, the hothouses covered an area of twenty-six acres, but it seems reasonable to assume that this also included kitchen gardens. There was a house for the head gardener near by, and the school for young gardeners, which Maria Fyodorovna had established at Pavlovsk, was moved here in 1819. In addition to these hothouses there was also the Woodland Orangery, which was one of the finest buildings in the park, as early twentieth-century photographs show.[55] Brenna was probably the architect. It was badly damaged during the German occupation, but some restoration has taken place.

Near to the Woodland Orangery an amphitheatre, designed by Nikolai Lvov, was constructed in the late 1790s. It was surrounded by an earth rampart 11½ feet high, which enclosed a circular space 213 feet in diameter. Spectators sat on turf benches on the ledges which descended to the arena. It appears to have been intended for contests, perhaps gladiatorial, but little seems to be known about what took place there, except that it is recorded that it was the setting of a fancy dress festival in the middle of the nineteenth century, and there is a a tradition that cockfights were staged there.

South-east of the park by the Black Lake, Lvov's Priory Palace is of exceptional interest for the method of its construction, which had been developed by the architect and had already been used successfully elsewhere. While the foundations and the tower are of local limestone, the rest of the building is mainly of compressed earth, which was beaten down between removable panels with a lime solution added every two or three inches, resulting in a very hard and durable material. Moulded earth bricks of similar composition were used at the points where two floors of the building met. The walls were fairly thick – 30 inches at the level of the windowsills on the ground floor, but gradually reducing above that.[54] Lvov was not only an exceptionally talented architect and inventor. He was also a notable poet, musician and artist.

Paul, as we have seen, was Grand Master of the Sovereign Order of the Knights of Malta. The Prince de Condé, now a refugee from the French Revolution and serving in the Russian army, was Prior of the Order[55] and the Priory Palace was built as a place where he could hold court.

Paul and Maria Fyodorovna were often at Gatchina, usually in the autumn, where she took a great interest in the garden, but was always concerned that it might outshine Pavlovsk. She was impressed by the technique of Paul's head gardener, Sparrow, and she described in detail to Kuchelbecker his method of planting lime trees and roses, which she considered much superior to that of her Pavlovsk gardener from Württemberg, Wisler:

> I have just this minute got back from Gatchina, where I observed with the most careful attention Sparrow's method of planting trees, and I must tell you that I was very surprised to see the difference between the pains he takes and the trivial care shown by Wisler. Sparrow plants the limes in black earth, waters every lime every other day and covers the roots with plenty of pine twigs. He treats rose bushes in the same way and they have all come into leaf although they have only been planted a week. Women are used for watering the trees. Try to find some here for this work and direct that all my limes and newly planted rose bushes are watered as from tomorrow. Twelve limes will be delivered to you today to replace those which died in my small garden. I entreat you to oblige Wisler to show more effort, more care and more finish in his work. Tell Henry, too, about Sparrow's method and about his success. I have given instructions that 500 wild rose bushes are to be bought for my small garden and for Henry.[56]

> I am very pleased with the good news which you give me about the work. Gatchina is a very dangerous rival and all your industry and care will be necessary for Pavlovsk to bear comparison with it.[57]

On other occasions:

> I have seen many avenues of planted trees here [Gatchina almost certainly] but they are better secured than ours with three stakes: I think that must be better.[58]

The Priory Palace, built by Nikolai Lvov for the Prince de Condé, Prior of the Sovereign Order of the Knights of Malta when Paul I was Grand Master.

As the beds of flowers are extremely skilfully done here, I thought I would send you a drawing of them with their exact measurements. This drawing will guide you a little with those you are going to make for me. Remember that there must be lilacs and wild roses in the middle of these flower beds. I hope to find some fine clumps of tall trees planted.... And I hope the Chinese kiosk won't be damaged when it's taken down, since I've already found a new place for it.[59]

During the fortnight we were away from here the road round the lake has been made which is more than a mile long. It is a feature of great beauty for Gatchina, but knowing your zeal and your love for Pavlovsk, I am persuaded that you will not remain behind and that I will find wonders on my return.

    I send you ten roubles so that you can give vodka to the workers in case of need if they get wet.[60]

I forgot to tell you, my good Kuchelbeker, that I don't want anyone to work on Easter morning. If they go back to work in the afternoon that will do, but the morning is intended for God.[61]

Visits to British Gardens

Between 1814 and 1818 four of the children of Paul I and Maria Fyodorovna visited the United Kingdom and British gardens.[62] The Grand Duchess Catherine Pavlovna, young widow of the Duke of Oldenburg and future Queen of Württemberg, was the first, arriving in March 1814, and she was joined ten weeks later for a short stay by Alexander I, enthusiastically greeted – a little prematurely, it turned out – as the principal saviour of Europe from the tyranny of Napoleon. They were followed by their brothers, the Grand Duke Nicholas, later Nicholas I, in 1816–17, and the Grand Duke Michael in 1818.

'I am enchanted with the countryside,' Catherine wrote to her brother on 1 April, 'the houses have a comfortable, clean and pleasing appearance, which is delightful, and what you see in the prints isn't at all exaggerated, but, on the contrary, perfectly exact.'[63] She was less favourably impressed by the Prince Regent, whom she found insupportably licentious and lewd. 'He has a way of looking quite shamelessly where eyes should never go.'[64] During her stay the Grand Duchess visited, in addition to Kew Gardens, Windsor, Oatlands, Blenheim, Coombe House, Richmond Park and the nursery grounds of Messrs Lee and Kennedy at Hammersmith.[65]

Three years later Baron von Nicolay, Maria Fyodorovna's former Secretary, who had travelled widely in the United Kingdom, was asked to accompany the Grand Duke Nicholas on an extensive tour. On his arrival from Calais on board the *Royal Sovereign* on 21 November 1816, it was reported that Nicholas spoke English very well and had 'very little the appearance of a foreigner. He has light hair without powder.' He was a guest at Windsor, Claremont, Blenheim, Woburn Abbey, Warwick Castle, Chatsworth, Harewood and Alnwick Castle, and later 'expressed to his Royal Highness the Prince Regent, in the highest terms of gratitude and approbation, the pleasure he had experienced from the hospitality and marked attention of the nobility and public bodies throughout the whole of his tour in Great Britain'. On entering the park at Chatsworth 'his Imperial Highness and suite were most agreeably surprised at seeing the grand avenue leading to the house, lighted by men on horseback with lanterns and flambeaux'. 'He was only to have staid one night,' recorded William Spencer Cavendish, 6th Duke of Devonshire, in his *Thought Book*,[66] 'but he remained for several, one day he went out shooting and killed 40 head of game in the paddocks. Another day we went to Hardwick, and he saw Haddon Hall.' A close and lasting friendship was established and between 21 January and 16 March 1817 they met in London almost every day. 'I was pestered by letters from Ladies who wanted to know him, and the notorious H. W. fell in love with him and wrote endless abominations to me about him.'[67] In later years they met on a number of occasions both in London and St Petersburg, where the Duke of Devonshire was a guest at Pavlovsk and at Yelagin Palace.

Maria Fyodorovna took a great interest in Nicholas's tour and received regular reports in letters from Baron von Nicolay. His letters have not been traced, but her replies are in the von Nicolay Collection at the University of Helsinki. On 30 December 1816 she wrote thanking him for letters from Warwick and Newcastle and expressing her great satisfaction at the attention being paid to the Grand Duke and the good impression he had made 'on all classes'. She was particularly pleased at 'the choice of an officer as distinguished as Colonel Congreve to accompany him'. On 24 March 1817 she thanked von Nicolay again for all his letters up to number 27.

In 1844, when Nicholas was in London as Emperor, there was still an enthusiastic response from the opposite sex. The Duchess of Sutherland, in a letter to the Duke of Devonshire, referred to 'a brow of such expanse, eyes like large blue lakes, and a chest that would bear the globe. He is very attractive, and if he has resisted all the effects of this colossal power of pleasing, he is very respectable.' The Duke had hoped that the Emperor would be able to visit Chatsworth to be the first to see the new Emperor Fountain – 'this new wonder of the Peak. It is magnificent, I saw through the dusk a river dart into the sky. It rises higher than 260 feet' – but it couldn't be fitted into Nicholas's itinerary, and an entertainment was arranged for him at Chiswick instead, where he might have been surprised to see four giraffes by the side of the River Chiz.[68]

The Grand Duke Michael's visit in 1818 lasted from June to October and was part of a grand tour of Europe planned for him by the imperial tutor La Harpe.[69] Twenty years old, he was said to be 'good-looking ... stout made, and of a fair complexion'. He, too, was accompanied by Baron von Nicolay (at the age of eighty!) and by Sir William Congreve, a close associate of the Prince Regent, who had been made a Knight of the Order of St Anne by Alexander, in recognition of the unnerving effect the rocket invented by him had had on the French at the Battle of Leipzig.[70] Many country seats were visited, not only in England but in Scotland, Wales and Ireland during the Grand Duke's extensive tour. He must have had his grandmother's example in mind when he visited Chamberlain's porcelain factory in Worcester[71] and ordered a breakfast and tea service,

> on each piece of which are to be faithfully delineated views of the several noble mansions and principal towns visited during his tour through the United Kingdom; twelve months are allowed to collect the most accurate representations of these objects, and so anxious is his Imperial Highness to have them perfectly correct, that where printed views are not to be obtained sufficiently descriptive, Messrs C. have received orders to send artists of the first eminence to sketch from nature, in the particular point of view his Imperial Highness wishes them to be taken.[72]

Barrow's Worcester Journal also informed its readers that the Grand Duke had been greatly impressed by 'the exquisite delicacy of texture and transparent clearness of their lately discovered *Regent Porcelain*'. Chamberlain's *Journal* for the years 1817–24 shows that this order took just over a year to execute, for on 30 October 1819 there is a list of the ninety-six pieces of the Grand Duke Michael's breakfast and tea service 'with views'.

The Grand Duke's movements were followed with interest by *The Times* and the provincial press, and it is possible to reconstruct much of his itinerary from these sources. He arrived at Dover on 5 June – without the Dowager Empress, who had been expected – and spent the first six weeks in or near London. He was entertained on a number of occasions by the Prince Regent at Carlton House, Hampton Court and Windsor and he was present at the Prince's State Procession to Parliament. He

was also entertained by the Earl of Liverpool at Coombe House; by the Earl of Pembroke (married to the daughter of Count Vorontsov) at Richmond, where he was taken in the Admiralty barge; and by Prince Leopold at Claremont.

On Friday 17 July, after visiting the artist B.R. Haydon to see his *Christ's Entry into Jerusalem*, he set off on his tour of the provinces. He stayed first at Oxford, wishing to see the University, and then went on to Blenheim 'where he was equally delighted with the pictures and the gardens'. The following day he went to Stowe, 'but the Marquis of Buckinghamshire not expecting the arrival of his illustrious visitor till the next day, was not at home', and it was left to the chaplain to conduct him through the house and gardens. From Stowe he went on to Warwick, visiting the castle, and then to Birmingham, stopping at Kenilworth Castle on the way. At Matlock the Grand Duke and his entourage stayed at Cummings Hotel and, having acquired a copy of Moore's *Picturesque Excursions in the Vicinity of Matlock* and all the available ponies, they explored 'romantic beauties of the place, and particularly the Grand Rutland Canyon. Their *set out* for this excursion formed a very singular and laughable spectacle; the Grand Duke mounted on a donkey, which scarcely raised his feet from the ground, seemed to enjoy it much.'[73]

He was so impressed by Matlock that he decided to postpone his visit to Chatsworth for a day. When he arrived there he was elaborately entertained and commemorated his visit by planting a tree near to the tree planted by his brother Nicholas the previous year.[74]

An inspection of the Castle Inn at Castleton encouraged them to spend the night there before viewing the Peak Cavern the following day.[75] Moving further north, they stopped briefly in Sheffield, 'viewed everything worth seeing in Leeds and York', dined with Lord Carlisle at Castle Howard and visited Durham, Newcastle and Alnwick Castle.

In Liverpool he saw the Exchange, the docks, 'that stupendous mass of machinery the patent cable manufactory', St Philip's Church and the School for the Blind. After 'inspecting the numerous branches of manufacture in which the blind are employed' he went to the music room, where the pupils delighted him with a rendering of the Imperial Russian Anthem. Elsewhere in Lancashire a discordant note was struck by one of the partners in an unnamed 'eminent manufactory', which they had applied to visit. It was readily agreed that the Grand Duke himself could be admitted but not 'his followers who are probably some of them machinists or draughtsmen, *disguised as noblemen*, and sent here for the purpose of copying our most valuable inventions and machinery.'[76]

Pieces of Grand Duke Michael's breakfast and tea service supplied by Chamberlain's porcelain factory in Worcester, photographed in a store room at the Hermitage.

His journey south took him through Northwich (for the salt mines), Kidderminster, Worcester, Cheltenham, Gloucester, Bath, Bristol and Plymouth, where he spent two days at Mount Edgcumbe. 'On landing in Barn Pool the Russian standard was hoisted. His Imperial Highness was welcomed by the noble owner in person, as well as by a royal salute from the battery; and after wandering through the flower garden, with which he was exceedingly gratified, dined with his Lordship.' Travelling along the south coast he passed through Sidmouth, Weymouth and Portsmouth and called at Arundel Castle before reaching Brighton, where he was entertained at the Pavilion. After a tour 'almost unexampled for celerity of travelling' he arrived back in London on 24 September.

This does not cover fully the Grand Duke's itinerary, but it is sufficient to indicate the range and importance of the places, and particularly the parks and gardens, which were included. Sixty pieces of the Chamberlain Worcester breakfast and tea service survive in the State Hermitage Museum. On each piece the name of the place is printed under the view and the name of the owner and the county is inscribed on the base. An escorted visit through a series of locked and sealed doors made it possible, through the kindness of R.S. Soloveichika, the former Keeper of Western Art, to make a list of the views and the inscriptions, which was subsequently published in *Garden History*.[77]

When the Mikhailovsky Palace (now the Russian Museum) was built for Grand Duke Michael in the 1820s, the Scottish architect Adam Menelaws contributed to the landscaping of the grounds.[78] In 1828, on the death of his mother, it was Michael who inherited Pavlovsk, the world's greatest 'English' park.

Alexander I and Antonin Carême
The Emperor Alexander's visit to England was brief, but he spent a good deal of time in Paris where he secured the services of the celebrated Antonin Carême as his *chef de cuisine*. While 'Capability' Brown brought the landscape park up to the walls of the house, Antonin Carême, '*le Palladio de la pâtisserie*',[79] took the picturesque right inside and on to the dining table. Carême was born in Paris in 1783 and given the name Marie-Antoine, but he chose to be called Antonin. His father was a common labourer and a '*chaud lapin*',[80] the number of Antonin's siblings being variously reported as twelve, fifteen and twenty-five. Whatever their precise number, there were too many mouths to feed, and in his tenth year Antonin was turned out into the world, without any formal education, to fend for himself. He was lucky to find shelter and employment in a cook-shop and remained there for some six years, laying modest foundations from which he was to rise to the highest pinnacle of French culinary art.

When, in 1814, Alexander entered Paris at the head of the victorious allied armies, Carême was working as chef for Talleyrand. Alexander stayed for a time with the latter at the Hôtel des Relations Extérieures and then moved to the Elysée Palace, taking Carême with him. After Alexander had left Paris Carême resumed working for Talleyrand, but, following

Napoleon's return from Elba and the Battle of Waterloo, the Russian Emperor was back in Paris in 1815, and Carême again took charge of his kitchens for the duration of his stay there. In 1818, at the Congress of Aix-la-Chapelle, Carême was once more engaged by Alexander. At the end of the Congress, the Controller of the Imperial Household, Muller, invited him, not for the first time, to take a permanent position in St Petersburg, but he chose instead to go to Vienna as *chef de cuisine* to the British ambassador, Lord Stewart, a war hero and Castlereagh's half-brother. When Stewart returned temporarily to England and Carême was staying in London, he received further approaches from Russia and decided to visit St Petersburg, ready to consider the post of *maître d'hôtel*, only to discover when he got there that the conditions of service were not such that he could accept. Before leaving Russia he helped prepare a dinner at Pavlovsk to celebrate the birthday of the Dowager Empress Maria Fyodorovna.[81]

Carême's career was outstandingly successful. As a chef he was prized above all others by the rich and famous, while his carefully researched books – *Le Pâtissier royal parisien*, *Le Pâtissier pittoresque*,[82] *Le Maître d'hôtel français* and *Le Cuisinier parisien* – were all acclaimed and they exerted considerable influence on his contemporaries. And yet, if he had been in a position to choose, he would have become an architect – '*mes moyens pécuniaires m'empêchèrent de me livrer à cette belle carrière*'.[83]

Le Pâtissier pittoresque is of interest to garden historians as an example of the influence of garden architecture on another field of design. 'Les beaux-arts sont au nombre de cinq, à savoir: la peinture, la sculpture, la poèsie, la musique, l'architecture, laquelle a pour branche principale la pâtisserie,' Carême wrote. Carême had discovered the print room of the Bibliothèque Nationale early in his career and was a regular visitor there, finding inspiration for new confections and kindling his passion for architecture – and this at a time when he was still learning to read:

> The Bibliothèque was the object of all my thoughts, and on Tuesdays and Fridays, which were public days, I never failed to spend a few hours there. The main print room inspired me with a good feeling for emulation; and I gradually emerged from the obscurity into which fate had caused me to be born. . . . I had soon travelled from pole to pole, without altogether understanding the narration; but whatever was relevant to design had great influence on my imagination. Egypt, Greece and Italy inspired in me a taste for architecture.[84]

Grande Chaumière russe, Pavillon moscovite and *Hermitage russe*: designs for table decorations by Antonin Carême, *chef de cuisine* to Alexander I when the latter was in Paris.

Of the 125 plates in the third edition of *Le Pâtissier pittoresque*
110 are designs for picturesque pavilions, temples, ruins, towers,
belvederes, cottages, hermitages, mills, cascades, etc., to adorn
fashionable tables. Transported into the warm climate of the
dining room, they are no longer tied to the vegetation of their
countries of origin, and palm trees may spring up in unlikely
settings. In the text Carême records that before creating these
designs he had returned to the Bibliothèque Nationale to look
again at travel and topographical books covering India, China,
Egypt, Greece, Turkey, Istria, Dalmatia, Germany, Switzerland,
Spain, Russia, Poland, Sweden, England and Ireland.[85] He
probably also studied such works as J.C. Krafft's *Plans des plus
beaux jardins pittoresques de France, Angleterre et d'Allemagne*,
Le Rouge's *Détails de nouveaux jardins à la mode: Jardins anglo-
chinois*, William Chambers' *Dissertation on Oriental Gardening*,
and, perhaps, the publications of W. and J. Halfpenny and
W. Wright. And one would expect him to have known at first hand
the *fabriques* in the Parc de Monceau, the Désert de Retz,
Bagatelle and the Folie Saint-James.

Detailed instructions are given for making and colouring the
materials needed to execute his picturesque designs – principally a
paste made from flour, sugar and the whites of eggs, almond paste,
and a paste made from starch and gum tragacanth. For the benefit
of young pâtissiers he added a brief history of architecture with a
description and illustrations of the five orders of Vignola and of
the Caryatid, Paestum, Egyptian, Chinese and Gothic orders. In
his view those who sought to practise his art needed a sound
architectural background if they were to succeed.

P. 83.

Grande Chaumière russe.

P. 22.

Pavillon moscovite.

P. 64.

Hermitage russe.

But he was ambitious to create something in materials more durable than sugar, flour and ground almonds, and he took lessons from the architect Charles Percier.[86] Then, between 1821 and 1825, he published in fascicles three small collections of designs for architectural monuments, a total of fifteen, magnificently engraved and printed. Apart from two lighthouses which were for Calais and Bordeaux, they were intended to add new lustre to Paris and St Petersburg. The collection of designs for St Petersburg was dedicated to the Emperor Alexander with his consent, the giving of which, accompanied by a ring, delighted the author:

> See how delicate the Emperor is! He was not able to recompense me for an art where I pleased him; and he has recompensed me for another art to which I have devoted all the leisure hours of my life and the aptitude I had from my early days for the design of ornament.[87]

These designs and those for Paris were for commemorative columns, temples and fountains, which were all to be embellished with sculptural groups and other ornament. Carême believed that the larger they were the greater the impression they would make, and some of them were to be more than 200 feet high. While he suggested that there could be some flexibility on this point – '*Si l'élevation de ces monuments semblait trop colossale, on pourrait les réduire d'un quart*'[88] – it is, perhaps, not altogether surprising that these projects are still waiting to be realized.

Yelagin Island
Maria Fyodorovna was a benevolent employer and a dedicated supporter of charitable causes. When there was sickness and some deaths among workers at Pavlovsk she wrote to Kuchelbacker: 'These deaths distress me very much. In God's name spare no money, no expense, no pains to prevent these illnesses, and urge Rittmeister to redouble his efforts to save these poor men.'[89] For Kuchelbecker himself she showed every consideration: 'As my sons have measles, you had better not come to see me to avoid giving it to your children, but write to let me know how the work is going at Pavlovsk.' And again: 'I beg you in God's name to take care of yourself and if you go to the new place where the colonnade and the cascade will be, go in the cabriolet. Don't go in the drozhki, the jolting could be harmful to you.'[90]

In 1806, after meeting an acquaintance walking in the park with her deaf-and-dumb nephew, and learning that he had a deaf-and-dumb brother and sister, Maria Fyodorovna determined to establish the first school in Russia for deaf-and-dumb children. A visit to St Petersburg was arranged for an experienced Polish teacher, Father Sigmund, and, in 1807, he opened a school for six boys and six girls at Pavlovsk in the Empress's first small house, Marienthal, which Paul had turned into the fortress Vip. Alexander Meller, the small boy she had met in the park, made excellent progress, which was rewarded

by a gold watch, and was later employed in the Empress's service, as were many of those who were educated with him. The school continued in Pavlovsk until 1810, when it was transferred to St Petersburg.[91]

In the town at Pavlovsk she had established a hospital and homes for wounded veterans of 1812. In St Petersburg she paid monthly visits to the institutions she supported there – the schools for the daughters of the Semenovsky and Preobrazhensky Regiments, the St Catherine Institute for Girls, the Institute for the Orphans of Soldiers, the Foundling Hospital, the Hospital for the Poor, and the Deaf-and-Dumb School. As she grew older she found the journeys from Pavlovsk increasingly difficult, and Alexander bought Yelagin Palace on Yelagin Island as an occasional residence for her.

Yelagin Island, in the estuary of the Neva, is linked to the shore by a bridge. It was called Melgunov in the 1760s, when A.P. Melgunov built a large house there, which had a pleasant garden, with pavilions, statues and flowerbeds. The name was changed when it became the property of I.P. Yelagin, a leading Court official, who built a new house, set in a remarkable formal garden with landscaping beyond. In an impresive orangery and various hothouses, a wide range of exotic flowering and fruiting plants was cultivated, among them pineapples, peaches and grapes; while in the wooden-framed winter garden, measuring 180 × 48 feet, and said to be reminiscent of Prince Potemkin's winter garden at the Tauride Palace, there were singing and ornamental birds and statues as well as rare plants. Other features included grottoes, pavilions and a temple with a statue of Catherine by Shubin. Yelagin Island was a favourite resort of the people of St Petersburg, for they were free to visit the park in summer. 'The company amuse themselves in walking and dancing, for which the proprietors keep a well-conducted Turkish band of music, in fishing and playing at bowls; and in the evening a firework display is generally exhibited. M. Yelagin himself usually takes part in the amusements he so liberally dispenses to others, and his daughters at times open the ball with some gentlemen present.' In winter, heated rooms were available to those who arrived in sledges, and they were allowed to walk in the winter garden.[92]

In June the northern point of the island was, and still is, the best place in St Petersburg to experience the 'white nights':

> This is the favourite place of the citizens of St Petersburg, where, every June evening, they gather in picturesque groups to watch the magnificent sunset and to spend the night, which lasts at most for half-an-hour. What produces the greatest effect is the moment when daylight is transmuted to the dark red, vividly outlined sphere, as it seems to sink into the depths of the gulf, casting farewell rays of violet light to nature and to the onlookers. Then silence reigns, and with it a bewitching chiaroscuro which scarcely succeeds in descending to earth, and then already, on the opposite side of the horizon, you see the blue glimmer of a new dawn.

Nature, having fallen asleep for a moment, comes back to life, greeting the emerging day with the rustle of leaves, a diversity of birdsong, the drone of insects. A light breeze, soughing through the trees, chases from the shore to the water the white clouds of vapour brought forth from the earth by the first rays of the rising sun. It is still only one o'clock in the morning, yet it's light enough to read a book if you want to. But this is no time for reading with such an enchanting view of the awakening morning. Without any feelings of sleep or tiredness, all you want is for what you have just seen to appear before your eyes again.[95]

Yelagin died in 1796. A later owner, Count G.V. Orlov, continued to make improvements and engaged Joseph Busch, son of John, to landscape the park, and Peter Buk to take charge of the flower gardens and hothouses. Their services were retained when Alexander bought it from Orlov for 350,000 roubles. (Busch was also in charge of the gardens of Alexander's palace on Kamenny Island.) Carlo Rossi, who had worked at Pavlovsk for Maria

Fyodorovna and at the palace of Tver for Catherine Pavlovna and the Duke of Oldenburg, was invited to rebuild the palace. His classical palace, which retained some of the framework of the earlier house, is placed by the river opposite Kamenny Island and at the eastern end of the Maslyany (Butter) Meadow, so called because it was a favourite place for promenading during the festivities of Shrove-tide, for which the Russian is *maslyanitsa* (butter week). Two service buildings on the north side of the meadow, the stables and the kitchen, look like large park pavilions with nothing on the outside to indicate their actual function. All the windows are concealed within inner courts. The semi-circular southern façade of the kitchen building has, where windows would have been, fourteen niches with statues of ancient gods and heroes by Pimenev. Rossi also designed the elegant orangery and seven pavilions, of which the music pavilion is particularly impressive. This palace and its

Yelagin Palace and some bold herbaceous planting, illustrated here in *c*.1820.

associated buildings form one the most outstanding complexes of park buildings in Russian architecture.

Joseph Busch's landscaping involved the moving of an astonishing amount of earth and altered not just the appearance of the island but even its shape and size. In Yelagin's time an earth wall had been built round the island to protect it from flooding, and a drainage canal had been dug. Under Busch a series of nine interconnecting pools was excavated, amounting to a fifth of the area of the island, and the very considerable spoil was used to raise the level of the marshy areas, to extend the shoreline and to build a substantial embankment carrying a carriageeway. This circled the island except between the palace and the river, where the old wall was removed to open the view to Kamenny Island. This work took several years to complete.

Thousands of trees – limes, oaks, elms, ash, birch, maple and larch – were planted. Among the trees there were open glades, and much attention was paid to the way that trees of different species were grouped for effective contrasts of form and colour. Particular care was taken in planting round the sinuous, newly constructed pools to achieve picturesque effects, and the still

water of the pools contrasted effectively with the swiftly flowing river near by.

The Maslyany Meadow, which had previously been crossed by five radial avenues, was extended as a large, informally shaped space, bounded by trees – chiefly oaks and limes – to the south, and by the palace and its associated buildings to the east and north. It continued to be frequented by the public. The garden by the palace was surrounded by metal railings, designed by Busch and painted white, with gates designed by Rossi. Contemporary watercolours show attractive herbaceous borders, for here was another opportunity for Maria Fyodorovna to indulge her love of flowers. There was also a smaller private garden between the orangery and the palace with many rare and exotic plants displayed both in the garden and in the orangery. All this would have been done in consultation with the Dowager Empress. By 1826 Bode was the gardener at Yelagin and she was very impressed by his work.

But when she was staying in Moscow it was to Pavlovsk that her thoughts turned. In a letter to General Friderits in May 1826 she asked:

> Are the lilacs in bloom? Is the small garden beautiful? How are the roses? Are the nightingales singing? Have you bought any trees and shrubs at the market? I'm afraid that the site for the orangery was not well chosen. Remember me when Wisler says that it has had no sun and that it is not good. You must consult old Bode from Yelagin. He's a skilful and experienced gardener.[94]

In September 1828 she was making plans for work in the garden and the park in the following year. On 10 September she approved a report on proposals to repair the small hunting lodge Krak by the Slavyanka and for the construction of new hothouses in the garden. But her health had been failing, and she died on 24 October, deeply mourned by her family, the imperial household and by the many thousands who had benefited from the charities she supported.[95]

The Grand Duke Michael inherited Pavlovsk with an endowment of 1,500,000 roubles to be invested in perpetuity for its upkeep. It was a condition that he should maintain, in their then state, the palace, the gardens, the park, the hothouses, and the hospital, the homes and the institute his mother had established on the estate for wounded veterans of the war of 1812. He was to keep what he wanted of the botanical collection and give the rest to the Imperial Botanic Garden.[96]

Left above: Rossi's Kitchen Building.
Left below: Rossi's Music Pavilion.
Right: Memorial to Maria Fyodorovna at Pavlovsk. The semi-rotunda was designed by Carlo Rossi in 1816 but was not constructed until almost a century later when ferro-concrete was the material used. V.A. Beklemishev provided the model for the bronze statue, which was cast in 1914.

6

LANDSCAPE PARKS IN AND AROUND ST PETERSBURG

While John Busch was landscaping the park for Catherine at Tsarskoe Selo, William Gould from Ormskirk arrived in St Petersburg in 1776 to lay out the garden and park at Prince Potemkin's palace, later called the Taurida Palace, built at Catherine's expense for the most important man in her life. This was the year in which, at her request, he was created Prince of the Holy Roman Empire by the Emperor Joseph II. Eleven years later he was to become Prince Potemkin-Tavrichesky (Taurida) in recognition of his military successes against Turkey and his development of the Crimea (Tauris in antiquity), where he founded the cities of Odessa, Sebastopol and Kherson, as well as building the Black Sea fleet.

Potemkin had first come to Catherine's notice as one of the Guards supporting the coup which put her on the throne. In 1774, soon after her break with Orlov, he became her lover. When, some two years later, they both decided it was time for a change, he combined the amorous and, it seems, successful pursuit of his nieces (five of them[1]) with the duty of helping to recruit, over a period, a relay of young and virile replacements to serve in the imperial bed. Their service was handsomely rewarded with large sums of money, vast estates and thousands of serfs – just what was needed to make new parks. Potemkin is said to have been spectacularly well endowed; and it is also reported that a life-size porcelain model of the endowment survived the prince and may well be stored away somewhere in the Hermitage.[2] He continued to be Catherine's closest associate for the rest of his life, and it is widely believed that they were secretly married. His achievements for Russia were immense, as was the wealth he acquired in the process.

According to the 1827 edition of Loudon's *Encyclopaedia of Gardening*, Gould, Potemkin's English gardener, 'had a character in some degrees analogous to that of his master; he lived in splendor, kept horses and women, and gave occasionally entertainments to the nobility.'[3] Someone may have complained, since we read in the 1834 edition that 'he kept horses and carriages'.[4] Potemkin owned a vast amount of property in various parts of the Russian empire, and Gould laid out English gardens for him in Astrakhan, by the Caspian Sea; in two of the new towns he founded on land taken from the Turks in the south, Ekaterinoslav (now Dnepropetrovsk) and Nikolaev; and, in the Crimea, at Artek, Massandra and Alupka. When Catherine travelled to the Crimea in 1787, on the tour arranged for her by Potemkin, Gould created English gardens for the palaces which were prepared for her at Simferopol, Bakhchiserai, Sebastopol and Karasubazaar.[5] 'In one of the prince's journeys to the Ukraine,' according to Sir John Carr,

An early nineteenth-century watercolour of the exceptional landscape at Mon Repos with von Nicolay's house to the left and Paulstein, the pavilion which served as his study, on the higher ground to the right of it.

Gould attended him with several hundred assistants, destined for operators, in laying out the grounds of Potemkin's residence in the Crimea. Wherever the prince halted, if only for a day, his travelling pavilion was erected, and surrounded by a garden in the English taste, composed of trees and shrubs, divided by gravel walks, and ornamented with seats and statues, all carried forward with the cavalcade.[6]

The author of an article recently published in Russia claims that while working in the imperial archives he had chanced on a petition to the Empress by Gould in 1793, which gives details of all the gardens he had worked on in Russia.[7] They include several properties in and around St Petersburg and Moscow, some of which Potemkin had owned only briefly, as well as properties in Belorussia, Moldavia, Ukraine and the Crimea. Unfortunately the archival reference quoted for the petition turns out to be erroneous, and since it is not possible to check the information against the alleged source it must be taken as unreliable.

While Potemkin had larger properties in Ukraine and the Crimea, the Taurida Palace with its park and garden was the most important. Martin Call, Gould's successor at the garden, contributed this description of it to Loudon's *Gardener's Magazine* in 1827:

The garden was planned and superintended by William Gould, from Lancashire, who displayed great judgement in forming the ponds, out of which he got sufficient materials to make an agreeable variety of swells and declivities. The ponds are well supplied with water, which is brought upwards of twenty miles in a small canal, cut by Peter the First, to supply the fountains in the summer garden of St Petersburg. . . . The grounds consist of a pleasure garden, small park, or enclosure for grazing, reserve-ground, nurseries, &c; and forcing gardens.[8]

The outstanding feature at the Taurida Palace was the quite exceptional winter garden, which the historian Heinrich Storch described at the beginning of the 1790s:

Along one side of the vestibule is the winter garden, an enormous structure disposed into a garden, only separated from the grand hall by a colonnade. As from the size of the roof it could not be supported without pillars, they are disguised under the form of palm trees. The heat is maintained by concealed flues placed in the walls and pillars, and even under the earth leaden pipes are conveyed, incessantly filled with boiling water. The walks of this garden meander amidst flowery hedges, and fruit-bearing shrubs, winding over little hills, and producing, at every step, fresh occasions for surprise. The eye of the beholder, when weary of the luxuriant variety of the vegetable world, finds recreation in contemplating some exquisite production of art: here a head, from the chisel of a Grecian sculptor, invites to admiration; there a motley collection of curious fish, in crystal vases, suddenly fixes our attention. We presently quit these objects, in order to go into a grotto of looking-glass, which gives a multiplied reflection of all these wonders, or to indulge our astonishment at the most extraordinary mixture of colours in the faces of an obelisk of mirrors. The genial warmth, the fragrant odours of the nobler plants, the voluptuous stillness that prevails in this enchanted spot, lull the fancy into romantic dreams; we imagine ourselves in the blooming groves of Italy; while nature, sunk into a deathlike torpor, announces the severity of a northern winter through the windows of the pavilion. In the centre of this bold creation, on a lofty pedestal, stood the statue of Catherine II, surrounded by the emblems of legislatrix, cut in carrara marble. It was thrown out of the building on its being made into a barracks.[9]

Far left: Prince Potemkin's Taurida Palace.

Left: The outlines of William Gould's landscaping in the Taurida garden are still clearly visible.

The last sentence refers to the action of Paul I after his mother's death, when he expressed his loathing for her and Potemkin by having the palace turned into a barracks for a regiment of Horse Guards and the winter garden into their stables.[10] Gould then returned to England but was back in St Petersburg in 1802 to restore the garden for Alexander I before retiring to Ormskirk in 1806.

Both Alexander and Nicholas I enjoyed the use of the palace and garden, which was still producing a remarkable range of fruit in considerable quantities in the early 1840s:

> The hothouses and orangery of the Taurian palace, which are among the most spacious in Petersburg, supply the imperial table. I visited them on the 28th February. Thirty rooms of various dimensions were filled with flowers, vegetables, and fruit trees. The vines are planted in long rows, and form alleys of luxuriant overhanging foliage, resembling those of the vineyards of the Rhine. They were partly in bloom; from some the blossom had gone off and the small grapes were set. These grapes were expected to be ripe in the beginning of June; and during that month it was estimated that fifty hundredweight of fruit would be gathered. In other alleys were ranged rows of apricot and peach trees in full blossom. . . . It was expected that twenty thousand apricots would be ready for gathering by the end of May. There were fifteen thousand pots of strawberry plants, most of them bearing fine fruit; and the gardener had already sent two crops to the imperial palace. . . . Without doors the winter snow, like Nature's winding sheet, was to overspread the ground for the space of six weeks longer, whilst in the magical parterres within, magnolias and lilies, like flakes of summer snow, were peeping from among verdant leaves, and looking as though they had been accidentally dropped in the rude North from the cornucopia of Flora.[11]

Dachas on the Peterhof Road

The word 'dacha' is used today for the millions of usually modest out-of-town retreats which are enjoyed by so many Russians; but it originally denoted 'something given' and was used for the plots of land, in and outside St Petersburg, given to courtiers by Peter. They were then required to develop them, without much delay, to a standard appropriate for his expanding new city. The favoured location outside the city was the Peterhof Road by the Gulf of Finland, leading to Peter's great palace. The plots were fairly uniform in size, usually measuring 100 × 1,000 sazhens (700 × 7,000 feet). During the early years the Peterhof end of the road was the more fashionable; but after the building of the Winter Palace, the imperial family spent most of the time there, and the city end became the first choice. Towards the end of the century Heinrich Storch described one section of the road as

more like a pleasure-ground than a highway. An uninterrupted series of country seats and villas ornamenting both its sides. Magnificence and taste, expense and art, have here occurred to convert a wilderness into a paradise, the charms whereof are heightened by the striking diversity of dispositions and ideas. Magnificent villas, Dutch villages, hermitages, ponds, islands, rural prospects, in ceaseless vicissitudes. The traveller, surprised at seeing himself suddenly transported from the fenny forests of Ingria into this highway, thinks himself in the region of fairyland, where nature and art dance in magical mazes about his carriage.[12]

The two dachas which most impressed were those belonging to the Naryshkin brothers, Alexander and Lev. Krasnaya Myza, generally known as 'Ba! Ba!', 4 versts (about 2½ miles) along the road from St Petersburg, belonged to Alexander, high cup-bearer to Catherine and later director of the imperial theatres. The house, set among trees with a lawn in front, was on one side of the road. The landscape park, on the other, said to be one of the first in Russia, was the largest on the Peterhof Road and extended to the shore of the Gulf. There were wide channels of water with many islands, a pavilion where newspapers were provided, a pavilion with a camera obscura to capture the picturesque views, and various other buildings. There were gondolas on the water and pelicans, swans and exotic ducks. Music, dancing, swings, skittles, refreshing drinks and sweetmeats were freely available. It was open on Sundays in summer to all respectable people and attracted many visitors. One of them doubted if there could be a place as beautiful in England.

Lev Naryshkin's dacha was called 'Ga! Ga!' and, as was the case with his brother's, the house was on one side of the road, with orangeries and a small orchard, and the landscape park on the other down to the Gulf. It was probably first laid out in the late 1760s. There was a pool, a temple, a mandarin's house, a Russian peasant's house, a Dutch peasant's house, a hermitage, summerhouses, a Chinese mountain pavilion, a Chinese house, a deep cave, a shepherd's hut and a column commemorating one of several visits by Catherine. A raised structure concealed musicians, and from it hares were released with dogs to pursue them. A French diplomat referred to flowerbeds, kiosks, numerous comfortable garden seats, conventional and floating bridges, handsome gilded boats and gardeners dressed in Chinese costume. Catherine visited 'Ga! Ga!' in 1777 with the Swedish King Gustav III and with the Austrian Emperor Joseph II in 1780, when there was a theatrical performance and a ballet. Every citizen of St Petersburg was also welcome. One visitor commented caustically: 'Naryshkin's house is different in that the most motley company visit it every day. The owner was content with the crowds who came, although they were all sorts of riff-raff.'[13]

Gardens on the Islands

There were other impressive gardens on the islands in the Neva estuary:

> The grand-ducal island, Kamennoi-ostrof, has not only a great many fine private gardens, but all people are allowed the liberty of amusing themselves here in a becoming manner. The romantic wildness of the island, its situation between other rival places of amusement, the fishing and a well furnished house of entertainment draw a great number of people hither on fine summer days. Another island, Krestovsky-ostrof, belonging to Count Razumovsky, is one continual forest, cut through in various places into large and noble vistas. Here likewise one is permitted to enjoy the beauties of nature. On Sundays and holidays are seen a great confluence of citizens of the lower classes, taking their pleasures unmolested.[14]

Yelagin Island, as we have seen (pages 140–2), was another very popular place of public resort.

English Landscaping on Rural Estates

In 1762 Peter III had issued an edict releasing the nobility from compulsory service, and the Charter to the Nobility of 1785 encouraged owners to settle on their estates and to develop industry and agriculture there. When they turned to making gardens, the English landscape style, emblematic of freedom, was the natural choice. Some owners of estates had been to England and had visited English parks; others were influenced by what they had seen at Tsarskoe Selo, Pavlovsk and Gatchina. 'Rural beauties and romantic scenes, assembled with so much taste in English gardens' were more in accord with the spirit and aspirations of the times than 'the sculptured hedges, stiff Dutch walks, wild-beast boxwood, pond Neptunes and seashell bowers of Europe'.[15] 'Till of late the taste of gardening among the great was confined to fruits,' wrote James Meader to his correspondent in England,

> but the Nobles who have been to England are so much enraptured with the English pleasure gardens that they are cried up here. This has set them all gardening mad. Any of the Nobility will give £100 pr Ann for an English gardener. I have been applied to for more than one but we few who are already here are not desirous of seeing any more arrive lest one scabby sheep spoil the whole flock.[16]

The Revd William Coxe was very impressed by the Englishness of Count Peter Panin's park at Mikhalkovo near Moscow:

> The grounds are prettily laid out in the style of our parks with gentle slopes, spacious lawns of the finest verdure, scattered plantations, and a large piece of water fringed with wood. We could not avoid feeling extreme satisfaction that the English style of gardening had

Top: Giacomo Quarenghi's drawing of Krasnaya Myza, Alexander Naryshkin's dacha on the Peterhof Road.

Above: A coasting hill on Kamenny Island, from a painting by I.V.G. Bart (*c*.1810).

penetrated even to these distant regions. The English taste, indeed, can certainly display itself in this country to great advantage, where the parks are extensive, and the verdure, during the short summer, uncommonly beautiful.[17]

Apart from their sentimental appeal, landscape parks also made better economic sense. There were about four hundred estates around St Petersburg, and many of them were developed more simply and without the benefit of English gardeners. Some of the main buildings have survived, though in less than pristine condition, and have been put to some communal use. Few garden features remain, but something of the designed landscape can still be appreciated and can be fascinating to explore. Even in their present rather melancholy condition many of the old estates have a considerable appeal, as two of their devoted admirers have eloquently testified:

> Today almost all the old estates are neglected, the buildings are decayed and falling into ruin, the parks are overgrown with young wood; but walking in them proves to be a beneficial and salutary exercise and soothes the spirit. How beautiful the old trees have become with their magnificent crowns and mighty trunks, and the copses that have been there for many years, the ancient groves, the spreading, shady avenues, the pools choked with weeds, the brightly lit meadows with a dense standing of grass. In these unrestored, uncared for estates we see before us a world of time past of unpretentious appearance. In their neglected state there is beauty and sadness. They give rise to reminiscences about our forbears, help us to a keener appreciation of their feelings and thoughts, mellowed in the conditions of the world of the estate. And among them not only people who actually existed, but also the heroes of the classics of our literature.[18]

Taitsy

The land at Taitsy once belonged to Abram Petrovich Hannibal, the Ethiopian great-grandfather of Alexander Pushkin. It later became the property of A.G. Demidov, whose grandfather's ironworks in the Urals had made the family's fortune, and he commissioned I.E. Starov, who also worked on Demidov's dacha on the Peterhof Road, to transform the estate. The park was created at the end of the eighteenth century and beginning of the nineteenth. Although it has long been completely neglected, the original outlines can still be perceived. There was a formal area near the house and increasingly natural landscaping beyond. Old oaks contrast with larches and the white trunks of birches. There was once a gardener's cottage, a summerhouse with a thatched roof, an aviary and other ornamental pavilions. These are all gone, but the Gothic gateway has survived. At the end of the nineteenth century Taitsy became a sanatorium for patients suffering from diseases of the lungs and there seems to have been little or no maintenance of the garden and park since then.[19]

Top: The garden and park at Taitsy have been neglected for more than a century with self-sown trees allowed to grow around the house. It was a home for old Bolsheviks in the 1980s, and this photograph was obtained by trespass.

Above: The Gothic gateway still survived in the park.

Right, above: Restoration was in progress on the house at Marino in the 1980s.

Right: The landscape park was badly in need of attention.

Far right: The neo-gothic church was a considerable ornament in the park before the German occupation.

Marino

About 25 miles south-east of St Petersburg near the village of Adrianovo, Marino dates from the early nineteenth century. It was called Marino after Maria Nikolaevna, the daughter of Nicholas I and widow of the Duke Maximilian of Leuchtenberg. She secretly married Grigory Strogonov, President of the Academy of Arts, knowing that her father would strongly disapprove.[20] A.N. Voronikhin, assisted by his pupil I.F. Kolodiny, Strogonov's serf architect, built the house and other estate buildings and laid out the park. There were once numerous architectural features in the park by the serf artist Ermolai Esakov and an impressive 'ruin-pavilion' by Kh.F. Meier, but these have all disappeared. The neo-gothic church, by P.S. Sadovnik, remained a prominent ornament in the park until the German occupation during the last war when it suffered the same ruinous damage as the house.[21]

Gostilitsy

The land at Gostilitsy, a few miles from Oranienbaum, belonged briefly to Robert Erskine, physician to Peter I, but after his death Peter gave it to Burchard-Christof Minikh, a soldier and hydraulic engineer, as a reward for his work on canal systems. During the twenty years of his ownership Minikh used his professional skills to build dams in the bed of the River Gostilka and created pools of a considerable size, cascades and fountains. With a system of five cascading pools it became a splendid water garden. Minikh's career continued to prosper under Anna, and he became a count, a general-field marshal and President of the War College; but when Elizabeth came to the throne he was arrested, his estate was confiscated, and he was sent into exile.

In 1743 Elizabeth gave Gostilitsy to her favourite, Alexis Razumovsky, who was also given the title of count, followed three years later by the rank of field marshal. He introduced a wildlife enclosure at Gostilitsy, which probably contained deer and elk, since these were the animals he and Elizabeth are known to have hunted. He also arranged magnificent firework displays for the Empress, who frequently stayed at Gostilitsy, as did Grand Duke Peter and Grand Duchess Catherine. Among the buildings he added to the estate were a new palace and the church. He also installed a *katalnaya gorka* (sliding hill).

When Alexis died in 1771 his brother Kirill inherited all his property. Kirill must have found his brother's baroque palace behind the times and replaced it with a new one in Palladian-inspired classical style. A new park building, the Tea House, stood at the top of a slope above the river, facing the palace. Near by, the Hermitage Pavilion, in the form of an ancient temple, was placed on a hill. The various colours of the stained glass in its doors and windows were projected by sunlight on to the white walls inside. A bell tower was a striking feature on another hill, and lower down there was a dark, cool grotto with seats to retire to on hot summer days.

In 1803 Kirill's son Peter succeeded him and increased the size of the estate, creating a new area of parkland with more large pools, and planting many trees. After his death in 1823 his brother Andrei, who lived abroad and served as Russian ambassador in Naples, Copenhagen and Stockholm, sold Gostilitsy in 1825 to Alexander Potemkin, Prince Potemkin's nephew. It was then probably the finest private estate in the environs of St Petersburg, and the Potemkins were rich enough both to maintain it and to enhance it. They entertained on a grand scale with receptions for many guests. Kirill Razumovsky's palace was not designed for such occasions, and in 1842 Potemkin commissioned Stakenschneider to build a new one, which was inspired by English country houses in the neo-gothic style. He had built a villa for Tatyana Potemkina's close friend, Maria Nikolaevna, Nicholas I's daughter, secretly married, as we have seen, to Grigory Strogonov.

On both sides of the River Gostilka, which had been simply landscaped, cascades, fountains, pavilions, elaborate flower gardens and, in summer, orange trees in tubs brought a more formal splendour to the scene. Elsewhere in the garden, too, there were striking floral displays, with hydrangeas, campanulas, stocks, daisies, dahlias, as well as roses, mentioned by contemporaries. There had been orangeries at Gostilitsy since the days of Minikh, but Potemkin's three orangeries were each about 300 feet long. One was devoted to vines, another to plums, peaches and apricots, and the third to rare flowering plants and plants from southern countries.

A mill, built by Minikh and converted to a tavern by Alexis Razumovsky, was replaced by a Turkish Pavilion, and not far away from it, in the 1850s, a fortress with towers, furnished with cannon, was erected, and its battlements were the scene of firework displays, continuing a Razumovsky tradition.

'It was a wonderful place to stay for the summer,' wrote Tatyana Potemkina's niece, Elena Khvoshchinskaya, many years afterwards,

> the splendid park, the garden, all kinds of flower beds, lots of fountains, cascades, pools with swans and pure, clear streams with trout swimming – it all seemed like fairyland. That time has long since gone when I rejoiced in the beauty of Gostilitsy, sitting on a bench somewhere, listening to all the varied splashings and murmurings of the fountains and cascades.[22]

Until the Second World War most of the estate buildings retained their external appearance, but fierce battles were fought over the park and considerable damage resulted. The palace, the fortress, the Tea House and the grotto were among the casualties, but the church survived and has been restored. Nature won back much of the territory it lost to the Potemkins, and although the park has long been neglected, it still has considerable charm with its lakes, pools, streams, river, waterfall, meadows and old oaks. It deserves expert attention and adequate funding.[23]

Zhernovka

In *Sredi kollektsionerov* (*Among Collectors*) Nikolai Lansere wrote in 1924 of the estate and garden at Zhernovka on the River Okhta near St Petersburg, which was then in a ruinous condition:

> In its heyday there was a succession of seignorial buildings around the garden and in the garden, namely: a beautiful two-storey stone house by the river, where there was a landing stage and a wooden building with a kitchen, wash-house cellar and ice-house; a large wooden single-storey house and a house half-stone, half-wood with three rooms; a large wooden house with a cart-shed, stables and ice-house; then the gardener's house, again with ice-house, cart-shed and stables; three stone orangeries and a wooden house for cherries; further on a stone threshing barn; a bakery covered with tiles, baths, a large wooden house for the steward and a whole series of wooden agricultural buildings – barns, stores, ice-houses, wood-sheds, stables, threshing floors. This list shows how rich and splendidly appointed this estate was.
>
> On the other side, the front of the residence, it faced a small but intricate English garden. Literally two paces from the wall of the house there was a pool with a bridge and an island, on which there was a summerhouse in the form of a mushroom installed over the grave of a dog of one of the owners. The banks of the pool and the island were overgrown with bushes and birch trees. The path from the portico, turning sharply behind the bridge, led to a vast old oak tree recently cut down. There was an avenue round the garden, now birch, now lime, in part by an overgrown roadway, in part by a gully with a stream flowing down to the river. A second avenue along the beautiful bank of the Okhta led to a charming stone building – an old landing stage, or rather a pavilion, a belvedere with enchanting views up- and downstream. In the centre of the garden on the greensward were groups of ancient trees, oaks and limes, sometimes forming circles on artificial mounds where iron benches once stood. . . . There used to be other pieces of fancy in the garden which no estate could manage without. There was a little birch house but nothing remains of it. Even such a utilitarian building as a threshing barn was not built simply but with decorations in the Chinese style. In all this the imitation of the taste of the court could be perceived, originating at Tsarskoe Selo, Pavlovsk or Gatchina.

The Monument to the Parents at Aleksei Arakcheev's Gruzino.

Gruzino

Another park with echoes of Pavlovsk and Gatchina was Count Aleksei Arakcheev's Gruzino. Count Arakcheev was a general in the artillery who played a leading part in reorganizing the Russian army for Paul I and afterwards served his close friend Alexander I. When he was still Grand Duke, Paul had singled out Arakcheev as a young officer at Gatchina and gave him every opportunity to demonstrate his outstanding ability both there and with the garrison at Pavlovsk. Rapid promotion followed the death of Catherine, and he was given the valuable estate at Gruzino in Novgorod province. In 1825 he suffered a double blow with the deaths of his companion, Nastasia Minkinaia – his marriage had been unsuccessful – and of the Emperor to whom he was devoted. In the following year he retired to his estate where he died eight years later with his eyes fixed, it is said, on a portrait of Alexander. In accordance with the terms of his will, he was buried at Gruzino beside the memorial he had erected to Paul and wearing a shirt which Alexander had given him many years before.

The park reflected its owner's career and allegiances. There were busts of both Paul and Alexander; a pavilion with a statue of St Andrew by Martos was modelled on the Pavilion of the Three Graces at Pavlovsk; there was a monument to Arakcheev's parents, a vase commemorating his mother's visit to Gruzino in 1800 and another in memory of Nastasia Minkinaia. Two statues of dogs remembered 'faithful' Zhuchka and 'dear' Diana; while

the bust of an old man challenged credulity with the inscription: 'In memory of 125-year-old Isaac Konstantinov, who planted the trees when he was young, born 1681, died 1806.' There were many statues in the park, among them Diana, Hope and Truth, and the terrace overlooked a winding lake with several islands, on one of which stood a Temple of Love. There was a grotto under the terrace with Etruscan-style vases.

When the garden historian Kurbatov visited Gruzino there were still two summerhouses. 'An open-work iron summerhouse, made to the design of Semenov, is intact. Another summerhouse also exists near the landing stage. The latter is, in fact, a pedestal for three eagles holding a hoop, in which was probably placed a chafing-dish for heating resin when there were illuminations.'[24]

Mon Repos

We have already met Baron Ludwig von Nicolay as Maria Fyodorovna's secretary and as one of the escorts of the Grand Dukes Nicholas and Michael on their visits to Britain in 1816 and 1818. We now meet him as man of letters and maker of parks and gardens.

Ludwig Heinrich Nicolay, a French citizen whose first language was German, was born in 1737 in Strasbourg, where, in deference to his father's wishes, he successfully studied law at the university and was briefly a professor of law; but his main interests were in literature – he published his first book of poems in 1760 – and the arts generally, including parks and gardens. During his travels around Europe, he met Prince D.M. Golitsyn in Paris and acted as his secretary during a diplomatic mission in Vienna. He had to return to Strasbourg shortly afterwards on account of the failing health of his father, but in 1766 he was invited by K.G. Razumovsky to become tutor to his son, Aleksei, during a long tour of western Europe, accompanied by Count I.I. Shuvalov, an important figure in Russian government circles and one of the founders of Moscow University. In 1768–9 Nicolay accompanied Aleksei and his brothers Pyotr and Andrei on a visit to England.[25] These contacts led to a recommendation to Catherine and to his appointment as one of the five tutors to Grand Duke Paul. Nicolay's close friend from his student days and fellow poet, Franz Hermann Lafermière, had preceded him to St Petersburg in 1765 as Paul's librarian. In 1773 Nicolay became secretary to Paul and his first wife, Natalia Alekseyevna, and then, after the latter's early death and Paul's remarriage, he became secretary to Maria Fyodorovna. He accompanied them on their visit to western Europe as the Comte and Comtesse du Nord in 1781–2 and, at Paul's request, was ennobled by Joseph II in Vienna. When Paul became Emperor, Nicolay became a counsellor of state and member of the cabinet and had the title of Baron conferred on him. In 1798 he became President of the Imperial Academy of Sciences. In 1803 Alexander reluctantly allowed him to retire and settle on his estate, Mon Repos, near Vyborg, which he had acquired in 1787.[26] This was Finnish territory which Sweden had ceded to Russia by the Treaty of Nystad in 1721.

Although he must have found life at the Russian court very fulfilling, von Nicolay had always dreamed of a simple life in the country. In a poem, *Das Landgut* (*The Country Seat*), published in 1778, he had asked Fortune to grant him two small hills, framing a peaceful valley with woods, winding streams and green meadows, and with rocks and the sea near by:

> O Schicksal, räume mir zwey kleine Hügel ein,
> Die, ungleich hingestreckt, ein stilles Thal verbauen,
> Lass sie nicht ohne Wald, nicht ohne Quelle seyn. . . .
> So laufe leicht gekrümmt, voll geschlängter Bäche,
> In beyder Hügel Schoss die lange Wiese hin;
> Jedoch ein krauser Baum, ein Weg, ein Brücklein breche,
> Zufällig angebracht, der Wiese fettes Grün. . . .
> Ein andrer Ausgang führt dem gesuchten Strande
> Zum malerischen See, der mein Gebiet beschliest.
> Hier nagt er trüb und laut am dunklen Felsenrande,
> Da er, wie flüssig Glas, die Blumen dort begiesst.[27]

Fortune treated him well. Mon Repos, near Vyborg, is on the very rocky and extremely picturesque island of Linnasaari, four kilometres long and joined to the mainland by a bridge. There were only small farmsteads there until the late 1750s when Peter von Stupischen, the Governor of Vyborg, decided to acquire part of it and to make a summer residence there. He built a house and an orangery, laid out a landscape garden and changed the name from Lill-Ladugard to Charlottendahl, in honour of his wife, Charlotte. After the death of Stupischen in 1782 the property seems to have been acquired from his beneficiaries in 1784 on behalf of Catherine, who bestowed it on Prince Friedrich of Württemberg, Maria Fyodorovna's brother, who had been appointed Governor of Vyborg. Sharing his sister's experience of outstanding family gardens and her enthusiasm for making new ones, he embarked on an ambitious programme of improvements. He acquired a further forty acres, built a new residence, a large new orangery, a gardener's house, stables, a coach house and other outbuildings. New paths were made, many trees – mainly limes but some oak and birch – were planted, pavilions were built, and the name was changed to Mon Repos. But he left Russia in 1797 and returned to Württemberg (he was to become King there in 1806), selling the estate to von Nicolay.[28] It was the perfect answer to the latter's dreams, and he wrote to his son Paul, who was at school at Eutin in north Germany, about his purchase:

Right, above: Design for a Birch Prospect Tower at Mon Repos.

Right: The British architect Charles Heathcote Tatum designed a 'Saxon-Gothic Tower' for the island which became known as Ludwigstein, where Ludwig and Johanna von Nicolay and a number of their descendants were buried.

a fine large house with many good outbuildings, also a good road, with trees planted on both sides, between here and the town. . . . Behind the house there's a large garden with an orangery, and all near to the sea, with some islands which belong to it, and beyond only bare romantic rocks. … You will be very pleased with it. You will have a lot to lay out and plant when you come here. The garden converges with the sea. One part of the garden has large rocks and trees, quite wild, and really appropriate English paths wind through them, and one of them leads onto a cliff which stands out quite precipitately against the sea, and there's a wonderful view to enjoy from it. I shall build a little temple of Apollo there. On the left hand side of the garden there's a fine rose field, which is enclosed on one side by a stone wall so high that the deer can't jump over it. On the sea side there's an island with a rock face, much higher than in the garden. You reach it by a bridge and climb by steps to the top. The view from there is quite different. But there are other islands without rocks but with nice turf and plenty of trees. You get to them by boat.[29]

Von Nicolay was well equipped to undertake the further development of his park. He had visited many parks and gardens in western Europe, had been closely involved with the development of the parks at Pavlovsk and Gatchina, and would have been well acquainted with Tsarskoe Selo, Peterhof and other parks in the vicinity of St Petersburg. In addition he was widely read on the subject. He had a remarkable library of 10,000 volumes at Mon Repos, which he and Franz Lafermière

The coastline of the island abounds with granite rocks.

had collected together from their student days with the understanding that it would finally be the property of whichever of them survived the other. Among the British authors represented in English editions were Milton, Pope, Shenstone, Gray, Thomson, James Macpherson, William Gilpin, William Mason, Horace Walpole, Humphry Repton (*An Enquiry into the Changes of Taste in Landscape Gardening*), William Chambers and Richard Payne Knight, and there were several architectural works with designs for garden features.[30] Works in French included Jacques Delille's *Les Jardins* and C.C.L. Hirschfeld's *Théorie de l'art des jardins.* There were copies of Edmund Burke's *A Philosophical Enquiry into the Origin of our Ideas of the Sublime and the Beautiful* in both English and French.[31] Von Nicolay's books are now in Helsinki University Library.

His first years at Mon Repos had to be devoted to preliminary work. Vast quantities of stone were used to form a rampart to keep out cattle from the relatively small area of the island which was not part of his property. To prevent seawater reaching the garden, two long dams were built from the island granite (which also provided fifty-six columns for the interior of Kazan Cathedral in St Petersburg). An extensive area around the residential buildings had to be cleared of stone. Many birch trees and some limes and oaks were planted in the park. An admirable gardener, Bisterfeld, was appointed. To help with the planning and development von Nicolay invited an old friend from Italy, G.A. Martinelli, to Mon Repos, where he spent several months in 1798. Martinelli was a painter and picture restorer, who had spent eight years working at the Hermitage. He designed and helped construct a number of features in the park and contributed to changes to the house. Marble statues of Jupiter, Neptune and dolphins are known to have been obtained for von Nicolay from Italy by Vincenzo Brenna, who may also have been the source of other sculpture at Mon Repos – Cupid, Apollo, Bacchus, Narcissus, a head of Medusa and a Pietas.[32]

Near the gateway to the property a viewing platform was constructed on a high rock with a large Chinese parasol – an idea of Paul's – perhaps not so much to protect those viewing from the sun as to indicate to approaching visitors that they were getting near to their destination. Beyond the gateway the road passed large, formally laid-out vegetable and fruit gardens, an orangery, a farmhouse, cowsheds, stables and a coach-house. Before reaching the courtyard and von Nicolay's residence there was a formal flower garden for rare plants and cut flowers. Prince Friedrich's house had been extended and given a wooden façade in Palladian style, which did not meet with universal approval, but the interior was admired. On the north and east sides of the house there were lawns with flowerbeds, marble busts, shrubs and trees and then the park and the sea. One of the flowerbeds had arches for climbing plants, perhaps influenced by Repton, as the Finnish garden historian Eeva Ruoff has suggested.[33]

Von Nicolay's guests were usually taken on a tour of the western side of the park in the morning and the eastern side in the afternoon, a division designed to make the best use of the light. The morning tour began with the monument to Franz Lafermière, who had died in 1795 on the estate of Count Semyon Vorontsov, where he was buried. The monument was a gift from Maria Fyodorovna and bore the inscription *Monument d'estime, confié a l'amitié*. Von Nicolay intended to be buried near by. Not far beyond the monument, Paulstein, the first pavilion he added to the park, served as his study.

A well-spring was the setting for a love story in verse by von Nicolay, featuring a beautiful nymph, Sylmia, the *genius loci* of Mon Repos, and Lahrs, a goatherd, representing the poet, blinded by his tears. After renouncing his love for Sylmia the water from the well restored his eyesight. Auguste de Montferrand, the architect of St Isaac's Cathedral in St Petersburg, designed a framework for the well-spring with a marble statue of Narcissus reclining on a stone bench by a small granite bowl and a larger marble bowl, from where a stream was

formed to carry the water to the sea. It was believed that it had curative properties.

A hermit's hut with a thatched roof, hidden from sight by densely planted trees, was another contribution from Paul. And then, at the furthest point of the park, World's End was reached, not signalled by a column as at Pavlovsk, but just massive rocks overhanging the sea.

A statue of Apollo met those who crossed the bridge to Mon Repos's largest neighbouring island, but it did not announce the kind of pastoral scene usually associated with Apollo. The island, with its vertiginous rock faces and often rough seas, was then

Right: The Chinese Pavilion, *der Marienturm*, which Maria Fyodorovna gave to her brother, Prince Friedrich of Württemberg, probably in the 1780s. Engraving by L.-J. Jacottet (*c*.1840).

Below: An enormous erratic boulder in the area of the park known as Pampuschinka, Joanna von Nicolay's name for Paul when he was an infant. Lithograph by L.-J. Jacottet (*c*.1840).

called Erichstein, because von Nicolay intended to build a castle-ruin there, where the ghost of the mad King Erik XIV, who ruled Sweden from 1560 to 1568, might rage his way through time. This was never built, but there was a Grotto of Medusa where her sculpted head was displayed. The sentimental visitor was expected to feel some trepidation here. A classical temple with the Roman deity Pietas on the peninsula east of Erichstein offered a return to tranquillity.

The first feature on the eastern side of the park was another temple, the Temple of Love. The problems of love are clearly underlined by placing it next to a towering rock representing the Leucadian rock, from which Sappho flung herself when her love for Phaeon went unrequited.

The Chinese pavilion – *der Marienturm* – which Maria Fyodorovna had given to her brother for the park, remained one of its most striking features. Above its unmistakably Chinese roof was a small viewing platform, approached by a long external flight of wooden steps, with its own small Chinese roof with a weather-cock in the form of a dragon. Maria Fyodorovna had personally decorated the interior of the pavilion in Pompeian style,[34] where visitors were protected against the elements by glazed windows. Near by, in an elevated position on a peninsula, a tall Tuscan column was erected bearing the inscription *Caesar nobis haec otia fecit* ('the emperor made possible this repose' – a variation of *Deus nobis haec otia fecit*, in the first of Virgil's *Eclogues*), which was an expression of thanks to the emperors Paul and Alexander for making possible his peaceful and fulfilling retirement. At the northern end of this peninsula, an enormous erratic boulder, resting quite safely but apparently precariously on a slope, was one of the sights of the park shown to visitors. This area of the park was called Pampuschinka, which was Johanna von Nicolay's pet name for Paul when he was an infant.[35] On a small island linked to the south of the peninsula by a path along a dam, a Turkish tent was placed by the water's edge, another spot to rest and enjoy the view.

Von Nicolay wrote a long poem about Mon Repos, *Das Landgut Monrepos in Finnland*, which was published in Berlin in 1804, with a detailed plan, as a guide to the park. In it he discussed theories of park and garden making, gave an account of the work involved in transforming his park, described the features that had been created and those which he still intended to add. He continued to live there happily until 1820, when Johanna's death was followed by his death soon afterwards at the age of eighty-two.

Paul von Nicolay had always taken a keen interest in the development of the garden. When he was still at school he had followed its progress not only in the letters of his parents but by corresponding with Bisterfeld, the gardener. After completing his studies at the University of Erlangen he entered the diplomatic service and worked with distinction in the Russian embassies in London (where he became a close friend of the Vorontsovs), Stockholm and Copenhagen. The Order of St Anne and the title of Baron were conferred on him. While working

abroad he travelled to Mon Repos as often as he could and spent all his retirement there.[36]

After the death of his parents he was granted special permission to bury them on the island which had been called Erichstein and now became Ludwigstein. The monument to Lafermière was moved from its original position and placed near by. In 1822 the British architect Charles Heathcote Tatum (1771–1842) designed a 'Saxon-Gothic Tower', which was built on the island. Busts of Ludwig and his wife were placed in a small hall, where there was also a table and a visitors' book. Paul's wife, Princess Alexandrine de Broglie, died in childbirth in Copenhagen in 1824 and she was buried near to his parents. Ludwigstein was to be the burial place for members of the family for decades to come.

When the Temple of Love, which was of wooden construction, showed considerable signs of wear Paul chose not to renew it. In 1827 he had an obelisk, also designed by Tatum, erected in its place in memory of his brothers-in-law, Auguste de Broglie and Charles de Broglie, who had fallen in the war against Napoleon at Austerlitz in 1805 and Kulm in 1813.[37]

The distinguished Russian scholar Dmitri Likhachev (1906–97) believed that two Russian parks, Mon Repos and Alupka, were influenced by Ossianism and thought that Sophievka in Ukraine may also have been. In 1762 James Macpherson published *Fingal, an Ancient Epic Poem* 'composed by Ossian, the Son of Fingal, translated from the Gaelic Language'. It celebrated the heroic deeds of brave warriors in battles long ago, fought in wild northern landscapes. Although its authenticity was questioned, and much of it may well be an original composition of Macpherson's, it took Europe by storm. Translated into numerous languages, it had considerable influence on the Romantic movement in literature and art. It inspired Byron and Hugo, and Goethe considered Ossian to be greater than Homer. It also inspired Russian poets, among them Derzhavin, Zhukovsky, Kuchelbecker, Pushkin and Lermontov.[38]

Parks, too, came under the influence of Ossian. In the Scottish picturesque park at Dunkeld there was formerly an elaborately theatrical shrine with a 'picture of the aged Ossian, singing, and some female figures listening to tales of the days that are past', with Ossian's Cave and Ossian's Seat near by. Hawkstone, in Shropshire, with its vertiginous cliffs, Red Castle, Giant's Well, Awful Precipice and its Hermitage, may be seen to provide a suitable haunt for the ghosts of ancient heroes. The best example of Ossianic influence on a park was at Alton Abbey (later Alton Towers) in Staffordshire, where the 15th Earl of

An engraving (1874) of the statue of Väinämöinen, a hero of early Finnish folk poetry, which was influenced by illustrations of Ossian in early editions of the Ossian poems by James Macpherson. It was the work of the Finnish sculptor Takanen and survived until the late 1930s.

Shrewsbury must have had Ossian in mind when he installed a blind Welsh harper (Ossian, too, was blind) and planted Scotch pines on Ina's Rock, towering above the woodland drive, near the site of a fierce battle fought in AD 716 between Ceolred and Ina, the kings of Mercia and Wessex. The entrance hall of the Abbey was 'hung round with swords, spears, helmets, shields and various other implements of war [and] here, seated in an ancient gothic chair, may generally be found an old Welsh bard, the minstrel of the mansion, habited in a picturesque costume, striking his harp to songs of other days.' In the armoury beyond were the figures of fifty knights, armed to the teeth and surrounded by assorted weaponry, all dimly lit by the light from stained-glass windows. 'Nothing is palpably and distinctly seen, but sufficient is developed to fill the mind with images of days, and scenes and customs long since departed.'[39] And just across the valley of the Churnet there were the remains of the ancestral castle 'with its stern-looking embattled walls, calling to mind those bygone days when the "stout Lord Talbot" rode to the wars with all his mighty following of knights, esquires and men-at-arms'.[40] On the other side of the garden the druidical monument, inspired by Stonehenge, evoked a more distant past. 'This gloomy structure, the powerful characteristic of a barbarous age, carries the mind irresistibly back to the era of fable, when all was dark, uncertain, and savage.'[41]

'Typical Ossianic landscape, which influenced parks and gardens of the end of the eighteenth and beginning of the nineteenth centuries, was exhibited by wild, rocky Scotland with its rocks, waterfalls, firs, oaks and pines. In the Russian empire the role of the northern wild and freedom-loving country, analogous to Scotland in Great Britain, was played by Finland.

. . . And so for Russian poets Finland was their own Scotland. It is therefore natural that the park at Mon Repos was created at the end of the eighteenth and beginning of the nineteenth centuries in the spirit of the poetry of Ossian,' argued Likhachev.[42]

The *Kalevala* was a collection of early Finnish folk poetry, relating heroic and supernatural deeds, which had been passed on orally from generation to generation. During the first half of the nineteenth century, perhaps inspired by the example of Ossian, it was collected from the lips of peasants by Elias Lönnrot, who organized and welded together thousands of verses from a wide range of sources into a single cohesive work which was published in 1849. There were translations into English, Swedish, German and French. Longfellow used the metre of the German translation for *Hiawatha*. The Kalevala were the three sons of Kaleva (Finland) – the ancient Väinämöinen, inventor of the sacred harp Kantele, Lemminkainen and Ilmarinen. Paul von Nicolay probably had Ossian in mind when he installed a statue of Väinämöinen in a particularly rocky part of the park at Mon Repos. In a Finnish article, illustrations of Ossian, taken from early editions of the poems, and later illustrations of Väinämöinen, each with a harp and with his left arm raised, demonstrate the influence of the former on the latter in the posture of the body.[43] The statue of Väinämöinen at Mon Repos was certainly reminiscent of images of Ossian. To this extent Likhachev was right in claiming Ossianic influence at Mon Repos, but there seems to be nothing to suggest that Ludwig von Nicolay set out to create Ossianic scenes, although he had a copy of the Ossian poems in his library.[44]

Mon Repos survived unspoilt well into the twentieth century. There were desendants of Ludwig von Nicolay living there until 1939, although most of the property had been nationalized by the Finnish government in 1921. In 1940 it became part of the Soviet Union. It suffered little damage during the war, but from 1945 it was used as a military rest home and the park buildings were wantonly damaged and pillaged for materials. In 1954 Mon Repos became the Kalinin Park of Culture and Rest, which amounted to state vandalism and ensured much further damage to one of the great cultural monuments of Europe. More recently the park has suffered from rock climbing and motocross. Some restoration was undertaken in the 1990s, but much still needs to be done, and sufficient funds should be made available.

Alexandria, Aleksandrinsky, Kolonistsky and Lugovoi Parks
Several new landscape parks for the private use of the imperial family appeared at Peterhof during the first half of the nineteenth century. The park called Alexandria in honour of Alexandra Fyodorovna, the wife of Nicholas I, is situated on the coast between Peterhof and Strelna and covers 285 acres. In 1825, shortly before his death, Alexander had given the land to Nicholas, who was to succeed him, and the Scottish architect Adam Menelaws was chosen to lay out the park. He was assisted by the gardeners F. Wendelsdorf, P. Rodionov, A.I. Gombel and,

later, P.I. Erler with a large workforce. Two pools were formed, thousands of trees were planted, and the result was soon romantic and picturesque, with walks which offered constantly changing views. In the park there were busts of Peter I and Alexander I and a marble column in memory of the daughter of Alexandra and Nicholas, also Alexandra, who died young.

Menelaws was then commissioned to build for Alexandra, on a terrace facing the Gulf of Finland, the Cottage Palace, a substantial, English-inspired seaside villa with gothic features.

Top: An early view of the Cottage Palace at Peterhof, designed by the Scottish architect Adam Menelaws for the Empress Alexandra, wife of Nicholas I.

Above: The Cottage Palace following restoration after the 1941–5 war.

He also designed the furniture and much of the interior detail, where gothic was much more in evidence. After the death of Menelaws, Stakenschneider extended the building and added a terrace with a fountain. There was a flower garden with a pavilion, and these had wonderful views of the Gulf.

Menelaws also designed the farm which was subsequently transformed by Stakenschneider into the Farm Palace. It has been described as 'English Gothic', but it was less gothic than the Cottage Palace. It had a splendid flower garden, enclosed on three sides by a pergola in which a statue of Night was placed. Near by, buildings for children were added – a traditional *izba* (wooden house), a watchtower and a fortress with trenches and cannon.

The other major building in the park is K.F. Schinkel's impressive Gothic Alexander Nevsky Chapel. The Cottage Palace and the Gothic Chapel have been restored.[45]

South of Alexandria, the Aleksandrinsky Park, again called after the Empress, was landscaped by Menelaws. It was planted with a variety of conifers and some groves of oaks. The main feature was a large artificially formed lake with inlets and promontories and three islands. There was a metal pavilion with a bust of Alexandra Fyodorovna and a flower garden on one of the islands, and a Swiss Cottage by I.I. Charlemagne on another. These buildings have not survived. In 1917 the name was changed to Proletarsky Park.[46]

Below: The ferry across to Tsarina's Island.

Bottom: The Lugovoi (Meadow) Park with natural landscape, the water course leading from Ropsha to the Peterhof fountains and associated pools.

The Kolonistsky Park owed its name to German immigrants who had settled there. In the 1830s a marshy area was drained and the large Olgin Pool was formed (called after Nicholas's daughter Olga), which provided water for some of the fountains in the Lower Park. There were two islands in the pool, each with a large pavilion, the Olgin Pavilion and the Tsarina's Pavilion. The latter was of considerable interest because it was an attempt to reproduce a Roman villa, inspired by the archaeological excavations at Pompeii. Marble and mosaic were lavishly used in the atrium, exedra and peristyle, and a small interior garden featured a marble seat with legs in the form of an animal's paws. Outside on the terrace a marble Narcissus sat at the centre of a marble basin with a fountain, surrounded by formal areas of grass and flowers.[47]

A path, 1¼ miles long, leads from the Upper Park to the Lugovoi (Meadow) Park, following the iron water-conduit which feeds the Peterhof fountains. In the second half of the nineteenth century the architect Stakenschneider, the engineer Mieczyslaw Pilsudski and the master gardeners P.I. Erler and P.G. Arkhipov all contributed to the park, which comprised open fields, natural landscape with wide stretches of water and buildings with gardens. The water course, eventually leading to Ropsha twelve or so miles away, is the main axis. In 1835 Stakenschneider created Nicholas's idealized, traditionally decorated, Russian wooden house, which served as a place of rest during imperial rambles. It still survives but without much of its carved decoration. Stakenschneider's Ozerki or Rose Pavilion followed ten years later with more echoes of ancient Roman and Greek architecture, a terrace with statues and vases, and a landscape park with three pools, picturesque groups of trees and winding paths. The pavilion was devastated during the German occupation. The Ruin Pool was formed in 1851 to Pilsudsky's plan, and an artificial ruin of the remains of a Greek temple, designed by Stakenschneider with guidance from Nicholas's sketches, was erected on a hill on an island, with pieces of masonry scattered on the slopes. This was another casualty of the war, though some of it may lie buried beneath self-sown trees and undergrowth.

The most important building in the park was Stakenschneider's Belvedere Palace (1850s), again prompted by Nicholas. This was built on a hill at the end of the park, ensuring wide-ranging views. It is a two-storey building, with the upper floor in the form of an ancient Greek temple, partly supported by caryatids. It was richly embellished with statues and vases and furnished in Grecian style. The garden of formal flowerbeds, which accompanied an earlier building on the site, was retained. After 1917 the Belvedere Palace, which had served as a place of rest and refreshment for the imperial family, became a rest home for workers. Restoration has been in progress for many years. The St Alexandra Church near by, which was set in a small garden of shrubs and winding paths, has not been restored.[48]

Right: The Belvedere Palace during restoration.

Opposite
Top: The ruin on the island.

Middle: The church with its small garden.

Bottom: The Belvedere Palace and the garden associated with it in the nineteenth century.

7

LANDSCAPE PARKS IN AND AROUND MOSCOW

We saw in Chapter Three that Count Nikolai Sheremetev lost interest in Kuskovo and turned his attention to his other Moscow estate, Ostankino. His main interest at Kuskovo had been the theatre, where his wife and former serf, Praskovya Kovalyova, was the leading actress and singer, and at Ostankino, in the 1790s, he built a palace which was also an exceptional theatre with a sculpture gallery and a picture gallery to serve as foyers.

The estate had a long history. Before the end of the sixteenth century there were groves of oaks and Siberian cedars, and in 1646 the then owner, Prince Cherkassky, Count Nikolai's ancestor on his mother's side, had three gardeners. During the early decades of the eighteenth century the garden covered 5 acres, and there were seven gardeners and two apprentices. A new formal garden was laid out during the second half of the century, but the orangeries were the most impressive feature. In 1761, after Johann Manstadt was appointed head gardener, an inventory was taken of the garden. There were then five wooden orangeries, and in them and in the open ground there were many lemon and orange trees, bay trees, myrtles, almonds, mulberries, fig trees, pomegranates, nuts of various kinds, oleanders, olives, apricots, pears, 'London' apples, foreign plums, grapevines, pineapples and eleven hotbeds with melons and watermelons. Espaliered paths featured gooseberries, barberries and cherries; and in the vegetable garden there were about five hundred beds of vegetables, strawberries and more than a thousand currant bushes. In the flower garden there were about a thousand rose bushes as well as jasmine, carnations, phlox, stocks, narcissi and tulips. There were supplies in abundance for Kuskovo and plenty to spare, with Catherine and Potemkin among the beneficiaries.[1]

Count Nikolai's new palace needed a new garden and park, and his serf architect A. Mironov produced a plan for what would have been a largely formal garden. Sheremetev saw the plan as old-fashioned and inappropriate in the 1790s and turned instead to his other serf architect P. Argunov, under the direction from time to time of Francis Reid. Now that the park at Tsaritsyno was approaching completion there was less work there for Reid, and he was allowed to accept other commissions. He was involved at Ostankino from 1792 to 1794 and was assisted by a very efficient serf gardener, Nikolai Kuverin. In 1796 another British gardener, Robert Manners, was engaged by Sheremetev and remained there for more than thirty years. He was twice sent to England to buy plants.[2]

Reid was responsible for the space near the palace, which was landscaped as an area of mown grass of irregular shape, with winding paths, groves, shrubberies and larches planted singly. It was no longer bordered by clipped trees but by freely spreading maples and limes. A quantity of treillage, which had been recently installed at considerable cost, was discarded. One small formally planned area was retained, but the vegetable garden was dispensed with.

A view of the park at Kuzminki, from *Vidy sela Vlakherinskovo* (*Views of Vlakherinsky Village*), engraved by André Durand from J.N. Rauch's watercolour.

Robert Manners laid out the rest of the park. Among the most picturesque features were the River Kamenka and the eight pools formed from it and stocked with fish. A large pool was excavated at the centre of the park, and the spoil was used to form Mount Parnassus, surmounted by an eight-columned roofless rotunda-ruin. Elsewhere in the park stood a temple, designed by Mironov, with a cupola and a four-columned portico displaying statues of Apollo and Venus in niches by the sides of the entrance. Inside the temple the statue of a weeping woman by an urn was the work of Triscorni.

When an inventory was taken in 1810 following the death of Count Nikolai there were 6,000 plants in the orangeries, and Ostankino continued to flourish for a time, but in the 1830s it was neglected and fell into decline. 'Lamps and coloured lanterns no longer illumine the English paths, now overgrown with grass, where myrtles and orange trees used to be set out,' wrote Pushkin after a visit.[3] By the end of the nineteenth century dachas were being built, as at Kuskovo, on part of the park and flowers were grown for sale in the orangeries. In 1917 Ostankino was put under state protection and became a State Museum of Serf Art in the following year. Though an area of modest size is retained by the museum, much of the Sheremetevs' former estate is now covered by the Dzerzhinsky Park of Culture and Rest, the Exhibition of Economic Achievements and the Botanical Gardens; while the palace, once architecturally dominant in the area, has been overwhelmed by the Cosmos Hotel, multistoried residential blocks and, above all, the Ostankino television tower.[4]

Yaropolets

At least the palace with its theatre survived at Ostankino and is well maintained for its present purpose. Of the hundreds of other former estates around Moscow the great majority have fared much worse, while Kuskovo and Arkhangelskoe are two of very few with restored parks and gardens. To discover what the rest were like in their heyday we must rely on contemporary descriptions, where they exist, on the archival research of mainly Russian garden historians and on the reports of enthusiastic researchers during the early Soviet period, who organized site visits and recorded what they found in *Sredi kollektsionerov* (*Among Collectors*). Many of them later paid dearly for their enthusiasm at a time when political incorrectness could result in a life sentence, as we shall see later.

In 1684 the village of Yaropolets, about sixty miles west of Moscow, was given to the Ukrainian hetman, P.F. Doroshenko, and then, in 1698, it was divided between his two sons. As a result there are two estates: in the south, Yaropolets of the Goncharovs, who acquired it in 1823, and in the north, Yaropolets of the Chernyshevs, which was acquired in the 1760s by Field Marshal Z.G. Chernyshev, who fought in the Seven Years' War and became Governor-general of Moscow.

During the second half of the eighteenth century the southern estate belonged to the Zagryazhskys, who replaced the existing wooden residence with a palace in Russian classical style, combining brick and white stone. In contrast, the entrance gates in the form of two towers, the composition of the *cour d'honneur*, part of the park wall and its towers, and the farm buildings are neo-gothic, perhaps inspired by Tsaritsyno. There were formal gardens in front of the palace and beyond them a large pool and a landscape park with park buildings extending to the banks of the River Lama. During the German occupation in 1941 the interior of the palace suffered considerable damage, including the room with its furniture where Pushkin stayed during visits to his mother-in-law. (His wife was a Goncharov.) The park was also badly damaged and the park buildings were destroyed.[5]

The Chernyshevs' imposing palace (perhaps by Pyotr Nikitin) with its formal garden was inspired by French architecture, which led to it being called the Russian Versailles. Axially laid out, the main axis linked the palace with the church (perhaps by Kazakov) and the line of the main avenue. Three terraces, with many lime trees and embellished with sculpture, descended to an excavated lake. An obelisk on the central terrace commemorated Catherine's visit to the estate in 1775.

There were many ornamental buildings in the landscape park, among them a Temple of Friendship, a Temple of Solitude, a bath house in Pompeian style, a building in the form of a mosque to celebrate the Russian victory against the Turks in 1774, an obelisk in honour of Field Marshal Pyotr Rumyantsev's rôle in that success, and a number of inscribed marble tombs robbed from a Turkish cemetery as war booty by Field Marshal Y.V. Dolgoruky and given to Chernyshev.[6] A temple dedicated to Catherine in a pine grove above the lake was reminiscent of the mausoleum to Paul at Pavlovsk. It was still well preserved in 1924, although the bust of Catherine was no longer there. The palace was then a hospital and the garden and park were completely overgrown, but the visitor who recorded this was still able to write: 'Anyone who ventures to these distant parts will experience great aesthetic pleasure.'[7] The park buildings were destroyed during the German occupation and the palace and other buildings suffered great damage.[8]

Chernyshev's brother Ivan, who was Russian ambassador in London from 1768 to 1769, planned to reproduce Lord Lyttelton's Hagley in Russia when he returned. Lord Lyttelton wrote in December 1770 to his architect, Sanderson Miller:

My dear Miller,

Count Czernichen, whom I entertained at Hagley last Summer was twelvemonth, when he was Russian Embassador at our Court, is going to build a Country House, and has writt me to beg a Plan of mine, which, he says, is the best he has seen in all his extensive Travels. As this does you great Honour, I hope you will not grudge the Trouble of sending it to him. He should have the Elevation of the four Fronts, with Plans of the three Stories distinctly marking the Dimensions of the several rooms. Those you gave to me are lost having been sent to the King and never returned.[9]

It would be interesting to know if a second Hagley ever appeared in Russia and, if so, what setting was provided for it. The house which had been built in 1762 for Chernyshev, on his estate by the Peterhof Road, was by the French architect, Vallin de la Mothe, and a view is preserved in a drawing by Quarenghi. It stood at the top of a slope above a pool and was in Russian classical style. The central block, with a columned portico and belvedere, was joined by glazed galleries to two identical wings.[10]

Otrada

The estate at Otrada, some 50 miles south of Moscow, was established by Vladimir Orlov, a younger brother of Catherine's favourite, Grigory Orlov. Educated at Leipzig University, Orlov's interest in science led to his appointment as Director of the Academy of Sciences to support its President, Count Razumovsky. After the fall from favour of the Orlovs, he was happy to retire to Otrada to develop his estate with its impressive residence, service buildings, church dedicated to St Vladimir, orangeries and English park.

He had visited England in 1772 when the English approach to landscaping had greatly impressed him, and he wrote in his diary: 'In making gardens the English try to imitate nature and to conceal the work which is necessary, and which is often more difficult than in formal gardens. In their gardens everything is scattered about – here a wood, there a copse, somewhere else a pool.'[11]

He employed a gardener from abroad, Piterman, and, in 1787, to make a plan for the whole area, he 'called in the British gardener-specialist from Tsaritsyno', which would have been Francis Reid. Streams and pools were formed from the abundant sources of water on the estate and were stocked with trout and sterlet. Encircled by tall trees, the Swan Pool with its island was considered to be the most picturesque. The pools were excavated by Turkish prisoners of war.

To add to the attractions of the park Orlov introduced nightingales. To get as near as possible to English models he acquired deer, but he seems to have overlooked the rigours of the Russian winter, which soon accounted for them.

Among the architectural features of the park were numerous pavilions, summerhouses and a picturesque farm. Between the church and the palace a bronze bust of Catherine stood on a tall plinth with the inscription 'Catherine the Great, benefactress of the Orlovs'. Large cast-iron lions on brick pillars stood on guard by one of the gates to the palace, while another gate was embellished with eagles (the name Orlov being derived from the Russian word for eagle). The garden by the palace was said to be 'enclosed by magnificent iron railings in the spirit of Versailles'.[12]

On the eve of the Revolution it was still possible to write: 'More than a century has passed, and the founder of Otrada and his brilliant brothers have long lain in eternal sleep, but, thanks to the solicitude of their descendants, the estate from the time of Catherine preserves with care and pride the memory of the first owner.'[13]

The Gardens of Nikolai Lvov

Nikolai Lvov (1751–1804), in addition to his many other talents, was both architect and landscape architect, and he worked in one or both capacities on many Russian estates, as well as designing churches and cathedrals. The work he did on his own estate, Nikolskoe-Cherenchitsy, some 120 miles north of Moscow, is instructive, since as architect and owner he was able to make all the decisions without having to debate them with a client. It was a fairly modest estate, his home since childhood, and there were no special landscape features.

Like Andrei Bolotov, who will be considered in the next chapter, Lvov believed that Russia needed neither English gardens nor French gardens but distinctively Russian gardens. He favoured the landscape style, but with some formality near the house, and that was his approach here. The new house, courtyard, orchard, rectangular pool and entrance drive were formally planned, but the rest was simply landscaped and followed the natural relief of the land. The south front of the house on a small hill had extensive views of meadows, ploughed fields and woods, while the porticoed north front looked across grassland and trees to pools and a cascade. Poplars, limes, willows, birch and larch were planted singly and in small groups in order not to impede the more distant rural views.

Lvov believed in combining utility with ornament. The ice house was beneath a pyramid; a grotto was also a bath; and a smithy was a picturesque structure of massive stonework with arched vaults, from where the furnace could add a romantic glow to the night sky. Other buildings included a pavilion-rotunda, a beaten-earth tower (the material we saw Lvov use at Gatchina), and the outstanding and surviving mausoleum with its cupola and surrounding colonnade. There were also agricultural buildings.

At Mutino, another modest property near Torzhok, Lvov built the house on a promontory, high above the River Tvertsa. Near by, a stream flowed through a series of excavated pools and cascaded into the river. There was a small formal garden by the house and, as at Nikolskoe, a smithy with arched vaults, built of rough stonework, and a pyramid, in this case over a wine cellar.[14]

A more important commission was at Vvedenskoe, 37 miles west of Moscow, where he built a large classical residence with two detached wings for Prince P.V. Lopukhin; he also built the church and laid out the park. It is an exceptional site, high above the River Moskva. After seeing it in winter Lvov wrote to Lopukhin:

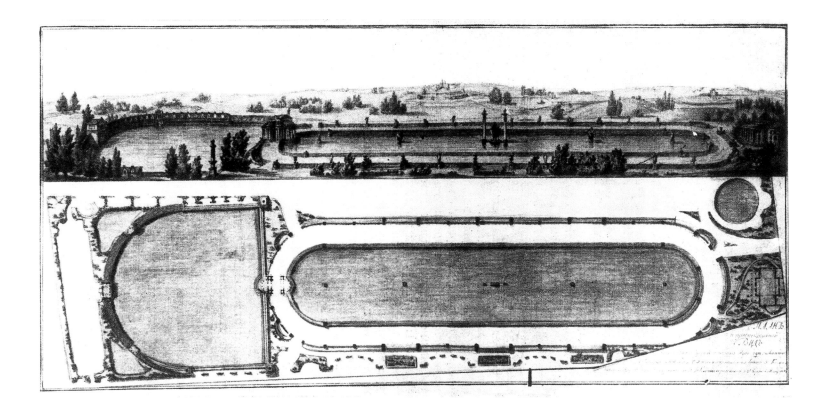

Lvov's plan (c.1798) to transform two large pools
into an arena where the games of ancient Greece
could be recreated.

Your property at Vvedenskoe is of such a kind that I was
quite overcome with delight, when, standing on the hill,
I looked down on the estate, where you had decided to
have the house built. What must it be like in summer?
When we take the work in hand, this place must become
the best of all the seats near Moscow. As regards Nature,
she has in fact done all she could, and yet left plenty for
the artist to do to show his talent.

He had looked for and found a supply of water which could be
brought to the site:

> In the park and on your cattle-farm there will be
> fountains everywhere; beside your house there will be
> magnificent cascades. . . . Take my word, the beautiful
> site of the place will be absolutely incomparable, all will
> come alive and be moving. I feel that romantic views
> without water can have only the beauty of a dead place.[15]

Iljin describes how Lvov planted pines in clusters on the sides
of the slope down to the river:

> This method of planting provides, during the subsequent
> strong growth of the crowns, the gigantic 'bouquets'
> which are so well known. So a kind of scenic wings was
> provided, distinguished by their silhouettes and strong
> colours, so necessary in the northward-facing situation
> of the park and house. Deciduous trees along the
> boundaries of the 'bouquets' accompanied the silhouettes
> to the level of the ground, covering the bare and reddish
> trunks of the pines.[16]

A vista was made through the park to focus on the splendid
distant view of the Savvin-Storozhevsky monastery at
Zvenigorod. On the other side of the house there was a birch
avenue, 1¼ miles in length, accompanied by formal planting.[17]

At Voronovo, 60 miles south-west of Moscow, Lvov designed
the palace for I.I. Vorontsov and extended the park in
landscape style with a series of terraces descending to a large
pool with an island. There were numerous small architectural
features – arbours, grottoes, pavilions – but only the Dutch
House, which was not by Lvov but Karl Blank, has survived. In
1812 the then owner, F.V. Rostopchin, the Governor of Moscow,
put a torch to his palace as the French army approached.[18]

Lvov's most remarkable plan for a park and garden was the
one he produced between 1797 and 1799 for the estate of Count
Alexander Bezborodko, Chancellor of the Russian Empire, by
the River Yauza in Moscow, where Giacomo Quarenghi was to
build the palace. Unfortunately Bezborodko died in 1799 and
nothing was realized; but eleven of Lvov's drawings of features
for the park have survived along with his explanatory text. He
again set out to combine the teachings of Kent and Le Nôtre,
and to bring together natural beauty and urban splendour.
The terraces in front of the palace were to be formal and
embellished by flights of steps, statues, flowing water, cascades
and the green of specially selected trees. Lvov chose to be
guided by

symmetry's little sister, leaving the big sister on the throne in Holland with her destructive sceptre made of scissors, with which, having mutilated myrtles, palms and even cypresses, she turned trees into bears, pyramids and dolphins, and filled our gardens with inert green monsters, which had become neither stumps nor trees.[19]

He promised that visitors would not be bored by finding that one half of the garden was a mirror image of the other half. Instead the overall outline would be formal, but there would be a variety of detail.

In the extensive area by the river there were two very large pools, part of an earlier garden, one square and the other a long rectangle. They were separated by a narrow strip of land, and it was Lvov's extraordinary ambition to transform them into an arena for the recreated games of ancient Greece. The square pool would become a semicircular *naumachia*, framed by an amphitheatre, for aquatic sports and mock sea battles. Two rostral columns would support beacons to illuminate the games when they took place after dark, and they could also be used for firework displays. In winter the pool would serve as a skating rink. The second pool would be divided into lanes for gondola races, and each lane would be terminated by a trophy serving as a reminder of a Russian naval victory. This pool would be at the centre of the hippodrome and surrounded by a track for chariot races.

On the central strip between the *naumachia* and the hippodrome would be two triumphal gates, through which the athletes would pass before competing. There would also be a temple displaying the busts of Russian heroes who had gained victories at sea, which would accommodate important guests as well as the judges who would make awards to the victors in the games.

A large area of the estate was to be landscaped, and, while Lvov venerated nature, a contribution from the landscape architect would also be necessary to open up vistas, to make groves either more or less shady, to dam streams in order to form pools, to make the fringes of woods more picturesque and to plant additional trees and shrubs where needed. While it was necessary to remain aware of the limitations of the Russian climate, the

Above: The temple in honour of victors at sea and the triumphal gates for victors on land.

Above right: Façade, cross section and plan for the aviary in the morning garden.

These illustrations are from Lvov's album of eleven drawings (1797–9) for the estate of Alexander Bezborodko.

Russian winter could add a special charm to the park. In conjunction with nature Lvov sought to produce scenes which would induce particular emotional reactions from the visitor.

There was an area for morning walks, another for walks in the middle of the day and a large area for evening walks. Lvov intended that there should be sweet scents from the turf and the flowers, and shelters and arbours placed where there were interesting views. The morning walk would be quiet and peaceful with the only movement coming from the stirring of the leaves. There would be one notable architectural feature at the end of a meadow, the aviary, from where there would be views of the Kremlin. Inside there was to be a dining room where the family could take breakfast or lunch while listening to the birds. The walk for the middle of the day would lead through wood and forest glade, with the trees providing ample shade from the sun without obscuring the surrounding views. An abundance of flowing and cascading water would refresh the air.

Since the owner, we are told, liked to share his pleasures, the evening walk was intended to be open to the public and to have a different character with wide and sometimes straight paths, the monotony of which would be interrupted by various pavilions and kiosks, some in the wood and some by the water. The main entrance would occupy a semi-circular space surrounded by a covered colonnade, under which several stalls would offer for sale haberdashery, confectionery, fruit, etc. By the second entrance there would be a coffee house in a Turkish kiosk, which would also sell cool drinks, confectionery and ice cream, and in its large central hall visitors would be able to pass the time in dancing when the weather disappointed.

When Count Bezborodko died at the age of only fifty-two Russia was deprived of its Chancellor and Moscow of a quite exceptional park.[20]

Estates near St Petersburg where Lvov worked included Murino for the Vorontsovs and Zvanka, the very large estate of his friend and fellow-poet Gavrila Derzhavin, whose career had flourished after the publication of the *Ode to Felitsa*, praising Catherine (see page 98).[21]

Bykovo

The house at Bykovo, 21 miles south-east of Moscow, was built and the estate laid out in the last quarter of the eighteenth century, probably by V.I. Bazhenov, for M.M. Izmaylov. As with many Russian estates, water was an important element, and the large pools and surrounding landscape are still there. While most of the park buildings, including the Hermitage and the stone landing stage, have gone, an exceptionally fine rotunda by one of the pools has survived. The cupola is supported by a circle of Corinthian columns. Three closed sections between pairs of columns were once ornamented on the outside by bas-reliefs, and there were niches with statues inside. The neo-gothic church is also most impressive.[22]

Troitskoe

Princess Catherine Dashkova (*née* Vorontsova) was among those responsible for putting Catherine on the throne in place of Peter III; this led to a warm relationship with the Empress, though it cooled towards the end of Catherine's reign. Two of Dashkova's brothers, Alexander and Simon Vorontsov, served as ambassadors in London, and, during visits to England, she became a great admirer of English gardens and of British life in general. In 1770, Painshill, Claremont, Longleat and Wilton were among the estates she visited. In 1776 she arranged for her son Paul to study at Edinburgh University and she lived in Edinburgh when he was there. While touring in Scotland she visited Blair Drummond, Taymouth Castle and Dunkeld. Through a friend she had met in Spa and stayed with in Ireland, a Mrs Hamilton, she later invited Martha and Catherine Wilmot, relatives of Mrs Hamilton, to visit her at Troitskoe, her estate some 50 miles south-west of Moscow. Martha arrived there in 1803 and stayed for five years, while Catherine was there from 1805 to 1807. They both kept journals as well as writing letters, and Martha persuaded the princess to write a short account of her life. These records provide interesting impressions of the garden at Troitskoe and of Dashkova at work as a gardener, both in her own garden and in the garden of her brother Alexander:

> The following year my brother came to stay with me at Troitskoe. He was delighted with my garden and with my various plantations and buildings, and when I visited him in the autumn he gave me full powers to change the layout of his garden, according to my own taste, and to carry on with the work of tracing out the plantations and walks on which I had been engaged during my stay with him in the previous year.
>
> On my return from Krugloe to Troitskoe I applied myself to the completion of the buildings I had begun, which, to me, made the garden pure delight. Every tree, every shrub had been planted either by myself or under my supervision in the exact spot where I wanted it. One is so apt to regard with affection the work of one's own hands, that I have no hesitation in saying that I found Troitskoe to be altogether one of the finest country estates I had ever seen in Russia or abroad.[23]

Right, above: The surviving rotunda at Bykovo is a particularly fine example of Russian eighteenth-century park architecture.

Right: The neo-gothic church remains an impressive feature in the overgrown landscape.

Far right: The house overlooking the park replaced its predecessor in 1856.

The Wilmot sisters were also impressed. Martha to her mother in July 1805:

> Troitskoe is now in its highest beauty. In one part of the Grounds there is a little Chinese Temple, and behind it a field of roses which is now in full bloom and fragrant beyond expression. One arrives at it suddenly from woods and walks quite in a different style and taste so that the contrast is uncommonly striking and pretty. I often sit in the lattice work arbour (for Temple is rather too grand a name for it) but am obliged to Guard my face with a *Zinzalière* against the swarms of Gnats and Wasps.[24]

Sukhanovo, once the home of the Princes Volkonsky, is now a rest home of the Union of Architects, with comfortable accommodation for visitors.

Catherine to a friend later in the same year:

> However Troitskoe is dead flat almost, and to the cultivation alone its beauty is attributable. An immense quantity of ground is laid out under shrubberies and all sorts of pleasure grounds completely in the English style. . . .
>
> The winding walk among the birches is a favourite one of the Princess because of it leading to the Monument of Granite erected on a Mount and dedicated to the remembrance of Catherine ascended the throne! Behind it is scoop'd a Hermit's Cell furnish'd with moss & rocky seats out of which You plunge into the depth of a Wood![25]

She was also impressed by the 'bath establishment' in one of the shrubberies, which

> is lovely & most perfectly arranged. The Women have nothing else to do but to heat the Furnace & keep

everything in order, and you know Bathing is with the Russians as with the Turks a religious observance as not one of the lower order would or could profane the Church without having been in the Hot Bath the Night before. This secures a universal ablution every Saturday regularly. The Bath here has three separate Chambers. In one is a gradation of stairs to increase the heat of a Vapour if you like it. There is a great Tub in which one sits up to the Chin & the Ceremony is to scour oneself with Horsereddish till you smart & then with Soap. You should first sit up to your knees in a composition of wormwood, Nettles, Grass-seed, Mint & Horsereddish! I have gone through this operation frequently.[26]

Princess Dashkova's nephew Michael Vorontsov, son of Simon the ambassador, was to make a great park at Alupka in the Crimea, as we shall see in the next chapter.

Sukhanovo

Sukhanovo, one of the most impressive estates in the vicinity of Moscow, belonged in the late eighteenth century to Aleksei Melgunov, a senator who was keenly interested in science and archaeology and related to the Melgunov who had given Yelagin Island its earlier name. His daughter, Ekaterina, married Prince Dmitri Volkonsky and after his death made her favourite nephew, Prince Peter Volkonsky, co-owner and her beneficiary. Thanks to their joint efforts and to the commitment of substantial resources, many improvements were made to the estate during the early years of the nineteenth century. Prince Peter enjoyed considerable influence thanks to his services at the courts of Alexander I and Nicholas I. The leading architects he invited to provide designs for Sukhanovo included Rossi, Zhiliardi, Stasov and Menelaws, but not all their designs got further than the drawing board.

The landscape park has survived quite well with its grass slopes, fine trees, the lake, pools and views of fields and woods beyond, but many of the buildings and other features have been lost. The orangery, the aviary, the tea house, a two-arched belvedere, the Hermitage pavilion, the sliding hill, the grotto, the church and the sphinxes by the lake have all gone. Also missing is the handsome cast iron, 23-foot-high obelisk erected in 1826, following the death of Alexander, a late commemoration of the defeat of Napoleon under his leadership, at the end of the campaign in which Prince Peter Volkonsky had taken part. It was ornamented with raised garlands and torches and surmounted by a two-headed eagle. There was a British contribution here, for the pedestal bore the name of Basil Clark, son of Mathew Clark, of the foundry responsible. It is thought to have been designed by V.P. Stasov, a close friend of the Clarks, with whom they worked frequently. Basil Clark married Stasov's daughter, Sophia. A memorial to the Empress Elizabeth, the wife of Alexander, who died in 1826, has also failed to survive.

Top: Fine trees combined with picturesque pools make a considerable contribution to the park.

Above: The mausoleum, still the most impressive building at Sukhanovo, now serves as a restaurant.

Of all the buildings at Sukhanovo the mausoleum, commissioned by Ekaterina Volkonsky in 1813, remains the most impressive, although it was brutally altered in 1935. Circular in plan with a cupola and a six-columned portico, it dominates the area of the park around it. D.I. Zhiliardi or A.G. Grigorev have both been suggested as the architect. It was originally flanked by identical, modest single-storey buildings, one serving as a small hospital and the other as an almshouse. In 1935 they were replaced by two-storey wings linked to the mausoleum by single-storey closed galleries, after the manner of early nineteenth-century palace buildings. The contrast of red brick and white stone, which had been very effective, was sacrificed to stuccoing. The colonnade and bell tower, which had stood behind the mausoleum, were destroyed.[27]

In a commanding position above a steep slope overlooking the lake, the Temple of Venus dates from the early nineteenth century and is a particularly elegant eight-columned open rotunda with symbols of hunting and music on bas-reliefs round the frieze. The statue of Venus is no longer present. A copy of Sokolov's fountain-statue of the milkmaid with the broken pitcher at Tsarskoe Selo also survives, but it now stands near the mausoleum instead of by a spring near the lake, where it was originally placed.

A group of neo-gothic service buildings contrasts strikingly with the classical style of the palace and the park buildings, but the associated gateway and towers have been demolished.

Sukhanovo is now a rest home for the Union of Architects with the mausoleum serving as a restaurant.

Petrovsko-Razumovskoe

In 1924, when it still seemed possible to show nostalgia and regret for the loss of so much of the great heritage of the country estates without risking one's liberty, Olga Chayanova wrote in *Sredi kollektsionerov* (*Among Collectors*) of Petrovsko-Razumovskoe in Moscow Province:

> Looking at the present-day park at Petrovsko-Razumovskoe with its scarcely defined avenues, lush, leafy, overgrown limes, with its governmental buildings of recent construction, it is impossible to imagine that the park, if not the creation of Le Nôtre as the legend has it, was at least in the Le Nôtre style – with clipped trees, with avenues sharply defined and fancifully arranged, with grottoes, a hermitage, a temple of Apollo, and everything which indisputably defines the last three decades of the 18th century. On the site of the present-day main building stood a wooden palace, closely adjoining the church. Probably they were joined by an interior passage. In the small garden to the left of the palace stood the temple of Apollo. 'On both sides,' says Professor Shreder, 'were small living rooms. The vault of the arch was embellished *al fresco* with a representation of the musical competition of the god with Marsyas, resulting, as is well known, with the loss by the latter of his skin, passing into the possession of the god.' The entrance to the park was to the right of the church or directly from the palace. The area in front of the palace was embellished with an allegorical marble group of the four seasons of the year. To the left of the palace there was until recently a pavilion called subsequently the ministry dacha. To the left, symmetrically with it, stood a pavilion with a through arch which led to the English park – now the 'Dendrologia'. All this was on the first terrace, demarcated from the second terrace by a balustrade on which were placed twenty-two marble figures. Twelve of them were busts of Roman emperors and the other ten mythological figures. Some steps led to the second terrace. Here the guests of Kirill and Lev Razumovsky came to watch the theatrical entertainment. Here, among combinations of trees in the form of arches, niches, columns, walls and so on was the summer theatre, the *coulisses* of which consisted of real trees and fences, while the stage and amphitheatre were of earth banks. Between them was the orchestra in a hollow.
>
> The orangery, which was near to the theatre, is not shown on the plan, and the menagerie is also not shown. In it, as required of an English park, wild deer ranged freely. The third terrace was closed in by a pool, which was excavated by Ukrainians, fellow countrymen of Razumovsky. On its bank stood a grotto, formed by an earth embankment embellished by a colonnade. This grotto is still there, but the arbour on it has not survived. A second more ingenious grotto with dark passages and a cave, was demolished after the student Ivanov was killed there by Nechaev.
>
> So this is all that is left of one of the earliest parks, only traces of its former splendour.[28]

In 1865 Petrovsko-Razumovskoe became the site of the Petrovskaya Academy of Agriculture and Forestry (hence the 'Dendrologia'), later the Timoryazevskaya Academy of Agriculture. Sergei Nechaev was an infamous revolutionary, who, in 1869, was seeking to organize a mass uprising. He secured the support of students of the Petrovskaya Academy, but one of them, Ivan Ivanov, failed to conform and was murdered by associates of Nechaev. Nechaev fled to western Europe.[29]

The handsome Temple of Venus with symbols of hunting and music on bas-reliefs round the frieze.

Rai-Semenovskoe

In the second decade of the nineteenth century Alexander Nashchokin established a spa resort with extensive gardens on his Rai-Semenovskoe estate some 30 miles south of Moscow in the Serpukhovsky district. A professor of chemistry had published an approving account of the waters there in Russian and in French in 1811 and had praised in the most enthusiastic terms the picturesque quality of the beautiful valley with its rich meadows, through which flowed the translucent waters of the River Nara.[30]

Before long there was a hotel with sixteen rooms – 'Restauration aux armes de seigneur' – and twenty-seven well-appointed peasant houses of various sizes to accommodate patients arriving for the water cure. There was also a bath house. An arbour marked the well-spring of the healing water, and a temple with a cupola supported by twelve columns stood in the centre of the valley. Entertainment was provided as well as board and the water cure. As each day was drawing to a close and the sun sank below the horizon a cannon was fired, signalling to the horn band[31] and the wind ensemble in different parts of the grounds that it was time to begin their evening programmes, which would continue until eleven o'clock. There was also a club and a green theatre. The formal garden was three quarters of a mile long with a lime avenue and a pool, but no detailed description seems to have survived. The English garden covered the slope with two terraces

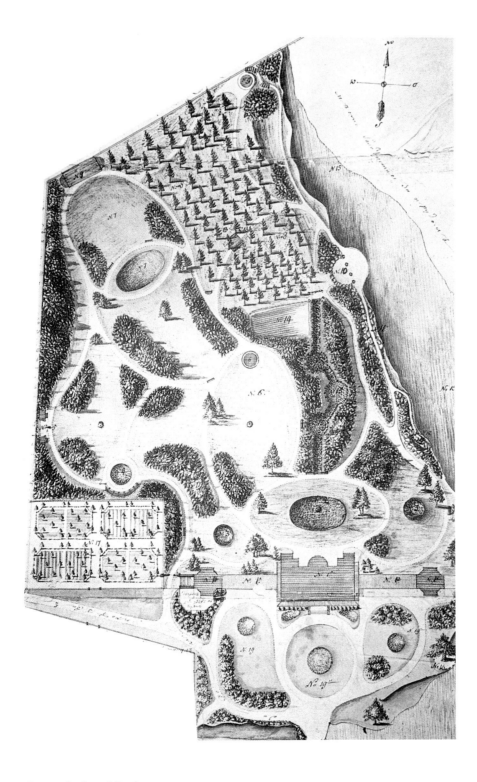

F. Melnikov's plan for the English garden at Ostafevo (1822).

The house at Ostafevo, which became a notable museum.

the main façade of the palace with rectangular boskets on either side. Beyond the lime avenue the path winds through an extensive landscape park to the north and on the west side of the garden. On the east side they were bounded by a large pool, where the reflections in the water were said to make this the most picturesque part of the park. The text accompanying the plan refers to a proposed belvedere and various other features. It is not known if the 'gallery with summerhouse on the pool' and the other summerhouses, referred to in the text, were ever built. A description of the property, soon after A.I. Vyazemsky's death in 1808, refers to the pool with a variety of fish, the River Desna half a verst (580 yards) away, the large English garden, the formal garden, the stone orangery with productive trees, a cherry house, pear trees and plum trees.

In front of the house there was a planted area with a sun cannon at its centre. In the barrel of the cannon there was an aperture with a magnifying lens leading to the powder. The cannon fired at midday when the sun's rays focused on the lens and ignited the powder. A number of European gardens had sun cannons in the middle of the nineteenth century. A good surviving example in full working order is a popular feature on the Swedish estate at Adelsnäs, near Åtvidaberg. It was restored under the direction of the late Baron Gösta Adelswärd in the 1980s.[33]

When travelling in Europe Vyazemsky fell in love with a Frenchman's Irish wife, Eugenia *née* O'Reilly, took her back to Russia and later married her. From their union the distinguished poet Prince Peter Vyazemsky was born. One of Andrei Vyazemsky's two illegitimate daughters, Ekaterina Kolyvanova, married the famous writer and historian Nikolai Karamzin, who lived at Ostafevo for fifteen years and wrote the *History of the Russian State* there. The presence of Karamzin and later Peter Vyazemsky made Ostafevo one of the country's leading cultural centres. Alexander Pushkin became a close friend of Vyazemsky, and other visitors included Vasily Zhukovsky, Konstantin Batyushkov, Alexander Griboedov, Nikolai Gogol, Denis Davidov and Nikolai Trubetskoy.

After the death of Andrei Vyazemsky – his wife had predeceased him – Karamzin acted as guardian to Peter. By the 1820s the latter was anxious to improve his property and, after repairing the house and the orangery, he engaged the architect F. Melnikov to produce a plan for a typical English pleasure garden. Melnikov's plan of 1821 was followed by a revision in 1822. The main avenue on the plan is no longer straight, but turns off to the right and then turns back again to resume its original course further on. New winding paths, labyrinths, glades and artificial undulations are shown. Different corners of the garden were called Field of Mars, Philosopher's Retreat, Delphic Oracle, Crocodile's Nest, etc. The plan shows sculptural ornaments, numerous summerhouses and pavilions, among them a raised pavilion from which to view the garden and the surrounding countryside. The outdoor rooms formed by the boskets could be used for 'dining, dancing or reading a book'. 'Skittles, swings, see-saws and summer sliding hills'

between the mansion and the river. On one side of the mansion there was a round temple and on the other a tall Chinese garden building, perhaps a pagoda. There was a pool on each of the terraces and by one of them a particularly attractive temple flanked by two interesting grottoes, one of which was marked 'Underground Entrance'. The green theatre was in the English park, skilfully formed by closely planted limes. There was also an animal reserve with wild goats and horses.

But what had seemed to be a promising venture turned to disappointment for the owners as the response failed to justify the outlay. Whether this was because patients generally were unimpressed by the water treatment is not clear, but one visitor, D.N. Sverbeev, recorded in his memoirs that his father, whom he had accompanied to the spa, went into terminal decline after taking the waters. Closure came in 1820. A visitor to Rai-Semenovskoe in 1924 found no traces of the spa buildings and the mansion altered beyond recognition. The formal garden and the English park were quite overgrown, the garden structures had disappeared and there were no wild goats; but impressive old trees remained, Kazakov's fine church still stood near by, and the surrounding countryside was as appealing as ever.[32]

Ostafevo

In the second half of the eighteenth century Ostafevo, 22 miles south of Moscow, belonged to K.M. Matveev, an industrialist who had a cloth factory there and built the church. In 1792 he sold the property to Prince Andrei Ivanovich Vyazemsky, who built the impressive palace in classical style with a belvedere and a six-columned portico, flanked by long open colonnades (which were closed later) leading to two-storey wings. A plan dated 1805 shows a lime avenue at right angles to the centre of

were suggested for the 'grove of entertainment'. On the bank of the pool there was to be a whimsical figure with a fountain and a cascade among rocks, on the Field of Mars a merry-go-round. Immediately in front of the palace a large oval lawn with a flowerbed and a statue of Flora was proposed and on each side of it a further lawn with special summer flowers 'but without statues'. It is not clear how far Melnikov's plan was carried out. Certainly the line of the main avenue was not altered, and, since Vyazemsky was ususally deeply in debt, it is unlikely that all the other proposed changes were made.

In 1861 Peter Vyazemsky made Ostafevo over to his son Paul, who was better able to afford to live there thanks to his wife's money, which must also have helped to build up the remarkable collection of art and antiques which he now brought to Ostafevo and arranged and catalogued there. A considerable programme of repairs to the palace and the park began in 1862. Paul arranged memorial rooms in the palace to his father, Karamzin and Pushkin, with archival collections. In the park he improved the planting and the paths and took a keen interest in the orangery and the hotbeds, where peaches, oranges and lemons were produced. Paul died in 1888 and was succeeded by his son Peter.

Peter Pavlovich preferred St Petersburg to Ostafevo and transferred furniture and many works of art to his house there. He neglected Ostafevo and wanted to sell it. Fortunately it was bought by his brother-in-law, Sergei Dmitrievich Sheremetev, who had married Ekaterina Pavlovna, Peter's sister. In 1899 they opened the palace as a museum, which proved extremely popular. It continued as a museum after the Revolution, but in 1930 the authorities in Moscow decreed that it should close, and its collections were transferred to other museums and to the state archives.

Between 1911 and 1916 monuments were erected in the park to Pushkin, Karamzin, Zhukovsky, Peter Andreevich Vyazemsky and Paul Petrovich Vyazemsky.[54] There is now a museum again at Ostafevo.

Marfino

In the early eighteenth century the estate at Marfino, 25 miles north of Moscow, belonged to Count Boris Golitsyn, a close associate of Peter the Great, who built a residence with a formal park and the first of the two Marfino churches. Golitsyn's son, Sergei, sold the estate in 1829 to Field Marshal Pyotr Saltykov, who was succeeded by his son Field Marshal

An 1840s lithograph by Chappuis and Bechebois, showing a view across the lake of the palace at Marfino and the outstanding neo-gothic bridge to the left.

Ivan Saltykov. During their time an impressive baroque palace was built, and Ivan Saltykov added several buildings in classical style, including a church, the kennels and the coach-house, which are all still there. Their formal garden covered 32 acres. Ivan Saltykov had many gardeners, and trees, mainly limes, and shrubs were precisely clipped to form pyramids, balls and green walls. Sculpture played an important rôle in the garden, and there were also grottoes and classical pavilions, of which two exceptional park examples have survived. The music pavilion is semi-circular in plan with Tuscan columns supporting a semi-cupola. The *Milovid* (belvedere) is a two-tiered rotunda on a steep slope overlooking the lake. An octagonal tower, with a Doric colonnade inside, is surmounted by a pavilion of eight Ionic columns supporting a dome, under which there still stands a statue of Apollo Belvedere. The buildings and the park were surrounded by the lake and a series of four pools at different levels, interconnected by water channels. A wildlife enclosure contained deer, hares, swans and peacocks, among other animals and birds. The orangeries produced lemons, oranges, apricots, peaches, grapes and dates.[35]

There were two theatres, one a wooden building in the formal park, the other an open-air theatre in a grove in the landscape park, where trees and shrubs provided the scenery for ballet, pastorales and vaudeville. More serious operatic and dramatic performances were staged in the covered theatre, where accomplished serf and amateur actors and musicians performed. Marfino was recognized as an important cultural centre, and celebrated visiting European artists were glad to appear there. The poet Ivan Dmitriev and Nikolai Karamzin were frequent guests. The latter wrote a play for the theatre, *Only for Marfino*, which he produced himself, playing the rôle of Count Pyotr Saltykov. The text of the play has not survived. After theatrical performances thousands of coloured lights illuminated the lake and the park, and these were followed by firework displays. During summer festivals there was boating on the lake with singers and musicians, and there were also literary entertainments and a merry-go-round. Horn music featured in these festivals, with a repertoire that included the overtures to Mozart's *Le Nozze di Figaro* and *Il Seraglio*.[36]

Disaster struck during the invasion of 1812, when French troops, who were stationed at Marfino, devastated the palace, took away most of the contents and caused great damage in the park. Ivan Saltykov fought with distinction against the French, was seriously wounded and died in 1813, when his sister

Below: The music pavilion.

Bottom: *Milovid*. A two-tiered rotunda with a statue of Apollo Belvedere.

Below, right: Winged griffins by the landing stage.

Countess Anna Orlova succeeded him. She lived abroad but gave instructions for restoration to proceed. This led to considerable expenditure, and, with the estate already deeply in debt, she sold it to her father-in-law, Count Vladimir Orlov in 1822. With the serf architect Fyodor Tugarov, he continued the rebuilding and did much to restore the formal garden. The work was approaching completion when he died in 1831. His daughter Sophia Panin inherited Marfino and decided on the reconstruction of the palace and other associated buildings.

The remarkable palace by M.D. Bykovsky (1800–85) which we see today was eventually completed in 1846 with elements of Gothic and English Tudor. It stands in an elevated position looking across the lake. Three terraces and a wide flight of steps lead down from the palace to the lake, where the landing stage is flanked by a pair of winged griffins. Near by, a group of children, with dolphins at their feet, support the shell-bowl of the spectacular Roman fountain. The palace is approached by Bykovsky's monumental and outstanding, colonnaded neo-gothic bridge in the combination of brick and stone associated with earlier Russian architecture.[37]

Kuzminki

In the first half of the eighteenth century the Kuzminki estate, which was then called Vlakhernskoe, some 6 miles south-east of Moscow, belonged to the Strogonovs, but it was bought by Prince Golitsyn in 1759 and belonged to a succession of Princes Golitsyn until the Revolution. The Golitsyns, like the Strogonovs and the Demidovs, owed their wealth to ironworks in the Urals, and iron was to make a large contribution to the park's furnishings and ornaments in the nineteenth century.

The compositional centre of the estate is the long irregular pool, surrounded by an extensive landscape park. The principal architectural features were placed around it and could all be viewed from the landing stage, ornamented with cast-iron lions and linked by a ferry to the other side of the pool. The classical main residence, which was built in the second half of the eighteenth century but refashioned in the nineteenth, was destroyed by fire and replaced during the Soviet period by a veterinary institute. The most important period of the park's development was between 1810 and 1850, when some notable structures were added by D.I. Zhiliardi, his cousin A.O. Zhiliardi and M.D. Bykovsky.

Particularly impressive is the Stable Yard. The Music Room, where a serf orchestra played and horn concerts were given, is at the centre of its main façade and is faced by a colonnade of four Doric columns, surmounted by a sculptural group of Apollo and the Muses and enclosed within a massive arch. This is flanked by two magnificent cast-iron rearing horses being restrained by attendants, the work of the sculptor P.K. Klodt and originally intended to embellish the Anichkov bridge in St Petersburg. The Propylaea, a portico with a double colonnade, each of six Doric columns, was built near the pool, opposite the main residence, and echoed the Propylaea in ancient Athens, which was the entrance to the Acropolis.

The kitchens were housed in the Egyptian pavilion, and Egyptian columns supported a ceiling covered with Egyptian images in the elaborate orangery. Egyptian features became popular in French gardens after Napoleon's campaigns in Egypt and then spread from France across Europe.

The splendid wrought-iron gates to the main courtyard, copies of gates made for Pavlovsk but incorporating the Golitsyn coat of arms, came from the Golitsyns' ironworks. They are flanked on each side by two tall torchères, each of which is accompanied by four cast-iron winged griffins. Lengths of wrought-iron railings round the courtyard

Left, above: A view across the lake and the ferry at Kuzminki to the house.

Left: A distant view of the Propylaea, echoing the Propylaea of ancient Athens.

Right, above: A view of the Stable Yard with the Music Room at the centre of the main façade.

Right: The church in the park at Kuzminki.

alternate with cast-iron lions mounted on stonework blocks. Lions were favourite ornaments in Russian parks during the first half of the nineteenth century.

Beyond the landscape park there was a large area of forest with twelve straight paths radiating from the centre, as was traditional for a hunting park.[38]

P.A. Demidov's Botanical Garden

The second half of the eighteenth century saw the development of some notable private botanical collections in Russia. P.A. Demidov, whose considerable wealth was based on the iron foundries his father had developed in the Urals, built up a famous collection on his estate, established in 1756 by the River Moskva. P.S. Pallas, the distinguished German naturalist who became Professor of Natural History at the Imperial Academy of Science in St Petersburg in 1768, catalogued Demidov's collection in 1780 when it contained 2,224 species. This figure later rose to 4,363. Many of the plants were from America, India and Siberia.

The garden was laid out on six rectangular terraces, each some 650 feet long, descending from Demidov's palace on the upper terrace to the river. On the three terraces below there were stone orangeries, sections of open ground and rows of fruit trees. On the next terrace there were boskets within which ornamental plants were grown, and on the terrace by the river a rectangular pool accommodated waterfowl. The terraces were bisected by a wide central avenue with flights of steps leading from the palace to the river.

After the death of Demidov in 1788 the garden and the collection of plants were neglected. The herbarium belonged to Pallas for a time but was later made over to the collection at Gorenki.[39] Pallas wrote of Demidov:

> It deserves to be recorded here, that the late PROKOP AKIMFIEVITCH DEMIDOV, counsellor of state, by his patriotic example, in importing, at his own expense, many foreign species of fruit trees, and liberally bestowing the treasures of his garden, has been principally instrumental in promoting this beneficial branch of industry. The inland provinces of Russia are also indebted to this beneficial man, for introducing several useful species of grain. But, alas! his spirit no longer animates the industry of the husbandman; his beautiful botanic garden, which I described in the year 1782 is now desolate; and the scarce and valuable plants which he had procured at a great expense from England, and bequeathed to the University of Moscow are shamefully scattered, insomuch that scarcely a vestige of his donation remains in its proper place.[40]

Left: D.G. Levitsky's portrait of P.A. Demidov in the Tretyakov Gallery, Moscow.

Right: The grotto at Gorenki.

Gorenki

The Gorenki estate belonged to the Dolgorukys in the early eighteenth century, but in 1747 it was given to Elizabeth's favourite, Alexis Razumovsky, and in the 1780s and 1790s it was redeveloped by his nephew, A.K. Razumovsky. The impressive palace and landscape park have been attributed to the Scottish architect Adam Menelaws, but Shvidkovsky believes that his rôle was secondary to that of Nikolai Lvov.[41] The palace was approached by a long semi-circular drive from two entrance gates with guard rooms, and the large semi-circular space it enclosed in front of the palace was landscaped with a wildlife enclosure and a pool for waterfowl. On the other side of the palace there was an extensive parterre with many marble statues, and beyond that a wide staircase, flanked by two iron eagles on pedestals, leading down to the landscape park with pools formed in the River Gorenki. The large stone grotto, half sunk in the ground, is still there, and on islands in the pools there are remains of two bridges which once gave access to the islands.

What made Gorenki famous was the remarkable botanical collection that Razumovsky assembled during the early years of the nineteenth century, ranging from medicinal herbs to exotic fruit trees and forest trees. While there were plants in the garden from as far afield as America and China, it aimed particularly to include all the plants known of in Russia. This was made possible by the work of collectors in Siberia, the Caucasus, the Urals, Crimea, Altai and Alaska (part of which was Russian territory until 1867). Many of the plants were in the open ground, but there were up to forty glasshouses with a combined length of about one mile. The large herbarium shared a building with a collection of minerals. Among the

distinguished botanists who worked there were Christian Steven and F.E.L. Fisher, who became directors of the Nikitsky Botanical Garden, near Yalta, and the Imperial Botanical Garden in St Petersburg. The cost of maintaining the garden and park at Gorenki amounted to 70,000 roubles a year. It is claimed that the number of introduced species there reached 7,000 in its final years. After the death of Razumovsky in 1822 the collection was broken up, and, while some of it went to the St Petersburg garden and the Moscow University garden, much of it was dispersed among private buyers.

The estate was bought by Prince Yusupov who removed some of the glasshouses to Arkhangelskoe, while a calico factory was installed in the palace, and manufacturing continued there until 1910. The palace was reconstructed in 1916, but the then owner was left with little time to enjoy it. During the Soviet period there was some restoration of the palace, which became a sanatorium.[42]

J.C. Loudon found Gorenki 'remarkable for its botanical riches, and an immense quantity of glass. The grounds are of great extent, but the surface is flat, and the soil a dry sand. A natural forest of birch and wild cherry trees clothes the park, and harmonises the artificial scenes. The mansion built by an English artisan, is highly elegant; and the attached conservatories and stoves, and decorated lawn, form a splendid and delightful scene, unequalled in Russia.'[43]

Neskuchnoe

The park at Neskuchnoe, on the right bank of the River Moskva, was laid out in the middle of the eighteenth century for N.Yu. Trubetskoy by the architect D.V. Ukhtomsky with a residence of modest size, service wings, an orangery, an aviary, a grotto, a wildlife enclosure, a number of park pavilions and a large formal garden divided into a number of enclosures, all framed by clipped hedges, well illustrated in 1753 by P. Nikitin. A later plan of the estate shows that some of the clipped hedges were extended and trained over the allées to form covered ways. Beyond the residence and towards the river there was a further area of formal garden.

An estate of the Golitsyns was contiguous with Neskuchnoe. Beyond the Golitsyn estate lay an estate of the Orlovs, which included the site of Demidov's botanical garden, where a landscape park had been created and Demidov's palace had been rebuilt. In 1828 these three estates were united into a single estate, which continued to use the name Neskuchnoe, and the classical Aleksandrinsky Palace was built as a summer residence for Alexandra Fyodorovna, the wife of Nicholas I. In 1834 the gardens of the three former estates were replanned under gardener Peltsel, resulting in an extensive landscape park.

In 1928 a large area of Neskuchnoe became the site of the first Park of Culture and Rest. In the 1920s there was a museum of furniture in the Aleksandrinsky Palace, but in 1934 it became the Presidium of the Academy of Sciences. Two pleasing small buildings, the bath house by the Elizavetinsky Pool and the Summer Cottage, survive in the park.[44]

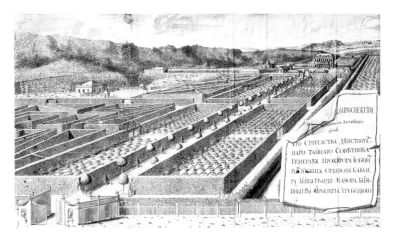

Top: A bridge in what survives of Neskuchnoe park.

Middle: The bath house by the pool in the park.

Bottom: P. Nikitin's 1753 drawing of the Neskuchnoe garden before it was landscaped.

Gorki

Gorki, later Gorki Leninskie, is pleasantly situated, some twenty miles south of Moscow, overlooking the valley of the River Pakhra, among hills, woods and meadows. In 1812 it belonged to General Pisarev, who fought against Napoleon, and the buildings on the estate date from then. Towards the end of the century it had become run down and was acquired by I.A. Prokofev, who restored the house in 1888–9. He extended the central lime avenue and the avenue of firs to the south, and planted an avenue a mile long to the north with white birches. In 1909 it became the property of Z.G. Morozova-Reinbot, who added the veranda on the south side of the house and a winter garden on the north side; while the walls were embellished with bas-reliefs featuring scenes from Greek mythology. In the garden lilac and jasmine were planted, lawns, flowerbeds and a fountain added. Two rotundas, one with Ionic columns the other with Doric, commanded views of the surrounding countryside. Beyond the formal area near the house informal landscaping with pools on the slopes led towards the river.

Lenin first came to Gorki Leninskie in 1918 while recovering from the attempt to assassinate him, and it was here that he spent the last two years of his life until his death on 21 January 1924. The Lenin Museum was opened in 1949 within a scheduled conservation area of 23,500 acres. The sculpture by S. Merkurov, *Funeral of the Leader*, with the body of Lenin borne by a grieving party of eight, is an impressive addition to the park. One of the exhibits in the garage is Lenin's Rolls-Royce, equipped for winter roads with its front suspension mounted on skis and the rear suspension on caterpillar tracks.[45]

Gorki Leninskie, where Lenin spent the last two years of his life.

8
SOME LANDSCAPE PARKS IN THE PROVINCES

Of the many hundreds of parks far removed from St Petersburg and Moscow, very few remain; the best of them are in Ukraine and the Crimea, where Sophievka and Alupka are world class. In this chapter we shall also consider the parks associated with Pushkin, Turgenev and Tolstoy, which are good examples of minor parks and among the few to have survived. But first we must look at Bogoroditsk and the work of Andrei Timofeevich Bolotov (1738–1823).

Bolotov was the most prolific and influential Russian writer on agriculture and gardening in a career which was made possible in 1762 by Peter III's manifesto freeing the aristocracy from compulsory service. This enabled Bolotov to resign his commission in the army and to retire to his small estate at Dvoryaninovo in Tula province south of Moscow. He had served in the Seven Years' War and had been stationed for four years in Königsberg in East Prussia, where he mastered German, studied natural sciences, practised drawing, attended lectures on philosophy and began to collect a library.[1] In peaceful seclusion at Dvoryaninovo, he was able to build on this foundation, which was to lead over the years to the publication of many hundreds of articles, at first in the *Proceedings of the Free Economic Society* and *Country Dweller*, and then in the *Economic Magazine*, the journal which was edited and published by Nikolai Novikov and issued as a supplement to *Moscow News* in the 1780s. Bolotov's articles covered such subjects as fertility, crop rotation, the application of manures, fruit cultivation (he described more than six hundred varieties of apples and pears), experiments with hybridizing, silviculture and landscape gardening.

Dvoryaninovo was a modest, run-down estate, with an old wooden house, rather primitive associated buildings, an unplanned, overgrown garden and an inconveniently scattered landholding. But there were two woods and some handsome old oaks as well as birches and other trees. All gardens at that time were formally laid out, among them the famous examples Bolotov had seen in St Petersburg, and, summoning all his serfs and the peasants living near by, he set about making one to his own design. Long straight avenues crossed by transverse avenues were planted with thousands of limes, and it seems that the hundreds of apple trees he acquired were planted in the spaces framed by the avenues. He was pleased with the result and enjoyed showing it to admiring neighbours.

The following year he turned his attention to the garden by the house, where the few survivors of the fruit trees planted by his forbears were surrounded by self-sown birch and aspen. Here too his approach was formal, with an arbour at the centre surrounded by a group of birches, where two crossing paths divided the garden into four squares. He became keenly interested in flowering herbaceous plants and made long flower borders. A great deal of labour was required to convert his grandfather's fishpond into an ornamental pool. Eventually the rest of the neglected family garden was transformed, and he added an octagonal summerhouse followed by a circular pavilion on an artificial hillock formed from the spoil resulting

The waterfall at Sophievka created by Ludovic Metzel for Felix Potocki.

from the excavation of a further ornamental pool. He also built an unpretentious wooden house on the crest of a hill with pleasant views of the surrounding countryside.[2]

A new phase in his life began when he was recommended by the Secretary of the Free Economic Society to Prince S.V. Gagarin as a suitable person to act as steward of imperial property intended for the future Count A.G. Bobrinsky, the illegitimate son of Catherine and Grigory Orlov. At first his duties were at Kiyasovka, south-east of Moscow, where he arrived with his large family in 1774. There were two neglected and overgrown formal gardens. He quickly restored these and then made another by the steward's house with numerous fruit trees and bushes and a flower parterre in front of the windows. In June he found glow-worms in the woods and ordered a quantity to be collected. He got 'almost a hatful', which he arranged on salient features of the parterre. When darkness fell he was delighted with the result when seen from the windows of the upper floor or from the roof, but it lasted only a few days.[3]

In 1776 Prince Gagarin wrote to tell him that, following the death of the steward at Bogoroditsk in Tula province, he was appointed to succeed him. The impressive palace and church at Bogoroditsk, both by I.E. Starov, were then almost completed. Bolotov was to spend twenty years there and to make a considerable contribution to the palace, the park, the town and the surrounding area. The year after he arrived the village of Bogoroditsk was listed to become a town, and Bolotov was involved in planning its layout facing the palace on the other side of the large pool which was formed from the river. He arranged the principal streets so that they all radiated from the main hall of the palace. On the level ground by the palace he designed a large formal garden with boskets, ornamental basins, fountains, flower parterres and other features. The very uneven ground beyond, with steep slopes and gullies, called for a quite different approach.[4]

Although it seems that Bolotov did not visit St Petersburg between the 1760s and 1803, he must have known about the new English landscape style which had been introduced by Catherine to her parks. He met many owners of estates around Moscow and it would be surprising if the new style were not discussed. Some of them may even have visited gardens in England. He seems to have been feeling his way towards the landscape style in a neglected wood at Bogoroditsk, which he sought to transform to a place people would visit for pleasure. It was cleared of litter and broken trees, and, over the years, many new trees and plants were introduced. Numerous avenues and paths were cut through the trees, a pool was made picturesque and pleasant views from the edge of the wood were opened up. Several clearings were made and, strangely, these added a formal element to the otherwise rather natural landscaping, since, in the interests of variety, some were round, others oval, quadrangular and triangular. Many benches and turf seats were provided for visitors.

In his autobiography he attributed his conversion to the natural style to his purchase of the first four volumes of Hirschfeld's great work *Theorie der Gartenkunst* during a visit to Moscow early in 1784. (Volume V was published in 1785.) These volumes were published in German and in French between 1779 and 1785, and in view of his contacts and his mastery of German, and since he was an avid collector of books, it is perhaps a little surprising that he had not found them earlier. Having acquired them he was so captivated that he could hardly put them down until he had finished them.

> Before this I was devoted to the system of Le Nôtre and loved formal gardens, but now quite the opposite, I have completely ceased to love formal gardens and have acquired a taste for gardens in the new style, called irregular, natural, for it would be a sin to call them English. And Herr Hirschfeld so delighted me with them that I am dying to see a garden laid out according to these principles.[5]

In the years which followed he published translations of numerous extracts from Hirschfeld and many articles influenced by Hirschfeld in the *Economic Magazine*, advocating the landscape style, but not that of the English landscape park.[6] Western formal and landscape gardens were unsuitable models for Russians to follow, he argued, and western books on park and garden design were of little value, since they were not written for the Russian climate and circumstances. He was writing for the owners of modest estates without unlimited means and advised them that formal gardens should be avoided, since they need continuous and careful maintenance and gardeners with appropriate experience. Foreign gardeners should also be avoided, since they would make gardens as they were made in their country of origin. He advised symmetry near the house and near the entrance, with parterres, borders of fragrant plants, topiary, statues, vases and arbours. At some distance from the house there should be a wide, straight avenue leading away from it and terminated by a pavilion or an arbour; and there should be two or four narrower, radiating avenues. Winding paths should lead from the avenues to features of interest – park buildings, pools, hills, etc. Avenues should be planted with limes; wide paths with limes and elms; narrow paths with rowan, birch, acacia, maple and hazel.

Parks, he argued, are a combined effort of nature and man, with nature playing the major rôle. Man has to bring out the best from what nature has already provided. Attractive views should be opened up of distant hills, meadows, groves, villages, churches, water. Water is particularly important, and when not already there, streams and pools should be introduced. It should be borne in mind that the pleasant sound of a stream varies according to the size of the stones it flows over. Unpleasant views should be screened by dense planting. Many former estates in central Russia were influenced by his articles, and traces of the parks which were created still survive.[7]

When he returned from Moscow to Bogoroditsk with his

volumes of Hirschfeld, Bolotov waited impatiently for the snow to clear sufficiently for him to walk over the ground and to plan where to plant trees, where there should be water, where meadow, where to introduce rocks, where to make avenues and paths, where to place bridges, park buildings and resting places. He visualized how it would look when the work was completed and when the trees had grown, and he made landscape sketches of the way he expected it to develop. He had a workforce of two hundred, a number of them with horses, and while some moved earth to reshape the landscape and transported rock to the places in the park where it was going to be used, others fetched a great quantity of saplings and wild flowering plants from nearby woods to be planted in the park. Care was taken to retain the soil around the roots of the saplings, and they were all placed upright on the carts which carried them. They were planted with great care with plenty of water and they were also continually watered afterwards when there was no rain. Those who planted the saplings were used to formal gardens and Bolotov had difficulty at first in getting the random arrangement he wanted, but he solved the problem by marking with a handful of sand the place where each was to be planted.

Bolotov wanted to create an elaborate water system with streams, pools, cascades and waterfalls, but the nearest spring he could find was 1¼ miles away and issued at a level considerably lower than the ground over which he wished to divert it. This problem was again solved with sand – a great quantity was piled over the spring, and it then flowed out 10 feet

Below: A ruin and caves hewn out of sandstone at Bogoroditsk.

Bottom: A view in the park at Bogoroditsk created by Bolotov for Count Bobrinsky, the illegitimate son of Catherine and Grigory Orlov.

From the series of watercolour views of the park by Bolotov and his son, Pavel, which are in the Museum of History in Moscow.

Below: A rotunda in the park, with the pool formed
by the river and the town beyond.

Bottom: A view across a pool to Count Bobrinsky's
palace.

From the series of watercolour views of the park
by Bolotov and his son, Pavel, which are in the
Museum of History in Moscow.

higher. Other problems were also ingeniously solved, a great
deal of labour was committed, and eventually what appeared to
be a natural stream carried the water through the park. Later
he found another nearer source of water, which enabled him to
create further pools to add to the beauty of the park.

As was often the case with romantic-sentimental gardens, a
series of changing scenes was provided for the visitor, designed
to evoke changing moods. A path through dense and gloomy
planting led to a melancholy scene with a small hill
surmounted by a black pyramid with a white inscription,
apparently an epitaph. This was followed by a cheerful scene
with pleasant planting by a wide open space leading up a slope
to a domed rotunda and then to a rocky hillock with a circular
pavilion, and, near by, the glistening surface of a pool with
islands and bridges.

It must be said that some of the features in the park were
rather incongruous and owed nothing to Hirschfeld. What
appeared in the distance as a ruined monastery was found on
closer inspection to be a stage set made of laths, boards,
sandstone and rubble. A grotto was intended to appear as an
underground cave, but the walls were embellished with gold
and silver decorations, shells, coloured sandstone and bottle

glass. It received natural light from a glass lantern above, on which stood a marble statue. An angled mirror in the lantern gave the visitor below a view of the town across the water.

Bolotov liked to surprise and to play tricks. A small hill was formed with a winding path to the top, and while visitors were there, a sluice was opened, surrounding the hill with water. When the victims called out for help a bridge was thrown across to rescue them.

A building in the Echo Valley, with its cascade of pools, came to be known as the Abode of the Echo and was a popular source of entertainment. Two separate, identical structures, one intended for bathing, the other for use as a rest room, were built side by side, and the space between them was covered by an arched roof. The vaulted space below was found to produce an echo of sounds coming from a particular point eighty paces away which was regularly visited by those anxious to put it to the test.[8]

Bolotov seems to have kept a record of every compliment paid to him for his work at Bogoroditsk. General Mikhail Krechetnikov, the viceroy of Tula and Kaluga, to whom he was answerable, seems to have been very impressed when he was taken on a tour of the garden, and Bolotov was able to report in his autobiography:

> All these fine scenes so amazed the viceroy that he didn't know which to contemplate first and which to delight in first. He even stopped and stood in one place for several minutes repeating: 'How very good it all is. How well-placed this stone pavilion is standing on the hill; what a splendid meadow, and how pleasing these woods are with their sinuous edges; and how these little hills adorn the scene, encircling the water, and how right are these groups of trees which are growing on them. And this rotunda, how fine it looks and how it enlivens the whole place, and how natural this stone hill on which it stands, looking like a cliff; and this pool with the little islands — how fine it is!!' And so on!![9]

Bolotov had completed his work on the park in only two years, an extraordinary achievement, but he remained in his post until 1797, when, at the age of almost sixty, he returned to Dvoryaninovo and lived there until his death in 1823. His final years were contentedly spent in writing, in continually improving his very productive orchards and, no doubt, in another round of landscaping. In recent years there has been some restoration at Dvoryaninovo of the house, the garden and the pool, but not of Bolotov's great collection of apple trees.

Although the architectural features at Bogoroditsk disappeared long ago, much of the framework of the park remains, and a good record of the scenes Bolotov created survives in the album of paintings he executed with his son, Pavel, which is now in the Museum of History in Moscow.

Nadezhino

The palace and park at Nadezhino, some 375 miles south-east of Moscow, were developed by Prince Aleksandr Kurakin on land which had been given to his great-grandfather, Prince Boris Kurakin, by Peter. Boris Kurakin had played a notable part in the campaigns against the Turks, had fought at Narva, had commanded the Semyonovsky lifeguards at Poltava and later served as ambassador in England, France and Holland. He was also Peter's brother-in-law, having married the sister of Eudoxia Lopukhina, the Tsar's first wife. Aleksandr had a successful career at court until he crossed Catherine, as a result of his association with the Grand Duke Paul, and was required to live at Borisoglebskoe, as the estate was then called.

To ease the pain he built a splendid palace with an extensive park which would be the social centre of a wide area, and, aspiring to a recall to St Petersburg, he named it Nadezhdino (Hope). The identity of the architect has not been definitely established. The perception of Palladian influence led to Nikolai Lvov being considered — he translated the first volume of Palladio's four-volume work on architecture — but Giacomo Quarenghi is generally thought to be more likely. Kurakin himself claimed responsibility for much of the design of the palace,[10] which was built in a commanding position on a high plateau above the River Serdova. He had visited gardens in England in 1771 and, while they had made an impression, he was not completely won over by them:

> Everything is peculiar and accords with the strange taste they have adopted. There are just vast meadows dispersed with hills, groves, flower parterres, fields, groups of trees, single trees, or, now and then, stone monuments of antique architecture. Wandering along the walks one is certainly struck by the novelty of the spectacle. The scene changes at every step. Everything is different.[11]

But the English style soon became fashionable in Russia, and, while at Nadezhdino there were plenty of straight paths, formality was blended with 'natural' landscaping. On the river side of the palace there was just a steep, apparently landscaped slope leading to a landing stage and a pavilion. On the other side a wide straight avenue led away from the courtyard to a circular area 820 feet to the north. From there five straight avenues radiated on the eastern side, the central one leading to a second circular area, from which further avenues radiated. One of the avenues was named Antoinette and there was also an Antoinette Pavilion. Other avenues were named Cesarovich, Peter Molchanov, Gatchina, Brother Alexis, Katina, Sophina and Alyona.

In the landscape park a network of paths wound their way among groves, glades, meadows and pools. Among the sentimentally named park buildings were Temples of Friendship (echoing Pavlovsk), Truth, Fidelity, Harmony, Patience and Fame and a Storehouse of Eternal Sentiments,

The Chinese Pavilion at Nadezhdino.

There was also a Chinese pavilion and an obelisk in memory of Marie Antoinette.

After the death of Catherine, Kurakin was able to resume his career in St Petersburg with the post of procurator general and paid little further attention to Nadezhdino. By the middle of the nineteenth century the park was in a state of general decay.[12]

Sophievska

Stanislas Shchensky (Felix) Potocki was born in 1751, the son of a wealthy Polish nobleman Salezi Potocki who, in Kristanopl (now Chervonograd), had one of the finest residences in Poland. At the age of twenty, on the death of his father, Felix inherited vast estates and enormous debts. In 1774 he married Josephine Amalia Minshek and moved to his Tulchin estate, since Kristanopl had ceased to be part of Poland. A splendid palace was built there in 1782, and a large park was laid out with native and exotic plants. During a visit to Italy he bought many seedlings of Lombardy poplars (*Populus nigra* 'Italica'). Potocki had 3,700,000 acres and 130,000 serfs. He took a great interest in agriculture and forestry, growing varieties of wheat, rye and oats which had not been grown in Poland before, and extending his woodlands. He took steps to ensure that his serfs had satisfactory dwellings with fruit trees on their plots of land, and when they worked on his estates they were paid in cash. Together with his second wife, Sophia, he was to make one of the world's greatest parks.

Sophia Constantine was born in 1760 in Turkey to Greek parents of modest means. After the death of her father her mother married an Armenian, who died soon afterwards. When her house was destroyed in a fire she was left without any means of support and, in 1777, she became a courtesan and took Sophia to the Polish ambassador, Carol Boskamp, who gave her a home and found a French teacher for her. On social occasions in the diplomatic circles of Istanbul her beauty and charm attracted much attention. In 1779, having claimed, it seems, that she was of noble birth and connected with the Greek royal family, she married an army officer, Major Witt, son of the Governor of the Polish Fortress of Kamenets Podolsk. He was to become General Witt on the death of his father in 1785. When they travelled around Europe she was univerally admired and warmly accepted in high society. In 1781 she was the guest for two months of King Stanislaus II Augustus of Poland, and later met King Frederick II of Prussia in Berlin and the Austrian Emperor Joseph II in Spa. The latter wrote enthusiastically about her to his sister, Marie-Antoinette, who received her in Paris, where she also met two future kings of France – Louis XVIII and Charles X. In 1788 she travelled to Russia with Field Marshal Prince Charles-Joseph de Ligne, who had advised Marie-Antoinette on the Petit Trianon, the Duc de Chartres on the Parc Monceau and the Baron de Monville on the Désert de Retz, and was the author of *Coup d'oeil sur Beloeil et sur une grande partie des jardins d'Europe*. In Russia she met and impressed Prince Potemkin, who arranged for her to be

presented to Catherine, by whom she was received in a very friendly manner and with gifts in 1791.[13] In the same year she met Potocki, who was completely captivated. She became his mistress and, when they had obtained divorces, his wife.

In 1795 she stayed with Helen Radziwill at Nieborów, where she was taken to see Arkadia, the famous park created by Radziwill in a Romantic style with elements of Greek mythology. Sophia was inspired by it and wrote to Potocki:

> After dinner we went to see Arkadia. It's difficult to imagine anything better or more romantic. You know Arkadia, but you saw it ten years ago. Imagine how much young trees must have grown in ten years and how much has been done to improve it. . . . I am madly in love with Arkadia. . . . Arkadia reminds me very much of the Crimea. You know, with your means in those parts we could have the same in two years, and perhaps something even more beautiful.[14]

But Potocki was not quite as rich as Sophia imagined, partly because of the debts he had inherited and partly because of Josephine's extravagance.

On a number of occasions in 1795 Potocki went hunting on his estate at Uman with Ludovic Metzel, a former captain in the Polish engineers and the illegitimate son of Potocki's brother-in-law, General Briulov, and he decided that the valley of the river Kamenka (as it came to be called), with its picturesque hills and granite rocks, was an excellent foundation for a landscape park, which would be the largest and most beautiful in Europe, and which he would dedicate to Sophia. Metzel was obviously keenly interested in parks and may well have had some experience of making them, since he was commissioned by Potocki to create the park which would be called Sophievka. He travelled abroad to visit and to study parks and to investigate the machinery available to overcome the problems which granite presented to the landscaper.

No plans or sketches seem to have survived. Metzel designed the complex and impressive water system. The Upper Pool (21 acres) serves as a reservoir for the remarkable waterfall, fountains and canal. To make the Lower Pool the granite bed was excavated with explosives, and the granite it yielded was used for rock features in the park, the relief of which was altered by the spoil from both pools. Grottoes were excavated with enormous effort by stonemasons. While the construction work proceeded, many native trees were planted and, in certain places, exotic plants from distant parts of the world. Many Lombardy poplars were brought from Tulchin. Marble statues were ordered from Italy. Metzel had the assistance of a very able gardener, Oliva, from Germany and a workforce which usually numbered about eight hundred.

Sophievka is a recreation of classical mythology in landscape. There is a Mount Parnassus and a terrace of the Muses with a Hippocrene stream, which was said to have flowed from a rock struck with his hoof by the winged horse Pegasus.

Left, above: Granite rocks excavated by Metzel in making the pools were used effectively in the landscape.

Left: The Grotto of Venus with a statue of Venus. It was originally the Grotto of Thetis.

Right: Metzel's impressive waterfall.

The Grotto of Diana represents the legendary grotto, where Actaeon, hunting in the forest, saw the goddess bathing and was turned into a stag and torn to pieces by his own hounds. The Grotto of Venus, where the statue of Venus has been placed in recent years, was formerly the Grotto of Thetis, the sea nymph. Her statue was once accompanied there by four sea monsters, all of which are thought to have been destroyed in a flood in the nineteenth century. The Grotto of Terror and Doubt related to the Greek myth of Tantalus, who betrayed the secrets of the gods and stole ambrosia and nectar from their table to give to mortals. For this he was condemned to stand for ever up to his neck in water, which subsided when he tried to drink, while fruit-laden branches just above his head swayed away when he stretched out a hand. There was formerly a statue of Orpheus in the park, a reminder of his descent into the underworld, where, through his music, he persuaded Pluto to allow Eurydice, who had died from a snake bite, to follow him back to earth. He gave an undertaking not to look back which, to his cost, he failed to keep. Later, when he was torn to pieces by crazed Bacchantes, his head fell into a river and was carried by the water to the island of Lesbos, and the place of its burial became an oracular shrine. Lesbos, represented by the half-submerged rock in the Lower Pool, was where the Greek poetess Sappho lived, and it was there that she threw herself from the Leucadian rock when her love for Phaeon went unrequited:

> Il rappelle Leucade et son rocher fameux
> D'où pour finir leurs maux les amans malheureux,
> Ranimant dans leurs coeurs un reste d'espérance,
> Cherchaient au fond des flots un terme à leur souffrance.[15]

Near by, the Caucasian Hill relates to the fate of Prometheus, who had stolen fire from the gods to give to mortals and was chained to a rock in the Caucasus, on the orders of Jupiter, and suffered daily visits from an eagle, which fed on his liver. The Cretan Labyrinth at Sophievka recalls Theseus' slaying of the Minotaur. The statue of Paris reminds us of the beauty contest between Venus, Juno and Minerva, when he awarded the apple to Venus, who had described Helen, the wife of King Menelaus of Sparta, to him as an available reward. His successful abduction of her from Sparta brought about the Trojan War; and the Snake Fountain represents the snakes which killed the Trojan priest, Laocoön, and his two sons after he had warned the Trojans not to take the wooden horse into the city. The Elysian Fields, the Vale of Tempe, sacred to Apollo, the Valley of Giants and the Athenian School are all featured in the park. The statue of Euripides has been there since 1800. After the Revolution, Homer, Socrates, Plato and Aristotle were removed from Talnovsky Park, once owned by Sophia's son-in-law Count Shuvalov, and were taken to the Uman Regional Museum, from where, in 1957, they reached Sophievka. The most remarkable recreation is the Styx, the river of the underworld, which is represented by a canal in a tunnel more than 650 feet long, along which gondolas ferried visitors.[16]

The Snake Fountain, representing the snakes which killed the Trojan priest Laocoön and his sons.

The central part of the park seems to have been completed by May 1802 for an opening ceremony on Sophia's name day. Sadly Potocki died in March 1805, when, although more remained to be done, a masterpiece had already been achieved. Metzel continued to work at Sophievka until 1813, when he was appointed to an important administrative post in Warsaw. Oliva remained at Sophievka until his death in 1827.

Stanislaw Trembecki, the Polish poet, who was living at Potocki's residence in Tulchin, celebrated Sophievka in a long poem, *Sophiowka*, which was published in 1806, though apparently written three or four years earlier. It served as a guide to the park and went into many editions. He compared Sophievka with the groves of Tusculanium on Cicero's estate; with Tivoli, celebrated by Horace, where there were waterfalls and cascades on the River Arno, which was a popular hunting resort in summer; and with Pavzilippo, the mountain near Naples through which there was a tunnel ⅔ mile long, leading to marvellous landscape. Sophievka, he declared, surpassed them all.[17]

In 1811 Comte Auguste de Lagarde stayed at Tulchin, and Sophia asked him to translate Trembecki's poem into French. His translation was published in 1815 in an expensively produced edition with seven views of Sophievka by a Scottish artist, V. Allen. The Emperor Alexander and his wife and other crowned heads were among the subscribers. Sophia and her son, General I.O. Witt, subscribed for thirty copies and must also have contributed liberally towards the cost of publication. De Lagarde also wrote this admirable account of the park in 1811:

> This garden was intended by the count to serve as a monument of his attachment and affection for the beauteous Sophia. . . . The plan of this garden was conceived by Mr Metzel, formerly a captain of Polish engineers. . . . Previous to the commencement of his undertaking Mr Metzel had travelled to Prussia, Silesia and Saxony, for the purpose of witnessing the operation of machinery of which he had only read the description and calculated the probable effects. The models he afterwards rendered subservient to the works at Sophioffka, and with such improvements, that rocks which seemed as if no earthly power could ever be capable of shaking, were completely removed from their bases. The perseverance of the count, the inventive resources of Metzel's genius and the immense means placed at his disposal finally produced that magic work Sophioffka.
>
> The approach to the place is announced by an obelisk of 60 feet in height, cut out of a single piece of granite on which are engraved in large Greek characters *Eros toi Sophia*. Love to Sophia. An immense sheet of water comes next, on the borders of which an uninterrupted avenue of willow trees has been planted. Not far from this spot the river Kamionska has been made to precipitate itself from a prodigious height, on a mass of

rocks, from whence it rebounds in foam to continue its course; it is a torrent which falls and one which rises – an admirable specimen of opposite movements. The river is crossed further down over an iron bridge of admirable workmanship, which leads to a space surrounded by several grottoes cut into immense rocks, which seem as if suspended in the air and so disposed as to show the grand cascade in a thousand different points of view. A path cut in the rock leads to an elevation which overhangs the sheet of water, and is intended as an imitation of the Leucadian rock immortalised by so many of the victims of love. A temple formed of trunks of trees, not deprived of their external covering, represents the early monuments which human piety consecrated to the Divinity. From here a sloping path leads into a deep cavern, whence an abundant spring sends forth its frothy waters. This grotto is dedicated to happiness, as words to that effect in the Polish language announce. Next is a sort of amphitheatre, surrounded by a double row of Italian poplars: it has several circular rows of seats, similar to the places which in Greece were dedicated to the discussions of the learned. It has been called here the Athenian School. An avenue of acacias leads to a marble pillar, the base of which is bathed in a stream. This solitude, consecrated to painful recollections, contains the tombs of three of the countess's children, snatched from her at an early age. Following the course of the stream, one is led to an Egyptian temple, which is in every sense enveloped in a sheet of water; it is only through an underground passage that it is accessible. During the hottest days of summer, the freshness of this place relieves one from the effects of the sun's burning rays. Not far off is situated an extensive aviary, containing birds from every part of the globe. Proceeding on the ascent of a gentle hill, shaded by tall and splendid trees, whose origin appears to date from of old, you enter on its summit an avenue which leads to a lake, where a boat in imitation of a Genoese gondola is to be found. Four oarsmen take you rapidly across the lake into a subterranean channel, where for twenty minutes you proceed in almost total darkness under masses of immense rocks. At the other extremity you enter another lake, the limits of which are hardly visible to the naked eye. A yacht, whose gilt masts and silk cordages are meant to give a resemblance to the vessel in which the Egyptian queen proceeded on her voyage to Tarsus, takes you up, sails in various directions, and finally lands you on an island, where, amidst trees and flowers, are one day to rest the remains of Trembecki, the author of the Polish poem Sophioffka, written in celebration of this place and the woman whose name it bears. At another end of the lake you are set down in a vast garden, where the fruits of the whole world have been made to grow in immense abundance, and in all the perfection required in their native soil. . . . A great number and variety of statues and other works of sculpture, of different and picturesque views, and of waterworks, are interspersed and reproduced in these extensive grounds. Imagination can never form a conception of the reality, and human ingenuity will never go further in any attempts to produce the imitation of an earthly paradise.[18]

The distinguished Russian scholar Dmitri Likhachev was convinced that the parks at Mon Repos, which we have considered, and Alupka which will be considered later, were influenced by Ossianism, and he thought that Sophievka may have been as well.[19] The waterfall, the enormous boulders and the cave-like grottoes at Sophievka may certainly remind one of Scotland, and it was a Scottish artist who provided the views for de Lagarde's translation of Trembecki's poem, but there is no evidence that Ossian was in the minds of Potocki and Sophia. Although they would have been acquainted with the Ossian poems, classical mythology alone appears to be the source of their inspiration. The first reference to Ossian came from de Lagarde in his translation of Trembecki's poem, where he asks if it is Malvina, widow of Ossian's warrior son Oscar, who is leading the aged and blind poet across the rocks:

> Sur ces âpres rochers, n'est ce pas Malvina
> Conduisant Ossian au palais de Selma?

In an endnote de Lagarde explained that he had seen Trembecki, at the age of eighty, being guided by Sophia across the rocks at Sophievka, and this had transported him to Scotland, seeing in his mind's eye 'Malvina, sole supporter of the Scottish Homer, leading Ossian to the Palace of Fingal and blending her sweet voice with the plaintive sounds of the harp of the bard'.[20]

In 1820 the Emperor Alexander visited Sophievka and must have admired the Lombardy poplars, since Sophia sent him some saplings the following year.[21] She was by then incurably ill and died in Berlin in 1822. Her son Alexander Potocki succeeded her at Sophievka, and it continued to be well maintained, but it was confiscated by the government in 1831 and came under the control of the War Ministry, when it was established that he had supported a Polish revolt. Perhaps surprisingly, the park seems not to have suffered at the hands of the army, possibly because Nicholas I had visited it twice and decreed that it should be kept in the same exceptional state as before. In 1836 General I.O. Witt, Sophia's son by her first marriage, became responsible for Sophievka, and it was at this time that it became known as the Tsarina's Garden.

The provisions made for staff are interesting. The head gardener was paid 800 roubles a year, his senior assistant 400, his junior assistant 240 and the administrator (an army officer) 400. There were 10 master gardeners, 12 trainee gardeners and 20 auxiliary workers. In addition a temporary workforce of 60 was taken on for a month in the spring and a month in the

autumn for such tasks as repairing paths and renewing the sand and gravel. In the 1840s the Flora Pavilion was added to the park, as well as a pavilion in the Chinese style and another in the form of a mushroom.

Théodore Themery, a French citizen who lived in Uman for twenty-two years and was the director of an academy for young ladies, published a detailed guide in French to Sophievka in 1846. He supported his text with quotations from de Lagarde's translation of Trembecki's poem, quotations from Jacques Delille's *Les Jardins*, with verses of his own and nine views of the park and a plan. In addition to providing information about the classical myths which had inspired features in the park, he built on de Lagarde's reference to Ossian and suggested that legendary Scottish heroes from the poems of Ossian might have found an appropriate setting at Sophievka. He explained who Ossian was and provided a French translation of some of the poems.[22]

Nicholas I visited the park in 1847 and ordered the building of the Gothic turrets by the entrance gates and the replacement of a building on an island by a pavilion in the Byzantine style, and commissioned A.I. Stakenschneider to design both. He promised to provide a statue of his wife, Alexandra Fyodorovna, in whose honour the park had been renamed, which was placed on the Caucasian Hill.

It is not known whether he was tempted to take the waters for which curative properties were claimed. A hydropathic establishment was established by the entrance, which drew favourable comment in a Kiev newspaper in the year of Nicholas's visit:

> You rest in silence, broken only by the song of the nightingale and the sound of the fountains and cascades. Add to this the splendour, elegance and luxuriance of the garden in all its meanders, the wealth of hothouse trees and plants, the multitude of flowers – you can picture to yourself how much comforting tranquillity is offered here to the patients.[23]

The fruit in the hothouses might also have been mentioned, for there were 'large lemon trees, very good pineapple plants which produced up to 3,000 fruit a year, peaches, grapes, apricots and bananas' under the care of the head gardener.

The army's record as custodians of the park for twenty-eight years was very impressive, but in 1859 Alexander II decreed that the Main School of Horticulture should be moved from Odessa to Uman and that thenceforth the park would be known as the Uman Garden Main School of Horticulture. Forestry was taught as well as horticulture, and then, in 1868, it became the Uman School of Husbandry and Horticulture. The career prospects of ornamental gardeners declined after the abolition of serfdom in 1861, since many landowners were no longer in a position to employ them. The 1870s and early 1880s were difficult because of floods and lack of funds, but V.V. Paskevich, who was head gardener from 1885 to 1892, brought new distinction to the park through his work on the introduction of decorative plants. He also established an arboretum and an apple orchard with a large collection of varieties. He later worked at the Nikitsky Botanical Garden near Yalta and at the Botanical Garden in St Petersburg. In the early years of the twentieth century the school became a hotbed for revolutionaries, and the director and a number of others were found guilty of subversive activities.[24]

The park suffered considerable damage during German occupation in two world wars. Among the many statues lost during the second was one of Lenin, which had been placed in the park in 1939. Most of the other statues were damaged. Now only a few of the statues of the early years remain, and hardly any of them are in their original places. Sadly, too, there are no Stygian ferry trips by gondola, but Sophievka is still a most impressive park and worth travelling a long way to see.

Sokirentsy

The estate at Sokirentsy, 90 miles or so east of Kiev, was given to Ignaty Ivanovich Galagan in 1716 by Peter the Great, and his descendants lived there until the Revolution. In the eighteenth century there was a wooden house which had a formal garden with clipped limes and a covered way leading to a pavilion decorated in Pompeian style. In the 1820s Count Pavel Grigorevich, who took a great interest in architecture, built a larger and more imposing house in classical style and laid out a landscape park of some 150 acres. The entrance to the estate is flanked by monumental gate-towers and attractive lodges from which a straight avenue leads through lines of tall trees. The latter were still clipped to form green walls when Georgi Lukomsky visited Sokirentsy in 1914, and this helped to lead the eye to the large white house with its eight-columned portico and flattened dome, 325 yards away. An unusual feature is the gentle ramp, the *pente douce*, which leads gracefully down from the first floor of the garden front of the house to the large meadow at the heart of the composition of the park. The ramp widens as one descends between diverging balustrades embellished with vases and statues of goddesses. Below the meadow lies the lake and beyond that wooded parkland with varied and picturesque relief. The ancient oak trees are a major element and are supported by birches, limes, white poplars, hornbeams, maples, larches, pines and chestnuts. The architect P.A. Dubrovsky (probably a pupil of Zhiliardi or Kazakov), along with an experienced gardener named Bisterfeld, worked at Sokirentsy for Count Pavel, but it has been suggested that the Count himself designed some of the garden buildings, including a gothic bridge, a gothic temple and an eight-columned rotunda. The latter was placed on an artificial mound and was further raised by a stone base of twelve steps. Looking out from the meadow across the lake it makes a very effective contribution to the composition of the park. The late-eighteenth-century church with a fine iconostasis was built by Count Grigory Ivanovich, Count Pavel's profligate father. There is also an orangery on the estate. Sokirentsy is a particularly

Top: The gentle ramp leading down from the first floor of the house at Sokirentsy to the meadow.

Above: The rotunda at Sokirentsy.

good example of a well-planned Russian estate which continued to be well maintained by the same family (the Lamsdorf-Galagans when the male line died out) long after many estates had fallen into disrepair. Since the Revolution it has been somewhat marred by inappropriate planting and building, but it is designated as a monument of park and garden art and one hopes that its character will be fully restored.[25]

In the 1980s there was a statue of Lenin in front of the house wearing Stalin's greatcoat. It was originally a statue of Stalin, but after he was posthumously denounced by Nikita Kruschev at the Twentieth Party Congress in 1956, his head was removed and replaced by Lenin's.[26]

Aleksandria

Count Branicki's romantic park at Aleksandria, on the outskirts of Byelaya Tserkov in Ukraine, was created between the end of the eighteenth century and the middle of the nineteenth in a landscape of woods and meadows by the River Ros. There were formal elements near the palace – parterres, sculpture, fountains and straight avenues. Among the picturesque architectural features in the park were a Turkish cottage, a Chinese bridge and an artificial ruin of two arches which provided a support wall for a dam, gave rise to a waterfall and served as a viewing platform. The Echo Colonnade is a semi-circular colonnaded gallery with remarkable acoustics. In 1829 a fraternal monument was erected in the park to fellow Slavs in Bulgaria, suffering under the yoke of the Turks. It took the form of two blocks of stone bound together by a hoop and was once accompanied by a piece of sculpture. But most important of all in the park were the trees: a wide range of species was planted very effectively.

The abolition of serfdom brought an end to further development of the park and a decline in maintenance, with self-sown trees adversely affecting the quality of the earlier planting. The years of the civil war, followed later by the German occupation, brought considerable further damage. In 1946 Aleksandria was given special state protection, and in the 1950s an impressive programme of restoration was undertaken. Park buildings were rescued from the ruinous condition they had been reduced to; the earlier landscaping was largely restored; additional areas were landscaped, new paths were introduced and the water system was improved. Trees continue to be the outstanding feature of the park and there are six hundred species and forms. With the range of herbaceous plants numbering seven hundred, Aleksandria vies with botanical gardens in its variety and has regained its place as one of the outstanding parks of Ukraine.[27]

Kachanovka

The palace and park at Kachanovka date from the eighteenth century and are situated 4½ miles from Parafievka in the Chernigov district of Ukraine. In 1770 the considerable estate was given to Field Marshal Rumiantsev-Zadunaisky by Catherine II. It was for him that the Moscow architect Karl Blank designed the palace, while M.K. Mostipanov, a pupil of V.I. Bazhenov, laid out the park on part of the estate's considerable area of ancient woodlands and pools. In 1824 the estate passed into the ownership of the Tarnovskys – Grigory Stepanovich, Vasily Vasilievich and his son, also Vasily Vasilievich – and it was during their tenure that Kachanovka became notable for its patronage of the arts. The writers Gogol and Shevchenko, the artists Repin, Ge and Vrubel and the composer Glinka were among the many who were invited to stay and work there. It was at Kachanovka that Glinka heard parts of *Ruslan and Ludmilla* performed for the first time by the resident serf orchestra.

The palace is approached along a wide, straight avenue, which also links the palace with the church. The area round the

Left: The statue at Sokirentsy of Lenin wearing Stalin's greatcoat.

Above: The Echo Colonnade at Aleksandria.

Right: View across the Maiorsky Pool at Kachanovka to the palace (right) and the Glinka Pavilion (left).

palace was formally laid out on the approach side with a large circular space of mown grass in front of the entrance, where two Cossack cannon once stood, and there were flowerbeds and statues. A straight transverse avenue crossed the approach avenue at right angles, and it was also crossed at the same point by straight radial paths. On the other side of the palace the view is of wooded landscape parkland with a wide central clearing leading down to the lake-like Maiorsky Pool. The area of water surfaces in the park is about 250 acres. Many winding paths lead through the park with a number of brick bridges crossing paths at a lower level. The principal trees in the park are oaks, maples, elms, limes and birch, but there are also groups and single trees of larch, fir, Weymouth pine, thuya and horse chestnut, with a total of fifty species of trees and shrubs recorded. The avenues are lined with limes, chestnuts, maples and birches. Numerous natural and manmade hillocks once served as viewing platforms but access is now restricted by self-sown trees and dense undergrowth. Two of their names have survived: the Hill of Love, where there was once a wooden summerhouse, and the Hill of Reverie. The outstanding viewing point in the park is the raised ground where the Glinka Pavilion still stands. By the Maiorsky Pool there is a rather ruinous structure which extends over three terraces: inside are dark, vaulted, underground passages, very large rooms, iron window-frames, iron rings on the walls and ceilings, and an atmosphere to disturb the nervous visitor. Its purpose was already a mystery in the late nineteenth century and remains so. Statues, fountains, seats and other small features were once distributed around the park, and there was a small theatre known locally as the Chinese Pavilion. The site of the Orangery has been established, but the location of the Winter Garden was still being researched a few years ago.

Vasily Vasilievich the younger seems to have made many improvements to the park and won the quite ecstatic praise of his nephew, M.V. Tarnovsky, writing in *Stolitsa i usadba*[28] in 1915:

> At every step one feels aware of the talent of the architect of this park and his infinite love for it. Vas. Vas. was a real master of garden making and a pure artist, who may with confidence be placed alongside such geniuses as Le Nôtre. On an expanse of 800 desiatins [2,160 acres] he created a fabulous park where every turn of a path revealed to the enraptured visitor one new view after another. Most valuable of all was the complete absence of anything trite or contrived. Nature did not lose the power of its presence, and all the grandeur was achieved with immense ability.

Sadly the lifestyle and the generosity to visiting artists of Vasily Vasilievich the younger led to financial difficulties, and he was forced to sell the estate in 1898.

After the Revolution, Kachanovka was given to the peasants, and the palace remained empty for some years, and then, from 1924 to 1933, it became an orphanage. During the years 1933 and 1934 a group of artists and architects from Kiev undertook some restoration of the palace and the central part of the estate, but between 1935 and 1941 it was occupied by Ukraine's sanatorium. During the last two years of the war it became an evacuation hospital and then a sanatorium for invalided officers. Between 1949 and 1982 it was again a sanatorium. In 1980 Kachanovka was declared a monument of historical-cultural importance, and since then some restoration has been undertaken. Kachanovka is one of Ukraine's most important parks, and one hopes that sufficient funds for this purpose will continue to be made available.[29]

Palaces in the Crimea

The annexation of the Crimea by Russia in 1783, masterminded by Potemkin, not only secured Russia's dominance over the Black Sea, but provided the richest and most powerful of the nobility with the opportunity to establish estates and to create parks in a much more benign climate than had previously been available to them in Russia, and in spectacular natural settings. 'Here you find rocks, ruins, mountains, cascades, woods, clumps, rills, torrents, mazy walks, flowering shrubs, slopes, hills, dales, seas, fruit trees, flowers, rich verdure; and, in short, we find in this country every beauty and every sportive arrangement of nature, on a great scale, which you have so wisely imitated on a small scale in your happy island,' wrote Maria Guthrie, a native of France, to her husband Matthew Guthrie, a surgeon in St Petersburg.[30]

Kachanovka Palace.

For Catherine's tour of her new territory in 1787 Potemkin had palaces prepared with pleasure grounds laid out by William Gould, which must have been the first Russian gardens in the Crimea. A few years later Maria Guthrie, in another letter to her husband, described 'one of those fairy palaces which arose as if by magic in the most romantic spots of the Tauride, by the secret arrangement of Potemkin, to surprise and charm Catherine II when she visited these acquisitions to her empire':

> Catherine, on arriving hither, with a quarter of her court, and some of the foreign ministers, was not a little astonished to find a large and elegant imperial mansion ready to receive her, in so romantic and charming a spot; while the light irregular form, most artificially given to imitate the Tartar style, added much to the novelty of the scene.
>
> It is placed on a bank of the limpid Karafu, which, after issuing in the form of a clear spring from the steep rocky wall of a fine neighbouring valley, winds round one side of this Tauro-Russian palace; while some noble hills seem placed on purpose to bound the view on the other.
>
> Here you see clumps of majestic trees, the Linnaean nobles of the forest, proudly lording it over the humble, though lovely flowering shrubs, which have taken shelter like ourselves from the midday ardour of the sun, under their spreading branches; and, I can assure you, we were happy to find shade in such fragrant company, in our sauntering across a fine and most extensive lawn, to gain a charming wood which makes part of the delightful pleasure grounds laid out by your countryman Gould . . . to adorn this fairy abode. How easy must his task have been here, and indeed in every part of the romantic Tauride where the Prince employed him, as Nature has furnished every rural beauty in such profusion, that Mr Gould could only have to prune away some of her luxuriance to give you a better view of the rest; and this we found he had done, more especially in the fine wood just mentioned, where a winding road led us insensibly to the view of every object worth attention, as we followed the meandering path.[31]

The garden was at Karasubazaar, now Beligorsk.[32]

Bakhchisarai

Maria Guthrie also visited Bakhchisarai, once the capital of the Crimean Khanate, and described the Khan's palace and garden:

> We enter this princely residence by a spacious court, and are struck in passing through it, with a view of the garden on one hand, hanging on the brow of a hill in the form of terraces, like the ancient gardens of Semiramis in Babylon, or those of the mountains of Egyptian Thebes. . . .
>
> Behind the exterior court there is a small interior one, which leads to a fine round vestibule paved with white marble, and ornamented with three fountains of cool, clear, and excellent water, from which rise five streams, ever playing and sparkling in the air, to cool the atmosphere of this delightful apartment. From this Arabian luxury you enter a charming little garden, where loaded vines, entwined with roses, form fairy bowers, wherein you may repose and eat the delicious fruit around you; for grapes, peaches, apricots, plums, cherries, etc. are all found here of a quality very superior to those growing wild in the valleys.[33]

Though she must have seen it in the Fountain Court, she failed to mention the Fountain of Tears – celebrated by Pushkin in a famous poem – which still survives:

The Fountain of Tears at Bakhchisarai.

In itself the fountain is highly symbolic. At the top is a five-petalled flower carved in marble whose centre resembles a human eye shedding tears. These fill a marble bowl, which symbolizes the heart. The water then overflows into two small bowls, tears bring relief. But this relief is only temporary: once more the water from the two small bowls gathers in a large one lying beneath them. And so forth and so on – sorrow forever alternates with relief.[34]

Alupka

Among Potemkin's acquisitions in the Crimea was the village of Alupka, surrounded by orchards and supremely well situated on the coastal strip between the mountains and the Black Sea, 10 miles south-west of Yalta. He ordered the planting of cypresses, planes, Italian pines and other ornamental plants from the Mediterranean, while almonds, pomegranates, olives, bays and mulberries were planted in the orchards. With the aid of Gould, he sought to create a private botanic garden, but after his death the estate changed hands more than once and lost this character.[35]

In 1824 the estate was bought by Count Michael Vorontsov who was then Governor-general of Novorossisk. He was the son of Count Simon Vorontsov, the Russian ambassador to England, and it was there that Michael was brought up and educated. His sister Catherine was the second wife of George Augustus, 11th Earl of Pembroke; while his wife, Elizabeth, may have been, briefly, the mistress of Alexander Pushkin.[36] He served with distinction against the French and was seriously wounded at Borodino, where he commanded a division of grenadiers in Prince Bagration's army. 'His courage at the siege of Leipsig impressed Bonaparte himself: "that's the stuff", he remarked, "of which marshals are made".'[37] Count Vorontsov was one of the richest men in Russia and by the 1840s owned more than 1,000,000 acres of land (including Massandra, Gurzuf and Cape Martyan in the Crimea) and 80,000 serfs. Hundreds of these serfs, among them skilled craftsmen and gardeners, were sent to work at Alupka from Vorontsov's other estates.[38]

Already in 1827 James Webster was enthralled by what he saw at Alupka:

> The gardens are singularly beautiful, having a lake, and, on the acclivity, quantities of large stones and rocks, heaped together. Some rocks, as that behind the mosque, are fifty feet, or more, in length. These gardens may be safely styled unrivalled! In the gardens of Versailles are rocks, which were brought together at a great expense; and the grottoes and overhanging precipices are pointed out as admirable objects – and such they are, as showing how far caprice and wealth can go in imitating nature. At every step in the gardens of Alupka, you meet with rocks far more imposing than the wonders of Versailles.[39]

Two years later another British visitor, Captain James Alexander, visited 'the delightful gardens of Aloopka':

> A white mosque and minaret were built near the village, and below was the country residence, in the Tartar style of architecture, with a Belvedere and flat roof, projecting eaves and verandahs. Here I spent the evening, and at an early hour wandered through the gardens, containing vines of many varieties, and flowers of the most brilliant hues; among the rocks were cascades and fishponds, in which last swans disported themslves among the water lilies. The Count created these gardens in the last few years, as if by enchantment, and the situation he selected is most picturesque. On looking up, a perpendicular mountain towers above the clouds, and below is the 'deep blue sea'.[40]

Michael Vorontsov had already made considerable progress with his park well before he began to build his new palace.

In the archives at Alupka there is a plan of an early scheme for the palace. It is on English paper with the date 1828 appearing in the watermark, the scale is in feet and there are inscriptions in English. It may be the work of Thomas Harrison (1744–1829), who had provided various plans between 1823 and

Above: The south front of Alupka Palace.

Right: The mountain peak Ai Petri towering above the trees in the park.

Top: The mountain peak Ai Petri beyond the garden by the palace.

Above: One of the six lions on the terrace and the rose 'Countess Vorontsova'.

1828 for Vorontsov's estates in Odessa and south Russia, but Francesco Buffo, an Odessan architect of Italian extraction, who designed Vorontsov's palace (1826–8) in Odessa, was responsible for the plan of the dining hall. This is also preserved in the palace archives. The laying of the foundations began in March 1830 and work on the walls in 1831, but in June of that year Vorontsov, who was then in England, sent instructions for the work to be halted. He had arranged for Edward Blore to produce a new plan for the palace, a plan which was to combine Tudor, medieval and Moresque styles, and work began on this during the following year, using the local grey-green stone, called diabase. It is the main, south façade, facing the Black Sea, which is Moresque with a dominant portal resembling the entrance of a mosque. The north façade suggests a rather austere Tudor mansion, while the west and east façades have the look of a medieval castle. No doubt the plans were the result of detailed consultations with Vorontsov, from whom the architect would have learned about the nature of the site. While Blore never visited Russia, an architect said to have been named Gayton[41] went to Alupka on his recommendation to supervise the work, but after the latter's sudden death in 1833 he was succeeded by another English architect, William Hunt, who remained there until the project was completed.[42]

William Hunt has been credited with the layout of the formal terrace garden in front of the south façade – the Lion Terrace – which has its roots in the Italian Renaissance, with parterres, marble fountains and vases, six splendid marble lions from the workshop of Bonanni flanking a grand stairway, clipped evergreens and flowering plants. Among the roses, the 'Countess Vorontsova' stands out. A fountain in an enclosed space near the library building echoes the Fountain of Tears at Bakhchisarai. Beyond the Lion Terrace a series of lower terraces descend to the sea. On the first terrace there are some small fountains, among them the Trilby Fountain, said to be 'in the English style', with the raised figure of a dog holding a cat in its mouth.[43] On the second terrace the principal feature is a fountain in the form of a shell. On another terrace roses and lilies were planted, of which a few years ago *Rosa bracteata* survived. There is a tea house near the landing stage built in the 1820s in the form of a Doric colonnade (the architect was Philip Elson[44]) surrounded by planes, laurels and oaks.

The romantic landscaping of the upper park behind the palace and towards the mountains is an outstanding example of the work 'of the hands, the taste and the spiritual concentration of the gardener of genius' Karl Kebach, who spent the last twenty-five years of his life there.[45] Work on the park began in 1831 when thousands of tons of rock were cleared from a wide area, vast quantities of black earth from Ukraine and fertile soil from mountain pastures were transported to the site, water courses with cascades were fashioned and mountain streams were diverted to feed them.

While the terraced garden in front of the palace has a social character, the upper park is a retreat from the world, a place of peace and solitude where one may wander, commune with nature and meditate. Vorontsov needed both a social stage and the means of escaping from it. 'Social order, to which architectural thought was answerable, was linked with the appearance in Russia of a particular way of cultural life. Along with Decembrist totality there developed a type of person who was divided, the civil servant-philosopher, the two sides of whose life remained not in clear harmony but as it were secret one from the other. . . . The distaste for empty social life appeared as natural as the need to plunge into it.'[46]

From the courtyard behind the palace a narrow winding path leads through leafy shade, past rocks covered in moss, grottoes, streams, waterfalls and cascades, a rather dark and melancholy area known as the Little Chaos. One of the grottoes contains the remains of Chelmik, a favourite dog of Vorontsov's, with a carved inscription in his memory. The path suddenly emerges into a wide glade with bright green grass and magnificent trees – pines, cedars and cypresses. The view of the mountain peak Ai Petri has been borrowed for the park with great effect. Cypresses, now very tall trees, were planted to frame it and to exclude the other mountains, and this seems to bring Ai Petri right up to the park. Elsewhere in the park it is used repeatedly to enhance the view. There are four glades: the Glade of Planes, the Glade of Chestnuts, the Glade of Contrasts and the Sunny Glade. In all of them there are quite exceptional trees – Italian, Mexican and Crimean pines, cedars of Lebanon, planes, chestnuts, cypresses, sequoias, silver firs, cork oaks, an araucaria and a Himalayan cedar. And in the spring there is a profusion of violets and primroses. In the centre of the upper park a series of three pools was created linked by a stream with

waterfalls. White and black swans, golden ducks and exotic fish provide animation and ornament.

Further up the slope, on the northern edge of the park, one reaches the Great Chaos, an enormous conglomeration of boulders deposited there by nature, a natural feature except that smaller stones have been removed to make the appearance more striking. On the summit there is an old grove of Aleppo and Italian pines, and from here one has a splendid view of the palace, the whole of the park and the mountains and sea beyond.

Alupka is the other Russian park believed by Dmitri Likhachev to have been influenced by Ossianism.[47] Michael Vorontsov would certainly have known of the poems and may even have visited Dunkeld with its shrine to Ossian, as his aunt, Princess Dashkova, had done. It seems quite possible that some of the landscaping at Alupka was inspired by Scottish scenery, which Vorontsov may have seen and which Edward Blore knew well – with Sir Walter Scott he was involved with the publication of *The Provincial Antiquities and Picturesque Scenery of Scotland*.[48] The author of an article on Alupka, apparently not aware that Blore never visited Russia, perhaps also had Ossian in mind when he wrote: 'Architect Edward Blore found in the landscape of the site and its surroundings an excellent inducement to develop a scheme based on the theme well known to him of wild mountainous Scotland, with its rocks, waterfalls, spruce, oak and pine, fanned into fashion by eighteenth-century Scottish ballads.'[49] He saw the summit of Ai Petri as a 'fantastic castle'. While there is no hard evidence that Vorontsov had Ossian in mind when developing Alupka, it is possible that Likhachev was right in this case.

The Nikitsky Botanic Garden, near Yalta, played an important role in the development of the park at Alupka. With the help of the director, N.A. Hartvis, plants and seeds were received from England, North and South America, Italy, the Caucasus, China and Japan. Through Wagner's nursery in Riga, Hartvis arranged for the purchase of camellias and magnolias originating in Loddiges' Hackney nursery. He wrote to Count Vorontsov on 20 July 1829 confirming that he had ordered six camellias '*des plus belles et nouvelles variétées*' and two magnolias. In November he wrote again to say that these plants had arrived, along with two rhododendrons, three azaleas and an arbutus, and that they were being overwintered in the orangery before being planted at Alupka in the spring. He added that he had read in Loudon's *Gardener's Magazine* that camellias had been successfully cultivated in the open ground in the London area. All these plants thrived after planting, but the rhododendrons and camellias perished in the severe winter of 1849. The magnolias continue to flourish on the second terrace and are now very large trees.[50]

During the Crimean War Alupka was granted immunity from attack by British naval forces. In May 1855, during the

The Great Chaos at Alupka.

siege of Sebastopol, a reconnaissance vessel was sent eastwards along the coast and among those on board was Captain S.J.G. Calthorpe, who had stayed at Alupka as Vorontsov's guest in 1851.

> So much has been heard and said of this place that it naturally excited the curiosity of all on board. The steamer was run as close to the land as was considered safe, that we might all get as good a view as possible of the beautiful structure and the lovely garden by which it is surrounded. Everything appeared exactly as when I had last seen it: the gardens as beautifully kept; the greatest profusion of flowers, whose fragrance we were near enough to enjoy; nothing seemed to indicate the absence of its owner, except that the window-blinds were all drawn.[51]

In February 1945 the British connection was resumed when Churchill stayed at Alupka during the Yalta Conference.

Nikitsky Botanic Garden
The Nikitsky Botanic Garden had been established in 1811 when a decree was signed in St Petersburg to establish an imperial botanic garden in the Crimea. In the following year work began on the site near the village of Nikita, 4 miles from Yalta. It was situated on a steep slope by the sea, and much rock had to be cleared, a vast amount of good soil introduced and a reservoir built. The rapid development of the Nikitsky Botanic Garden under its first two very able directors, Christian Steven (1812–26) and Nikolai Hartvis (1826–60), not only made considerable contributions to viticulture and fruit culture, but also led to the local availability of a wide range of ornamental plants for the great gardens being made along the Black Sea coast. Many new plants were introduced and acclimatized, and by 1824 there were 4,500 species in the garden.

The parks of the Crimea stand out above all for the splendour of their trees, and among the many new trees introduced by Steven were *Pinus pinea, P. halepensis, Cupressus sempervirens, Juniperus virginiana, Prunus laurocerasus, Buxus balearica, Sophora japonica, Quercus suber* and *Aucuba japonica*. Under Hartvis, while much attention was given to pomological and viticultural studies, the introduction of ornamental plants continued to be an important activity. Trees introduced during this period included *Cedrus atlantica, C. libani, Pinus wallichiana, P. montezumae, Abies pinsapo, A. nordmanniana, Libocedrus decurrens, Sequoia sempervirens, Sequoiadendron giganteum, Cupressus lusitanica, C. torulosa, Quercus ilex, Q. cerris, Paulownia tomentosa* and *Rhapis excelsa*.[52]

Left: The Goddess of the Night fountain-statue at Gurzuf.

Right: A view of the landscape from Mikhailovskoe.

The Nikitsky Botanic Garden is an extremely attractive garden to visit: it is not laid out along the usual systematic lines of botanic gardens; instead box-edged paths lead past a succession of impressive scenes, achieved by ornamental planting of a high order and supported by intermittent views of the mountains and the sea.

Pushkin Park at Gurzuf
The Duc de Richelieu, who had preceded Michael Vorontsov as Governor-general of Novorossisk and the Crimea, built a house on the slope of a hill near the sea at Gurzuf and surrounded it by a simple landscape park between 1808 and 1812. Pushkin stayed there for three weeks in 1820, and as a result of that visit the park is known as Pushkin Park. It was at first a combination of plantings of native trees and shrubs and meadows, but after the Nikitsky Botanic Garden was established many exotic plants were introduced. The area round the house was terraced, an orangery was built and an ornamental basin was constructed in a grove of pines. Pyramidal cypresses, marble fountains and balustrades with vases contributed to the formality. Later in the nineteenth century some particularly impressive fountains were added – the Goddess of the Night, Nymph and Rachel. The many large trees – Italian pines, cedars of Lebanon, planes, oaks, chestnuts and palms – give the park an enclosed character. They also go some way towards countering the presence in the park of the large buildings of the Ministry of Defence sanatorium.

Two other important Crimean parks, Livadia and Kharax, will be considered in the next chapter.

Alexander Pushkin Museum Park
Of the many minor estates and parks which existed in Russia in the nineteenth century, the few which have survived and have been restored and maintained are those associated with famous people. The three small estates Mikhailovskoe, Trigorskoe and

Petrovskoe, just a mile or two apart, along with the Svyatogorskoe Monastery, near Pskov, some 185 miles southwest of St Petersburg, became the Alexander Pushkin Museum Park and receive thousands of visitors throughout the year.

Mikhailovskoe was built by the poet's grandfather, Osip Abramovich Hannibal, son of Abram Hannibal, an enslaved Abyssinian prince who became one of Peter the Great's generals. Pushkin was a frequent visitor when his parents lived there, and between 1824 and 1826 he lived there in exile as a result of the libertarian views he had expressed in print. The modest manor house has been rebuilt more than once—most recently after its destruction during the German occupation – and every effort has been made to recreate the garden and the simple park. The flowerbeds – jasmine, acacia, wild roses, lilacs and hazel bushes near the house – reflect what is believed to have been there in Pushkin's time, as does the kitchen garden, poultry yard, orchard, hothouse, apiary and dovecote. There is a large circular area of grass in front of the house, which is approached by a straight avenue of firs, 275 yards long. There is also an old lime avenue. One of the pools among the trees surrounds the Island of Seclusion, once a favourite retreat of Pushkin's. Storks and herons nest in the trees, as they have done for centuries, and there are views across the River Rorot, the Lakes Kuchane and Malenets, and an idyllic landscape of water meadows and woods to distant hills.

Trigorskoe, the home of Pushkin's friends, the Osip-Wulfs, was often visited by the poet. It is on high ground overlooking the river and equally fine views of unspoilt landscape. The simple park of woodland and lime avenues dates from the late eighteenth century. A long rectangular clearing, framed by limes, was called the 'green ballroom'. There are pools, a bath house, an orchard and a tall pillar, which serves as a sundial, in a clearing. Petrovskoe was the home of Abram Hannibal, in whose time a manor house was built and the estate laid out with a simple formal park with straight avenues, trimmed limes, labyrinths, trellis arbours and an impressive park building combining a grotto and a summerhouse. Pushkin's tomb is by the Svyatogorskoe Monastery a few miles away.[55]

Semyon Geichenko, as Director of the Alexander Pushkin Museum Park, dedicated more than half his life to the restoration and recreation of these three small estates and the surrounding landscape after devastation during the war.

Spasskoe-Lutovinovo

The house and park at Spasskoe-Lutovinovo, once the home of the writer Ivan Turgenev (1818–83), a few miles north-east of Orel, was on land which had been given to his ancestor Ivan Lutovin by Ivan IV (the Terrible), at the end of the sixteenth century. Turgenev was deeply attached to the estate and to the country around it, which for him was the epitome of Russia. That part of central Russia is particularly attractive, with undulating landscape, oak and birch groves and rivers.

Almost the only formal part of the park were the lime avenues, the main group of which was planted at the very

Top: The house at Petrovskoe.

Above: The Island of Seclusion at Mikhailovskoe.

Right: A view across the Mikhailovskoe Pool to the water meadows and woods beyond.

beginning of the nineteeth century, to celebrate its arrival, in XIX formation. Otherwise the park was very informal with winding paths, old limes, birches, poplars, oaks and maples, alternating with meadows of king-cups, forget-me-nots, camomile, mint and wild strawberries; and not a statue in sight! Here and there was a wooden seat or a summerhouse, where Turgenev would sit and enjoy the woodland scents and listen to the birds. It was at Spasskoe as a boy that the peasants who became his friends taught him the names of the trees and the flowers and how to identify the birds from their song; and it was here, too, that he acquired his liberal views and his opposition to serfdom.

He never referred to the 'park', always the 'garden', but one of his biographers, writing at the beginning of the twentieth century, decided that it was neither park nor garden:

> No, all these many and various kinds of trees, brought together on this piece of land, can't be called 'garden', 'park' or 'wood' – it's all mingled together here, and in the blending something congruent, harmonious, full of artistic significance has been formed, for which there isn't a name. The creation of all this splendour has been formed in accordance with the taste of several generations, and to the power of nature has been added the travail of thousands of human hands – that is how what bears the name garden at the estate in the village of Spasskoe has come about.[54]

In a letter to Pauline Garcia-Viardot, the opera singer he so much admired, Turgenev wrote in 1868:

> All around was ravishingly beautiful; and if you ever come to Spasskoe I will take you to this seat. Two splendid pines of a rare kind are growing close together . . . in the middle of a lovely glade; beyond them, through the pendant branches of the birch, the pool can be seen, or rather the Spasskoe lake. . . . You will see that this is very beautiful. There are nightingales there, which unhappily have stopped singing, and there are warblers, blackbirds, golden orioles, turtle-doves, chaffinches, goldfinches and many sparrows and crows. There's a ceaseless chirruping, with which, from a distance, the sound of the quail in the rye mingles.[55]

A large pool in the garden, now dried up, was called the Savin pool after the actress Maria Savina, who appeared in Turgenev's plays. She had stayed at Spasskoe and had heard the nightingales:

> What a splendid garden there is there with amazing limes. Once at two o'clock at night he asked: 'Who wants to go to hear the night voices?' . . . And, heavens, what wonderful 'night voices'. It seemed as though every blade of grass and every bush was singing.[56]

Top: The home of Turgenev at Spasskoe-Lutovinovo.

Above: A woodland path on the estate.

When he was a student at the universities of Moscow, St Petersburg and Berlin, Turgenev was always glad to get back to Spasskoe for the vacations, and in later years he entertained fellow writers there, among them Nekrasov, Grigorovich, Fet and Tolstoy. During the years he spent in France and Germany his thoughts regularly returned to the 'garden', which frequently provided settings for his fiction, as with *Faust* (1856):

> The garden has grown wonderfully more beautiful: modest little plants of lilac, acacia and honeysuckle . . . had grown luxuriantly into substantial bushes; birches and maples had all grown taller and had spread out; the lime avenues had become particularly fine. I love these avenues, I love the soft grey-green colour and the delicate scent of the air under the vault of the branches. . . . My beloved oak sapling has now become a young tree. Yesterday in the afternoon I sat on the seat in its shade for more than an hour. I was very content. All around the grass was flourishing gaily; a golden light lay on everything, intense and mellow, it even penetrated the shade. . . . And what a sound of birds! . . . Birds are my passion. Turtle-doves cooed incessantly, now and then a golden oriole whistled, a chaffinch was making its usual pleasant call, the blackbirds were getting cross and chattering away, a cuckoo expressed his opinion from afar. Suddenly, like a lunatic, a woodpecker uttered its piercing cry. I listened and listened to all this soft fusion of sound and didn't want to stir.[57]

The house, which was destroyed by fire in 1906, was rebuilt in 1976 and is now a museum of the life and work of Turgenev. The oak, which he planted when he was fourteen, is now a feature in the park. While the park would benefit from a little more restoration, it is a very pleasant place to visit.

Yasnaya Polyana
Leo Tolstoy was born in 1828 on the family estate of Yasnaya Polyana, some 230 miles south of Moscow, and spent more than fifty years of his life there. It had been the estate of his grandfather, Nikolai Volkonsky, for whom a house was built, a formal park laid out and pools excavated. The main house in which Tolstoy was born is no longer there: he sold it in 1854 to pay off gambling debts, and it was dismantled and removed for reassembling elsewhere. An old foundation stone with an inscription marks the spot. Tolstoy returned to his estate in 1856 and settled in the north-east wing, which was extended several times to accommodate his growing family. The Literary Museum is housed in the other wing, which is unchanged and so preserves its original appearance.

From the towers at the entrance, the estate buildings are approached by a long straight avenue of birch trees. The formal park near the house is oblong in shape. Two intersecting lime avenues combine with two diagonally intersecting lime avenues to divide the space into eight triangles. Tolstoy's mother had planted these triangles with apple trees, and from time to time the height of the limes was reduced to allow sufficient light to reach them. Failure to follow this programme caused the apple trees to decline and encouraged the growth of undesirable weeds. At the centre, where the avenues crossed, there was a circular space, 30 feet in diameter, with a large elm tree and seats and music stands for the musicians who played for guests on special occasions.

In the landscape park shady avenues lead past a series of picturesque pools, through woodland with open glades, and meadows by the winding River Voronka. There are virtually no architectural features – just a simple wooden 'summerhouse tower', raised well above the ground for the view, and a wooden structure in one of the pools, serving as a bathing enclosure. What is said to be Tolstoy's favourite seat is a rustic construction of roughly trimmed lengths of birch.

In Tolstoy's time there were also hothouses, three large orchards amounting to 100 acres, and 620 acres of forest, to the planting of which he gave much time and thought. More birches were planted than any other species, but firs, limes, oaks, maples and ash also featured prominently. Tolstoy's grave is a simple green mound in the forest.[58]

When Tolstoy died in 1910 the fortunes of country estates and private parks were in terminal decline. Only seven years later their private ownership would be a thing of the past.

An avenue in the park at Yasnaya Polyana.

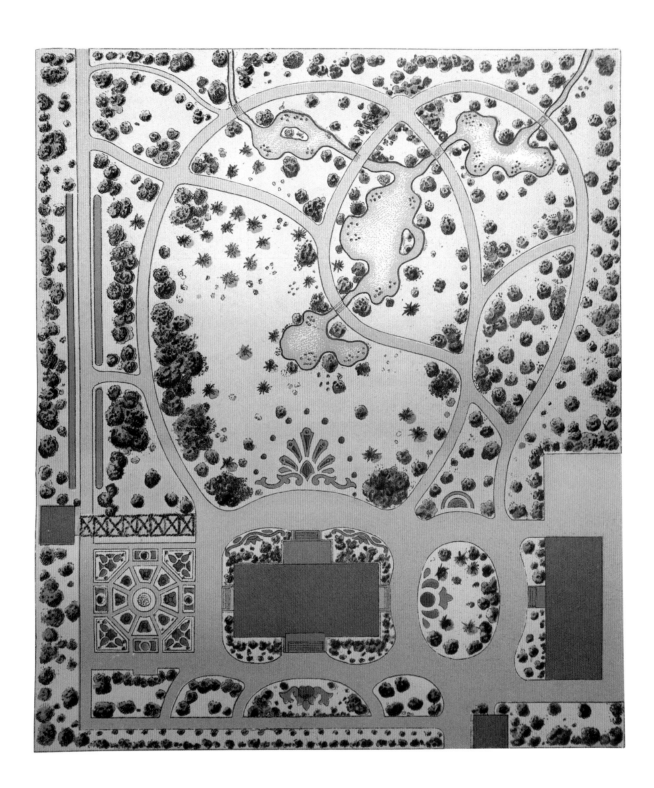

9
FROM THE EMANCIPATION OF THE SERFS TO THE REVOLUTION

A model plan for a garden, from A. Regel's
Izyashchnoe sadovodstvo i khudozhestvennye sady
(*Elegant Gardening and Artistic Gardens*) (1896).

The serfs had played an enormous role in the making of Russian parks: in no other country in Europe was it possible to employ labour on such a scale and at such little expense, Serfs were usually required to work three days a week for their owners in return for the plot of land allotted to them. 'The average land allotment per male soul in the north was 11½ acres compared to 8½ acres in the black earth belt' in the south where the soil was more fertile.[1] While many liberal aristocrats saw serfdom as iniquitous, most landowners were reluctant to give up their free labour. For some, like the Sheremetevs, it was not just free labour but a wide range of virtually free expertise, for their serf architects, artists, craftsmen, musicians and actors received only very modest rewards for their services.[2] But the violence committed by peasants during the revolt led by the Cossack Pugachev in the 1770s, when many landowners were massacred and their property was destroyed, was not forgotten. Further outbreaks had occurred from time to time, and the threat of more was ever present. The abolition of serfdom finally came with the Emancipation Edict in 1861, Alexander II having decided that 'it were better that the emancipation came from above, than from below'.[3] It was, however, only a limited benefit for the freed serf. He now had to buy the land allotted to him, admittedly on easy terms;[4] he had to pay the 'soul tax';[5] he was legally obliged to continue to reside in the same community; and there were other restrictions. Unrest was to continue.

For many owners of estates and parks this was the last straw. Their financial situation had been declining for some considerable time, usually due to their extravagant lifestyle. Westernization had generated expensive tastes, and fortunes had been spent touring western Europe, building and furnishing new palaces and creating appropriate new parks and gardens. Only a minority of the nobility could afford the expenditure they incurred; others fell deeply into debt, and many estates were heavily mortgaged. Most landowners were unable to increase the revenue from their property significantly, since agricultural practices in Russia lagged far behind those of western Europe. Moreover, few had the necessary entrepreneurial skills or an appetite for hard work. Factories were established on some estates, but were often unable to compete with goods produced by peasants or by the factories of the bourgeoisie.[6] Some sold parts of their estates for dacha development, others sold up altogether to those who could put the land to better agricultural or commercial use. As a result many parks virtually ceased to exist. Statistics show that between 1877 and 1905 the total area of land owned by the nobility fell by almost a third.[7]

Even the richest in the land were prepared to sell off parts of their parks for dacha sites, as we have seen with the Sheremetevs at Kuskovo and Ostankino. Still more surprisingly, the imperial family also disposed of substantial areas of important parks. Dachas were built on the wildlife reserve in the English Park at Peterhof, while the railway was allowed to pass through the southern end of the park. Part of the park was abandoned to dachas even at Pavlovsk, where neither the imperial family nor those employed to look after the park seemed to appreciate its artistic integrity. Taleporovsky wrote of its decline:

> The end of the 19th century, which is characterised by its lack of taste, succeeded in leaving a deep trace here. The later gardeners, enthusiastic for certain species and varieties of trees, had little understanding of the general landscape of the park. Obviously they were afraid of empty spaces, vistas, different perspectives – everywhere, even in small glades, they planted specimen cedars, larch and silver firs. For example, in the middle of the Botanical Avenue they planted a silver fir, which completely blocked the view of the Elizabeth Pavilion and the Old Chalet. Throughout the park (on the former Parade Ground, near the Temple of Friendship, near the Hermitage) cedars were planted in small, unattractive groups, and, quite inappropriately, mountain pines by the Amphitheatre, the Temple of Friendship and the Apollo Colonnade. The Labyrinth was swept away to make a tennis court. The cascade by the Apollo Colonnade was closed, and, in the upper pool which had fed it, commercial public baths were established.[8]

At Tsarskoe Selo the two main additions to the park were the play-farm and a model railway with bridges, tunnels and level crossings. Early in the twentieth century the park was badly neglected:

> The park is not well maintained. Only the paths and the immediate surroundings of the palace are kept tidy. The drainage ditches have become boggy. The woods are overgrown with wild scrub. No one ventures to undertake the necessary thinning. At the head of an imperial garden in Russia there is a general whose knowledge of garden art is not based on practical experience. The court gardeners can't undertake anything of their own accord. If the park gets too wild a specialist in garden art will be approached behind whose authority the general and all the officials can hide.[9]

There was no longer the same commitment to an ideal which had led to the making of great formal gardens and then to great landscape parks. Most of those making gardens in Russia in the later decades of the nineteenth century were not interested in combining a wide range of features, as had been the case with formal gardens and landscape parks. What interested them above all else were plants, and particularly brightly coloured flowering plants, striking trees and shrubs and the newly introduced species which were reaching Europe from around the world. 'Unity, totality and integrity of character, simplicity of decisions – all these were sacrificed to what was modish, to a superfluity of flowers and to the eccentricity of separate details.'[10] There was the same preoccupation with plants in England at the time, but there the climate was more helpful to gardeners than in most parts of Russia, where suitable winter protection was essential as well as a garden. Those without gardens could indulge their taste for plants indoors, where they were to be found

> in every dwelling, from the solitary rose-tree in the attic or cellar window of the seamstress to the most luxuriant exotic in the windows of her wealthier neighbours on the *bel étage*. Flowers and plants form an expensive item of household equipment in these climes. At the commencement of the season, arrangements are made with a florist to supply a certain number of shrubs and flowering plants in pots, which are replaced by others every month, for a certain sum, ranging from ten to a hundred silver roubles per month; these are disposed in broad sills, in niches, on pillarettes, in vases, and on numberless invisible contrivances.[11]

Livadia

While the parks around St Petersburg were in decline, important parks continued to be made for the imperial family by the Black Sea coast. The palace and park at Livadia were acquired in 1860 for the Empress Maria, wife of Alexander II. After the palace was destroyed by fire in 1882, the white palace, to the design of N.P. Krasnov, replaced it, and, together with two associated buildings, was completed in 1911. By this time the area of the park had been increased from 114 to 395 acres. It slopes steeply, with terraces, down to the sea.

The palace, 390 feet above sea level, stands on a wide terrace which had been formed in the 1860s. The Italian Courtyard, Florentine in style and surrounded on four sides by arcades, is particularly striking. Eight radial paths, leading to a central marble basin, divide the space into eight flowerbeds, each with a palm tree. Another small courtyard is Moorish in style.

The area in front of the palace is formally laid out with mown grass, flowerbeds and clipped box and yew, and there are no tall trees between the palace and the sea to obscure the view. The main avenues in the park are appropriately wide for an imperial residence, and there are viewing platforms from which to admire the Black Sea coast as far as Alupka, including views of the former parks at Oreanda, Gaspry, Koreiz and Miskhov, all now sanatoria.

There are some four hundred species and forms of trees and shrubs in the park. Many trees are planted in groves, some of mixed species, some of a single species. A grove of Italian, Corsican and Crimean pines reaches a height of 80 feet, one of Wellingtonias 115 feet. They grow against a background of many old native oaks.

Livadia Palace, where Stalin, Roosevelt and Churchill met for the Yalta Conference in 1945.

Among romantic features at Livadia are a grey marble column with an inscription in Arabic, some unusual small fountains, a Turkish Pavilion, a Rose Pavilion, the Tsar's Pavilion and other pavilions, and a long pergola supporting climbing plants which leads to a marble fountain. Natural streams with cascades flow down the slope between the palace and the sea, and there are pleasant paths offering shade, seats and drinking fountains.[12]

After the Revolution the palace buildings became museums. In February 1945 Livadia hosted the Yalta Conference, where Stalin, Roosevelt and Churchill met to discuss future strategy.

Kharax

The palace and park at Kharax, dating from the 1850s, also belonged to the Romanovs. The eastern part of the park is mainly natural woodland, but an area of 5 acres around the palace was formally laid out. A flower parterre of geometrical design was edged with clipped green box. The formality of the terrace, with its figured basins, flights of steps and a grotto, was accentuated by the planting of pyramidal cypresses. Of particular interest near by was a space outlined by antique columns with other architectural fragments; these were brought here in the nineteenth century following archaeological excavations at a local Roman fort. Other archaeological finds – terracotta vases and bas-reliefs – failed to survive the German occupation. A large part of the park (20 acres) extends over the western slopes of the headland of Ai-Todor, with juniper and oak predominating but accompanied by some two hundred species and forms of exotic introductions.[13]

An English guest at Kharax in 1913 was overwhelmed:

Harax, the palace of the Grand Duke, is enchanting. One turns through wrought iron gates down a drive lined with banks of flowers of every colour and scent, quite intoxicating. As you reach the house the banks vanish, and flights of white marble terraces smothered with roses, lilies and honeysuckle descend to the wide, dark sea. Clumps of cypress shade marble seats, over which hover bright butterflies. All is a scene of enchantment, one hardly dares to breathe lest it should all vanish like a dream.

Harax is more like a village than a palace in the usual sense. There is a main house where the family live, a guest house where we are staying, houses for servants and their families, laundries and other offices. All have red tiled roofs to remind the Grand Duchess of England of which she is so fond.[14]

Today Kharax suffers from the presence of sanatorium buildings and approach roads. It is not open to the public.

Top: The Italian Courtyard at Livadia.

Above: The pergola in the garden.

Opposite: White wistaria on the palace at Kharax.

Chekhov's Garden in Yalta

A much simpler garden was being made in Yalta around the turn of the century. Anton Chekhov was an enthusiastic, knowledgeable and discriminating gardener who took a great delight in his plants. He was already in failing health when he decided in 1898 to live in Yalta, hoping to benefit from the climate there. He bought a plot of land with an area of 800 sazhens – about ¾ acre – and built a house and made a garden in the few years that were left to him. Although he had the help of an experienced gardener, V.M. Krutovsky, he did much of the planting himself and kept a record of the plants he acquired. His principal sources were horticultural establishments in the Caucasus and Odessa and the Nikitsky Botanic Garden. Both his house and his garden have been given memorial status. Some of his plants still survive and those which have died have been replaced.

The plot, on a slope, was divided into three terraces, each fifteen to fifty feet wide. He made a start on the planting in 1898 with a hundred rose bushes, thirty lilies and camellias. In February of 1899, the year he wrote *Uncle Vanya*, he enthused in a letter to his sister, Maria Pavlovna: 'Yesterday I was planting trees in the garden and was literally in a state of bliss, so pleasant, so warm, so poetic. Simply rapture. I planted twelve cherries, four pyramid mulberries, two almonds and some others.'[15] In November in the same year he wrote to a friend, V.I. Nemirovich-Danchenko: 'I'm planting it myself with my own hands. Of roses alone I've planted a hundred, all of them of the noblest varieties. Fifty pyramid acacias, many

camellias, lilies, tuberoses and so on.'[16] In the following February he wrote to Olga Knipper, the actress who was to become his wife: 'In the garden only three of the seventy roses planted in the autumn have failed. Lilies, irises, tulips, tuberoses and hyacinths are coming up. The pussy-willow is green already, and the grass by the seat in the corner has been splendid for some time. The almond blossom is out. . . . I'm planting palms.'[17] Shortly afterwards he wrote to the writer M.O. Menshikov: 'A miracle has occurred. The camellias are flowering in my garden in the open ground. An unprecedented phenomenon in Yalta, it seems. They lived through the winter and survived eight degrees of frost.'[18]

When Arseny Shcherbakov, who had worked in the Nikitsky Botanic Garden, was working for Chekhov, the latter sent instructions from Moscow for his mother to pass on: 'Tell Arseny that he should dig round the olives and manure them . . . that he should water the birch tree once a week and the eucalyptus (it's between the chrysanthemums and the camellias) every other day. The roses once a week without fail. The azaleas and camellias with rain water.'[19] In 1901, the year of *The Three Sisters*, he planted some vines from the Nikitsky garden. But his health had deteriorated and in the following March he wrote to Olga Knipper: 'Yesterday and today I have been pruning roses, and oh dear! After each bush I had to rest. My health has obviously got sharply worse this winter.'[20]

He worked in the garden for the last time in the spring of 1903, the year of *The Cherry Orchard*. In 1904 he went to

A corner of Anton Chekhov's garden in Yalta.

Badenweiler in Germany to take the waters and died there on 2 July. His sister Maria continued to look after the garden, replacing dead plants with new ones. In the autumn of 1904 she planted a cypress, in memory of Chekhov, opposite the window of his study, where it can probably still be seen. It was she who founded the museum, which receives more than a hundred thousand visitors every year. One of the exhibits is the exercise book in which Chekhov kept a list of the plants in his garden. It included sixty-seven roses, among them 'Souvenir de la Malmaison', 'Gloire de Dijon', 'Maréchal Niel', 'William Henry Richardson' and *Rosa banksiae* 'Lutea'.[21]

Public Parks
Some early public parks were laid out during the first half of the nineteenth century, and many more followed in the second. In St Petersburg and Moscow gardens were made beside cathedrals and other public buildings and in many squares. The Aleksandrovsky Garden near the Admiralty in St Petersburg is impressive: its network of winding paths, with spacious lawns and accompanying flowerbeds, trees and shrubs, was designed by E. Regel. The scheme was later revised with the introduction of wide straight avenues. In Moscow the *Bulvardnoe Koltso* (Boulevard Ring), with its central promenade and flanking gardens, encircling a large central area of the city, is outstanding; as is the Aleksandrovsky Garden on the west side of the Kremlin. By the end of the nineteenth century most major provincial towns had at least one or two public parks. Numerous parks were laid out by the Crimean Black Sea coast in Yalta and other resorts; and notable parks were made in the Caucasus at Sukhumi and Sochi.[22]

Botanic Gardens
Considerable progress was made by Russia's botanic gardens in the nineteenth century, above all in St Petersburg. The botanic garden there dates from 1714 when Peter established a physic garden by decree on Apothecary Island in the Neva delta. Its purpose was to collect and cultivate medicinal herbs. Peter's physician, Robert Erskine, was its first superintendent, but he died in 1718.[23] In 1736, when it was called the *Meditsinsky Sad* (Medical Garden), a catalogue of plants was published listing 1,275 species. Horticultural plants were added to the care of the garden, with China, Mongolia and Siberia among the sources; but a further catalogue of plants in 1796 listed only 1,580 species, considerably fewer than in the private botanic gardens of P.A. Demidov and A.K. Razumovsky.

When Razumovsky died in 1822 it was hoped that his wonderful collection of plants, his herbarium and his library might be acquired for the St Petersburg garden, but the task of transporting them all by road from Moscow was too daunting, as were the prices sought by Razumovsky's heirs. The library and only a few rare plants were bought, but the services of F.E.L. Fisher, the eminent botanist who had been in charge at Gorenki, were also secured. According to an account in the *Gardener's Magazine* in 1826, this appointment was made 'through the intervention and influence of the Emperor's mother [Maria Fyodorovna], a great lover of botany, who herself possesses a very fine collection of plants'.[24]

Fisher was Director in St Petersburg from 1823, when the name was changed to the Imperial Botanic Garden, until 1850. Great progress was made during this period as he reorganized the garden along the lines of Gorenki. In 1824 'orders were given for ranges of greenhouses, conservatories and stoves':

> There are three principal houses, facing the south, each 700 feet in length, and 20 to 30 feet from back to front, placed in parallel lines, but at such a distance from each other that by two other houses of the same length, running from north to south, and placed at the ends of these, the whole forms a parallelogram, measuring 700 feet each way, intersected by a central house of the same length. The middle building is most lofty, being 40 feet high in the central part. The three that face the south have a sloping light in front reaching from the top to the ground. Those which run north and south have a double roof, are comparatively low, and have the path in the centre. All are heated by means of common flues, and with wood, principally birch. Water is raised by engines from the river, and cisterns filled in various parts of the houses, and in the most convenient situations. The large spaces of ground or areas between the buildings, are filled with shrubs and flower beds; only behind the most southern one is a splendid suite of apartments for the Royal Family. These have windows, opening from above into the house below, so that the plants may be seen to great advantage.[25]

In 1824 Fisher listed 5,688 species in the garden. Plants were acquired by purchase, by exchange and by collectors in the field:

> There is scarcely a garden in Europe, which will not, if it has not already, contribute to stock this superb establishment. The collection is, even now, very great. . . . During the last year . . . no less than 14,000 packages of seeds were sown in 60,000 pots. Dr Fisher paid a hasty visit to England and Scotland in last autumn, and collected so great a number of living plants (above 4,000), that he engaged Mr. Goldie of the Monkwood Nursery, near Ayr, to take charge of them during the voyage, and to assist in the transplantation. This was successful, and on Mr. Goldie's quitting St. Petersburgh in October, the whole collection was in a most thriving condition.[26]

In the 1830s thousands of pots with plants were delivered from Rio de Janeiro, where a branch of the garden was established.

Among other outstanding nineteenth-century directors were E. Regel (1855–66 and 1875–92) and E.R. Trautvetter (1866–75). Regel was both a distinguished botanist and an expert on ornamental gardening and landscaping, and he introduced many exotic plants into ornamental horticulture. It was largely through his initiative that the Russian Horticultural Society was formed.

Towards the end of the nineteenth century a new landscaped area was added to the generally formal arrangement of the beds which is customary in botanic gardens. This was an attempt to place plants in settings imitating actual natural landscapes. The result is still very pleasing.

The first palm house was wooden-framed and frequently needed repairs. In 1899 a most impressive new iron-framed palm house, with advanced air-conditioning, was erected to the design of the St Petersburg architect Hieronymous Küttner (1839–1929). At the centre it is 75 feet high, and there is an adjoining pavilion with a large basin to accommodate the giant water lily, *Victoria amazonica*.[27]

Nineteenth-century landscaping in the Imperial Botanic Garden in St Petersburg.

Left, above: The Palm House in the Imperial Botanic Garden in St Petersburg. It was designed by Hieronymous Küttner and erected in 1899.

Left: A pavilion adjoining the Palm House accommodates the giant water lily *Victoria amazonica*.

By 1917 there were about 5,000 species in the open ground, some 26,000 species and varieties under glass and 2,000,000 dried specimens in the herbarium. The garden was not adequately maintained during the first years after the Revolution, but then recovered. During the siege of Leningrad it suffered horrendous damage and losses, but eventually recovered again.[28]

Monasteries

The gardens of important monasteries underwent substantial changes in the nineteenth century, among them the Monastery of the Caves in Kiev, the Monastery of the Trinity and St Sergius in Sergiev (now Zagorsk), the Solovetsky Monastery in the White Sea and Valaam Monastery on Lake Ladoga. Their remote situation makes the last two particularly interesting.

The Solovetsky Monastery, one of the largest and once one of the richest in Russia, is remotely situated on an island in an archipelago in the White Sea, 95 miles south of the Arctic Circle. Founded in 1429, the monastery-fortress is surrounded by a high wall with towers, built in 1584–94. There was an armoury above the Holy Gate. In the sixteenth and seventeenth centuries the monastery served as a place of exile for church and state dignitaries who had fallen out of favour. In the 1660s, when the monks refused to accept the revision of the liturgy introduced by Nikon, the Patriarch of Moscow, the monastery was besieged for several years before being taken by storm in 1676 by the forces of the Tsar.[29]

The island is a place of considerable natural beauty, with many lakes and woods. While there were vegetable gardens and fruit trees at the monastery from an early date, it was not until the nineteenth century that serious landscaping began. Earlier roads became avenues, and a large area became a park, with sketes (retreats for hermits), chapels, and crosses serving as architectural features. A visitor in the late nineteenth century wrote:

> Every vista is terminated by an ornamented chapel, at every turn there appears a cross, well carved and painted dark red – and all these sites either commemorate some marvellous manifestation of divine help or bear witness to memorable events in the life of the monastery.[30]

In 1694 Peter had arrived on the island for a short stay after sailing through a life-threatening storm. 'As his personal thanksgiving, he made with his own hands a wooden cross ten feet high and carried it on his shoulder to the spot on the shore where he had landed after his ordeal. It bore his inscription in Dutch: "This cross was made by Captain Peter in the summer of 1694".'[31]

A remarkable garden was created around a hermitary built for Archimandrite Makary in 1822, 2½ miles north-west of the monastery. The site was particularly well chosen in a deep valley between two hills, sheltered from cold winds. Thanks to a microclimate, the warmth from a wax bleachery and considerable horticultural skills, some surprising successes were achieved.

It's a delightful spot, squeezed in among the wooded hills and the deep, green valley. . . . A gardener-monk of peasant stock suggested we should look at the greenhouses and hot-beds. Here there were melons, water melons, cucumbers and peaches. All in the hot-beds of course. The stoves were disposed to conduct heat under the soil where fruit trees were growing. In this way the heat was evenly spread. The greenhouse with flowers is delightful. The arrangement of the flower beds displays taste and an understanding of what's required. I was there for a long time attentively contemplating all the details of this place. It's a polar Italy, as one eminent visitor rightly called it.[32]

Before the First World War 10–15,000 pilgrims visited the Solovetsky Monastery every year. There was no charge for accommodation in the hospices but a donation was expected.[33] During the Soviet period it was to become a dreaded concentration camp: this was the Gulag Archipelago.[34]

Free accommodation was also available to pilgrims in the hospice of the Valaam Monastery; this was situated on a rocky island, surrounded by forty smaller islands, in Lake Ladoga. Baedeker (1914) suggested that a donation of one rouble or two marks would be appropriate. The monastery was founded when Novgorod was a major power, and there were orchards and vegetable gardens there in the thirteenth century.[35] Valaam suffered during the wars between Russia and Sweden, and when the monastery was destroyed in 1754 the monks abandoned the island for a time.

The present buildings date from the late 1880s, and most of the surviving planting dates from the second half of the nineteenth century. Larch, fir and oak were widely used in numerous avenues and groves over a wide area, and hazel, ash, chestnut and maple were also planted. Trees rare in the region were introduced and acclimatized, and then propagated in a tree nursery and planted around the island and other islands in the archipelago. Some were exported for sale in St Petersburg and Finland. A survey in the 1980s listed thirty-eight species of trees and shrubs which had been introduced to Valaam.[36] The addition of new trees into the surrounding landscape turned a wide area into a semi-wild park, with architectural interest provided by sketes and chapels on elevated sites.

Before the Revolution there were four hundred apple trees of sixty varieties in the orchards, and on one apple tree ten varieties had been grafted. Pears, plums, cherries, gooseberries and currants were also grown. Pumpkins weighing up to two poods (72 lbs) were recorded, and watermelons and some exotic fruit were produced in hothouses. In ornamental gardens, by the monastery and the cathedral, lilac, honeysuckle, bird cherry, acacia and a range of flowering plants were grown. There was also an apothecary's garden.[37]

Monastic life in Russia was to end with the Revolution.

War and Revolution

While English gardeners had been most in demand in the late eighteenth and early nineteenth centuries, German gardeners then took over and held most of the major gardening positions until the outbreak of the First World War. G. Kuphaldt, who had been working in Russia for a number of years, was then imprisoned for some time before being allowed to return to Germany, and he gave an interesting account of the state of gardening in the Russian Empire in an article in *Gartenflora* in 1916:

> In the past few years substantial sums had been made available for the laying-out and maintenance of gardens and promenades in large cities like Moscow, St Petersburg, Warsaw and Riga. In the bathing resorts on the Finnish and Riga gulfs there are small wooden houses between well-kept gardens. The great road on the Gulf of Finland from Strelna to Oranienbaum, resembles with its country houses the Elbe road from Ottensen to Blankenese. The art of gardening is of little importance in the small towns in the interior of the empire in the properties of officials and merchants. The German type of small residential town with tasteful stone houses secluded in the greenery of suburbs does not exist in Russia except in the Baltic provinces and Finland. The well-to-do Russian merchant considers a comfortable residence essential. Every Russian householder of the better sort has a faultless pair of horses and a coachman. The Russian is extremely hospitable to foreigners, to an extent we can't dream of, but he has little use for laying out and maintaining gardens in accordance with the highest principles of garden art. When he stays at his dacha the Russian is satisfied with a half-shaded, little-cared-for garden with some flowers, foliage, a see-saw, swing and sandpile for the children. The Russian has a great weakness for sunflowers and for bright and fragrant flowers. The flowers of the lilac will be torn off relentlessly. A lilac bush with its broken branches after flowering is a sorry sight. The simple Russian just cannot understand why he should not pick a flower which pleases him, and it is difficult to maintain public gardens in provincial towns in the interior of the country. All flowering plants and flower borders must be surrounded by a metre-high fence. The maintenance of a garden is not possible without a great many custodians. Poplars, limes, elms and birch in the north, robinias in the south provide the principal material for the planting of allées and gardens. A baked lawn, not rich in plants, with a tall carpet-bed and a dry fountain basin; a small music pavilion and foliage – these are the landmarks of a public garden of a small Russian provincial town. With the exception of vegetable cultivation, in which the Russians are unsurpassed masters, the practice of garden cultivation has been in German hands for centuries. The Germans have had a complete monopoly and almost everywhere have retained their language and customs. For the most part Germans came as estate gardeners and after acquiring some Russian worked their way up to head forester, estate steward or other positions for which only conscientious people could be employed. Some of the immigrants founded commercial gardens and nurseries or sought to practise landscape gardening. The owners of the greatest nurseries in Russia such as Wagner & Schoch (Riga), Eilers, Freundlic (St Petersburg), Mayer (Kiev), Bauer, Fehringer (Moscow), Rothe (Odessa), Ullrich (Warsaw) are or were Germans. The price lists were published in German, and this helped to retain the character of the whole gardening profession. The main gardening posts, such as city garden directors, directors of the botanic gardens and gardeners to the Court, were exclusively occupied by Germans until a few years ago. The Botanic Garden of St Petersburg reached the highest degree of perfection under the direction of Dr Regel who never learned Russian well in spite of the thirty years he spent in St Petersburg.[38]

The war, which brought an end to German employment in Russian gardens, also helped bring about the downfall of the discredited establishment and the Revolution. The unrest that had continued after the Emancipation was intensified in 1905 when at least two hundred peaceful protestors, seeking to hand in a petition to the Tsar at the Winter Palace, were shot because they failed to disperse. In the years which followed many revolutionaries were tried and executed. After the outbreak of war, a series of defeats for the Russian armies was accompanied by a serious economic situation and food shortages, which led to strikes, bread riots and violence. While the peasants in rural areas supported the revolutionaries – they were promised bread and land – urban industrial workers formed the vanguard and were joined by regiments returning defeated from the front. In October 1917 the Bolsheviks succeeded in gaining control of the government: the outlook for private parks and gardens was bleak.

Model plans for flower gardens, from A. Regel's *Izyashchnoe sadovodstvo i khudozhestvennye sady* (*Elegant Gardening and Artistic Gardens*) (1896).

10
THE SOVIET
PERIOD

Alexander Nikolsky's vision (1930s) for the sky at night over the stadium in the S.M. Kirov Park of Culture and Rest on Krestovsky Island. This illustration was provided by one of Nikolsky's former colleagues.

Before, during and after the Revolution most of the aristocracy fled abroad with what they could carry with them. The valuable contents of many estates were transferred to museums, but many other estates were pillaged and many of the buildings were destroyed. In December 1922 the Society for the Study of the Russian Estate was formed by a group of enthusiastic and knowledgeable amateurs who were concerned for the future of the surviving estates and were anxious to promote their protection and study. In April 1923 the Society was ratified by the People's Commissariat for Internal Affairs, and members 'felt that there was solid ground under its feet'. Concerts of estate music and lectures were arranged and enthusiastically attended, and before long there were around a hundred members. Regular excursions were made to estates and excellent reports were produced on the buildings, the collections and the parks and gardens.[1] Chapters Six and Seven included extracts from their reports, published in *Sredi kollektsionerov*, on Zhernovka (page 153), Rai-Semenovskoe (pages 176–7) and Petrovsko-Razumovskoe (page 175).

A.V. Lunacharsky, the Commissar for Enlightenment, was sympathetic to the aims of the Society, but after his death in 1928, and as Stalin tightened his grip on power, a wave of repression against the intelligentsia overwhelmed members of the Society along with many others. The first to suffer was the President, Aleksei Grech, who was arrested by the KGB and sent to Solovki, where monastery had become gulag: he was later shot. Six other leading members suffered a similar fate. Dmitri Likhachev, whose views on Ossianism have been considered in Chapters Six and Eight, was a fellow prisoner of Grech on Solovki and survived. In a newspaper interview in 1987 he said that Grech and the other members imprisoned there were accused of taking valuable objects from museums in order to hand them back, when an opportunity arose, to the original owners.[2] This was quite untrue. A number of members of the Society were sent into exile and were eventually able to return, while some were interrogated by the KGB and remained under threatening surveillance. Pavel Sheremetev, the son of Sergei who had established the museum at Ostafevo (pages 177–8), was a member of the Society. While Lunacharsky himself now occupied the main part of the palace at Ostafevo, Sheremetev was allowed to continue to administer the museum and to live in a wing with his family; but in 1927 they were obliged to leave the estate, when, as a former member of the aristocracy, he was deprived of his rights as a citizen and dismissed from his post. He was later under surveillance by the KGB for a considerable period. During the war he died of hunger.[3]

Dachas in the Twentieth Century

Soviet hostility to private ownership extended to the dacha. The history of the dacha has been impressively told by Stephen Lovell in *Summerfolk*. While in the eighteenth century dachas had been out-of-town residences for the élite on land given by the Tsar, by the nineteenth century they had become much more widely owned by those who could afford them as a retreat from the city. After 1917 virtually all those near large cities were municipalized and reallocated to manual workers, usually to house two or more families to meet the rule of 6 square metres (65 square feet) per person. Many dachas further away were also municipalized, particularly those of a substantial size and with good facilities. A few owners succeeded, usually through influence, in hanging on to their dachas. It helped if they could claim that there were numerous occupants.[4]

'In the early years of Soviet power dachas were commonly treated as an undesirable "remnant of the past" that had no place in a society informed by the principles of collectivism and Bolshevik self-denial';[5] but before long the new Soviet élite had abandoned self-denial and were enjoying exclusive new dacha developments with special facilities in protected compounds in favoured districts. Stalin had several dachas, as had his henchmen. Sometimes on the fall from favour of a leading Bolshevik his dacha became available. Even as Andrei Vyshinsky, the arch prosecutor in the show trials of the 1930s, was demanding the death penalty for one of his victims, he was already planning to acquire the unfortunate comrade's dacha.[6]

The *dachniki* – occupants of dachas – were not usually greatly interested in gardening in the 1930s. The plots on which their dachas were built served as outdoor rooms in summer, perhaps planted with one or two flowering shrubs, fruit trees or bushes. The Second World War brought a transformation as a result of the accompanying acute food shortages and failures of the supply system: intense vegetable gardening became vital for survival. Dacha plots and all available land in the cities were committed to food production, and in Leningrad a large area even of the Summer Garden was turned over to potatoes. By 1942 5 million Soviet citizens were gardening for food: by 1945 the figure had risen to 18½ million. Remarkable successes were reported, including a claim that one heroic allotment gardener had produced 2½ tons of vegetables on 180 square yards of land.[7]

Food shortage continued well after the war, particularly following the famine of 1946–7. In addition to allotments there were also garden plots, which were rather larger and became extremely popular. At first those who were allocated garden plots were not allowed to erect any structures, but in 1949 toolsheds were permitted by the Moscow soviet.[8] Structures much larger than necessary to house tools frequently appeared and were met with objections; but eventually modest dwellings (almost

Left, above: A dacha near Pavlovsk.

Left: A dacha at Izborsk.

Right: A dacha near Pavlovsk.

invariably self-built) were allowed, subject to size and design controls, and garden plots became modest dachas.[9] Both dachas and garden plots became virtually privately owned. The introduction of the two-day weekend in the 1960s added significantly to the use citizens were able to make of them. The number of garden plots soon far outstripped that of dachas, and 'by 1987, more than 4.7 million citizens of the Russian Federation had "second homes" on garden plots (as compared to a mere 55,000 with dachas proper).'[10]

In the 1980s many leading members of the Politburo continued to indulge in all the perquisites they could get their hands on, with dachas at the top of the list, and in 1983 Yuri Andropov, the party's more ascetic General Secretary, complained of the quite excessive number of dachas they had access to. The rising star Mikhail Gorbachev proposed that there should be an investigation into the 'disgraceful phenomena', but Andropov drew the line at that. After the fall of communism the country's new leaders continued to feather their nests in much the same way, as 'Yeltsin and his changing cast of associates found themselves cosy retreats in Barvikha, Kuntsevo, and other resorts preferred by high Soviet cadres.'[11]

Parks of Culture and Rest
The Soviet Union's contribution to park design was the Park of Culture and Rest, which was designed to provide, 'for tens of thousands of visitors, diverse kinds of cultural-enlightening work, relaxation, sporting activities and rest in optimum natural surroundings'.[12] The first Park of Culture and Rest was developed in Moscow in 1928 on a large part of the site of the Neskuchnoe estate and was later called Gorky Park. Gorky was among those who attended literary festivals there, along with Aleksei Nikolaevich Tolstoy, Aleksandr Fadeev and many others. Politics were very much on the agenda, and Fadeev was reported to have said of the park: 'The place, where in Russia before the Revolution there was a filthy rubbish heap, has been transformed to a splendid flower garden, in which millions of people find joy and happiness. Is this not a symbolic image characterizing our great fatherland, its remarkable journey from the rotting rubbish of tsardom to the radiant heights of socialism?' M.Ya. Ginsberg's plan for the park included a sports stadium; a road and a square for tanks; a theatre; a house of music; a house of physical culture; a circus; a building for science and technology; a library; a riding square; a cinema; corners for geography, mineralogy and geology; a childrens' section; a meteorological station; a boating lake; a big wheel; and bases for peace and quiet. Before long there were similar parks in many towns and cities of the Soviet Union and by 1985 the number exceeded 1,200. In the past Russia had imported park and garden fashions from western Europe, but now there was something to export, and Parks of Culture and Rest appeared in Hungary, Romania, Poland, Germany, Cuba and Japan.[13]

Gorky Park, the first Park of Culture and Rest, created in 1928.

The S.M. Kirov Central Park of Culture and Rest in Leningrad, on Yelagin, Kamenny and Krestovsky Islands, would have been the most interesting of all the Parks of Culture and Rest if Alexander Nikolsky's plans for Krestovsky Island had been fully realized. Krestovsky Island was to be a centre for physical culture, sport and 'mass festivities'. The S. M. Kirov football stadium (begun in 1933 and completed in 1950) within a vast oval mound is impressive, but it lacks the surrounding gallery, tower and other architectural details proposed by Nikolsky, which could have made it outstanding. On both sides of the main avenue leading to the stadium other facilities for a range of sporting activities were provided. On the south side of the island Nikolsky planned a beach for children with a Young Naturalists' Island; off the west coast he proposed an artificial archipelago of small islands; on the north side a summer theatre for music and drama with 1,500 seats, an open-air theatre for 'spectacular mass entertainments' with 12,000 seats, a cinema with 1,000 seats, a chess club, a water-course with a yacht club for sailing and rowing regattas, and the formation of two large artificial hills, lying just off-shore, the Lively Hills (*Vesyolie Gory*).

The Lively Hills, with their waterfalls, precipices, paths, terraces with trees, and viewing platforms from which to admire the landscape, were the most striking of all Nikolsky's proposals. Inside the hills, at various levels, were to be a cinema, a planetarium, an exhibition hall, restaurants with exits on to open terraces, and caves with 'all the wonders of the underground kingdom'. A suspended track would offer the aerial journey between the hills in a kind of cradle; boats would provide an exciting descent by water chute; and there were to be other attractions committed to 'invigorate the nervous system and to develop skills and self-control'.

Anticipating the transport that would be required for up to 160,000 visitors at a time, Nikolsky intended that trams would enter the park through tunnels to stopping-points under decorative pavilions in order to avoid noise, smell and possible danger to visitors. Restaurants and buffets were planned to accommodate 6,000 visitors at a time.[14] If the will and the means had been available the S.M. Kirov Central Park of Culture and Rest would have been serious competition for Disneyland and Alton Towers.

Yelagin Island suffered from being part of the park with the imposition of a big wheel and a network of straight concrete paths, but considerable improvements were made in the 1980s thanks to the efforts of the Park Engineer, Andrei Mets, who also established a gardening school for boys on the island. With the aid of nineteenth-century plans, he has identified groups of trees personally planted on Yelagin by Alexander I and Nicholas I which still survive.[15]

During the Soviet period a good deal of attention was paid to providing open spaces and green planting in towns and cities. After the defeat of the German army numerous victory parks were created, following the tradition, begun at Peterhof and

парк культуры и отдыха имени С.М.Кирова **ВЕСЕЛЫЕ ГОРЫ** на Кировских островах в Ленинграде

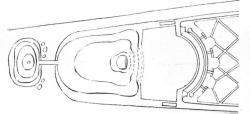

Nikolsky's unrealized scheme for the Lively Hills in the S.M. Kirov Park of Culture and Rest, with a cross-section. These illustrations were provided by one of Nikolsky's former colleagues.

continued at Tsarskoe Selo, of celebrating military victory in park architecture. Another sequel of the war was the very moving Piskaryovskoe Cemetery, resting place of the thousands of victims who perished during the siege of Leningrad. The simple Forest Cemetery on the outskirts of Tallinn is also impressive.

Many new botanical gardens were established. At the time of the Revolution there were twenty in the Russian empire: by 1984 there were 120 in the Soviet Union. Important among the new gardens were those in Riga (founded 1922), Minsk (1932), Kiev (1936), Alma-Ata in Kazakhstan (1932), Novosibirsk (1946) and the world's first polar botanical garden in Kirovsk near Murmansk (1931); but most important of all was the new Moscow Botanical Garden (1945), which became the coordinating centre for all the others.

The Moscow garden, one of the largest botanical gardens in the world, covers 890 acres and is pleasantly situated in north Moscow in the Ostankinsky Forest Park. The gently undulating site, crossed by the valleys of the rivers Yauza, Likhoborka and Kamenka, lends itself to the formation of interesting landscapes, while the varied soil conditions make it possible to cultivate a wide variety of plants.

One large section of the garden was designed to display the flora of the Soviet Union, and the visitor wanders through a succession of scenes, some with rocks and artificial hills, made to represent the terrain of European Russia, the Caucasus, Central Asia, Siberia and the Far East, each with a comprehensive range of the native trees and plants. Another major area (125 acres) is untouched forest, mainly oak with some aspen, birch and rowan, which is allowed to grow and regenerate naturally. The arboretum (185 acres) accommodates a large collection of trees from various parts of the world which have successfully adapted to the climate of Moscow. The exhibition of ornamental plants has large collections of roses, narcissi, tulips, hyacinths, lilies, peonies, gladioli and phloxes. The hothouses contain some five thousand species of tropical and sub-tropical plants.

A wide range of scientific work is carried out by the staff of the garden, with particular emphasis on the introduction and acclimatization of plants and the effective use of plant resources. N.V. Tsitsin, well known for his experiments with perennial wheat, was the first Director of the garden and continued in the post for thirty-six years.[16]

Post-war Restoration

The greatest achievement during the Soviet period of Russian landscape architects, along with architects and craftsmen, was the restoration of the great parks and their palaces at Peterhof, Tsarskoe Selo, Pavlovsk and Gatchina after the devastation suffered during the German occupation. The photographic record of 1944 bears witness to the enormity of the task which faced them, but when we visit the palaces today and walk in the parks, it is still hard to believe that all this has been recreated from what generally amounted to almost total obliteration.

The parks were restored not to their state in 1941 but to that of their heyday. Even before the war it had become clear that considerable work would have to be done in the eighteenth-century parks, since many of the trees were approaching the end of their lives, and since some of the changes which had occurred over the years had adversely affected the character of the parks and needed to be reversed. The pioneers in the field were T.B. Dubyago, who worked on the restoration of the Summer Garden, and L.M. Tversky and L.D. Akopovaya, who made a study of the landscape areas of the park at Pavlovsk and worked out a method of landscape analysis. Their experience served as the foundation for the work embarked on after the war.[17]

An account has already been given in Chapter Two of the dreadful damage suffered at Peterhof and of the symbolic restoration of the Samson Fountain completed in 1947. During the following four decades the main palace, the three small palaces and the upper and lower parks with all their fountains were restored.[18]

At Tsarskoe Selo the palace was largely restored by 1961, and work on the park began soon afterwards under the direction of Natalia Tumanova. Near the palace much of the formality of the mid-eighteenth century, which had been abandoned when the landscaping style was introduced, was restored, although trees that had been allowed to grow freely and were still healthy were not removed. Evergreen hedges were again clipped to form green walls.

The parterre of embroidery reappeared in front of the palace. In the eighteenth century it was intended to combine sand, broken brick, charcoal, mown grass and low clipped evergreen plants. The latter were omitted in the first attempt at restoration, since box succumbs to the St Petersburg climate, but the result

The Marly Palace at Peterhof in 1945.

was seen to be unsatisfactory. A second attempt, with the broken brick replaced by mown grass, was much more successful. Throughout the park there was a great deal of replanting, vistas that had become obscured were reopened, and many park buildings were admirably restored.[19]

The palace at Pavlovsk was reduced to ruins during the occupation, the park buildings and bridges were destroyed or severely damaged, and more than half the trees in the park were felled. The palace was completely rebuilt by 1970, and the adjacent private garden was restored by 1982 under the direction of E.A. Komarova. She was also responsible for the restoration of the White Birches area (250 hectares), based on plans of 1828 and 1856 and an aerial photographic survey of 1935. By the 1980s most of the park buildings and the park had been restored.[20]

Left: The restoration of a formal area in the park at Tsarskoe Selo.

Below: The wooden structure on which to train a covered way at Peterhof.

Right: Restoration of the parterre at Tsarskoe Selo. The first version.

Right, below: Restoration of the parterre at Tsarskoe Selo. The final version.

During the German occupation the palace at Gatchina was burnt down, many of the park buildings were destroyed or badly damaged, bridges were blown up, and hundreds of trees were felled. The restoration was not undertaken until much later than that of the other parks, but the palace was eventually restored, and the restoration of the formal gardens was completed by the late 1980s by I.A. Erf. Much of the park was also restored in the 1980s by L.A. Gerasimenko and A.G. Lelyakov.[21]

After the fall of communism there was a further dramatic rise in the number of garden plot dachas in the 1990s,[22] and they continued to be an important source of the nation's food. In 1999 a new public holiday was declared: Gardeners' Day. There has also been a much greater interest in ornamental horticulture, catered for by garden shops, small garden centres and new horticultural magazines. Considerable quantities of plants are being imported from abroad, particularly from Holland and Germany. A number of impressive roof gardens have been created on buildings in Moscow and St Petersburg.[23] Many of the pretentious new three- and four-storey dachas, which, in total disregard of green-belt conservation, have been added to the landscape around Moscow, stand on small featureless plots; but some have professionally designed gardens, and once again private owners are employing gardeners. In St Petersburg new buildings have obliterated many of the open spaces with green planting between blocks of housing, which were such admirable features of Soviet urban planning; and new development has even been allowed in the Primorsky Park, the best of the twentieth-century victory parks.

The most promising development has been the proposal by Moscow University partially to restore the old botanic garden in Moscow, founded by Peter the Great as the Apothecaries' Garden in 1706, but also to recreate it as a centre of gardening where plants and a wide range of garden equipment, materials and furniture will be available. It is intended to stimulate an interest in gardens generally and to encourage the restoration of other historic gardens. Many of the plants available will be historic species and varieties which have traditionally been planted in and around Moscow. Oleg and Nikita Yamein have designed buildings for the garden reflecting Russian architecture of the eighteenth and nineteenth centuries, and the English landscape architect Kim Wilkie has contributed to the overall design. Substantial progress has been made with the project under the direction of Dr Alexsei Reitum.[24]

Some very large private gardens are now being planned, and it will be interesting to see what develops during the next few years.[25]

Top: A model for the restoration of part of the park at Pavlovsk.

Middle: The Rose Pavilion at Pavlovsk during rebuilding.

Bottom: The interior of the Rose Pavilion during restoration.

Right: The restored Samson Fountain at Peterhof and the water flowing away along the canal to the sea.

PLANS

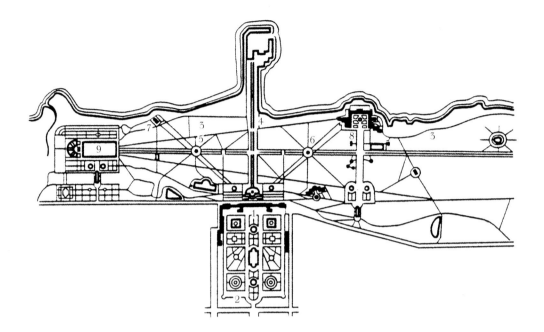

PETERHOF

1. The Great Palace
2. The Upper Garden
3. The Lower Park
4. The Samson Canal
5. The Eve Fountain
6. The Adam Fountain
7. The Hermitage
8. Monplaisir Palace
9. The pool by the Marly Palace

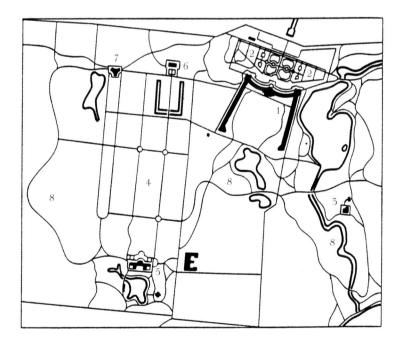

ORANIENBAUM

1. The Great Palace
2. The Lower Garden
3. Peterstadt
4. The area laid out in association
   with the Chinese Palace
5. The Chinese Palace
6. The Stone Hall
7. The Coasting Hill Pavilion
8. Landscaped area

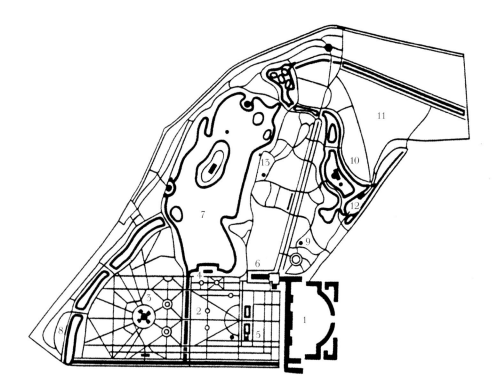

TSARSKOE SELO

plan of the Catherine Park

1. The Catherine Palace
2. The Old Garden
3. The Hermitage
4. The Grotto
5. The Upper Bath
6. The Cameron Gallery
7. The Great Lake
8. Cascading Pools
9. The Kagul Obelisk
10. The Small Pools
11. The Rose Field
12. The Chinese or Creaking Pavilion
13. The Milkmaid Fountain

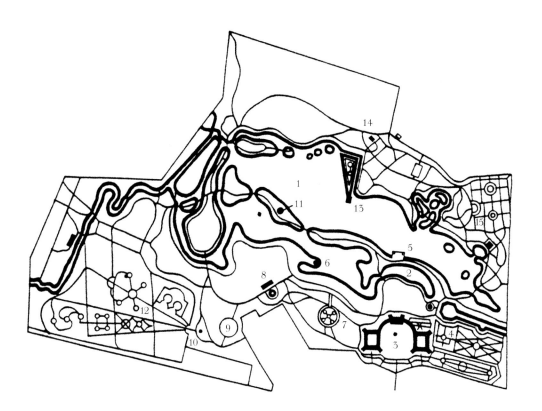

GATCHINA

1. The White Lake
2. The Silver Lake
3. The Palace
4. The Dutch Garden
5. The Terrace Quay
6. The Chesmensky Obelisk
7. The Turkish Summerhouse
8. The Woodland Orangery
9. The Amphitheatre
10. The Eagle Column
11. The Eagle Pavilion
12. Sylvia
13. The Temple of Venus
14. The Little Birch House
15. The Botanical Garden

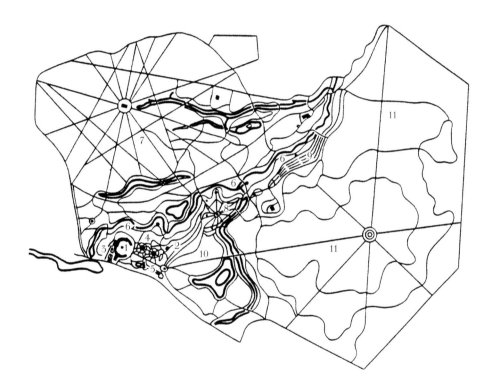

PAVLOVSK

1. The Palace
2. The gardens by the Palace
3. The Private Garden
4. The Great Circles
5. The Aviary
6. The Slavyanka valley
7. The Great Star and the Valley of the Pools
8. The Old Sylvia
9. The New Sylvia
10. The parade ground area
11. The White Birches

NOTES

1. THE EARLIEST RUSSIAN GARDENS

1. Dubyago, 7–8.
2. Vernadsky 110.
3. Riasanovsky, 40.
4. Ignatieva, 'The mystery', 69.
5. Dubyago, 9.
6. Riasanovsky, 95.
7. *Ibid.*, 103.
8. Dubyago, 11.
9. Palentreer, 80.
10. Dubyago, 19.
11. Hamilton, 149–50.
12. Porter, 88–91.
13. Information from Dmitri Shvidkovsky.
14. Dubyago, 22–7; Palentreer, 80–104.

2. THE FORMAL PARKS AND GARDENS OF ST PETERSBURG

1. Marsden, 51–2; Massie, R.K., 361–2.
2. Evelyn, v, 284.
3. *Ibid.*, v, 284, 290:

    Feb. 6 1698 'The Czar of Moscovy, having a mind to see the Building of Ships, hired my House at Says Court, & made it his Court & palace, lying and remaining in it, new furnish'd for him by the King.'

    June 9 1698 'I went to Deptford to viewe how miserably the Tzar of Moscovy had left my house after 3 moneths making it his Court, having gotten Sir Cr: Wren his Majesties Surveyor & Mr. London his Gardener to go down & make an estimat of the repairs, for which they allowed 150 pounds in their Report to the L: of the Treasury.'

    Diary editor's note: 'The Tsar had left England on 21 April. By 6 May Benbow petitioned the king for an allowance for reparation. Reports on the garden, the fabrics and the furnishing were drawn up by George London and two other men on May 9, and were forwarded by Wren to the Treasury on 11 May. A warrant for payment was issued on 21 June. As Benbow's tenancy was expiring shortly, Evelyn was allowed £107. 7s. for damage to the house and £55 for the garden; Benbow £133. 2s. 6d. for the furnishings.' It would seem that the king had not provided the furniture.
4. Gothein, II, 189.
5. de Jong, 336.
6. Dubyago, 318, note 44.
7. *Ibid.*, 53.
8. Likhachev (1991), 127.
9. Le Blond had provided most of the drawings for the plates in A.J. Dezallier d'Argenville's *La Théorie et la pratique du jardinage*, first published anonymously in Paris in 1709. John James's English translation, *The Theory and Practice of Gardening*, was published in 1712. Henrey, III, 491–3.
10. Sometimes spelt Harnigfelt, but according to Reiman, p. 24, 'in 1709 a contract was concluded in Amsterdam with the gardening master Leonard Hernichfelt'.
11. Dubyago, 44–8.

12. Ignatieva conducted experiments with red whortleberry as an edging for parterres at the Forest Academy and the Upper Park at Peterhof in 1980–81 and published advice on cultivation and training. This pioneering work in authentic restoration has not been developed elsewhere. See Ignatieva (1982), 37–8; and Reiman, 24–5 and note 47. Red whortleberry seems also to have been used as a box substitute in Sweden. See Adelswärd (1994), 47–60, and Lundquist, 106–11.
13. Reiman, 22.
14. *Ibid.*, 56–7 and note 94.
15. Hughes, 211.
16. Dubyago, 322.
17. Kuznyetsova, 56–60.
18. Masson, 23.
19. Hughes, 231.
20. Hirschfeld *L'Art des jardins*, v, 332. Hirschfeld acknowledged his indebtedness to Jakob von Stählin for his descriptions of Russian gardens.
21. Aleshina, 417, and Dubyago (plans), 58–9.
22. Dubyago, 132–3.
23. *Ibid.*, 145–6.
24. Petrov (1983), 340.
25. *Ibid.*, 338.
26. *Ibid.*, 336.
27. *Ibid.*, 324.
28. *Ibid.*, 372–81.
29. Petrov (1983), 376–8; Raskin (1978), 144, 163, 202, 340.
30. Petrov (1983), 384.
31. Åberg, 185–8.
32. Petrov (1983), 382.
33. *Ibid.*, 412.
34. *Ibid.*, 434.
35. *Ibid.*, 426.
36. *Ibid.*, 410.
37. *Ibid.*, 390.
38. *Ibid.*, 388.
39. Tikhomirova, 83.
40. *Ibid.*, 97–104.
41. Tikhomirova, 388, lists the scenes on the bas-reliefs: Latona and Jupiter; The Abduction of Deianeira; The Fall of Phaethon; The Rape of Proserpine; Perseus and Andromeda; The Contest of Apollo and Marsyas; The Golden Age (Aphrodite receiving gifts); The Rape of Europa; A Bacchic Scene; Allegory of Successful Navigation (Neptune on the sea-shore); Narcissus changed into a Flower and Echo; The Triumph of Neptune; The Contest of Atalanta and Hippomenes; The Sacrifice; A Woman abducted by a Triton; A Child abducted by a Triton; The Triumph of Aphrodite; Diana and Actaeon.
42. N.V. Dydykin sculpted the Tritons, I.V. Krestovsky the River Volkhov and V.V. Ellonen the Neva.
43. Dubyago, 115.
44. *Ibid.*, 124–5.
45. Hallström, 3–13.
46. Dubyago, 128.
47. *Ibid.*, 183.
48. *Ibid.*, 183–90.
49. *Ibid.*, 105–14.
50. *Ibid.*, 239–42.
51. *Ibid.*, 245–60.

52. *Ibid.*, 101–4.
53. Raskin, Gorod, 22.
54. Dubyago, 219–20.
55. Petrov (1964), 90–2; Benois, 198-204.
56. Benois, 223–4.
57. *Ibid.*, 225–30, Petrov (1983), 60–5.
58. Löwenwolde had acquired the garden from the nephew of Admiral F.M. Apraksin, the original owner, who was a close associate of Peter. The admiral obtained the sculpture for his garden from Italy at the same time as it was being bought by Peter for the Summer Garden. Dubyago, p. 250, quotes from a letter to Peter in 1717 from Savva Raguzinsky: 'Today we have contracted for 24 statues and 20 busts gilded, namely 12 statues of the chief Roman emperors and 12 emperors' wives – the same are contracted for by the Count-Admiral if they are not agreeable to you.'
59. Dubyago, 230.
60. Storch, 419.
61. [Ward], 146.
62. Duzhnikov, 50–55.
63. Troyat, 133.

3. THE FORMAL PARKS AND GARDENS OF MOSCOW AND THE PROVINCES

1. de Jong, 332.
2. *Ibid.*, 340.
3. *Ibid.*, 338.
4. *Ibid.*, 310.
5. *Ibid.*, 309–11.
6. Dubyago, 281–3.
7. *Ibid.*, 284.
8. Coxe, I, 269.
9. Dubyago, 288.
10. *Ibid.*, 286–8.
11. The text on Kuskovo which follows includes information from Dubyago, 297–305; Bakhtina, 44–7; Tikhomirov, 90–93; and Baranova, pages not numbered.
12. There is also a Dutch House (1760s) by the architect Karl Blank at Voronovo (45 miles south-west of Moscow).
13. Ségur, III, 189.
14. Quoted in Baranova without stating the source.
15. Dubyago, 305–12; Rapoport, 18–23.
16. In 1918 Livonia was divided between Latvia and Estonia.
17. Dubyago, 207–15.
18. *Ibid.*, 319.
19. Kuuskemaa, 5–51; Dubyago, 214–18.

4. CATHERINE THE GREAT AND THE ENGLISH STYLE OF LANDSCAPING

1. de Madariaga, 3 ff.
2. Poniatowski, vol. 1, 120.
3. Quoted by Cross, *British Art Treasures*, 80.
4. Raskin, Gorod, 22 ff.
5. Petrov (1983), 532–3.
6. Storch, 67.
7. Raskin, Gorod, 9.
8. Loudon, 1834, 245–6.
9. Cross, *British Art Treasures*, 83.
10. He signed himself variously as Johann Busch, John Busch and John Bush. His family who

survived him in England retained the German spelling.

11. Conrad Loddiges was a major exporter of plants and issued catalogues in English, German and French. He probably supplied plants and seeds to Busch at Tsarskoe Selo.

12. The certificate Loddiges received on completing his apprenticeship in Hanover is in the Hackney Archives Department.

13. John Bartram (1699–1777) was an early American plant-collector. He supplied many plants to Peter Collinson (1694–1768), who had a botanical garden at Mill Hill.

14. Extract from a letter provided by Marcus Köhler from the Harbke estate papers in the State Archives in Magdeburg; and Köhler, 114.

15. Köhler, 114; and other information provided by Marcus Köhler from the Harbke estate papers in the State Archives in Magdeburg.

16. Cross, *British Art Treasures*, 21.

17. Lord Coventry had frequently purchased plants from the Hackney nursery and continued to do so after it was acquired by Conrad Loddiges. There are ten invoices in the Croome estate archives for plants supplied by Busch from Hackney and more than twenty for plants from Loddiges.

18. This would have been John Fothergill (1712–80) who practised medicine in Lombard Street and had a notable botanic garden at Upton House, West Ham. He sold his large collection of natural history drawings, which included many flower paintings, to Catherine the Great. Information from Ray Desmond, *British and Irish Botanists and Horticulturists* (London, 1977).

19. *Vaccineum vitis-idaea*, red whortleberry, was sometimes used as a substitute for box in Russia.

20. This letter is in the archives of the Croome Estate, reference 192, and is used here with the permission of the Trustees. The signature appears to be in a different hand from the rest of the letter, and it may be that Busch's first wife, Ann, was acting as his secretary for English correspondence. There is no evidence in the archives of any later consignments of plants from St Petersburg.

21. Catherine's letter of 25 June 1772, *Sbornik Imperatorskogo Russkogo Istoricheskogo Obshchestva*, XIII (1874), 256.

22. Wedgwood Mss in Keele University Library, 18452-25.

23. *Ibid.*, 18453-25.

24. Illustration in Kennett, 77.

25. Filosofov, 18.

26. Rothstein, 37.

27. Harris, 231.

28. Loudon (1834), 246.

29. Cross, *An English Lady*, 70–1.

30. Cox, 104.

31. Yakovin, III, 169–78.

32. Shvidkovsky, *The Empress*, 100.

33. Cross, *By the Banks of the Neva*, 268.

34. Kurbatov, 518. Karavaeva states, p. 13, that the engravings taken to Russia by Neyelov included views of Stowe, Kew and Wilton as well as Studley Royal.

35. Petrov (1964), 95.

36. Bunatyan, 65 ff.

37. Riasanovsky, 266.

38. Shvidkovsky, *The Empress*, 11 ff.

39. Yakovin, III, 380–93.

40. Shvidkovsky, *The Empress*, 34, 102.

41. Seeley, 28.

42. [Bukh, K.A.], 20.

43. Seeley, 14.

44. Cross, *An English Lady*, 54.

45. Carr, 392.

46. Cross, *An English Lady*, 54.

47. King, 19.

48. Vil'chkovskii, 189–97.

49. *Ibid.*, 198–9.

50. *Ibid.*, 190.

51. Shvidkovsky (1996), 226–37; Cross (1997), 297–305.

52. Shvidkovsky, 'A Grandmother's', 107–13.

53. Bunatyan, 27 ff.

54. Translation of lines quoted by Andrei Ariev in Losseff, 51.

55. Translation of lines quoted by Sonia Ketchian in Losseff, 131.

56. [Watson], 6.

57. Cross, *The Lords Baltimore*, 85 ff.

58. Calvert, liii.

59. *Ibid.*, xxvi–xxv (the pagination is confused).

60. *Ibid.*, lxiii–iv.

61. *Gentleman's Magazine*, vol. 74, pt. 2, 1105 (1804), quoted by Henry, II, 358.

62. Hitt, 6 of the preface and facing 360.

63. Cross, *Banks of the Neva*, 277. Meader had provided the designs for a greenhouse, a pineapple stove and a grape house in Hitt. Text on 7–8 of the preface, plates facing 438, 491 and 495.

64. Cox, 105. Letters he wrote in Russia, copies of which have survived, seem to have been to his successor as head gardener at Syon Park. This extract is from one of them.

65. *Ibid.*, 109.

66. *Ibid.*

67. Swinton, 414.

68. Cox, 111.

69. Glezer, 105–21.

70. A.B. Granville quoted by Loudon (1834), 245.

71. [Smith], I, 106–7.

72. The remarkable but dilapidated palace built in 1667–71 for Tsar Aleksei Mikhailovich was demolished on Catherine's orders. Catherine's palace was badly damaged during the French invasion of 1812 and was demolished in 1816. A palace for Alexander I was built on the site in 1825, but was demolished in 1878.

73. Mineeva, 25.

74. Mikhailov, 104.

75. *Ibid.*, 105.

76. Andrei Rayevsky, quoted by Mineeva, 106.

77. Mineeva, 105.

78. Montefiore, 489. The price paid was a generous 935,288 roubles.

5. THE LANDSCAPE PARKS OF PAUL I AND MARIA FYODOROVNA

1. Merkle, *Segensreiche*, 8–10; Berger-Fix, 94–5.

2. d'Oberkich, *Mémoires*, I, 44.

3. Merkle, *Jugendjahre*, 43.

4. Berger-Fix, 48.

5. Hirschfeld, *L'Art des jardins*, v, 414.

6. d'Oberkirch, *Mémoires*, 81.

7. Clinchamp, 89.

8. d'Oberkirch, *Mémoires*, 1952, II, 10–13.

9. Karavaeva, 14–15.

10. Semevskii, 393.

11. Berger-Fix, 112.

12. Ivanova, O.A., 17.

13. Shvidkovsky, *The Empress*, 117.

14. *Ibid.*, 141.

15. Semevskii, 250.

16. This was the dairy at Hohenheim which is illustrated in Hirschfeld, *L'Art des jardins*, v, 413.

17. Semevskii, 354.

18. Letter, 8 July 1786.

19. Shvidkovsky, *The Empress*, 117–18.

20. Semevskii, 345–6.

21. *Ibid.*, 39.

22. In *Les Jardins* Delille considered the merits of the formal garden and the landscape garden, comparing them through the work of Le Nôtre and William Kent, and decided that the latter is the higher form, knowing that landscape had God on its side;
Aimez donc des jardins la beauté naturelle;
Dieu lui-même aux mortels en trace le modèle.
Regardez dans Milton, quand ses puissants mains
Préparent un asile au premier des humains,
Les voyez-vous tracer des routes régulières,
Contraindre dans leur cours des ondes prisonnières?
The advice he subsequently gave throughout the poem on how to make a garden in the image of Nature was widely followed at home and abroad.

23. First complete English version (translator not identified), 1789, 92, translating these lines from the original:
Mais j'en permis l'usage, et j'en proscris l'abus.
Bannissez des jardins tout cet amas confus
D'édifices divers, prodigués à la mode,
Obélisque, rotonde, et kiosk, et pagode,
Ces batimens Romains, Grecs, Arabes, Chinois,
Chaos d'architecture, et sans but, et sans choix,
Dont la profusion stérilement fécond
Enferme en un jardin les quatres parts du monde…
La ferme, le trésor, le plaisir de son maître,
Réclamera d'abord sa parure champêtre.
Les Jardins, 1801, 92–4.

24. *Poema Sady, ili ukrashat' sel'skie vidy*, translation by Petr Karabanov, (St Petersburg, 1804); *Sady*, translation by A. Palitsyn, (Kharkov, 1814); *Sady, ili Iskusstvo ukrashat' sel'skie vidy*, translation by A.F. Voeikov (St Petersburg, 1816); *Sady*, translated by I.Ya. Shafarenko, (Leningrad, 1987). Delille made only a brief general mention of Russian gardens, and Voeikov added sixty-five lines of his own to his translation with descriptions of Kolomenskoe, the Taurida garden, Tsarskoe Selo, Arkhangelskoe, Kuskovo, Lyublino, Neskutchnoe and Savinskoe.

Voeikov's version was reprinted along with Shafarenko's translation in 1987. A hundred thousand copies were printed! *Les Jardins* has also been translated into Polish, Italian, German and Portuguese.

25. Semevskii, 109–13; Shvidkovsky, *The Empress*, 163.

26. First complete English version, 1789, 88–9, translating these lines from the original:

Ne craignez point d'offrir des urnes, des tombeaux;
D'offrir de vos douleurs le monument fidèle.
Eh! qui n'a pas pleuré quelque perte cruelle?
Loin d'un monde léger, venez donc à vos pleurs.
Venez associer les bois, les eaux, les fleurs
Tout devient un ami pour les âmes sensibles;
Déjà pour l'embrasser de leurs ombres paisibles,
Se penchent sur la tombe, objets de vos regrets,
L'if, le sombre sapin; et toi, triste cyprès,

27. Semevskii, 356–7.

28. Taleporovskii, 10.

29. 1789 English translation, 88, 100, translating these lines from the original:

Mais de ces monuments la brillante gaieté,
Et leur luxe moderne, et leur fraîche jeunesse,
D'un auguste débris valent-ils la vieillesse?
L'aspect désordiné de ces grands corps épas,
Leur forme pittoresque attache les regards;
Par eux le cour des ans est marqué sur la terre…
…mortels, hâtez-vous de jouir;
Jeux, danses et bergers, tout va s'évanouir.
Les Jardins, 1801, 90, 100.

30. Semevskii, 395–6.

31. *Ibid.*, 561.

32. *Ibid.*, 522.

33. *Ibid.*

34. *Ibid.*, 544. 'These cherry-houses are carefully closed and coated with pitch, and it is only in the warm summer season that the trees are exposed to the fresh air by the removal of the glazed roofs and wooden walls.' Kohl, II, 231.

35. Semevskii, 520.

36. 22 February 1782.

37. *Arkhiv knyaz'ya Vorontsova*, (Moscow, 1883), xxix, 280.

38. Würtemberg, 342–3, 358.

39. Carter, 47.

40. *Ibid.*, 48–78

41. 'Biographical Sketch of John Fraser, the Botanical Collector', *Companion to the Botanical Magazine*, 1837, v.2, 300.

42. *Ibid.*, 300–2.

43. Semevskii, 128–9.

44. *Arkhiv knyaz'ya Vorontsova*, (Moscow, 1883), xxvii, 356–7.

45. Semevskii, 256–7.

46. *Ibid.*, 59–61.

47. *Ibid.*, 176–81; Taleporovskii, 13.

48. Petrov (1983), 278; Lansere (1995), 18; Cross, Neva, 270.

49. Richardson, 400–3.

50. Lansere (1995), 44–5.

51. *Ibid.*, 49.

52. *Ibid.*, 47.

53. Petrov (1995), 289.

54. *Ibid.*, 310.

55. Golovine, V.N., 172.

56. Semevskii, 345.

57. *Ibid.*, 536.

58. *Ibid.*, 547.

59. *Ibid.*, 525–6.

60. *Ibid.*, 544.

61. *Ibid.*, 534.

62. Reports which appeared in the Court Circular column of *The Times* are the source of my information concerning the tours of the Grand Duchess and the Grand Dukes unless another source is given.

63. Romanov, Perepiska, 178.

64. *Ibid.*, 180.

65. During or shortly after Catherine Pavlovna's visit to England, the excellent Russian apple 'Borovinka' was introduced to British horticulture and named 'Duchess of Oldenburg'. It became very popular and may still be obtained from the Brogdale Horticultural Trust in Faversham, Kent.

66. In the archives at Chatsworth.

67. Lees-Milne, 33, identifies 'H.W.' as 'the notorious courtesan Harriette Wilson', who embarrassed numerous aristocrats when she published her memoirs, a best-seller. See her entry in the *Dictionary of National Biography*.

68. From one of two long letters from the 6th Duke to Princess Lieven giving a long account of the Emperor's visit. Recorded in the Duke's *Thought Book*, in the archives at Chatsworth.

69. Editor I.E. Andreevskii and others, *Entsiklopedicheskii slovar'* (St Petersburg, 1890–1906), xix, 485.

70. *Dictionary of National Biography*, iv, 934.

71. The Grand Duchess had visited the Royal Porcelain Manufactory of Messrs Flight, Barr and Barr in Worcester in 1814 (*Worcester Herald*, 14 May 1814). The Grand Duke Michael may have been encouraged to buy Worcester porcelain by the long article which had appeared in *The Times* on 8 July, when he was in London.

72. *Barrow's Worcester Journal*, 10 September 1818.

73. *Derby Mercury*, 30 July 1818.

74. *Ibid.*, 6 August 1818.

75. *Ibid.*

76. *Manchester Mercury*, 22 September 1818.

77. Volume 13, 1, (Spring, 1985), 30–2.

78. Taranovskaya, 115–16.

79. So described by the Marquis de Cussy. Bernier, 95.

80. Bernier, 89.

81. *Ibid.*, 178.

82. 1815, dedicated 'à Monsieur Muller, l'un des Maîtres-d'Hôtel, Contrôleur de la Maison de Sa Majesté l'Emereur de toutes les Russies'.

83. Carême, 18–19.

84. *Ibid.*, 18–19.

85. *Ibid.*, 56.

86. Bernier, 187.

87. *Ibid.*, 186.

88. Quoted in *L'Art culinaire au xix siècle: Antonin Carême* (exhibition catalogue, 1984), 41–2.

89. Semevskii, 538.

90. *Ibid.*, 522, 538.

91. *Ibid.*, 525–6.

92. Storch, 439.

93. Plastov, A., 'Pis'ma provintsiala iz Peterburga', *Semeinyi krug*, 1860, no. 26. Quoted by Nemchinova.

94. Semevskii, 561.

95. *Ibid.*, 235.

96. *Ibid.*, 567.

6. LANDSCAPE PARKS IN AND AROUND ST PETERSBURG

1. The five Engelhardt sisters. Montefiore, 185–95.

2. Montefiore, 115–16.

3. Loudon, *Encyclopaedia* (1827), 61.

4. Loudon (1834), 265.

5. Montefiore, 305, 353.

6. Quoted by Loudon (1834), 249.

7. Vorontsov, A.V.

8. Loudon, *Gardener's Magazine*, 1827, 388.

9. Storch, 50.

10. Kennett, 80.

11. Kohl, I, 238–9.

12. Storch, 62–3.

13. Gorbatenko, 123–4.

14. Storch, 439.

15. Guthrie, 135.

16. Cox, 109.

17. Coxe, I, 312–13.

18. Murashova and Myslina, 6.

19. Gogolitsyn, 154–7.

20. According to A.F. Tyutcheva, the daughter of the poet F.I. Tyutchev and a maid of honour to the Empress Maria Aleksandrovna, 'This marriage exposed her to real danger if it became known to her father. Fortunately he had no suspicion of the event… the wedding took place in the private church of Lady Potemkin.' Quoted by Murashova, 62.

21. Gogolitsyn, 172–5.

22. Quoted by Murashova, 71.

23. Murashova, 40–74; Shapovalova, 42–5.

24. Kurbatov, 610–11.

25. Cross (1980), 311, note 58.

26. Ruoff (1992), 36 ff; Kishchyk (2001), 30 ff.

27. Quoted by Ruoff (1992), 37.

28. Kishchyk (2001), 23 ff.

29. Ruoff (1992), 36.

30. *Ibid.*, 53, note 55. The architectural works included: John Soane, *Designs in Architecture consisting of Plans, Elevations, and Sections for Temples, Baths, Cassines, Pavilions, Garden-Seats, Obelisks and Other Buildings*; J. Taylor, *Decorations for Parks and Gardens. Designs for Gates, Garden Seats, Alcoves, Temples, Baths, etc.*; N. Wallis, *The Carpenter's Treasure, a Collection of Designs for Temples, etc., in the Gothic Taste*; C. Middleton, *Designs for Gates and Rails suitable to Parks, Pleasure Grounds, Balconys &c.*

31. Information from Helsinki University Library.

32. Ruoff (1992), 40–1.

33. *Ibid.*, 41; and the plan in Nicolay.

34. Ow, 279.

35. Ruoff (1992), 46.

36. Kishchyk (2001), 43–4.

37. Ruoff (1992), 50–1 and 'An Anglomaniac', 64–5.

38. Likhachev (1991), 312.

39. Ebenezer Rhodes, *Derbyshire Tourists' Guide* (1837), 226 ff.

40. *Journal of Horticulture and Cottage Gardener* (1870), v, 287.

41. W. Adam, *Gem of the Peak*, 5th edition (1851), 231.

42. Likhachev, (1991), 312–13.

43. Talvikanta, 240–69.

44. Information from Helsinki University Library.
45. Gorbatenko, 246–51; Petrov (1983), 444–53.
46. Petrov (1983), 454; Gorbatenko, 250–1.
47. Petrov (1983), 454–9.
48. *Ibid.*, 461–7.

7. LANDSCAPE PARKS IN AND AROUND MOSCOW

1. Elizarova, 48.
2. Mikhailov, 104–5; Elizarova, 50.
3. Anikst, 333.
4. Elizarova, 51–3; Vergunov, 192–3.
5. Al'tshuller, I, 40–4; Toropov, 45–8.
6. Roosevelt, 93.
7. Toropov, 48.
8. Altshuller, I, 44–7; Toropov, 45–8.
9. *An Eighteenth-century Correspondence, to Sanderson Miller, Esq., of Radway.* Edited by Lilian Dickens and Mary Stanton, (London, 1910), 440.
10. Gorbatenko, 146–7.
11. Kondakov, 5.
12. *Ibid.*, 6.
13. *Ibid.*, 1–7.
14. Vergunov, 351–8.
15. Iljin, 103.
16. *Ibid.*
17. Al'tshuller, II, 81–4.
18. *Ibid.*, II, 121–3.
19. Vergunov, 384.
20. *Ibid.*, 383–6.
21. *Ibid.*, 114.
22. Al'tshuller, II, 162–4.
23. Dashkova, 246, 248.
24. Wilmot, 145.
25. *Ibid.*, 199, 209.
26. *Ibid.*, 202.
27. Dunaev, 25–35; Pilyavskii, *Sukhanovo*, 39–52; Al'tshuller, I, 313–16.
28. Chayanova, 48–50.
29. Saunders, 323–4.
30. F.F. Reis, *Description et analyse chimique des eaux minérales, qui se trouvent dans la terre de M. le Conseilleur privé A. de Nachtchokin à Semenovskoe, gouvernement de Moscou, district de Serpouchoff.*
31. In a Russian horn band each horn produces only a single note!
32. Denike, B., 'Rai-Semenovskoe', *Sredi kollektsionerov*, September–December, 1924, 31–8.
33. Adelswärd, *Middagsskott*, 49–52.
34. Dunaev, 36–62; Agal'tsova, 83–100; Vergunov, 204–9.
35. Kvyatkovskaya, 27–47.
36. *Ibid.*, 50, 62.
37. *Ibid.*, 68 ff.
38. Tikhomirov, 269–82; Vergunov, 122–3; Bakhtina, 40–3.
39. Vergunov, 203.
40. Pallas, I, 7.
41. Shvidkovsky, *The Empress*, 228–9.
42. Al'tshuller, I, 8–11; Vergunov, 200–3; Tikhomirov, 116–20.
43. Loudon (1834), 250.
44. Bakhtina, 52–5; Vergunov, 200–4.
45. Vergunov, 213–17.

8. SOME LANDSCAPE PARKS IN THE PROVINCES

1. Lyubchenko, 10.
2. *Ibid.*, 22–31.
3. *Ibid.*, 32–3.
4. *Ibid.*, 38–9.
5. Bolotov, III, 1134
6. Hirschfeld (I, 83) called for gardens which were German in their inspiration, not mere copies of English gardens and Chinese oddities:
   Es mag hie und da wohl einzelne unüberlegte Copien der Engländischen Manier, selbst einige Nachäffungen chinesischer Seltsamkeiten geben. Aber im Ganzen scheint doch die angenehme Erwartung durch, dass jetzt ger Geist der Nation sich auch hier einer eigenen Ueberlegung und Thätigkeit überlassen will, und dass wir Gärten gewinnen werden, die mit dem Gepräge des deutschen Genies bezeichnet sind.
7. Lyubchenko, 42–9.
8. *Ibid.*, 70–86.
9. Bolotov, IV, 39.
10. Roosevelt, 48.
11. Translated from the French quoted in Cross (1980), 248.
12. Ezhova, 69–105.
13. Kosenko, 39 ff.
14. *Ibid.*, 44.
15. Trembecki, 65.
16. *Ibid.*, 84 ff.
17. *Ibid.*, 21–2.
18. De Lagarde (1831), 104.
19. Likhachev (1991), 312–20.
20. Trembecki, 160.
21. Kosenko, 52.
22. *Ibid.*, 79–80
23. *Ibid.*, 58, quoting from the *Kievskie gubernskie vedomosti*. No date given.
24. *Ibid.*, 60–63.
25. Rodichkin, 100–2.
26. Information provided locally.
27. Rodichkin, 95–7.
28. *Stolitsa i usadba* (*The Capital and the Estate*) was Russia's equivalent of *Country Life*.
29. Tarnovskii, 121–9; Rodichkin, 132–5; Vergunov, 297–9; and a typescript by Bela Timofeeva, the architect in charge of the restoration.
30. Guthrie, 134. A series of letters written in her native French by Maria Guthrie, 'formerly acting directress of the imperial convent for the education of the female gentry of Russia', which were translated and no doubt embellished by her husband.
31. *Ibid.*, 204–6.
32. Montefiore, footnote, 377.
33. Guthrie, 75–6.
34. Volobuyev, 26.
35. Timofeev, 72; Golubeva, 5.
36. Montefiore, 497.
37. Crook, 513.
38. Timofeev, 35–6.
39. Webster, 65.
40. Alexander, J.A., 279–80.
41. Or perhaps Hayton or Heiton. The initial letters G and H are both transliterated by a Russian G. Possibly a relative of Andrew Heiton (*c*.1793–1858), an architect who practised in Perth (Colvin, 411).
42. Timofeev, 36–7; Crook, 513–15. Where these two accounts differ I have generally accepted the former since the authors would have had access to material which would not have been seen by the author of the latter.
43. Vergunov, 329.
44. Tsarin, pages not numbered.
45. Annenkov, 43; Vergunov, 326. Kebach was also responsible for Gurzuf, Massandra, Oreanda, Gaspra, Miskhor, Foros and Tessel. He died in 1851 and from then until 1861 the head gardener was Ivan Bishkovich. He was succeeded by Kebach's son Anton, who had studied at the School of Horticulture in Uman.
46. Annenkov, 43.
47. Likhachev (1991), 294.
48. Colvin, 115.
49. Rodichkin, 114.
50. I am indebted to Anna Galichenko, the Curator of the museum at Alupka, for this information and for these extracts from letters of N.A. Hartvis to Michael Vorontsov:
   le 20 juilet 1829
   M'ayant chargé de demander de Riga pour son jardin d'Aloupka des Camellias et des Magnoliers, je viens de recevoir de la part du jardinier Wagner de Riga l'annonce qu'il a reçu à la fin de Mai un superbe envoi des plus belles et nouvelles variétées de Camellia de l'établissement de Loddiges à Hackney près de Londres, très bien conservées dont il offre le plant à 20–30 roub: / prix de Loddiges sur place 15 shill / : Il y a parmi elles la Camellia oleifera. je écrit de suite à Wagner et l'ai chargé de m'envoyer pour la somme fixée pour votre Excell., six camellias, 2 Magnolias et quelques autres arbisseaux toujours vert que nous manquons encore. Tout cela doit arriver au mois d'Aôut ou septembre et j'aurois soin de bien hiverner ces plantes à Nikita dans l'orangerie pour les planter en Avril ou mai à Aloupka.
   Nikita 2 Nov 1829
   Quelques jours avant ma maladie arrivèrent les belles plantes que votre Excellence m'a chargé de faire venir pour Aloupka du jardinier Wagner de Riga, nommément six belles Camellias, au nombre de quelles, la Camellia oleifera et C. sasanqua, les autre quatre à fleurs pleines de plusieurs couleurs, deux Rhododendron, trois azalées et un arbousier de Provence. J'aurois soin de faire hiverner ces plantes dans l'Orangerie pour pouvoir les planter à Aloupka au point temps – je viens de lire dans un journal anglais d'horticulture (le Gardeners Magazine de Mr Loudon) que l'on commence à cultiver avec succès parfait aux environs de Londres les Camellias en plein air; ce seroit pour nos bosquets toujours vert une acquisition magnifique les feuilles aussi belles que celles de laurier-cerise et des grands fleurs magnifiques de toutes couleurs!
51. I am indebted to Elinor Witshire, formerly of Intourist Moscow Ltd, for the information in this paragraph.
52. Lypa, 53–6.
53. Geichenko, 1–199.

54. I.F. Rynda, '*Zabytaya usad'ba*', *Cherty uz zhizni Turgeneva*, 67, (St Petersburg, 1903), quoted by Agal'tsova, 150–1.
55. Bogdanov, 70.
56. *Ibid.*, 128, quoting from a letter to V.I. Bazilevsky, 1895.
57. *Ibid.*, 86.
58. Borisov, 134–7.

9. FROM THE EMANCIPATION OF THE SERFS TO THE REVOLUTION

1. Pipes, 146.
2. Roosevelt, 246.
3. Robinson, 61.
4. Pipes, 165. 'The government advanced to the landlords on the peasants' behalf 80 per cent of the price of the land, as determined by assessors, which the peasant had to repay over a period of forty-nine years in the form of "Redemption Payments". The remaining 20 per cent of the purchase price the peasant paid the landlord directly; in money if he had it, in services if he did not.'
5. A tax introduced by Peter and imposed on all adult males.
6. Robinson, 56.
7. *Ibid.*, 15. 'In 1877, the personal possessions of the nobles totalled 73,077,000 *desiatinas*; in 1905, only 52,104,000.'
8. Taleporovskii, 14.
9. Kuphaldt (1916), 74.
10. Vergunov, 135.
11. [Smith, M.A.P.], I, 69–70.
12. Rodichkin, 117–20; Vergunov, 335–7.
13. Vergunov, 344.
14. I am indebted to Anthony Pasley for this record of his grandmother's.
15. Chekhov, M. and M., 128.
16. *Ibid.*, 128–9.
17. *Ibid.*, 129.
18. *Ibid.*
19. *Ibid.*
20. *Ibid.*
21. *Ibid.*, 108–9, 130.
22. Vergunov, 142–51.
23. Cross, Neva, 124.
24. Loudon, *Gardener's Magazine* (1826), 84.
25. *Ibid.*, quoting from *The Edinburgh Journal of Science* (1824), No. 6, 356, 358.
26. *Ibid.*, 85.
27. Küttner, 57–60.
28. Lebedev, 4–26; Lapin, 30–41.
29. Baedeker, 336.
30. Medvedeva, 88, quoting Grigorevskii, M., *Stavropigial'nyi pervoklassnyi Solovetskii monastyr'*, (Archangel, 1897), 70.
31. Massie, R.K., 130.
32. Medvedeva, 89, quoting Nemirovich-Danchenko, V.I., *Solovki. Vospominaniya i rasskazy iz poezdok s bogomol'tsami*, (St Petersburg, 1875), 326.
33. Baedeker, 336.
34. For an early account of the horrors of the Solovetsky gulag see Duguet.
35. Vergunov, 154.
36. Kuchko, A.A. and others, *Ekosistemy Valaama i ikh okhrana*, (Petrozavodsk, 1989), 127–52. Referred to by Medvedeva, A.A., 91.
37. Medvedeva, A.A., 90–1; Bagratid (pages not numbered).
38. Kuphaldt (1916), 70–1.

10. THE SOVIET ERA

1. Kartavtsov, 54–5.
2. Ivanova, L.V., 323–4.
3. *Ibid.*, 326–7.
4. Lovell, 122–5.
5. *Ibid.*, 159–60.
6. *Ibid.*, 154.
7. *Ibid.*, 165. Report in the periodical *Ogonek* in 1948.
8. *Ibid.*, 166.
9. *Ibid.*
10. *Ibid.*, 214.
11. *Ibid.*, 211–12.
12. Gorokhov, 133.
13. Gorokhov, 133–60; Lunts, 16–21.
14. Ol', 87–111.
15. Information in a letter from Mets.
16. Tsitsin, 1–30; Lapin, 14–27.
17. Il'inskaya, 6–8.
18. *Ibid.*, 78–93.
19. *Ibid.*, 108–21.
20. *Ibid.*, 158–49.
21. *Ibid.*, 122–38, 152.
22. 'Overall, the number of owners of plots in the Russian Federation rose from 8.5 million in 1991 at the start of land reform to 15.1 million in 1997.' Lovell, 216.
23. Titova, 54–9.
24. Hayden (1997), 17–19.
25. Information from Dmitri Shvidkovsky.

BIBLIOGRAPHY

SOURCES PUBLISHED IN RUSSIA, UKRAINE AND ESTONIA

Agal'tsova, B.A., *Sokhranenie memorial'nykh lesoparkov* [The Conservation of Memorial Forest Parks] (Moscow, 1980)

Aleksandrona, I.A., and others, *Sadovo-parkovoe iskusstvo Leningrada v proizvedeniyakh khudozhnikov i arkhitektorov XVIII-XX v.v.* [The garden-park art of Leningrad in the works of artists and architects of the XVIII–XX centuries – exhibition catalogue] (Leningrad, 1983)

Aleshina, L.S., *Leningrad i okrestnosti* [Leningrad and its Environs], (Moscow, 1979)

Al'tshuller, B.L., and others, *Pamyatniki arkhitektury Moskovskoi oblasti* [Architectural Monuments of the Moscow District] (Moscow, 1975)

Anikst, M.A., and Turchin, V.S., *Vokrestnostyakh Moskvy* [On the Outskirts of Moscow] (Moscow, 1979)

Annenkov, Anatoly, and Galichenko, Anna, 'Park v Tavride' [The Park in the Crimea], *Dekorativnoe iskusstvo* (Moscow, July 1979)

Bagratid, L.V., *Valaam* (Petrozavodsk, 1991)

Bakhtina, I.K., and Chernyavskaya, E.N., *Zagorodnye usad'by v Moskve* [Estates in the Suburbs of Moscow] (Moscow, 2002)

Baranova, Olga, *Kuskovo* [English text] (Leningrad, 1983)

Benois, A.N., *Tsarskoe Selo v tsarstvovanie imperatritsy Elizavety Petrovny* [Tsarskoe Selo in the reign of the Empress Elizabeth Petrovna] (St Petersburg, 1910)

Bogdanov, B.V., *Dusha moya, vse mysli moi v Rossii* [My soul, all my thoughts are in Russia] (Moscow, 1985)

Bolotov, A.T., *Zhizn' i priklyucheniya Andreya Timofeevicha Bolotova*, 4 vols [The life and adventures of Andrei Timofeevich Bolotov] (Moscow, 1873)

Bolotova, G., *Letnii sad* [The Summer Garden] (Leningrad, 1981)

Bondar', Yu.A., *Landshaftnaya rekonstruktsiya gorodskikh sadov i parkov* [The Landscape Reconstruction of Urban Gardens and Parks] (Kiev, 1982)

Borisov, Sergei, *Yasnaya polyana* (Moscow, 1981)

[Bukh], *Tsarskoe Selo* (St Petersburg, 1840)

Bunatyan, G.G., *Gorod muz* [The Town of Poets] (Leningrad, 1987)

Chayanova, Ol'ga, 'Park i vozdushnyi teatr Petrovsko-Razumovskoe' *Sredi kollektsionerov* July–August 1924, 48–50

Chekhov, Maria and Mikhail, *The House-Museum of A.P. Chekhov in Yalta* (Moscow, 1963)

Denike, B., 'Rai-Semenovskoe' *Sredi kollektsionerov* September–December 1924, 51–8

Dubyago, T.B., *Russkie regulyarnie sady i parki* [Russian Formal Gardens and Parks] (Moscow, 1963)

Dunaev, M.M., *Kyugu ot Moskvy* [To the South of Moscow] (Moscow, 1986)

Duzhnikov, Yu.A., *Ropsha* (Leningrad, 1973)

Elizarova, N.A., *Ostankino* (Moscow, 1966)

Elkina, A.S., *Gatchina* (Leningrad, 1980)

Ezhova, I.K., *Zubrilovka. Nadezhdino* (Saratov, 1979)

Fedoruk, A.T., *Sadovo-parkovoe iskusstvo Belorussii* (Minsk, 1989)

Filosofov, M., 'K istorii serviza s zelenoi liagushkoi' [Towards the History of the Green Frog Service] *Sredi kollektsionerov* May–June 1924

Gamaleye, Henrietta, *Kolomenskoye* [English text] (Leningrad, 1986)

Geichenko, Semyon, *Alexander Pushkin Museum Park* (Moscow, 1982)

Geirot', Aleksandr Fyodorovich, *Opisanie Petergofa* [A Description of Peterhof] (1999 reprint in Leningrad of 1861 edition)

Glezer, E.N., *Arkhitekturnyi ansambl' angliiskogo parka* [The Architectural Ensemble of the English Park] (Leningrad, 1979)

Gogolitsyn, Yu.M., Gogolitsyna, T.M., *Pamyatniki arkhitektury Leningradskoi oblasti* [Architectural Mouments of the Leningrad District] (Leningrad, 1997)

Golubeva, I.V., and Kuznetsov, C.I., *Nikitskii botanicheskii sad* [Nikistky Botanic Garden] (Simferopol, 1985)

Gonzague, P.G., *La Musique des yeux et l'optique théâtral* (St Petersburg, 1807)

Gorbatenko, *Petergovskaya doroga* [The Peterhof Road] (St Petersburg, 2002)

Gornostaev, F.F., *Dvortsy i tserkvi yuga* [Palaces and Churches of the South] (Moscow, 1914)

Gorokhov, V.A., and Lunts, L.B., *Parki mira* [Parks of the World] (Moscow, 1985)

Ignatieva, M.E., 'Brusnichnik v parkakh' [Red Whortleberry in Parks] *Leningradskaya panorama* No. 9, 1982, 36–8

Il'inskaya, N.A., *Vosstanovlenie istoricheskikh ob'ektov landshaftnoi arkhitektury* [The Restoration of Historic Examples of Landscape Architecture] (St Petersburg, 1993)

Il'in, M., and Moiseeva, T., *Moskva i podmoskov'e* [Moscow and the Surrounding Area] (Moscow, 1979)

Ivanova, L.V., 'Tragicheskie sud'by chlenov Obshchestva izucheniya russkoi usad'by' [The Tragic Fate of Members of the Society for the Study of the Russian Estate] 321–7, *Russkaya usad'ba* ed. L.V. Ivanova (Moscow, 1994)

Ivanova, O.A., *Pavlovsky park* [Pavlovsk Park] (Leningrad, 1956)

Karavaeva, E., 'Vse k razmyshlen'yu zdes' vlechet…', [Everything Here Induces Reflection] *Yunyi Khudozhnik* V, 1984, 12–15, (Moscow, 1984)

Kartavtsov, I., 'Obshchestvo Izucheniya Russkoi Usad'by' [The Society for the Study of the Russian Estate] *Sredi kollektsionerov* July–August 1924, 54–55

Kishchyk, A.A., *Park Monrepo v Vyborge* [Mon Repos Park in Viborg] (St Petersburg, 2001)

—— and others, *Okhrana i ispol'zovanie pamyatnikov sadovo-parkovogo iskusstva* [The Protection and Use of Monuments of Garden-Park Art] (Moscow, 1990)

Klabunovskii, I.G., *Podmoskovnye usad'by* [Some Estates near Moscow] (Moscow, 1946)

Kondakov, S., 'Otrada', *Stolitsa i usad'ba*

[The Capital and the Estate] 30 August 1917, 1–7

Korshunova, M.F., *Arkhitektor Yurii Felten* [The Architect Yuri Felten – exhibition catalogue] (Leningrad, 1982)

——, *P'etro Gonzaga* [exhibition catalogue] (Leningrad, 1980)

Kosenko, I.S., and others, *Dendrologicheskii park Sofievka* [The Dendrological Park Sophievka] (Kiev, 1990)

Kostochkin, V., *Drevnerusskie goroda* [Ancient Russian Towns] (Moscow, 1972)

Kurbatov, V.Ya., *Sady i parki* [Gardens and Parks] (Petrograd, 1916)

Kuuskemaa, Jüri, *Kadriorg: the 18th-century Palace and Park* [English translation from Estonian] (Tallinn, 1985)

Kuznetsova, O.N., and Borzin, B.F., *Letnii sad* [The Summer Garden] (Leningrad, 1988)

Kvyatkovskaya, N.K., *Marfino* (Moscow, 1985)

Kyuchariants, D.A., *Khudozhestvennye pamyatniki goroda Lomonosova* (Leningrad, 1985)

Lansere, Nikolai, 'Zabytaya prigorodnaya usad'ba XVIII veka' [A Forgotten Estate of the 18th Century] *Sredi kollektsionerov* July–August 1924, 36–44

—— and others, *Gatchina pri Pavle Petroviche tsesareviche i imperatore* [Gatchina in the Time of Paul Petrovich as Tsarevich and Emperor] [articles from *Sredi kollektsionerov*] (St Petersburg, 1995)

Lapin, P.I., *Botanicheskie sady CCCP* [Botanical Gardens of the USSR] (Moscow, 1984)

Lebedev, D.V., Lipschitz, S.J., and Lodkina, M.M., *An Outline of History of V.L. Komarov Botanical Institute (1714–1961)* (Moscow-Leningrad, 1962)

Likhachev, Dmitri, 'Sad i Kul'tura' [The Garden and Culture] *Dekorativnoe iskusstvo*, No. 12, 1982, 38–45

——, *Poezia sadov* (St Petersburg, 1991)

Lunts, L.B., and Mikulina, E.M., 'Parki SSSR' [Parks of the Soviet Union] *Stroitel'stvo i arkhitektura* [Building and Architecture] 2/1985

Lyubchenko, O.N., *Est' v Bogodoritske park* [In Bogodoritsk there is indeed a Park] (Tula, 1984)

Lypa, A.L., *Introduktsiya i akklimatizatsiya drevesnykh rastenii na Ukraine* [The Introduction and Acclimatization of Trees in the Ukraine] (Kiev, 1978)

Medvedeva, A.A., 'Sadovo-parkovoe iskusstvo ostrovnykh monastyrei Severo-Zapada Rossii' [The Garden-Park Art of the Island Monasteries of North-west Russia] (Solovki, Valaam, Konevets) *Nasledie monastyrskoi Kul'tury* Part 2 (St Petersburg, 1997) 86–94

Mikhailov, E., 'Sadovnik Frensis Rid v Tsaritsyno i Ostankino' [The Gardener Francis Reid at Tsaritsyno and Ostankino] *Arkhitektura SSSR* No. 4, 1990

Mikulina, E.M., *Vzaimodeistvie goroda i okruzhayushchei sredi* [The Interaction of the Town and its Suroundings] (Moscow, 1985)

—— (editor) *Gorod i landshaft* [Town and Landscape] (Moscow, 1985)

Mineeva, K.I., *Tsaritsyno: dvortsovo-parkovyi ansambl'* [The Tsaritsyno Palace-Park Ensemble] (Moscow, 1988)

Murashova, N.V., and Myslyna, A.P., *Dvoryanskie usad'by Sankt-Peterburgskoi gubernii* [Estates of the Nobility in the St Petersburg Province] (St Petersburg, 1999)

Nemchinova, D., *Elagin Ostrov* [Yelagin Island] (Leningrad, 1982)

Nesin, V.N., and Sautkina, G.N., *Pavlovsk Imperatorskii i Velikiknyazheskii* [Imperial and Grand-Ducal Pavlovsk] (St Petersburg, 1996)

Ol', G.A., *Aleksandr Nikolsky* (Leningrad, 1980)

Palentreer, S.N., 'Sady 17-ogo veka v Ismailove' [Gardens of the 17th Century in Ismailovo] *Soobshchenie instituta istorii iskusstva* No. 7, 1956

Petrov, A.N., *Dvortsy i parki* [Palaces and Parks] (Leningrad, 1964)

—— and others, *Pamyatniki arkhitektury prigorodov Leningrada* [Architectural Monuments in the Environs of Leningrad] (Leningrad, 1983)

Pilyavskii, V.I., *Sukhanovo* (Leningrad, 1986)

——, *Dzhakomo Kvarengi* (Leningrad, 1981)

Poniatowski, Stanislas-Auguste, *Mémoires du roi Stanislas-Auguste Poniatowski* (St Petersburg, 1914)

Pylyaev, M.I., *Staryi Peterburg* (Leningrad, 1990)

Rapoport, Valery, *Arkhangelskoye* [English text] (Leningrad, 1984)

Raskin, A., *Petrodvorets* [Peterhof] [English text] (Leningrad, 1978)

——, *Gorod Lomonosov* [The Town of Lomonosov], (Leningrad, 1979)

Regel, A., *Izyashchnoe sadovodstvo i khudozhestvennye sady* [Elegant Gardening and Artistic Gardens] (St Petersburg, 1896)

Rodichkin, I.D., and others, *Sady, parki i zapovedniki ukrainskoi SSR* [Gardens, Parks and Nature Parks of the Ukrainian SSR] (Kiev, 1985)

Rogotchenko, A.P., *Umanskoe chudo* [The Wonder of Uman] (Kiev, 1977)

Romanov, Nikolai Mikhailovich, *Perepiska Imperatora Aleksandra I s sestroi Velikoi Knyaginei Ekaterinoi Pavlovnoi* [The Correspondence of the Emperor Alexander I and his Sister the Grand Duchess Catherine Pavlovna] (St Petersburg, 1910)

Rothstein, Nikolai, review of G.C. Williamson's *The Imperial Russian Dinner Service* in *Starye gody* February 1910, 37 ff.

Semennikova, N., *Letnyi sad* [The Summer Garden] (Leningrad, 1969)

——, *Pushkin, dvortsy i parki* [Pushkin, Palaces and Parks] (Leningrad, 1987)

Semevskii, M.I., *Pavlovsk: ocherk istorii i opisanie 1777–1877* [Pavlovsk: Notes of History and Description 1777–1877] (St Petersburg, 1877)

Shafarenko, I.Ya., *Sady* [a new translation of Jacques Delille's poem *Les Jardins*], (Leningrad, 1987)

Shuiskii, V.K., *Vinchentso Brenna* (Leningrad, 1986)

Shvidkovskii, D.O., *Gorod russkogo prosveshcheniya* [The City of the Russian Enlightenment] (Moscow, 1991)

Sverbeev, D.N., *Zapiski* [Memoirs] (Moscow, 1899)

Taleporovskii, V.N., *Pavlovskii park* (Leningrad, 1923)

Taranovskaya, M.Z., *Carl Rossi* (Leningrad, 1980)

Tarnovskii, M.V., 'Kachanovka' *Stolitsa i Usad'ba* Nos. 40–1, 1915, 121–9

Themery, T., *Guide de Sophiowka, surnommé la merveille de l'Ukraine* (Odessa, 1846)

Tikhomirov, N.Ya., *Arkhitektura podmoskovnykh usad'eb* [The Architecture of the Estates in the Environs of Moscow] (Moscow, 1955)

Tikhomirova, M., *Pamyatniki, lyudi, sobytiya* [Monuments, People, Events] (Leningrad, 1984)

Timofeev, L.N., and Tsarin, A.P., *Alupka: putevoditel'* [Alupka: a Guide] (Simferopol, 1985)

Titova, N.P., *Sady na kryshakh* [Gardens on Roofs] (Moscow, 2003)

Toropov, C., 'Zametki: Yaropoltsy' [Observations: Yaropolets] *Sredi kollektsionerov* July–August 1924, 45–8

Tsarin, A.P., *Alupkins'kii palats-muzei* [Alupka Palace-Museum] (Kiev, 1982)

Tsitsin, N.V., and Lapin, P.I., *Glavnyi botanicheskii sad AN SSSR* [The Main Botanical Garden of the USSR] (Moscow, 1975)

Tumanova, N.E., *Ekaterininsky park* (St Petersburg, 1997)

Ushakova, Yu.S., and others, *Okhranyaetsya gosudarstvom* [Protected by the State] (Leningrad, 1983)

Vagner, G.K., *Starye russkie goroda* [Ancient Russian Towns] (Moscow, 1984)

Vergunov, A.P., and Gorokhov, V.A., *Russkie sady i parki* [Russian Gardens and Parks] (Moscow, 1988)

Vil'chkovsii, C.N., *Tsarskoe Selo* (St Petersburg, 1992, reprint of 1911 edition)

Vityazeva, V.A,. *Nevskie ostrova* (Leningrad, 1986)

Vladimirov, V.V,. and others, *Gorod i landshaft* [Town and Landscape] (Moscow, 1986)

Volobuyev, O., *Greater Yalta* (Moscow, 1979)

Voronikhina, A.N., and others, *Arkhitekturnaya grafika Rossii – pervaya polovina XVIII veka* [Architectural Graphic Art of Russia – first half of the 18th century] Hermitage collection (Leningrad, 1981)

Voronikhina, L.N., *Serviz s zelyonoi lyagushkoi* (Leningrad, 1962)

——, 'O peizazhakh "Serviza s zeyonoi lyagushkoi"' [About the Landscapes of the 'Green Frog Service']. *Muzei* No. 9 (Moscow, 1988)

[Vorontsov], *Arkhiv knyaz'ya Vorontsova* [The Archive of Prince Vorontsov] (Moscow, 1870–95)

Vorontsov, A.V., 'Vil'yam Gul'd, sadovnik knyazya Potemkina-Tavricheskogo' [William Gould, Gardener of Prince Potemkin-Tavrichesky], *Nevskii arkhiv: istoriko-kraevskii sbornik IV,* (St Petersburg, 1999), 143–166

Yakovin, Ilya, *Istoria sela Tsarskogo* [The History of Tsarskoe Selo] 3 vols (St Petersburg, 1831)

OTHER PUBLISHED SOURCES

Adelswärd, Gösta, 'Vad menade André Mollet? Ljung eller lingon?', *Lustgården*, 1995, 47–60

——, 'Middagsskott i romantisk park', *Lustgården*, 1987–8, 49–52

Alexander, J.A., *Travels through Russia* (1830)

Alexander, John T., *Catherine the Great: Life and Legend* (New York and Oxford, 1989)

Anonymous, 'Biographical Sketch of John Fraser, the Botanical Collector', *Companion to the Botanical Magazine* 1837, v.2, 300–3

Åberg, Alf, 'Fångars elände' *Natur och Kultur* (Stockholm, 1991)

Baedeker, Karl, *Russia* (London, 1914)

Bardowskaya, L.W., *Schloss- und Parkensichten der Stadt Puschkin* (Dresden, 1982)

Berger-Fix, Andrea, and Merten, Klaus (compilers), *Die Gärten der Herzöge von Württemberg in 18. Jahrhundert* [exhibition catalogue] (Worms, 1981)

Bernier, Georges, *Antonin Carême 1783–1833* (Paris, 1989)

Calvert, Frederick, *Gaudia poetica* (Augsburg, 1770)

Carême, Antonin, *Le Patissier pittoresque* (Paris, 1828)

Carr, John, *A Northern Summer* (London, 1805)

Carter, H.B., *Sir Joseph Banks and the Plant Collection from Kew sent to the Empress Catherine II of Russia* (London, 1974) [In fact the plants were requested by and sent to the Grand Duchess Maria Fyodorovna.]

Clarke, G.B. (editor), *Descriptions of Lord Cobham's Gardens at Stowe (1700–1750)* Buckingham Record Society no. 26 (1990)

Clinchamp, Comtesse Berthe de, *Chantilly 1485–1897* (Paris, 1903)

Colvin, Howard, *A Biographical Dictionary of British Architects* (London, 1978)

Cox, E.H.M., 'An English Gardener at the Russian Court, 1779–87', *New Flora and Silva* 1939, II, pt 2, 103–12

Coxe, William, *Travels into Poland, Russia, Sweden and Denmark* 5th edition (London, 1802)

Crook, J. Mordaunt, 'Xanadu by the Black Sea: The Worontzow Palace at Aloupka', *Country Life* 1972, 513 ff

Cross, Anthony, 'British Gardeners and the Vogue of the English Garden in Late-Eighteenth-Century Russia' and 'Cultural Relations between Britain and Russia in the Eighteenth Century', *British Art Treasures from the Russian Imperial Collections in the Hermitage* edited by Brian Allen and Larissa Dukelskaya (New Haven and London, 1996)

——, *By the Banks of the Thames* (Newtonville, Mass., 1980)

——, *By the Banks of the Neva* (Cambridge, 1997)

——, 'The Lords Baltimore in Russia', *Journal of European Studies* xviii, 1988, 77–91

—— (ed.), *An English Lady at the Court of Catherine the Great: The Journal of Baroness Elizabeth Dimsdale, 1781* (Cambridge, 1989)

Dashkova, E.R., *The Memoirs of Princess Dashkova* (Durham, NC and London, 1995)

Delille, M. L'Abbé [Jacques], *Les Jardins ou L'Art d'embellir les paysages* (London, 1801)

Demidova, D., 'Der Park auf der Yelagin-insel in St Petersburg', *Die Gartenkunst* 2/1992, 307–16

Duguet, Raymond, *Un Bagne en Russie rouge, Solovki, l'Ile de Faim, des Supplices, de la Mort* (Paris, 1927)

Evelyn, John, *The Diary of John Evelyn* (Oxford, 1955)

Firdsov, Gennady, 'Tragic fate of a great botanist', *Lustgården*, 1998, 37–40

Floryan, Margrethe, *Gardens of the Tsars* (Aarhus, 1996)

——, 'Alle tiders have. Billeder og betydning i Katherina IIs Tsaritsyno', *De lyse sale. Festskrift til Bent Skovgaard* (Copenhaen, 1990)

Golovine, V.N., *Memoirs of Countess Golovine* (London, 1910)

Gothein, Marie Luise, *A History of Garden Art* (London, 1928)

Guthrie, Marie, *A Tour, Performed in the Years 1795–6, through the Tauride, or Crimea* (London, 1802)

Hall, James, *Dictionary of Subjects and Symbols in Art* (London, 1974)

Hallström, Björn H., *Russian architectural drawings in the Nationalmuseum* (Stockholm, 1963)

Hamilton, G.H., *The Art and Architecture of Russia* (2nd edition, London, 1975)

Harris, James, *The Diaries and Correspondence of James Harris, First Earl of Malmesbury* (1844)

Hayden, Peter, 'British Seats on Imperial Russian Tables', *Garden History*, vol. 13, 1 (1985)

——, 'A note on Jacques Delille (1738–1813) and a new Russian translation by I.Ya. Sharfarenko of *Les Jardins*', *Garden History*, vol. 18, 2 (1990)

——, 'The Russian Stowe', *Garden History*, vol. 19, 1 (1991)

——, 'The Fabriques of Antonin Carême', *Garden History*, vol. 24, 1 (1996)

——, 'Tsarskoe Selo: The History of the Ekaterinskii and Alexandrovskii Parks', *A Sense of Place* 13–34, (USA, 1993)

——, 'Pavlovsk', *The Garden*, vol 107, part 6 (1982)

——, 'A Celebration of Water', *Landscape Design*, 162, 19–23 (August, 1986)

——, 'Planting a new prospekt', *Landscape Design*, 259, 17–19 (April, 1997)

Henrey, Blanche, *British Botanical and Horticultural Literature before 1800* (London, 1975)

Howard, Jeremy, and Kuznetsov, Sergei, 'Scottish Architects in Tsarist Russia', *History Today*, February, 1996, 35–41

Hirschfeld, C.C.L., *Théorie der Gartenkunst* (Leipzig, 1779–85)

——, *Théorie de l'art des jardins* (Leipzig, 1779–85)

Hitt, Thomas, *The Modern Gardener* (London, 1771)

Hughes, Lindsey, *Russia in the Age of Peter the Great* (New Haven and London, 1998)

Hyams, E., and Macquitty, W., *Great Botanical Gardens of the World* (London, 1969)

Ignatieva, M.E., 'The mystery of ancient Russian gardens', *Lustgården*, 1997, 69–78

Ignatieva, M.E., Reiman, A.L., Vorontsova, L.J., 'Troubled by water. Tavrichesky Garden in St Petersburg', *Lustgården*, 1996, 39–46

Iljin, M, 'Russian Parks of the Eighteenth Century', *Architectural Review*, February 1964, 100–11

Jackman, S.W. (ed.), *Romanov Relations* (London, 1969)

James, John, *The Theory and Practice of Gardening*, 'Done from the French original [of A.J. Dezallier d'Argenville] printed at Paris, anno 1709.' (London, 1712)

Jones, W. Gareth, *Nikolai Novikov: Enlightener of Russia* (Cambridge, 1984)

de Jong, Erik, 'Virgilian Paradise: a Dutch Garden near Moscow in the Early 18th Century', *Journal of Garden History*, vol. 1, no. 4

Kennett, Audrey, *The Palaces of Leningrad* (London, 1973)

King, John Glen, *A Letter to the Right Reverend the Lord Bishop of Durham containing some Observations on the Climate of Russia and the Northern Counties* (London, 1778)

Knapas, Rainer, 'Mon Repos vid Viborg – det förlorade paradiset', *Lustgården*, 1996, 47–58

Kohl, J.G., *Russia and the Russians* (London, 1842)

Köhler, Marcus, '"Wenn wir erst einen ins Wilder angelgtaen Garten zu sehen gewohnt sind…"', *Die Gartenkunst*, 1/1993, 101–25

Kuphaldt, G., 'Der Garten am Winter-Palais in St. Petersburg', *Die Gartenkunst*, V, 1903, 186–9

——, 'Die Gartenkunst in Russland, besonders in den baltischen Provinzen', *Gartenflora*, LXV, 1916, 70–79

——, 'Der Park von Schloss Marino bei Iwanowskoje Gouvernement Kursk', *Die Gartenkunst*, VII, 1905, 19–24

Küttner, Juri, 'Ett palmhus i förfall', *Lustgården*, 1997, 57–60

Lagarde, A. de, *Voyage de Moskou à Kiev* (Paris, 1824)

——, *Journal of a Nobleman* (1831)

Langley, Batty, *New Principles of Gardening* (London, 1728)

Lees-Milne, James, *The Bachelor Duke* (London, 1991)

Le Rouge, Georges Louis, *Détails des nouveaux jardins à la mode: Jardins Anglo-Chinois* (Paris, 1776–87)

Lönnrot, Elias (compiler), *The Old Kalevala*, translations and foreword by Magoun, F.P. (Cambridge, Mass., 1969)

Loseff, Lev, and Scherr, Barry (editors), *A Sense of Place* (Columbus, 1993)

Loudon, J.C., *Encyclopædia of Gardening* (1827 and 1834 editions)

—— (editor), *Gardener's Magazine* (London, 1826–44)

Lovell, Stephen, *Summerfolk: a History of the Dacha 1710–2000* (Ithaca and London, 2003)

Lundquist, Kjell, 'Om lingon som buxbomsersättning', *Lustgården*, 1995, 106–11

de Madariaga, Isabel, *Russia in the Age of Catherine the Great* (London, 1981)

Marsden, Christopher, *Palmyra of the North* (London, 1942)

Massie, R.K., *Peter the Great* (London, 1982)

Massie, Suzanne, *Pavlovsk: The Life of a Russian Palace* (Boston, 1980)

Masson, Georgina, *Italian Gardens* (London, 1961)

Meader, James, *The Planter's Guide* (London, 1779)

Medvedeva, Anna, and Gannibal, Boris, 'A Monastery park on lake Ladoga', *Lustgården*, 2001, 119–124

Merkle, J., *Jugendjahre der Kaiserin Maria Feodorovna* (Stuttgart, 1892)

——, *Segensreiche Wirksomkeit durch vier Generationen* (Stuttgart, 1893)

Mollet, André, *Le Jardin de plaisir* (Stockholm, 1650)

Montefiore, S.S., *The Life of Potemkin* (London, 2000)

Newlin, Thomas, *The Voice in the Garden: Andrei Bolotov and the Anxieties of Russian Pastoral, 1738–1833* (Evanston, Ill., 2001)

Nicolay, L.H., *Das Landgut Monrepos in Finnland* (Berlin, 1804)

d'Oberkirch, *Mémoires de la Baronne d'Oberkirch* (Paris, 1853)

——, *Memoirs of Baroness d'Oberkirch* (London, 1852)

Ow, Meinrad von, 'Schloss Monrepos unterm Sowjetstern', *Schwabische Heimat*, 1984, v. 35, 275 ff

Pallas, P.S., '*Travels through the Southern Provinces of the Russian Empire in the Years 1793 and 1794* (London, 1802)

Pipes, Richard, *Russia under the Old Régime* (2nd edition, London, 1995)

Porter, Robert Kerr, *Travelling Sketches in Russia and Sweden* (London, 1809)

Raeburn, M., Voronikhina, L., and Nurnberg, A. (eds), *The Green Frog Service* (London, 1995)

Reiman, Andrei, 'Vegetation for Russian Formal Gardens', *Die Gartenkunst des Barock*, in the Journal of the German National Committee of Icomos, XXVIII, 20–26 (1997)

Riasanovsky, N.V., *A History of Russia* (4th edition, Oxford, 1984)

Richardson, William, *Anecdotes of the Russian Empire* (1784)

Rhodes, Ebenezer, *Derbyshire Tourists' Guide* (1837)

Robinson, G.T., *Rural Russia under the Old Régime* (New York, 1949)

Roosevelt, Priscilla, *Life on the Russian Country Estate* (New Haven and London, 1995)

Ruoff, Eeva, 'Das finnische Monrepos', *Die Gartenkunst*, 1/1992, 35–53

——, 'Notiser från Monrepos', *Lustgården*, 2001, 33–40

——, 'An Anglomaniac in Finland', *Country Life*, February 15, 2001, 62–5

Saunders, David, *Russia in the Age of Reaction and Reform 1801–81* (London and New York, 1992)

Seeley, Benton, *Stowe: A Description of the Magnificent House and Gardens* (1769)

Ségur, Comte de, *Memoirs of Count Segur* (London, 1825–7)

Shapovalova, E.F., 'Gostilitsy: A Country Estate in Russia', *Landscape Design*, April, 1991, 42–5

Shvidkovsky, Dmitri, *The Empress and the Architect* (New Haven and London, 1996)

——, 'Cameron Discoveries', *Architectural Review*, no. 2, 1982

——, 'Adam Menelaws', *Apollo*, n.s. vol 135, 1992

——, 'A Grandmother's Tale', *Garden History*, Vol. 19, no. 1 (1991)

[Smith, Mary Ann Pellew, according to the British Library catalogue], An English Lady, *Six Years Travel in Russia* (1859)

Storch, Heinrich, *The Picture of Petersburg*, 'from the German of Henry Storch' (London, 1801)

Swinton, A., *Travels into Norway, Denmark and Russia*, (London, 1792)

Talvikanta, Maija-Liisa, 'Ossiaanista soitta', *Kalevalaseuran vuosikirja*, 41, 1961

Terras, Victor (editor), *Handbook of Russian Literature* (New Haven and London, 1985)

Trembecki, Stanislas, *Sophievka*, [Polish text with French translation by the Comte de Lagarde], (Vienna, 1815)

Troyat, Henri, *Catherine the Great* (Henley-on-Thames, 1979)

—— *Alexander the Great* (Great Britain, 1984)

Vernadsky, George, *Kievan Russia* (New Haven, 1948)

[Ward/Rondeau/Vigor, Jane], *Letters from a Lady* (London, 1775)

[Watson, Sophia], *Memoirs of the Seraglio of the Bashaw of Merryland By a Discarded Sultana* (London, 1768)

Weber, F.C., *The Present State of Russia* (1723)

Webster, James, *Travels through the Crimea, Turkey and Egypt* (1830)

Wiebenson, Dora, *The Picturesque Garden in France* (Princeton, 1978)

Williamson, G.C., *The Imperial Russian Dinner Service* (London, 1909)

Wilmot, Martha and Catherine, *The Russian Journals of Martha and Catherine Wilmot* (London, 1934)

Wilson, Andrew, *The Ukrainians: Unexpected Nation* (New Haven and London, 2002)

von Württemberg, Carl Eugen, *Tagbücher seiner Rayssen* (Tübingen, 1968)

INDEX

Page numbers in *italics* refer to captions.

Abercrombie, John 100
Adelsnäs 177
Aiton, William 125
Akhmatova, Anna 99
Akopovaya, L.D. 233
Aleksandria 200, *200*
Aleksandrinsky Palace 184
Aleksandrinsky Park 161
Aleksandrovsky Garden (Moscow) 220
Aleksandrovsky Garden (St Petersburg) 220
Alekseevsky 18
Alexander, Captain James 205
Alexander I 74, 98, 103, 109, 126, 127, 136, 138, 140,
    148, 153
Alexander II 215
Alexander Palace 96, *96*
Alexander Pushkin Museum Park 209-10
Alexandershantz 73
Alexandria 160-1
Alma-Ata 233
Alton Abbey 158-9
Alupka 145, 158, 204-9, *204, 206, 207*
Andreev, Tit 10
Andropov, Yuri 231
Anhalt-Bernburg-Zerbst, Prince of 84
Anna Ivanovna, Empress 44, 57
Annenhof 43, 57
Annensky, Innokenty 99
Apothecary's Garden
    Izmailovo *9*, 15
    Moscow 10, 236
Arakcheev, Count Aleksei 153
Argunov, Fyodor 60, 65
Argunov, Nikolai 65
Argunov, P. 165
Arkadia 193
Arkhangelskoe 7, 67-73, *67, 69, 71*, 184
Arkhipov, P.G. 162
Artek 145
Astrakhan 145

Bakhchisarai 145, 203-4, *203*
Baltimore, Frederick Calvert, 6th Lord 99-100
Banks, Sir Joseph 125
Baratta, Pietro 20
Barattini, Giovanni and Giuliano 27, 74
Batyushkov, Konstantin 177
Bazhenov, Vasily 104-5, 106, 170
Beklemishev, V.A. *142*
Belvedere Palace 162, *162*
Benois, N.L. 67
Bergholz, Friedrich von 42, 44
Berlin
    Charlottenburg 17
    Monbijou 17
    Oranienburg 17
Bezborodko, Count Alexander 168
Bezborodko estate 168-70, *168, 169*
Bidloo, Govert 53
Bidloo, Lambert 53
Bidloo, Nicolaas *4*, 53-4, *53, 54*, 56

Biron, Ernst-Johann 57
Bisterfeld
    gardener at Mon Repos 156, 158
    gardener at Sokirentsy 199
Blank, Ivan 23, 33
Blank, Karl 58, 60, 168, 200
Blenheim 137
Blore, Edward 206, 207
Bobrinsky, Count A.G. 188
Böckler, G.A. 18
Bogolyubsky, Prince Andrei 9
Bogoroditsk 188-91, *189, 190*
Bolotov, Andrei Timofeevich 187-91
Bonazza, Antonio 20, 24
Bonazza, Giovanni 33
Borisov, Anton 24, 27
Borisovo 10
botanical collections 220-1, 233
    Gorenki 183-4
    Imperial Botanic Garden 184, 220-3, *221, 222*, 224
    Moscow Botanical Garden 233
    Nikitsky Botanic Garden 184, 207, 209
    P.A. Demidov's garden 183
    Pavlovsk 126
Boulevard Ring 220
Brants, Christoffel 17
Braunstein, Johann 18, 24, 30, 32, 33, 46
Brenna, Vincenzo 110, 113, 117, 120, 121, 123, 127, 134,
    156
Brocket, Denis 42, 43
Brown, Lancelot ('Capability') 82, 84, 138
Bruyn, Cornelius de 53, 58
Buffo, Francesco 206
Buk, Peter 141
Busch, John *49*, 82, 84-5, 87, 96, 117, 128, 145
Busch, Joseph 141, 142
Bykovo 170, *170*
Bykovsky, M.D. 180

Call, Martin 147
Calthorpe, Captain S.J.G. 209
Cameron, Charles 89, 90, 92, 93, 98, 109, 110, 113, 116,
    117, 123
Carême, Antonin 138-40
Carr, Sir John 145, 147
Catherine I 43, 44, 46
Catherine II (Catherine the Great) 7, 46, 50, 77, *77*,
    128, 130, 148, 203
    see also English Park; Oranienbaum; Tsaritsyno;
    Tsarskoe Selo; Winter Palace
Catherine Pavlovna, Grand Duchess 126, 136
Caus, Salomon de 18
Chamerlain's porcelain factory 137, *137*
Chambers, Sir William 89, 110, 139, 156
Chantilly 110, 120
Charlemagne, I.I. 103, 161
Charlemagne, Ludovick 21
Charlottenburg 17
Chatsworth 136, 137
Chayanova, Olga 175
Chekhov, Anton 219-20
Cherkassky estates 58
Cherkassky, Prince 165
Chernyshev, Ivan 166-7
Chernyshev, Z.G. 166

Chesme, Battle of 85, 87, 92, *92*
Chesme Palace and Church 85
Chevakinsky, Savva 46
Chinese parks and buildings 89
Cipriani, Sebastiano 40
Clark, Basil 173
Cloase, Thomas 82
coasting hills
    Gostilitsy 152
    Kamenny Island *149*
    Oranienbaum 81, 82, *82*
    Tsarskoe Selo 49-50, 96, *96*, 99-100
Condé, Prince de 134
Congreve, Sir William 136-7
Constantine Pavlovich, Grand Duke 77, 92, 98, 100
Cottage Palace 160-1, *160*
Coxe, Revd William 57, 149-50
Crimea 145, 202-9

dachas 215, 216, 228, *228*, 231
    garden plot dachas 228, 231, 236
    Peterhof Road 148
Dannecker, Johann Heinrich von 98
Dashkova, Princess Catherine 170
Davidov, Denis 177
Davydov, Ivan 23, 33
Delille, Jacques 120, 123, 124, 156
Delvig, Anton 98
Demidov family 7
Demidov, A.G. 150
Demidov, P.A. 183, *183*
Derzhavin, Gavril 98, 170
Devonshire, William Spencer Cavendish,
    6th Duke of *109*, 136
Dézallier d'Argenville, A.-J. 73
Dimsdale, Elizabeth 87, 96
Dimsdale, Dr Thomas 94
Dmitriev, Ivan 179
Dolgoruky, Prince Yuri 9, 10
Dubki 42
Dubrovsky, P.A. 199
Dubyago, Tatyana 22, 40, 42, 56, 233
Dunkeld 158, 207
Dvoryaninovo 187-8, 191
Dzerzhinsky Park of Culture and Rest 166

Egotov, I. V. 106
Egyptian garden features 180
Ekaterinhof 43-4, *43*
Ekaterinoslav (later, Dnepropetrovsk) 145
Elizabeth Petrovna, Empress 21, 44, 46, 49, 50, 57
    see also Ropsha
Elizavethof 43
Elmsall, William 27
Elson, Philip 206
England
    Alton Abbey 158-9
    Blenheim 137
    Chatsworth 136, 137
    Kew 87, 110, 125, 126
    Longford Castle 85
    Painshill 102
    Russian visits to 17, 125, 126, 136-8, 170
    Stowe 77, 87, 89, 92, 93-6, *93, 94, 95, 96*, 137
    Studley Royal 89
Englez, Peter 10

English landscape style 7, 21, 82, 85, 87, 149–50, 188, 191
  see also landscape parks
English Palace 100, *100*, 103, *103*
English park 100–3, *100*, 215
Erf, I.A. 236
Erler, P.I. 160, 162
Erskine, Robert 152, 220
Esakov, Ermolai 152
Etupes 109–10
Evelyn, John 17

Fisher, F.E.L. 184, 220–1
Fock, Bernhard 27
Fontana, Giovanni 45
Forest Cemetery 233
France
  Chantilly 110, 120
  Marly 17, 18, 22, 27
  St Cloud 17
  Trianon 17, 120
  Versailles 17, 18, 22
Fraser, John 125–6
fruit gardens 10
  Izmailovo 15
  Ostankino 165
  Pavlovsk 125
  Ropsha 50
  Tsarskoe Selo 46
funerary monuments
  Alexandria 160
  Arkhangelskoe 73
  Gruzino 153–4, *153*
  Mon Repos 157, *158*
  Pavlovsk 123, *123*, *142*
  Sukhanovo 175

Gatchina 126, 128–36
  amphitheatre 134
  Eagle Pavilion 130, *131*, 133
  hothouses 134
  hunting park 130
  Island of Love 133
  Little Birch House *132*, 133–4
  plan 240
  Priory Palace 134, *134*
  Private Garden 130, *130*
  restoration 236
  Temple of Venus *131*, 133
  White Lake *128*, 130, *132*, 134
  Woodland Orangery 134
Geichenko, Semyon 210
George III of England 125
Gerasimenko, L.A. 236
Gibbs, James 89
Ginsberg, M.Ya. 231
Glinka, Mikhail 200, *201*
Godunov, Boris 10
Gogol, Nikolai 177
Golitsyn family 7, 180
Golitsyn, Count Boris 178
Golitsyn, Prince D.M. 67, 154
Golovin, Fyodor 56
Golovinsky Garden 56–7
Golovkin, Count Gabriel 44
Golovkin, G.I. 50

Gombel, A.I. 160
Gonzaga, Pietro 73, 110, 120, 121, 123, 127
Gorbachev, Mikhail 231
Gorenki 183–4, *183*
Gorki (later, Gorki Leninskie) 185, *185*
Gorky Park 231, *231*
Gostilitsy 152
Gothic Revival architecture 85, 89, 161
Gould, William 103, 145, 147, 148, 203
Graefer, Johann Andreas 84
Great Northern War 17
Grech, Aleksei 227
Green Frog dinner service 85, *85*, 87
green theatres 46, 65, *65*, 177
Greig, Admiral 92
Grenville, Captain *92*, 93
Grey, Thomas 50
Griboedov, Alexander 177
Grigorev, A.G. 175
Grigorevich, Count Pavel 199
grottoes
  Alupka 207
  Gorenki 185, *183*
  Kuskovo 60, *62*, 64, 67
  Peterhof 24
  Petrovsko-Razumovskoe 175
  Sophievka *194*, 196, 197
  Strelna *41*, 42
  Tsarskoe Selo 49, *49*
Gruzino 153–4, *153*
Guêpière, Philippe de la 109
Guerne, Charles de 69
Gumilev, Nikolai 99
Gurzuf 209
Guthrie, Marie 202, 203, 204

Hackett, James 130
hanging gardens 9
  Kremlin Palace 10
  Riga 73
  Summer Garden 21
  Tsarskoe Selo 92, 93
Hannibal, Abram Petrovich 150, 210
Hannibal, Osip Abramovich 210
Harris, Sir James 87
Harrison, Thomas 204
Hartvis, Nikolai 207, 209
Helmholz, F. 130
Hermitage
  Kamenny Island 44, *44*
  Kuskovo 60, *60*, 67
  Peterhof 30, *30*, 37
  Tsarskoe Selo 46, *46*
Hernichfelt, Leonard 18, 24, 27, 32
Het Loo 17
Hirschfeld, C.C.L. 20, 188
Hitt, Thomas 100
Hohenheim 110, 118, *118*
Honselaarsdijk 17
hothouses
  Gatchina 134
  Taurida Palace 148
  Tsarskoe Selo 87
  Yelagin Island 140
Hunt, William 206

hunting parks
  Ekaterinhof 44
  Gatchina 130
  Tsarskoe Selo 46

Imperial Botanic Garden 184, 220–3, *221*, *222*, 224
invasion of Russia (1812) 7, 67, 71, 179
Istra 10
Ivan I 10
Ivan III 10
Ivan IV (Ivan the Terrible) 10, 210
Ivanov, Nazar 10
Izmailovo 13, 15, 18, 53
  Apothecary's Garden *9*, 15
  maze 15
  menagerie 15
  Pleasure Palace *14*, 15
  Prosyansky Garden 15
  Vineyard Garden *14*, 15
Izmaylov, M.M. 170

Joachim, Patriarch 10, 15

Kachanovka 200–2, *202*
Kadriorg 74–5, *74*, *75*
Kalevala 160
Kalinin Park of Culture and Rest 160
Kamenny Island 44, *44*, 149, *149*
Karamzin, Nikolai 89, 177, 179
Karasubazaar (Beligorsk) 145, 203
Kazakov, Matvei 106
Kebach, Karl 206
Kekerekeksinensky Palace 85
Kew 87, 110, 125, 126
Kharax 218, *218*
Khvoshchinskaya, Elena 152
Kiev 9, 233
King, Revd John Glen 96
Kirovsk 233
Kiyasovka 188
Klein, Roman 73
Klodt, Piotr 21, 180
Kolodiny, I.F. 152
Kologrivov, Yuri 64
Kolomenskoe 13, 18, 104
Kolonistsky Park 162, *162*
Komarova, E.A. 234
Kovalyova, Praskovya 65, 165
Kozlovsky, Mikhail 27
Krafft, J.C. 139
Krasnaya Myza ('Ba! Ba!') 148, *149*
Krasnov, N.P. 216
Krasov, Andrei 46
Krechetnikov, General Mikhail 191
Kremlin Palace 10
Krestovsky Island 231
Krutovsky, V.M. 219
Kuchelbecker, Wilhelm 98, 117, 118, 125, 136, 140
Kuphaldt, G. 224
Kurakin, Prince Aleksandr 191, 193
Kurakin, Prince Boris 191
Kuskovo 58–67, *58*, *59*, *60*, 165
  Dutch House 60, *60*, 67
  green theatre 65, *65*
  Grotto 60, *62*, 64, 67

Hermitage 60, *60*, 67
Italian House 64, 67
Menagerie 64, *64*
Orangery *59*, 65, 67
Küttner, Hieronymous 221, *222*
Kuverin, Nikolai 165
Kuzminki *165*, 180–3, *180*

Lafermière, Franz Hermann 125, 154, 156, 157
Lagarde, Comte Auguste de 197–8
landscape parks 144–213
Aleksandria 200
Aleksandrinsky Park 161
Alexander Pushkin Museum Park 209–10
Alexandria 160–1
Alupka 145, 158, 204–9
Bezborodko estate (plans) 168–70
Bogoroditsk 188–91
Bykovo 170
English park at Peterhof 100–3, *101, 102, 103*, 215
Gorenki 183–4
Gorki 185
Gostilitsy 152
Gruzino 153–4
Kachanovka 200–2
Kolonistsky Park 162
Kuzminki 180–3
Livadia 216–18
Marfino 178–80
Marino 152
Mikhalkova 149–50
Mon Repos 154–60
Nadezhino 191–3
Neskuchnoe 184
Nikolskoe-Cherenchitsy 167
Ostafevo 177–8
Otrada 167
Peterhof Road 148
Petrovsko-Razumovskoe 175
Pushkin Park 209
Rai-Semenovskoe 176–7
Sokirentsy 199–200
Sophievka 158, 193–9
Spasskoe-Lutovinovo 210–13
Sukhanovo 173–5
Taitsy 150
Taurida Palace 146, 147–8
Troitskoe 170, 172–3
Voronovo 168
Vvedenskoe 167–8
Yaropolets 166–7
Yasnaya Polyana 213
Yelagin Island 140–2, 231
Zhernovka 153
see also Gatchina; Pavlovsk; Tsarskoe Selo
Lane, Joseph 102
Langley, Batty 82
Lansere, Nikolai 153
Lavrentyev, P.P. 38
Le Blond, Jean-Baptiste Alexandre 18, 20, *21*, 22, 24, 27, 32, 33, 40, *41*, 43, 73
Le Nôtre, André 18, 175
Lee, James 125
Lefort, François 56
Lefort Garden 56, *56*
Lelyakov, A.G. 236

Lenin, Vladimir 185, 200, *200*
Likhachev, Dmitri 158, 159–60, 198, 207, 227
Linnaeus, Carl 99, 124
Livadia 216–18, *216, 218*
Loddiges, Conrad 82, 84, 125, 207
Lomonosov, Mikhail 98
Longford Castle 85
Lönnrot, Elias 160
Lopukhin, Prince P.V. 167
Loudon, J.C. 102, 184
Löwenwolde, Count Reinhold 49
Lunacharsky, A.V. 227
Lvov, Nikolai 98, 134, 167–70, 183, 191
Lyttleton, Lord 166–7

Macpherson, James 158
Manners, Robert 165, 166
Manstadt, Johann 165
Marfino 178–80, *178, 179*
Maria Fyodorovna 7, 98, 109, 110, 115, 117, 118, 123, 124, 125, 126–7, 134, 136, 140, 142, 154, 157, 158, 221
see also Gatchina; Pavlovsk; Yelagin Island
Marino *150*, 152
Marly 17, 18, 22, 27
Marly Palace *29*, 30, 37
Martinelli, G.A. 156
Martos, Ivan 27, 123, 153
Massandra 145
Mattarnovy, Georg 20
Matveev, Ivan 18
Matveev, K.M. 177
Mawe, Thomas 100
Meader, James 82, 87, 100, 102, *102*, 149
Meadow Park *161*, 162
Meier, Kh.F. 152
Melgunov, Aleksei 173
Meller, Alexander 140
Melnikov, F. 177
menageries
Izmailovo 15
Kuskovo 64, *64*
Marfino *179*
Oranienbaum 81
Peterhof 32–3
Tsarskoe Selo 98
Menelaws, Adam 98, 138, 160–1, 183
Menshikov, Prince Alexander 44, 45, 73
Merkurov, S. 185
Mets, Andrei 231
Mettenleiter, Yakov 133
Metzel, Ludovic 193, 197
Michael Pavlovich, Grand Duke 82, 136, 137–8, 142
Michetti, Nicolo 18, 20, 24, 27, 32, 33, 40, *41*, 42, 74
Mikhailov, Nikolai 38
Mikhailovich, Aleksei 13, 15
Mikhailovskoe 209, 210, *210*
Mikhalkova 149–50
Minikh, Burchard-Christof 152
Minsk 233
Mironov, A.F. 60, 165, 166
Mon Repos *145*, 154–60, *154, 157, 158*
monastery gardens 10, 223
Monastery of the Trinity and St Sergius 13
New Jerusalem Monastery 13

Solovetsky Monastery 223
Valaam Monastery 223
Monastery of the Trinity and St Sergius 13, *13*, 15
Monbijou 17
Monighetti, I.A. 98
Monplaisir 30, 32
Montferrand, Auguste de 157
Morozova-Reinbot, Z.G. 185
Moscow and environs 53–60, 164–85
Annenhof 43, 57
Apothecary's Garden 10, 236
Arkhangelskoe 67–73
Bidloo Garden 53–4
Bykovo 170
German Suburb 53
Golovinksy Garden 56–7
Gorki 185
Gorky Park 231
Kremlin Palace 10
Kuskovo 58–67
Kuzminki 180–3
Lefort Garden 56–7
Marfino 178–80
Mikhalkova 149–50
Moscow Botanical Garden 233
Neskuchnoe 184
Ostafevo 177–8
Ostankino 66, 165–6
Otrada 167
Petrovsko-Razumovskoe 175
public parks 220, 231
Rai-Semenovskoe 176–7
Sukhanovo 173–5
Troitskoe 170, 172–3
Tsaritsyn Meadow 10
Tsaritsyno 104–7
Vasiliev Garden 10
Voronovo 168
Vvedenskoe 167–8
Yaropolets 166–7
Mostipanov, M.K. 200
Mothe, Vallin de la 167
Munro, Ian 105–6
Murino 170
Musin-Pushkin, Count Aleksei 82, 100
Mutino 167

Nadezhino 191–3, *192*
Napoleon Bonaparte 7, 67, 71, 204
Nartov, A.K. 49
Naryshkin, Alexander 148
Naryshkin, Lev 148
Nashchokin, Alexander 176
Nechaev, Sergei 175
Neskuchnoe 184, *184*
Netherlands
Het Loo 17
Honselaarsdijk 17
Ouderhoek 17
Petersburg 17
Rijksdorp 17
Watervliet 17
Zorgvliet 17
Nevsky, Alexander 9
New Jerusalem Monastery 10, *10*, 13
Neyelov, Ilya 96

Neyelov, Ivan 89
Neyelov, P. 102
Neyelov, Vasily 84, 87, 89
Nicholas I 103, 136, 148, 160, 198
Nicolay, Baron Ludwig von 117, 124, 136, 154, 156, 157, 158, 160
Nicolay, Baron Paul von 158, 160
Nikitin, P. 184, *184*
Nikitin, Pyotr 166
Nikitsky Botanic Garden 184, 207, 209
Nikolaev 145
Nikolskoe-Cherenchitsy 167
Nikolsky, Alexander 227, 231, *232*
Nikon, Patriarch 10, 13, 223
Noe, George 125
Novaya 103
Novgorod 9
Novikov, Nikolai 106
Novosibirsk 233

orangeries
Arkhangelskoe 67
Gatchina 134
Gostilitsy 152
Kuskovo *59*, 65, 67
Marfino 179
Ostankino 165, 166
Peterhof 33
Ropsha 50
Tsaritsyno 106
Oranienbaum 45, *45*, 77, 78–82, *78*
Chinese Palace *78*, 81
Coasting Hill 81–2, *82*
Coasting Hill Pavilion 81, *81*, *82*
menagerie 81
plan 239
Oranienburg 17
Orlov, Count Grigory 7, 96, 128, 130
Orlov, Count Vladimir 167, 180
Orlova, Countess Anna 179–80
Ossianism 158–60, 198, 207
Ostafevo *176*, 177–8, *177*
Ostankino 66, 165–6
Otrada 167
Ouderhoek 17

Painshill 102
Pallas, P.S. 183
Panin, Count Peter 149
Parks of Culture and Rest 231
Paskevich, V. V. 198–9
Paul I 57, 94, 103, 109, 110, 121, 123, 130, 134, 148, 153, 154
see also Gatchina; Pavlovsk
Pavlovsk 7, 109, *109*, 110–28, *110*, 138, 140, 216, *236*
Apollo Colonnade 115–16, *116*
Aviary 113, 115, *115*
charcoal-burner's hut 118
Dairy 117–18, *117*
fireworks and celebrations 126–8
fruit gardens 125
Maria Fyodorovna memorial *142*
Mausoleum for Paul I 123
Monument to the Parents 123, *123*
New Sylvia 20
Old Chalet 118, *118*

Old Sylvia 120, *120*
Pavilion of the Three Graces 113, *113*, *115*
Peel Tower 118, *118*, 120
plan 241
plant collections 125–6, 142
Private Garden 113, *113*
restoration 234, *236*
Rose Pavilion 127, *127*, 128, *236*
Ruin Cascade 123–4, *124*
Slavyanka valley 116–17, *117*, 123
Temple of Friendship *112*, 113
Peter I (Peter the Great) 7, 15, 17–18, 53, 223
see also Dubki; Golovinksy Garden; Kadriorg; Peterhof; Riga; Ropsha; Strelna; Summer Garden
Peter II 44, 57
Peter III 45, 50, 77, 78, 104, 149
Peterhof (Petrodvorets) 7, 22–39
Adam and Eve Fountains 33, 37
Cottage Palace 160–1, *160*
Dragon and Dolphins Fountain 23, *23*
English Palace 100, *100*, 103, *103*
English park 100–3, *100*, 215
Favoritka Fountain 33, *34*
Great Cascade 24, *24*, 27
Hermitage 30, *30*, 37
Hermitage Cascade *17*
Lion Cascade *17*
Marly Cascade 27, *28*, *29*, 37
Marly Palace *29*, 30, 37, *233*
menagerie 32–3
Monplaisir 30, 32
Neptune Fountain 23–4, *23*
Oak Fountain 24
orangery 33
plan 239
Pyramid Fountain 33
restoration 37–8, 233
Roman Fountains 33
Ruin Cascade 27
Samson Fountain and canal 27, *27*, 37–8, *38*, *236*
Sun Fountain 32, *32*
trick fountains 32, *32*
Peterholm 73
Petrovsko-Razumovskoe 175
Petrovskoe 210, *210*
Pilsudski, Mieczyslaw 22, 162
Pisarev, General 185
Piskaryovskoe Cemetery 233
Pitt, William 94
Platon, Patriarch 13
Pokrovskoe-Rubtsovo 13
Pokrovsky Monastery 10
Poniatowski, Stanislaus Augustus 77
porcelain services
Chamberlain service 137, *137*, 138
Green Frog dinner service 85, *85*, 87
Potemkin, Alexander 152
Potemkin, Prince Grigory 7, 92, 107, 145, 147, 204
Potocki, Sophia 193, 198
Potocki, Stanislas Shchensky 193, 197
Preobrazhenskoe 13
Prokofev, I.A. 185
Prokofev, I.P. 27
Proletarsky Park 161
Prosyansky Garden 15
Pugachev, Emelyan 104, 215

Pushkin, Alexander 71, *73*, 98–9, 166, 177, 203, 204, 209, 210
Pushkin Park 209
Quarenghi, Giacomo 96, 100, *100*, 167, 168, 191

Rachette, Jean Dominique 27
Radziwill, Helen 193
Rai-Semenovskoe 176–7
Rastrelli, Bartolomeo 18, 23, 24, 40, 46, 49, 57
Rastrelli, Carlo 18, 23, 24, 27, 30, 40
Razumovsky, Field Marshal Count Alexis 7, 50, 152, 183
Razumovsky, A.K. 183, 220
Razumovsky, Kirill 152
Regel, A. *215*, *224*
Regel, E. 220, 221, 224
Reid, Francis 105–6, 165, 167
Reitum, Dr Alexsei 236
Repton, Humphrey 126, 156
restoration, post-war 37–8, 233–6
Revolution 7, 224, 227
Richelieu, Duc de 209
Riga 73, 233
Alexandershantz 73
Peterholm 73
Rijksdorp 17
Rinaldi, Antonio 57, 78, 81, 82, 89, 128
Ritter, Christoph 24
Rodionov, P. 160
Romodanovsky, Prince 50
roof gardens 236
Winter Palace 103–4, *104*
Roosen, Jan 18, 46, 58
Ropsha 22, 50–1, *51*, 162
Rossi, Carlo 21, 110, 141, 142
Rousseau, Jean-Jacques 130
Rumiantsev-Zadunaisky, Field Marshal 200
Ruoff, Eeva 156
Rusca, Luigi 42

Sadovnik, P. S. 152
St Cloud 17
St Petersburg and environs 17–51, 144–63
Aleksandrinsky Park 161
Alexandria 160–1
Dubki 42
Ekaterinhof 43–4
Gostilitsy 152
Gruzino 153–4
Imperial Botanic Garden 184, 220–3, 224
Kamenny Island 44
Kolonistsky Park 162
Marino 152
Mon Repos 154–60
Monplaisir 32
Oranienbaum 45
Peterhof (Petrodvorets) 7, 22–39
public parks 220, 231
Ropsha 50–1
Strelna 40–2
Summer Garden 18, 20–2
Taitsy 150
Tsarskoe Selo 7, 46–50
Vasilevsky Island 44
Winter Palace 103–4, *104*
Yelagin Island 140–2, 231

Zhernovka 153
see also Gatchina; Pavlovsk
Saltykov, Field Marshal Ivan 178, 179
Schädel, Gottfried 45
Schedrin, Feodosy 27
Schinkel, K.F. 161
Schlüter, Andreas 18, 20
schools of gardening 18, 24, 126, 134, 198, 231
Schröder, Conrad 46
Scotland 158, 159, 207
Sebastopol 145
Second World War 7, 37, 71, 236
Seeley, Benton 77, 87, 93, 94
Ségur, Comte de 65
serfdom 7, 65, 179, 215
Sergiev 13, 15
Shcherbakov, Arseny 220
Sheremetev family 58, 215
Sheremetev, Field Marshal Count Boris 7, 58
Sheremetev, Count Nikolai 65, 66, 165
Sheremetev, Pavel 227
Sheremetev, Sergei Dmitrievich 178
Shubin, Fedot 27
Shuvalov, Count I.I. 154
Simferopol 145
Simonov, Vasily 37, 38
Slavyanka valley 116–17, 117, 123
S.M. Kirov Central Park of Culture and Rest 231, 232
Sochi 220
Society for the Study of the Russian Estate 227
Sofia 92
Sokirentsy 199–200, 199
Sokolov, P. 98
Solovetsky Monastery 223, 227
Sophievka 158, 187, 193–9, 194, 196
Sovereign Order of the Knights of Malta 123, 134
Soviet period 227–36
spa resorts 176–7, 198
Sparrow, Charles 82, 128, 134
Sparrow, John 130
Spasskoe-Lutovinovo 210–13, 212
Stakenschneider, Andrei 17, 23, 27, 103, 152, 161, 162, 198
Stalin, Joseph 200, 218, 227, 228
Starov, I.E. 150, 188
Stasov, V.P. 89, 173
Sterne, Laurence 102, 103
Steven, Christian 184, 209
Storch, Heinrich 147, 148
Stowe 77, 87, 89, 92, 93–6, 93, 94, 95, 96, 137
Strelna 40–2, 41
Strogonov family 7
Strogonov, Grigory 152
Studley Royal 89
Stupischen, Peter von 154
Sualem, 27
Sukhanovo 172, 173–5, 173
Sukhumi 220
Summer Garden 18, 18, 20–2, 20
Summer Palace 20, 21
sun cannons 177
Surmin, Ilya 74
Suzdal 9
Svyatogorskoe Monastery 210
Swieten, Steven van 42
symbolism 18

table decorations, garden architecture and 138–9, 138
Taitsy 150, 150
Taleporovskii, V.N. 216
Tallinn 74
Tarnovsky, M.V. 202
Tarnovsky, Vasily Vasilievich the Younger 200, 202
Tatum, Charles Heathcote 158
Taurida Palace 146, 147–8, 147
Telyatevsky, Ivan 10
Themery, Théodore 198
Thomon, Thomas de 123
Tikhomirova, Marina 37
Tolstoy, Leo 213
Trautvetter, E.R. 221
Trembecki, Stanislaw 197, 198
Treptow 109
Tressini, Domenico 18, 20, 21, 21, 44, 50
Trianon 17, 120
Trigorskoe 209, 210
Triscorni, Paolo 115, 115, 166
Troitskoe 170, 172–3
Trombara, Giacomo 69
Trubetskoy, Nikolai 177, 184
Tsaritsyn Meadow 10
Tsaritsyno 104–7, 104, 106
Tsarskoe Selo 7, 46–50, 46, 82–100, 84, 216, 234
    Agate Pavilion 90, 93
    Alexander Palace 96, 96
    Alexandrova dacha 98
    Arsenal 98
    Baths 90
    Cameron Gallery 90, 90, 96
    Catherine Palace 82
    Chinese Village 88, 89
    Coasting Hill 49–50, 96, 96, 99–100
    Creaking Pavilion 88, 89
    Ekaterinsky Park 98
    Granite Terrace 98
    green theatre 46
    Grotto 49, 49
    hanging garden 92, 93
    Hermitage 46, 46
    hothouses 87
    menagerie 98
    Milkmaid Fountain 98, 99
    Mon Bijou 46, 49, 49, 98
    New Garden 46, 96
    Palladian Bridge 89, 95
    plan 88, 240
    pyramid 94, 94
    restoration 233–4
    Sofia 92
    Stowe, influences of 93–6
    Temple of Memory 93–4
    Turkish Bath Pavilion 98, 98
Tsitsin, N.V. 233
Tugarov, Fyodor 180
Tumanova, Natalia 22, 233
Turgenev, Ivan 210, 212–13
Tuvolkov, Vasily 22
Tversky, L.M. 233
Tyazhelov, Fyodor 67
Tyurin, Evgraf 73

Ukhtomsky, D.V. 184
Ukraine 200–2

Väinämöinen 158, 160
Valaam Monastery 223
Vasilevsky Island 44
Vasiliev Garden 10
Velten, Yuri 21, 30, 51, 85, 89
Vere, James 84
Versailles 17, 18, 22
Viau, Théophile de 120
Viestura 73
Vineyard Garden, Izmailovo 14, 15
Vladimir 9
Volkonsky, Prince Peter 173
Voronikhin, Andrei 17, 27, 42, 110, 127, 152
Voronovo 168
Vorontsov, I.I. 168
Vorontsov, Count Michael 173, 204, 206, 207
Vorontsov, Count Simon 125, 126
Vvedenskoe 167–8
Vyazemsky, Prince Andrei Ivanovich 177
Vyazemsky, Prince Peter 177, 178
Vyshinsky, Andrei 228

Wailly, Charles de 58
Wassoult, François 27
Watervliet 17
Webster, James 204
Wedgwood, Josiah 85
Weinman, Ivan 126
Wendelsdorf, F. 160
Whately, Thomas 89
Wilkie, Kim 236
Wilmot, Catherine and Martha 170, 172–3
winter gardens
    Kuskovo 65
    Taurida Palace 147
    Winter Palace 104
    Yelagin Island 140
Winter Palace 103–4, 104
    roof garden 103–4, 104
Wolfe, General 93
Wren, Christopher 54
Württemberg, Carl Eugen, Duke of 110, 125
Württemberg, Friedrich, Prince of 154
Württemberg, Friedrich Eugen, Duke of 109, 123

Yalta 219–20, 220
Yamein, Oleg and Nikita 236
Yaropolets 166–7
Yasnaya Polyana 213, 213
Yelagin, I.P. 140, 141
Yelagin Island 140–2, 141, 231
Yeltsin, Boris 231
Yusupov, Prince Nikolai 71
Yusupov, Nikolai F. 73
Yusupov Mausoleum 72, 73

Zagorsk 13
Zemtsov, Mikhail 18, 20, 30, 33, 74
Zhernovka 153
Zhiliardi, A.O. 180
Zhiliardi, D.I. 175, 180
Zhukovsky, Vasily 177
Zorgvliet 17
Zvanka 170

ACKNOWLEDGMENTS

I began to collect material for this book more than twenty years ago, when Russians were still wary about contacts with visitors from the West. I was planning a tour of the great parks around Leningrad for enthusiastic members of the Garden History Society, which gave me an acceptable reason to contact Russian specialists, and I succeeded in getting the necessary clearance from the political officer of the Union of Architects. I am grateful to the Union of Architects in Moscow, St Petersburg and Kiev for help and hospitality.

I was very fortunate to meet the late Olga Ivanova, who then chaired the landscape architects' section of the Union of Architects in Leningrad, and her colleague Natalia Ilinskaya, who succeeded her in that post. I am very much indebted to them for their friendship, hospitality, books, other material and help on many occasions. I am similarly indebted to the present chairman, Andrei Reiman. I remember with gratitude the late Inga Barsova and her husband, who took me to Gatchina, when it was out-of-bounds to western visitors, and to other parks which I would not otherwise have seen. During a tour on foot of the outlying parks at Peterhof she enabled me to see the interior of the Belvedere Palace by introducing me to the caretaker as 'this professor from Estonia'. With Andrei Mets and Elena Shapovalova, Inga hired a coach to take me to Ropsha. For visits to Pulkovo, Marino, Gostilitsy, Strelna and Mon Repos I am also grateful to Elena Shapovalova as well as to Maria Ignatieva; while Andrei Mets provided help and hospitality on Yelagin Island where he was the Park Engineer. The Director of Yelagin Palace, another Maria Fyodorovna, allowed me to take photographs of the park from the roof. To Marina Fleet, the Curator of the park at Pavlovsk, to Tatyana Shulkina, formerly of the Komarov Botanical Institute, to E.V. Komarova, who was responsible for the restoration of the park at Pavlovsk, and to the late Natalia Tumanova, who restored the park at Tsarskoe Selo, I am indebted for help on numerous occasions. I am grateful to the late R.S. Soloveichika and to Ludmilla Voronikhina for their kindness and help at the State Hermitage Museum. Also in St Petersburg Boris Kokno, Andrei and Alyona Shreter and the late Login Shreter gave me valuable assistance.

It was Elena Mikulina in Moscow, to whom I had written for advice, who put me in touch with Olga Ivanova, and I owe her thanks for help on many occasions, for the gift of Tatyana Dubyago's invaluable book on Russian formal gardens and for the apple pie she baked for members of the Garden History Society. I first arranged to meet Dmitri Shvidkovsky after his article on Charles Cameron had appeared in the *Architectural Review*. I learned the day before that he was in hospital and that his mother would take me there to see him, but the hospital preferred to allow him to go home for the day. We have since met frequently both here and in Moscow, and I thank him for a great deal of help, including visits to parks, enabling me to obtain many of the historical illustrations for this book, and for introducing me to various home-made vodkas and other Russian delicacies. I am also grateful to his late father, Oleg Shvidkovsky, to his mother Vera Kalmykova, and to his wife Katya Shorban. I thank Nina Titova, designer of gardens, for her help and friendship, and I remember with gratitude the late Yuri Gershevich, who worked on the restoration of Tsaritsyno. Tanya Panova at Intourist Moscow Ltd I thank for all her help with the tours she arranged for me, which included places not usually on Intourist itineraries; and I thank Marina Golovchenko who acted as our guide on most of them. In Moscow I am also indebted to Elena Semyonova-Prozorovskaya, Taisia Wolftrub, Anna Persits and Vladimir Chekmaryov.

After I had taken part in 'British Days in Kiev' in 1991 at the invitation of the Foreign Office, the late Natalia Abesinova, then chair of the landscape architects in Kiev, arranged a series of visits to parks in Ukraine. I remain very grateful for that and for the hospitality she and her husband, Yuri Pedan, provided. I thank Bela Timofeeva for the material she gave me about the park at Kachanovka, and Igor and Olga Rodichkin for the excellent book they gave me about the parks of Ukraine, to which they were major contributors. Anna Galichhenko, the Curator of the palace-museum at Alupka, and Anatoly Annenkov, formerly at the Nikitsky Botanic Garden, were both of considerable help during my visits to the Crimea.

For all I have learned about Mon Repos and for other help I am indebted to Eeva Ruoff. Marcus Köhler, Margot Lutze and H.W. Lack in Germany, Sirkku Dölle and Sirkka Havu in Finland, Andrzej Kostołowski in Poland, the late Gösta Adelswärd, Siv Söderlund and Inga Hemelin-Jungstedt in Sweden, Margrethe Floryan in Denmark and Barry Scherr, Anna Ljunggren and Albert Schmidt in the United States have all been very helpful.

I have gained much from the publications of Anthony Cross and Priscilla Roosevelt, and I am also grateful to John Roberts, John Simmonds, Michael Pearman, Gaye Blake Roberts, Harry Frost, Jenny Newman, Jeremy Howard, Elinor Wiltshire, Kate Hamblen, Sian Walsh and the late Ian Laurie. Among members of the Garden History Society I must single out Mavis Batey, Ray Desmond, Keith Goodway, Robert Oresko, Christopher Thacker, Anthony Pasley and Marion Waller, along with all those members who supported the tours I arranged to parks in Russia and Ukraine. I thank Susan Causey of the Prince of Wales

International Business Leaders Forum for information about the Solovetsky Monastery in the White Sea, where the Prince is supporting the restoration with the participation of landscape architect Kim Wilkie and archaeologist Brian Dix. I also remember with gratitude and affection the late Herbert G. Wright.

I must record my appreciation for help in the archives at Pavlovsk, Chatsworth, the Croome Estate Trust and the County Record Office in Matlock; at the State Hermitage Museum in St Petersburg, the Nationalmuseum in Stockholm, the National Museum of Finland, the Württemberg Landesmuseum, the Ashmolean Museum, the Wedgwood Museum in Barlaston and the Dyson Perrins Museum in Worcester; in the Saltykov-Shchedrin Library in St Petersburg, Helsinki University Library, Leiden University Library, Berlin Technical University Library, the Bibliothèque Nationale in Paris, the British Library, the library of the Royal Botanic Gardens in Kew, the library of the Linnean Society, the library of the Royal Horticultural Society, Keele University Library and Eccleshall Library; and at Moorlands Photo Laboratory in Burslem.

I owe a considerable debt to Gareth Jones, Emeritus Professor of Russian at the University of Wales, Bangor, and to my daughter, Sarah Annes Brown, Director of Studies in English and Fellow of Lucy Cavendish College, Cambridge, for reading the text and for many helpful suggestions. I thank Anne Fraser and John Nicoll at Frances Lincoln for their enthusiasm and encouragement, and Michael Brunström, my editor, and John Morgan, the designer of the book.

And I am particularly grateful to Jean, my wife, for her forebearance with my preoccupation.

I dedicate the book to all those friends in Russia and Ukraine who helped to make it possible.